LONDON
MAIN LINE
WAR DAMAGE

LONDON
MAIN LINE
WAR DAMAGE

B W L Brooksbank

Capital Transport

Acknowledgements

The content of this book depends fundamentally on the efficiency and dedication of the staff at the National Archives, Kew. I recognize and truly appreciate the value of their work. As well, I am indebted to the staff of the Reprographic Department for providing many of the photographs reproduced in this book.

I am very much indebted to the staff of the former Railtrack (South) for providing numerous copies of their archived photographs, and I warmly appreciate the help given by Allan Sibley of the Great Northern Railway Society, by Graham Kenworthy and David Taylor of the Great Eastern Society, also by Richard Durack of the Archives Library of the London Borough of Newham, for most of the LNER photographs.

I am most grateful to Mr P. C. Trewin of BRB (Residuary) Ltd for kindly allowing free publication of the wartime photographs which formerly belonged to the Main Line Railway Companies, then passed through the British Railways Board and so to the BRB (Residuary) Ltd.

I would like to express my gratitude to Jim Whiting for having sufficient interest to undertake the publication of this work and for all the trouble he has diligently taken over it. I give many thanks to John McCrickard for suggesting originally that in the London context I approach Capital Transport Publishing with my collection of documentation on wartime railway incidents.

Finally, I warmly thank Bernard Harding (a former officer of British Rail and London Transport) for his very thorough and professional reading of the text prior to my offering it for publication.

B. W. L. Brooksbank
January 2007

Abbreviations in this book

BB – Barrage balloon(s)
BDS(O) – Bomb Disposal Service (Officer)
C&W – Carriage and Wagon
DAB – Delayed-action bomb(s)
E&SB – Ealing & Shepherd's Bush Line
ELR – East London Line (LPTB)
EMU – Electric multiple-unit
FLY – Flying Bomb(s) (V-1)
H&C – Hammersmith & City Line
HE – High explosive(s)
HL – High Level
HSW – Hand-signal working
HT – High tension
IB – Incendiary bomb(s)
LB&SCR – London, Brighton and South Coast Railway
LC&DR – London, Chatham and Dover Railway
LCC – London County Council
LL – Low Level
LT&S – London, Tilbury and Southend
MWL – Metropolitan Widened Lines
NA – National Archives (formerly Public Record Office)
N&SWJ – North and South Western Junction Line
NLR – North London Railway (LMSR)
nwr – Normal working resumed

PAC – Pilotless aircraft – i.e. V-1 (FLY)
PLA – Port of London Authority
PMW – Pilot-man working
PW – Permanent Way
RCC – Railway Construction Company
RCH – Railway Clearing House
RCS – Royal Corps of Signals
RE – Royal Engineers
REC – Railway Executive Committee
S&T – Signal and Telegraph
SL – South London Line
SLW – Single-line working
SM – Stationmaster
SpR – Speed Restriction
T&H – Tottenham & Hampstead Line
TBW – Telephone Block working
TC – Track circuits
Telecom – Telephone and telegraph lines
TIW – Time-interval working
UXB – Unexploded bomb(s)
UXLM – Unexploded land-mine(s)
W&C – Waterloo & City Line
WLER – West London Extension (GWR, LMSR and SR Joint)
WLR – West London Line (GWR and LMSR Joint)

Contents

First published 2007

ISBN 978-1-85414-309-9

Published by Capital Transport Publishing
PO Box 250, Harrow, Middlesex, HA3 5ZH

Printed by CS Graphics, Singapore

Introduction

During the Second World War, London was naturally the prime target for air attack on Britain by Nazi Germany. It was not only the capital of the nation and Empire and seat of government but Britain's largest port and a centre of world-wide trade, a major manufacturing city, and the hub of most of its railway system. Moreover, after the Fall of France and the Low Countries, aircraft could attack London from the Continent by a relatively short approach, much of it across the sea.

The London Civil Defence Region (No. 5) corresponded fairly closely with the present-day Greater London Metropolitan Area, although embracing a slightly wider area of the suburbs including all of Middlesex and some boroughs on the fringes that are now in Surrey, Kent, Essex or in Hertfordshire. It had a population of 8,780,000 and was a major industrial area with about 1,300 'Key Points' – i.e. targets of importance in aerial warfare. A large proportion of the country's food-processing and of the lighter and more specialised manufacturing industry was carried out in the Greater London Area. Moreover, numerous factories were engaged in the manufacture and production of war material, the largest of which included the Royal Arsenal at Woolwich and the Royal Ordnance Factories at Enfield and Waltham Abbey. Major utilities included the largest electricity generating stations and gas works in the United Kingdom. The Port of London, comprising Dock installations with 10 miles of main frontage, stretched downstream for 15–20 miles from the City. In 1939 it was responsible for 17.5% of all imports (excluding oil) and 20.5% of all imported foodstuffs, while 34% of the country's food storage capacity in main ports and 63% of cold storage was in the London area. Railways centred on London served the major oil refineries and other installations, including the port of Tilbury, further down both sides of the Thames Estuary.

The Nazis claimed that they specifically forbade the targeting of urban areas in London itself (or other cities). Nevertheless, significant enemy bombing attacks on mainland targets began in mid-June 1940. The first bomb fell in the London Region at Addington near Croydon on 18 June 1940. Bombs fell in the London Region on six further occasions up to the middle of August, by which time the Battle of Britain was well under way. The German Air Force (Luftwaffe) was engaged in its mortal struggle with the RAF, attacking airfields, aircraft factories and oil refineries, and bombs were falling in the Region with increasing frequency and intensity.

This was the prelude to the large-scale and in effect indiscriminate 'Blitz' on Britain's industrial cities, ports and their population. By an unexpected switch of tactics at the height of the Battle of Britain, a major daylight attack was launched on 7 September on East London and its Docks by 348 bombers escorted by 617 fighters. It was intended to confuse and overwhelm the British defences, notably RAF Fighter Command – and it nearly did.[1] Unprecedented damage was done and the daytime raid was followed that night by another by 250 bombers. However, public reaction then and later did not – as the Nazis hoped – force the British Government to sue for peace: it had the opposite effect, resulting eventually in Hitler and his gang bringing about the destruction of many German cities instead.

The Luftwaffe soon discovered that, while daylight bombing was fairly accurate, it required massive fighter support to prevent crippling losses of bombers. On the other hand, their attacks in the dark were virtually unopposed other than by anti-aircraft fire and balloons, although these defences forced the bombers to drop their loads from a much greater height and what they hit was largely a matter of chance. So began the

systematic Blitz of London: until mid-November only a limited number of attacks were made by day (five of any significance), but at night the bombers attacked London on almost every single night. The Nazis believed that this alone would make Britain surrender, without an invasion that in any case by 17 September had to be postponed indefinitely[2] on account of the growing resistance of the RAF and the impending winter weather. In the end, throughout the war London endured 101 daylight attacks and 253 night attacks, but most occurred in the last four months of 1940, with 77 attacks in daylight and 102 at night. Including during the V-weapon offensives of 1944–45, a total of 29,800 people lost their lives in the London Region and 50,307 were seriously injured; 95% were civilians.

During September 1940 daylight attacks were continued until the 15th, but on each of ten nights in September at least 250 tons of bombs fell on London. The raids in October were to some extent hampered by the weather, although the Luftwaffe was now benefiting from its new navigational aids. Attacks on London continued nightly and were heavy on twelve of the nights in October. In November, there were raids on twelve of the first thirteen nights, being heavy on seven of them. London was being slowly worn down, but it seemed a routine experience to most people, for in early November still only 40% of the population was sheltering (9% in public shelters, 4% in the Underground stations and 27% in domestic shelters). However, London was too vast a city; the aircraft, bombs, skills and equipment of any air force at that time were incapable of paralysing London's key infrastructure. After 13 November, the capital was released from its continuous ordeal, but it was still raided heavily if intermittently on many nights in the ensuing six months, suffering its worst raids of all in the spring of 1941. Heavy raids occurred on four more nights in November, then on three in December, the Great Fire Raid of 29/30 December destroying large swathes of the City of London. Meanwhile, from mid-November, the enemy switched their main attacks to provincial industrial centres and ports, starting with Birmingham and Coventry.

In January and February 1941, the Luftwaffe was severely hampered by the weather, and London suffered raids on only six nights. However, in March the Blitz on Britain resumed with enhanced ferocity: larger bombs and now parachute mines, ever more incendiary bombs. The first major attack on London since 12 January was made on the night of March 8/9, then the next night, lesser attacks on 15/16, 18/19, and a heavy attack on 19/20. In April, London received its worst ever attacks on the nights of 16/17 and 19/20, when on each night some 700 bombers during 7–8 hours (some flying two, or even three, sorties) dropped about 1,000 tons of high explosives and over 150,000 incendiary bombs, and at least 2,400 people were killed in the two raids. In May the one raid on London on the night of 10/11 was nearly as bad, 571 sorties being flown over six hours and over 1,400 people killed. But after that the Blitz ceased, rather abruptly and unexpectedly, as the bulk of the enemy air force was withdrawn for the invasion of the Soviet Union.

The result of the Night Blitz over London from September 1940 to May 1941 was that 19,877 people had been killed and 25,578 seriously injured, many in shelters. Most raids had been aimed primarily at the Docks and enormous damage had been done there, but there was much devastation as well in the City, the West End and residential districts. Tens of thousands of homes had been destroyed and severe damage done to many public buildings such as museums, churches, hospitals, schools, department stores, shops and offices. Numerous factories, warehouses and major utilities had been destroyed or damaged, with thousands of tons of food, oil and other commodities lost. However, the effect – expected by the enemy to be decisive – on the ability of Britain to make war was definitely not seriously impaired. Perhaps the most important effect was that the Blitz kept in Britain over half a million men defending the country against the air assault, who would otherwise be engaged on more aggressive military operations overseas.

After the great raid of 10/11 May 1941, the Blitz was virtually over, and for a long time London endured no further heavy attacks until early in 1944. At that stage, the Luftwaffe finally attempted some small reprisal for the Allied Strategic Bombing Offensive on Germany. This was the 'Little Blitz' of 14 raids, of which those on the nights of 18/19 and 20/21 February 1944 were definitely heavy. In all, London received 71 major raids (i.e. with over 100 aircraft employed) by manned aircraft.

During the V-weapon offensives, London was the prime target, but as the targeting was crude in the extreme the damage and casualties achieved were very small in relation to the number of attacks and the weight of ordnance expended. Commencing 13 June 1944 and over the ensuing 102 days to 1 September, the Germans managed to ground-launch 8,081 Flying Bombs (V-1), of which 5,232 reached Britain and 2,340 fell in the London Region. The resulting casualties in the Region amounted to 5,126 killed and 14,712 seriously injured. The first two months of the offensive were the worst, because from mid-August the Allied armies were overrunning the launching-sites. However, between 5 September 1944 and 14 January, 1945 388 V-1s launched from the air came over and 66 reached London, then a further 52 came overland during March 1945 (the very last on 28 March) of which 13 reached London. The inefficiency of the V-1s and susceptibility to defences is shown by the fact that only 61% reached Britain and 46% of these were destroyed by our defences. On account of the surface blast effect of its 850 kg warhead, each bomb that landed in a built-up area did a great deal of damage; 1,074 affected the railways (including outside London) – in property mainly only by smashing glass, but they killed 54 railwaymen and injured 1,282. Including railways, there were 691 Key Points incidents, eight of them (on factories) being rated as 'High Grade'.

By an extraordinary coincidence one of the very first V-1s landed slap-bang on a bridge on the main railway line out of Liverpool Street. Whereas 414 'Red' i.e. 'Raiders Overhead' or 'Imminent Danger' Alerts were received in London in 1940 (including on each of 101 consecutive days, 23 August to 1 December), in 1944 there were 511 such warnings. In the 12 weeks ending 3 September, 'Red Alert' warnings were in force in London for 32% of the time and in the worst week (ending 9 July) for 60%. In 1944 Flying Bombs were mainly responsible, and warnings of these did not require lighting to be turned off. Disruption of railway operations by the very frequent Alerts in the summer of 1944 was perhaps more serious than any due to the explosions. A 'Red' warning was shown to drivers by signalmen and train speeds reduced to 30 mph. Lights were not extinguished, and shunting and other movements were not impaired to such an extent as in 1940/41.

The Rockets (V-2) began on 8 September 1944. Between then and 27 March 1945, 1,054 (each with one ton of high explosives) reached Britain. Of these, approximately 575 fell in the London Region, the monthly rate rising from 17 in September 1944 to 130 in March 1945. They killed 2,754 people (about 2,000 in London), including a sizeable number of railwaymen. There were only 71 Key Point incidents due to V-2s in the London Region, with just two rated as 'High Grade'. A V-2 caused about the same degree of damage and casualties as a V-1, and like them they were inaccurate in the extreme. The main difference was that as the V-2 came out of the blue there was no direct defence and no precautions could be taken. In the London Region, the

V-1s and V-2s together killed 7,988 people and seriously injured 20,905; they completely destroyed 29,400 houses and damaged – but not irreparably – 1,255,000. The last V-2 fell at Orpington (not on railway land) at 16.54 on 27 March 1945 and marked the very end of enemy bombardment of the UK. In all, the railways recorded 1,432 incidents as due to V-1 and V-2. To quote Bell (q.v.): "It is creditable to the railway staff of all grades that there were few absentees during these disquieting events and traffic was never brought to a standstill for any length of time."

The War in Europe came to an end on 7 May 1945. There was no more war damage to the UK Railways, but of course the conflict continued in the Far East against the Japanese until 15 August 1945.

Railways and the War

Prominent in the damage and disruption caused by the air raids was that on the railways, the subject of this account.

When war came the railways were absolutely essential to inland transport: foremost, for the movement of freight and minerals, especially the supply of coal to the public utilities, industry and the general population, the movement of foodstuffs and for the distribution inland of imported and manufactured merchandise (civil and military); secondly, for the movement of passengers over long distances and between their suburban homes and usually more central places of work; thirdly – often in priority – the movement of military personnel (on duty and on leave) and of military supplies. All of these transport requirements were enhanced much above peacetime levels, while road transport (local movement by bus or lorry to a lesser extent) was severely curtailed to conserve oil and rubber – both then obtained entirely from overseas. Several further factors acted to enhance railway traffic substantially: decentralisation of armaments manufacture and other requirements of the war effort; an immense increase in the Fighting Forces, multiplied after mid-1940 by the retention of most of the British and Dominions armies in the UK, and also from 1942 to 1945 the US Army; the enormous programme of airfield construction and their subsequent occupation and use by the Air Forces; the diversion to the railways of coastal maritime traffic from the North Sea and the Channel, owing to the menace of the enemy; the great increase in the imports from America of steel and of war material such as aircraft and tanks, which in turn required an unprecedented availability of special wagons.

Fortunately the prolific network of the railways often allowed for deviations to alternative routes from those obstructed by enemy action. This was especially valuable to 'commuting' passengers, although they could usually turn to the local bus services, either on regular routes or provided specially. However, there were several serious bottlenecks that critically affected long-distance freight traffic.

Preparations

At the outbreak of war in September 1939, the railways were ready, more or less, to meet the emergency. After the Munich Crisis in September 1938, the Ministry of Transport (War Transport from May 1941) appointed the Railway Executive Committee (REC) as an advisory body and stated that Government control would be taken of the undertakings of the Railways and the London Passenger Transport Board as soon as the country was in danger through enemy aggression, as had been done at the outbreak of the First World War in 1914. The members of the REC comprised the Chief Executives of the Big Four Railways (GWR – Sir James Milne; LNER – Sir Ralph Wedgwood [Chairman, succeeded in August 1941 by Sir Alan

Garrett Anderson]; LMSR – Sir William Wood; SR – Gilbert Szlumper, succeeded in September 1939 by Sir Eustace Missenden) and the LPTB – Frank Pick, succeeded in May 1940 by Lord Ashfield, with G. Cole Deacon as Secretary. Sixteen Consultative Committees were set up to deal with different aspects of railway matters and reported to the main REC. The most important, one which sat almost daily, was the Operating Superintendents' Committee, chaired by V.M. Barrington-Ward of the LNER. In the MoT the responsibility for railway matters was assigned to two Divisions: Traffic and Maintenance, the Heads of which were accountable to the Railway Control Officer, who provided the link with the REC.

Early in 1939 detailed instructions were drawn up in secret and circulated to General Managers for the 'Control of the Railways in the Event of Armed Conflict'. Plans were made well before the outbreak of hostilities to cope with immediate demands. These included evacuation from vulnerable areas – London in particular – of mothers with young children, schoolchildren and hospital patients; treasures, gold etc.; key Government and business departments; also such measures as the removal of naval ammunition from coastal depots and of perishables from the Docks to inland Cold Stores.

Naturally, a major aspect of the work of the REC in preparation for the war was concerned with Air Raid Precautions (ARP). Those undertaken by the Railways from mid-1938, much of it at Government expense, included the following.

Protective measures: the provision of shelters at principal stations and yards; protection of bridges, tunnels, administrative centres and other vital points, telephone exchanges, signalboxes and so on, including duplication of skeleton facilities. The REC was accommodated during the war in special bomb-proof offices made by conversion of the disused Down Street Underground station on the LPTB Piccadilly Line. The Head Offices and most of the District Control Offices of the Big Four were moved to requisitioned country houses and other rural locations, also specially protected against air raids: the LMSR at The Grove near Watford, the LNER at The Hoo near Knebworth, the GWR at Aldermaston and the SR at Deepdene House, Dorking.

Provision of materials for emergency repairs gave stocks sufficient for three months above normal consumption: Civil Engineers' material for permanent way and bridges, including baulk timber, steel trestling and steel sheet-piling; Signal & Telegraph (S&T) Department material; Mechanical Engineers' material (spare parts). Stocks of additional equipment for clearance and reconstruction work were also built up, such as 35-ton breakdown cranes, extra welding equipment, also material to provide telephone connections with GPO circuits.

Another ARP that had to be considered was external lighting. Its control had to be radically altered, to conform with the very severe limitations imposed – perhaps to excess – to avoid helping enemy aircraft to navigate at night. During 'Red' Alerts, all external lights were supposed to be extinguished, although after the introduction in July 1940 of the 'Purple' ('Hostile Piloted Aircraft Around') warning to the Railways, they were permitted a limited ('Category C') illumination. Associated with lighting controls were those pertaining to the movement and speed of trains, and judgment was needed to strike a balance between maintaining the flow of traffic and taking unnecessary risks.

Coping with Disruption

Most of the damage suffered by the railways was coincidental, the enemy at the time probably being aware that hitting specific railway targets was nearly impossible except in daylight from a low level. Disruption to railway working was caused less by high explosive (HE) and incendiary bombs (IB) than by unexploded bombs (UXB) – some of which were genuine delayed-action bombs (DAB). Other mishaps, due to crashing aircraft, barrage balloons and their cables, and by AA shells, were numerous and sometimes caused lengthy interruptions of train services, as well as damaging track or communications (telecom), especially telegraph wires. Indeed, the effect of physical damage to power or telecom cables often took longer to remedy[3] than the severance of track: a crater in plain track could be filled and the line restored in a few hours, but damage to bridges or tunnels was quite another matter. Fires, started by IB or HE, were the cause of much of the damage to buildings.

In one way or another, air warfare caused a great waste of manpower on the railways and reduced the amount of effective work done by locomotives, vehicles and appliances. A great deal of time was wasted in chasing round each suspected site trying to verify UXB/DAB, when in many cases there proved to be no bomb at all. Trainmen were on duty for exceptionally long hours when traffic operations could not proceed according to the regular programmes. Interference with the turnover of wagons in shunting yards and in goods warehouses was equally serious. The number of wagons shunted when a 'Red' warning was in force might be reduced to 30% of normal, and this had a knock-on effect on other yards and the running of trains. In terms of dealing with emergencies, the Railway authorities ensured that at Main and District Headquarters, Engineering staff were on duty each night, working alongside the Operating staff who collated particulars of incidents as they became available. By the morning following an attack, it was usually possible to determine the order of priority of repairs necessary and arrangements made for the concentration of men, materials, and equipment. The relative seriousness of any damage would be determined, then all possible arrangements made for dealing with it as soon as daylight arrived – or even before daylight, if possible. After consultation between the District Controllers and Engineers, a pronouncement could be made on the probable duration of any blockages. After it had been decided what train services could be run, the District Controller made the necessary arrangements with the District Passenger Manager with regard to passenger services. The latter fixed up any bus services required and arranged for the advising of the public by posters, blackboards and loudspeakers. Freight services were re-arranged by the District Controller in collaboration with the Divisional Superintendent of Operations.

The repair of damage was often beyond the capacity of the existing Engineering staff – perhaps depleted anyway by loss of men to the Services, so extra repair gangs were organised. This was not easy and often the assistance of the Military had to be solicited. As for UXB, an organisation was evolved for reporting them to the Regional Commissioners. They were then dealt with by the specially trained Bomb Disposal Service (BDS) of the Army; unexploded land mines (UXLM) – considered dangerous even if they were 400 yards from the railway – needed the Navy.

In September 1940 when severe air raids were occurring, the ARP plans made before the war were proving obviously inadequate. Much more money had to be spent on these measures and on additional ones: protective equipment, including now air raid spotters, and more shelters; provision of squads for cleaning, decontamination, rescue, demolition, breakdown and fire-fighting; removal or protection of glass at stations and other buildings; arrangements for the movement of trains through gassed areas; provision of alternative electricity supplies. The (feared) awful possibility of the enemy using (blister) gas especially as an act of desperation before D-Day did not arise, but the cost of the other measures justified the total of £11.5 millions that was eventually spent.

Repair of Air Raid Damage

Damage to track was often made good in a matter of hours, and damaged girders of many of the smaller bridges were also quickly replaced. The repair of the permanent way was usually straightforward. Earthwork from the neighbourhood, or kept in readiness in trains, was used for filling craters; likewise, rails and sleepers were moved from convenient stacking grounds. If crossing-work was damaged, at first plain track was usually substituted. If bombs had exploded underground and the ground had subsided, the running rails could be supported temporarily by extra rails fastened underneath the sleepers. The restoration of traffic over an underbridge was much more difficult. So the accumulation before the Blitz of stocks of steel trestling proved to be well worth while, as this was very useful for the rapid temporary repair of underline bridgework.

Even more than the permanent way, the signalling and telecommunication systems were easily disrupted but quite easily repaired, especially the simple wiring on poles. Likewise, cables carrying the electricity supply for traction, signalling etc. were very vulnerable if not put underground. So were the conductor rails on electrified lines, but were usually readily restored. On the other hand, modern signalling systems, because of their susceptibility to even minor damage and their complexity, gave rise to exceptional disruption: for example at Victoria on 21 December and Waterloo on 29 December 1940. Fortunately, with the exception of Blackfriars Junction Box on 19/20 April 1941, the several large power signalboxes in the London area escaped serious damage and consequent widespread and grave disruption. In fact the similar Boxes at London Bridge (8/9 December 1940) and Charing Cross (16/17 April 1941) had remarkable escapes, when parachute mines came down on each – without exploding.

With 4,105 miles of running lines, the SR had about 3,500 steel bridges and 5,600 bridge arches, a large proportion of these being located within 10 miles of the centre of London. Indeed, built on bridges and viaducts were: all the 5½ miles from Charing Cross via London Bridge to Greenwich and virtually all the five miles to New Cross/New Cross Gate, all the three miles Blackfriars to Loughborough Junction and from Victoria the 2¾ miles to Clapham Junction and 1¾ miles to Factory Junction, also some other stretches in South London. However, north of the Thames few railway lines were built over streets and houses, the 2½ miles of LMSR Broad Street to Dalston Junction being a notable exception.

The SR's emergency stock of joists and baulks was distributed at 18 depots throughout the system, five of them located 10–15 miles from London. Also stored at these depots were reserves of rails, sleepers, points and crossings, etc. and reserves of appliances in general use, with emphasis on heavy cranes. Filling material had also been dumped at convenient sites, particularly the refuse from the stone quarries supplying broken stone ballast for the track, for this type of material consolidated quickly when used to fill up bomb craters.

When the heavy attacks on London occurred, the severest damage was caused by large bombs dropped on brick viaducts and bridges. In one instance the main viaduct carrying the railway to Waterloo was so severely fractured that six out of eight tracks were put out of action over three arches each of 30ft span. Similar damage was caused in many other viaducts and that done to the steel girder work of bridges and to bridge abutments was sometimes considerable. The smaller craters in brickwork viaducts were easily bridged from the reserve joists already prepared, and after this type of damage traffic might be resumed inside 24 hours, at a reduced speed. For craters in embankments and cuttings the time needed to fill in and make good the track varied from about six to 48 hours. Occasionally a very large crater would take three or four days.

Where abutments of viaducts or bridges were severely damaged it was invariably necessary to erect temporary trestling, so as to enable the rapid resumption of traffic. Besides ordinary timber trestling, considerable use was made of steel trestling designed by the War Department, which consisted of standard sections of various lengths that could be quickly put together. This had the advantage that as soon as the permanent repairs had been completed at each bridge the sections could be dismantled and sent for re-use at other places. With damaged tunnels, the repairs were usually done on the cut-and-cover principle, the depth of overlying earth allowing, and concrete was utilised instead of brickwork in their reconstruction, as skilled bricklayers were scarce. Repair of damage sustained by bridges, viaducts and tunnels generally needed much technical skill and time, and so caused the greatest delay to traffic. The incidence of such damage was of course greater in an urban area where these structures were more closely spaced.

Documentation of Damage and Disruption in the London Region

The majority of Britain's main lines radiated from London, and traffic between the South-East quadrant and the rest of the country had to pass through the London area, crossing the River Thames at some point. What happened on the four Main Line Railways in London due to enemy action is presented in the following list, which is based on the Situation Reports (DSR) received by the REC and passed on to the Ministry of War Transport.[4] Those cited in this book refer only to the wartime London Civil Defence Region. Reports were actually sent in twice a day.

The times – where given – may often be those of receipt of the report and not the precise time of the incident, which would have been perhaps up to 30 minutes earlier. The DSR were later summarised by the Railways (Maintenance) Division of the MoWT and where disparities occur the latter has been quoted. Supplementary detail, particularly of the major incidents, has been added as found in various other contemporary reports.[5] In many instances, no precise times are reported, nor are the records on restoration by any means always complete. Therefore it has sometimes been difficult to discern the precise sequence of events and there will be gaps in the story.

This book deals only with London's main lines. However, many of those occurring on LPTB lines shared with or running alongside the main-line railways are cited.[6] Otherwise, with certain minor exceptions, all incidents due directly to enemy action on the main-line railways of damage, disruption and mishaps in the London Region are listed here. When many UXB remained to be cleared after raids – probably, but not inevitably – before lines could be reopened, they are listed separately in brief. Although they often entailed interruptions of traffic for a period of perhaps some hours, the closing of important lines for examination for damage or obstruction are not cited here if none was found. Other incidents, even those – sometimes very disruptive – due to drifting barrage balloons, are mentioned only if of special interest. As in peacetime, there were inevitably traffic accidents from time to time and these often caused blockages of important lines for a few hours,[7] but only the more serious are listed.

In the case of the SR,[8] there appear to be rather more records surviving at the National Archives (Public Record Office). The SR records include the hour-to-hour handwritten logs kept by various officers directly concerned,[9] which vary idiosyncratically in the extent and detail of their coverage.

To save space, an abbreviated language (as in the original reports) is applied. Less familiar abbreviations used are listed on page 4.

Clapham Junction Carriage Sheds. In the big daylight raid on the London Docks on 7 September 1940, one Luftwaffe bomber made a 'lucky strike' about 10 miles off target, achieving heavy destruction of SR main line stock.

1939 and the Heavy Bombing of 1940

No incident attributable to enemy action occurred on the railways in London – or anywhere else – for almost a year. However, the long period of the 'Phoney War' was far from easy for the railways.

First, on 1–4 September 1939, was the Evacuation. Though only undertaken because of the threat of enemy action, this big operation (to a pre-planned schedule) entailed considerable alteration of normal passenger services from and to London and curtailment of freight traffic. Commencing on Friday September 1st, the day Nazi Germany began its invasion of Poland, in four days over 617,000 people (mothers with young children, schoolchildren, teachers and other selected classes of adults) were conveyed from London to comparative safety in 1,577 special

trains, many of which left from suburban stations such as Ealing Broadway, Watford Junction, Bowes Park and Wimbledon.

Then, for about two weeks at the end of January 1940, the whole country was gripped in the 'worst/coldest weather in living memory', with numerous railway lines blocked by ice and deep snowdrifts, followed in early February by freezing rain and then floods. Even London was affected, and the Southern Electric trains had to be hauled by steam engines on several days owing to ice on the conductor-rails.

Although from mid-June 1940 some damage occurred on the railways in other Regions, it was not until the height of the Battle of Britain period that incidents were reported from the London Region.

August 1940

16/8/40

SR: Merton Park – Merton Abbey 17.23: Many HE on Merton Park station. 10ft crater at Abbey Junction. Both lines cut. Also two HE blocked Merton Abbey goods line and Line & Co.'s private siding; 17.35 goods Merton Abbey – Wimbledon blocked in. Shuttle service put on West Croydon – Mitcham. UXB feared at Merton Park.

Raynes Park – Motspur Park 17.30: West Barnes Crossing Box demolished and lines blocked until later in evening; all telecom cut. Traffic not affected.

Malden 17.30: HE on station, destroying booking-office, damaging both Up lines and Down Through, and cutting all colour-light signalling Raynes Park – Hampton Court Junction. Ten people killed, including three railway staff. 16.49 EMU Teddington – Waterloo machine-gunned from end to end and one passenger killed. Lines at Malden soon repaired, but Up Local platform unusable; trains stopped at Up Through platform instead. TIW Malden – Malden Crossing (Kingston line). All lines repaired during 17/8. Colour-lights restored, except on Up Through line at Malden, by 05.25 27/8.

18/8/40

SR: Purley 13.10: HE damaged Down Main. Engineers' hut burnt down. UXB at Purley Oaks station, in goods yard and near junction of Caterham/Tattenham Corner branches. All lines Purley – Croydon out of use. Up Slow trains terminating Merstham, Up Fast trains at Purley. Shuttle service on Tattenham Corner branch. Buses substituted as required. Some trains diverted via Horsham. Down Main repaired 20.30, then Down services run as booked, but Up services via Redhill and Up Local. Buses provided Coulsdon North – Purley – Croydon. Repairs completed by 05.00 19/8, but Caterham branch closed until 16.35 22/8 owing to UXB Kenley – Whyteleafe – cleared 22/8.

Riddlesdown – Woldingham 13.10: HE damaged track and telecom. UXB above tunnel, removed 05.00 19/8.

Merton Park 23.45: DAB exploded, damaging much track and cutting lines to Wimbledon and Tooting. Another UXB found near Tooting line. nwr 12.00 20/8.

24/8/40 (Saturday)

LMS: Upminster – Emerson Park 16.12: HE covered line with debris. Buses substituted until 12.50 25/8. Then at 16.30 a UXB found but soon removed.

LNE: Clapton Junction – St James Street 02.15: DAB on line exploded, damaging track. Down trains terminated at Hackney Downs, Up trains at Hoe Street. nwr 09.45 25/8.

SR: Coulsdon: HE beside Quarry line, blocking both lines with debris and 21.00 Newhaven – Bricklayers Arms freight ran into it. Traffic diverted via Redhill. Quarry Line clear 25/8 with SpR. nwr not until 5/9.

25/8/40 (Sunday)

LMS: Hackney Wick – Victoria Park 01.00: Telecom and Block cut. nwr 06.15.

LNE: West Green – Seven Sisters: HE cut telecom. Train service suspended owing to UXB, later found to have exploded. nwr 09.55.

Cambridge Heath 03.16: Locomotive and several coaches derailed after line damaged after near-miss by HE. All lines blocked. Trains diverted via Stratford. Slow lines repaired 16.30, others later. nwr 21.35 26/8.

SR: Bricklayers Arms Goods 00.00: Blast broke roof glass.
Staines – Windsor 02.15: HE cut telecom, until 11.35.

26/8/40

LMS: Elm Park – Hornchurch 15.40: Both Electric lines blocked, until 21.20. Steam trains not affected.

SR: Lower Sydenham 01.40: Near-miss damaged station, also brake van of passing goods train. Block failed, but repaired by 07.55.

27/8/40

Although no damage occurred, the LNER reported that 'Red Alerts' in the London area overnight had resulted in serious delay to traffic, including Mail and Newspapers which were held back at Offices, because goods yard and other staff took shelter.

SR: Chessington North: UXB believed near line. Trains terminated at Tolworth until 11.00, but it was a false alarm.

29/8/40

LNE: Churchbury – Forty Hill (goods line) 12.30: Two craters found. Lines blocked until 09.00 30/8.

SR: Gipsy Hill 00.40: UXB near line, declared safe 02.15.

30/8/40

SR: Clock House – Elmer's End 01.25: HE near-miss damaged telecom and threw debris on line. Cleared 03.40.

Norwood Loco Shed 21.25: HE damaged middle road and coal stage, derailing one locomotive[10] and perforating another. Three drivers injured. Damage repaired 1/9.

Feltham 21.30: IB caused fires in C&W Depot, Cripple Sidings and behind Loco Shed.

31/8/40 (Saturday)

LMS: Mill Hill 01.00: HE fell near Elstree Tunnel, also one UXB. All traffic stopped until 02.11 while tunnel examined.

Hornchurch – Elm Park 01.04: HE severely damaged Up line, but repaired by 20.10.

East Horndon: HE destroyed three railway cottages. One person killed. No damage to line, but water main burst.

Brondesbury – Brondesbury Park 02.20: HE severely damaged Up line. Broad Street electric service terminated at Finchley Road and buses substituted to Willesden Junction. Freight traffic between LNER and GWR diverted via Chalk Farm. Later a UXB reported. nwr 08.40, but Brondesbury station remained closed until UXB removed 12.40 4/9.

Katherine Road Box (Upton Park – East Ham) 04.55: DAB forced closure of Tilbury and LPTB District lines until 08.55. Underground trains reversed at Upton Park. Buses substituted.

LNE: Grange Hill (Fairlop Loop): UXB fell in night near station, another in goods yard approach. Station slightly damaged and trains and passengers cautioned. nwr 10.30.

SR: Crayford 18.10: HE damaged track. nwr 1/9.

September 1940

1/9/40 (Sunday)

LMS: Elm Park: UXB forced closure of station. Buses provided for passengers. Trains at caution. Reopened 18.30 4/9 – bomb was a 'dud'.

LNE: Leytonstone in night: HE smashed glass at station.

SR: Norwood Junction: HE damaged locomotive.[11]

2/9/40

LMS: Dagenham – Hornchurch 17.20: HE cut Block, until 19.45.

LNE: Winchmore Hill – Grange Park 11.40: UXB suspected on Down line. Services suspended until 16.55, but soon declared safe by BDO.

SR: Waddon Marsh, Pan-Britannia Sidings: Blocked by UXB, until 8/9.

3/9/40

SR: Beckenham Junction – Birkbeck 15.26: UXB near line. Shuttle service Crystal Palace LL – Beckenham Junction until declared safe 16.55.

5/9/40

LNE: Goodmayes 21.30: Several HE fell on and around station. Considerable damage to buildings and platforms. Fast lines blocked. Demolition of retaining wall blocked entrance to Down Yard. Nos 1–3 roads of Up Yard and 12 roads of Down Yard damaged. Loco of 21.00 Liverpool Street – Southend derailed in debris, but no injuries to passengers. Up and Down Through lines blocked. Three coaches of Casualty Evacuation train No. 21 standing in Up Yard damaged. Through lines in order by 17.00. All except five yard roads clear by 7/9. nwr 9/9.

SR: Chislehurst 10.10: HE near Chislehurst Goods Box, blocking Through lines. Police suspected UXB near Slow lines, so all lines closed and trains diverted via Lewisham Junction and Catford Bridge to Orpington. Buses substituted Grove Park – Orpington. Through lines clear by 17.15, but at 06.15 6/9 Up Through subsided. nwr (with SpR) 10.05.

Bromley North 22.47: Traffic stopped owing to HE in embankment.

Eltham Well Hall 23.00: Booking-office damaged by IB fire. nwr 00.15 6/9.

6/9/40

LMS: Elm Park – Hornchurch 22.10: Large number of IB obstructing lines. District Line trains reversed at Hornchurch until 23.20.

LNE: Gallions (PLA) 23.59: HE on station damaged arcade. Lines clear 05.55 7/9.

SR: Claygate – Hinchley Wood 00.55: HE threw debris over line. Clear 02.20.

Saturday 7 – Friday 13 September 1940

The first two major raids on London occurred in the afternoon (17.00–18.00) of 7 September and overnight (20.10–04.30) on 7/8 September. Altogether 649 tons of HE and over 100,000 IB fell on London. Most of it was dropped successfully on target. Very heavy damage was done, particularly in the Docks areas. There were nine conflagrations[12] – each requiring the attention of 100 pumps or more (three at West India/Millwall Docks, two at Surrey Commercial Docks, one each at London/St Katherine's Docks, Woolwich Arsenal and Bromley-by-Bow), 19 major and 40 serious fires. The largest was at Surrey Commercial Docks where the fire at Quebec Yard was a mile square and was attended by 300 pumps; another fire at the same docks required 130 pumps; that at the Woolwich Arsenal required 200 pumps. Fire reinforcements had to be brought in from as far as Birmingham and Nottingham. The area between North Woolwich Road and the Thames over about 1½ miles was destroyed, including much of Silvertown, where the population was surrounded by fire and had to be evacuated by use of the River Thames.

Some 29 Key Points – factories, mills, works, docks, public utilities, railways etc., were affected, with a number of dock warehouses destroyed or gutted. At the Surrey Docks 60–70% of the timber and storage was destroyed; likewise at East India and London Docks. The lock gates at King George V and Millwall Docks were damaged, and the rotary converter station supplying electricity to the whole of the Royal Docks received a direct hit. Shipping sunk amounted to over 28,000 tons and over 169,000 tons was damaged. Gas, electricity and water supplies were cut off from many East London boroughs. Casualties numbered 1,000 killed and 1,605 seriously injured.

A further heavy attack was made on the following night, 8/9 September (20.00–05.00), when 202 tons of HE and 70,000 IB were delivered. This time there were no less than 12 conflagrations (four in the City, two in Rotherhithe, two in Holborn, one each in London/St Katherine's Docks, West India/Millwall Docks, Hackney and Poplar), three major and 17 serious fires. Casualties were 412 killed and 747 seriously injured. Key Points affected were 17, including the virtual destruction of Fulham Power Station (190,000 kW). Notable buildings hit included St Thomas's and Fulham Hospitals, Madame Tussaud's and the Natural History Museum.

The railways in the area were very badly affected, especially the LNER and the SR, and the railwaymen showed great heroism. For example when Channelsea Sidings, Stratford, were hit and many carriages set on fire, shunters got to work, engines were coupled up and carriages were rescued from ten roads, so that in the end only 14 were lost.

7 and 8/9/40

GW: Poplar Goods: Direct hits by two HE along with IB destroyed Depot. No casualties, but 36 horses believed killed later reported to be safe.

South Lambeth: Crater in No. 2 Compound. Locomotive and wagons damaged.

Smithfield Goods: Access blocked by HE on Aldersgate station.

Paddington: Bomb in Harrow Road damaged retaining wall and threw debris on Up and Down Suburban and Goods lines. Cleared 14/9.

LMS: Plaistow 17.29:[13] Electric train on bay line damaged and partly lying on its side. 17.45: Electric train bombed approaching sewer bridge; two cars derailed and driver injured. Train again hit during the night and first coach blown on end. Another on Up line damaged and derailed. Third train on Down line sustained damage. Another bomb fell in middle of Loco Shed: front wall blown out and masonry strewn over running lines; rear wall severely cracked. DAB blew up at intervals throughout the night. Sewer bridge between West Ham and Plaistow damaged. All lines closed.

Stepney East (see also LNE): Lines damaged by big fire near station and all closed.

Dagenham 22.15: Empty electric train derailed at station owing to damage on line. All lines closed, and not reopened until 14.00 14/9.

Broad Street 23.30 7/9–00.45 8/9: HE on No. 1 platform affected also Nos 2–4. IB fell on Broad Street and Worship Street Goods Depots. Fire extinguished by staff – no serious damage and no delays. Electric train in Broad Street station slightly damaged. Skinner Street and New Inn Junction signalboxes hit by IB sustained slight structural damage. At 06.00 fire still burning near latter Box and signalman unable to work same. DAB on line, so Broad Street – Dalston Junction services suspended. Trains resumed (to Dalston only) from 09.00 (steam trains), electric trains only at 10.30 17/9.

Bromley: Factory adjacent to line hit by HE and masonry strewn across line. UXB lying on Up Through line. Line between Bow Road and Gas Factory Junction littered with debris. Steam and electric lines Bromley – West Ham damaged. All lines closed. Shuttle service provided on LT&S lines in to Barking. nwr 16.50 11/9.

West Ham: Up local line broken. DAB lying in Durban Road, beside railway. Later a DAB exploded under empty electric train on Up Local platform line; part of train blown onto Down Through line. At 06.00, 11 DAB still lying in West Ham Sidings. East Ham – Upton Park electric line broken. Steam lines intact although littered with debris. All lines closed. West Ham Station not reopened until 05.15 11/8/41 for electric services only.

Canning Town Goods: Shed demolished and offices considerably damaged, also many wagons.

Upton Park: Line Upton Park – East Ham littered with debris and several DAB reported lying on lines. All lines closed. nwr not until 14.00 14/9, when LPTB service resumed Upton Park – Upminster.

East Ham: Line near station littered with debris from explosions in adjacent properties. All lines closed.

Barking: Barking West Box out of commission. Local line Barking –
East Ham littered with debris. Barking No. 2 Box hit by IB
and slightly damaged. River bridge and electric cables
damaged. Nos 4 and 5 platforms at Barking Station
severely damaged. All services suspended.

Bow (Midland Division). HE fell on Goods Depot, but running lines
in order.

Poplar 'A' Goods: Bombs dropped during night and fire at Goods
Depot still burning at 06.00 8/9. Old and New Stations, PLA
and GWR warehouses gutted by fire. East Quay sustained
considerable damage and barges moored nearby burning.
DAB in traffic sidings, which are otherwise intact.

Devons Road: Adjacent factory on fire. Lines Devons Road – Poplar
closed until examination can be made; debris on line. nwr
19.30 8/9.

St Pancras, Islip Street Junction – St Paul's Road Junction: All lines
blocked, following DAB dropping on Up Fast line immediately after passage of 19.57 relief passenger train from
Bedford to St Pancras. At 04.45 8/9 a further bomb blew a
hole in boundary wall in Cambridge Street Sidings. Slow
and Fast reopened 19.00 9/9. nwr 01.15 10/9.

LNE (GE Section):

Forest Gate 23.30 7/9: Up Through and both Down lines damaged
by HE. Also UXB – cleared 06.45 8/9. Up and Down Through
lines reopened 14.00 9/9.

Temple Mills – Lea Bridge: HE caused closure of all lines for a few
hours.

Fenchurch Street – Stratford: Bow Road and Shadwell stations
damaged. Up and Down Fast lines blocked, but Up line
Bow Road – Stepney in order early 8/9 – but see Burdett
Road below (9/9). Down line Stepney – Bow Road blocked
by debris. Fast lines Stepney – Fenchurch Street also
affected by damaged arch at Shadwell. Slow lines in order
07.00 8/9. Down line restored 19.55 9/9; Slow lines Bow
Junction – Stepney 12.10 8/9; to Leman Street 11/9. Burdett
Road station safe, but UXB still preventing service to
Fenchurch Street. LMS resumed service in to Leman Street
15.30 12/9. Fast lines reopened to just outside Fenchurch
Street 12.00 14/9, into the terminus 17/9.

Limehouse – Blackwall line heavily damaged in night (7–8/9):
Poplar Dock Yard out of commission. Many wagons
destroyed by fire. Working over the line suspended.

Bethnal Green – Hackney Downs: Damage reported at London
Fields. All lines out of action. Cambridge main-line trains
diverted via Stratford. Full service run on Fast lines in
morning of 8/9, but owing to damage at Platform 1 at
Liverpool Street, only 'fog service' run 9/9 on Enfield,
Palace Gates and Chingford branches.

Stratford – North Woolwich: Section completely out of action. Six
signalboxes damaged, including Custom House, Canning
Town and Stratford South Junction. At Abbey Mills Lower
Junction signalbox demolished and tracks damaged.
Several bomb craters along branch. Many loaded and
empty wagons burned out at North Woolwich, Silvertown
and Thames Wharf. Silvertown Tunnel cracked. Silvertown
South Junction damaged. Thames Wharf Yard damaged.
North Woolwich station buildings, Stationmaster's house
and Goods Office completely demolished. Woolwich Pier
damaged and still on fire 8/9. Line also blocked owing to
flooding caused by fracture of Silvertown sewer. All services on the North Woolwich branch suspended. Lines to
Thames Wharf restored 13.00 14/9 to allow acceptance of
freight, but Goods lines still out of use. Coal traffic not
restored (over passenger lines) until 21/9. Restricted
goods service not restored to Millwall and Poplar Docks
until 23/9 and to West India Dock and Beckton 24/9.
Silvertown Tunnel not repaired and passenger services
restored to North Woolwich until 1/1/41.

Bishopsgate 00.15: Damage done to offices and goods warehouse
by fire and bombs. Many loaded wagons destroyed.

Working restricted. Hydraulics not restored until 27/9.

East London Junction 00.15: Junction damaged and transfer to SR
stopped; line also damaged at Surrey Docks and at
Shadwell. DAB at Surrey Docks exploded 13.20 on 13/9,
blowing up track. The EL Line was not restored until 18.15
on 7/10 – to New Cross, to New Cross Gate on 12/10.

Channelsea Sidings, Stratford: 18 coaches badly damaged by fire
(all spare stock).

Lea Bridge – Copper Mills Junction 03.36: Light engine testing road
derailed by running into bomb crater, blocking Up and
Down Main lines – reopened 17.50. Up Goods road not
affected. nwr 11.40 10/9.

Hackney Downs 04.10: Fast lines on London side buckled and
twisted by HE. Lines restored from London Fields 11.30
11/9, but service restricted pending restoration of Platform
1 at Liverpool Street

Garford Street, West India Dock Road: Bridge damaged.

Ilford: Signalbox burnt out.

General: Telecom damaged over a wide area.

LNE (GN Section):

King's Cross Potato Market 04.00: HE caused two fires and some
damage to points at No. 5 arch. nwr 11.30.

Cranley Gardens 04.10: Nearby HE caused blockage by debris
towards Alexandra Palace. Services terminated at Cranley
Gardens. nwr 08.50.

Royal Mint Street Yard 12.20: On fire.

SR (Western Section):

Waterloo 23.20: Lines blocked Waterloo – Vauxhall. Gap of 50ft in
six lines on viaduct and two remaining Up and Down lines
damaged. Station closed, until 19/9! Repairs not entirely
completed until 1/10.

Clapham Junction 02.40: Bombs dropped on Carriage Sheds. Six
roads out of use. Much stock derailed and damaged.

Norbiton 18.10: HE at station and beside line to Malden.

East Putney – Southfields 18.15: Services suspended owing to
DAB, which exploded 20.23. District Line trains resumed
09.25 8/9.

Worcester Park – Stoneleigh 18.30: HE blocked both lines.

Tolworth – Malden Manor 20.20: Damage caused to the lines by
German bomber crashing on the track.[14] A number of
bombs jettisoned, including DA type, two of which subsequently exploded blowing out foundations of track and
causing large crater. Electric cables and conductor rails
damaged, also underground cables burnt out. Lines reopened 19.05 11/9.

Wandsworth Town – Putney 20.50: HE dropped through overbridge
No. 11 onto the track, blocking all lines. nwr 08.55 9/9.

Wimbledon 23.09: HE dropped on north side of station as LPTB
train entering No. 1 road, causing damage to the platform
loop, also the train. Rails in No.1 road twisted and No.2
road damaged. Six passengers and one staff injured.
Platform 4 reopened 09.25, remainder later on 9/9.
(Clapham Junction – Wimbledon closed 00.50 for examination, until 08.00 9/9). nwr Wimbledon – Raynes Park on
9/9. North of Wimbledon track damaged by fire.

Wimbledon Park Sidings 23.10: HE bomb dropped on departure
road, damaging an empty train, breaking several windows
and making crater in track.

Waterloo – Vauxhall, Juxon Street Bridge: A heavy calibre bomb
pierced one of the arches and exploded beneath it. It made
a crater 50 x 30ft, shattering two piers and damaging a
third. The whole of the arch on the north side was shifted,
but on the south side (Up and Down Local lines) the arch
was only slightly affected and after testing two tracks
were opened for urgent traffic. With gangs working day
and night, timberwork was constructed to support the
damaged masonry and the space beneath the arches was
filled with well packed quarry refuse and stone chippings,
watered and tamped to ensure consolidation. Concrete
and brickwork retaining walls were built to retain the

filling, so converting a length of viaduct into a solid embankment. Nos 3 and 4 roads were reopened for traffic on 25/9, Nos 5 and 6 on 2/10. The remaining roads were reopened on 7/10. The work was done with the assistance of the Military and also a certain number of Contractors' men.

SR (Central and Eastern Sections):

Plumstead 17.35: Bomb fell – without exploding – on electric train passing through station on Up line. One casualty. Bomb exploded later, derailing two coaches. Both lines damaged.

Victoria 17.55: Electric traction and signalling plant failed. One driver killed; two firemen and one other staff seriously injured. Trains proceeded normally, but under HSW from Nos. 10 and 11 platforms. 01.30: Further HE fell. Station roof, water-crane, booking-office and other rooms damaged. Empty train set on fire and badly damaged. Station closed, Central Section reopened evening 8/9, except Platforms 10 and 11. Eastern Section not reopened until 13/9. Up Relief line Factory Junction – Victoria not restored until 14.00 1/10.

London Bridge – North Kent East Junction 17.55: Electric traction and signalling plant failed. Central Section main-line trains to London Bridge terminated at East Croydon and local services at Norwood Junction or Peckham Rye. Further HE fell on railway at 03.25 and both Eastern and Central Section lines were closed London Bridge – North Kent Junction.

North Kent East Junction, Factory Junction and Stewarts Lane 17.55: Signalling failure owing to loss of supply current. HSW instituted.

Elmer's End – Woodside 18.00: Lines blocked by debris from fallen chimney. Cleared 19.15.

Falconwood 18.25: HE on Welling side of station, damaging two coaches of an Up train and derailing a third. Both lines blocked. Train re-railed 07.45 8/9, but line still closed owing to DAB. nwr 10/9.

Nunhead 18.30: HE on station and goods yard. Both lines blocked. DAB dealt with and damage repaired 9/9.

Purley 20.49: Lines blocked. Main lines reopened 23.40, Caterham branch as far as Whyteleafe 01.12 8/9.

Lewisham Junction 21.15: Lines closed Lewisham – Blackheath owing to demolition of 16ft span bridge at country end. SLW next day. Permanent arch reconstruction not until 3/41. North Kent Line also blocked owing to damage at Plough Lane Bridge.

Abbey Wood 23.00: Lines damaged by UXB.

Spa Road 23.30: HE on track about one mile from London Bridge. All lines closed 00.00–01.30 for examination, then all except one Up and one Down on Eastern Section reopened. No. 2 Down line reopened 06.00, leaving only No. 3 Up out of use. All not clear until 23/9.

Angerstein Wharf 13.15: DAB exploded, damaging sidings, draw-ahead road and LPTB Siding. Extensive damage to works and plant. Five wagons derailed.

Peckham Rye Junction 23.55: Damage closed lines to Denmark Hill and to East Dulwich. Reported all clear 01.50. Empty train slightly damaged by fire.

Battersea Park 01.52: HE fallen near viaduct, so lines closed until 03.00.

Balham – Streatham Common 06.40: HE caused flooding from burst water main, but clear about 08.00.

Loughborough Junction 11.45: UXB detonated, blocking lines. Five S&T men injured. Power supply of signalling cut to Victoria, Blackfriars and Nunhead. Local lines reopened 16.40 (15 mph).

Tulse Hill – Streatham 22.40: HE fell on track at Leigham Junction, blocking all lines Tulse Hill – Streatham and Tulse Hill – Leigham Junction.

Victoria 23.43: HE bomb dropped on Grosvenor Road Bridge, rendering all lines unsafe. Victoria Station again closed. Central Section lines reopened 10.45 9/9. Up Through Eastern line not restored until 16.50 6/10, and Down relief to Stewarts Lane not until 16.00 17/11.

North Kent West Junction: Signal-box demolished. Lines blocked. Locomotive[15] damaged.

Bricklayers Arms Goods: HE damaged 'F' section shed and roof, also 7-ton crane. Hand crane also hit and hydraulic main damaged.

Deptford Wharf: Hydraulic plant, cranes etc. out of use owing to damage to water main. Timber siding on fire. Wagons damaged. Later, Grove Street Crossing damaged by DAB in hold of sinking SS 'Astwood'. Another DAB adjacent to siding.

Rotherhithe Road Carriage Sidings: Coaching stock in Up sidings damaged and water supply cut off.

New Cross Gate: Five HE in sidings. Three wagons derailed and coach burnt out. IB fell through roof of Loco Shed fitting-shop, causing slight damage. Driver killed and one other staff injured.

Hither Green – Parks Bridge Junction: Through lines blocked by masonry from wing of Bridge 124.

East Brixton: Station bridge burnt and Barrington Road bridge damaged. SL lines blocked.

Plumstead, White Hart Road Bridge: HE damaged bridge.

Other UXB: Penge East 18.00, cleared 15.00 8/9; Honor Oak – Nunhead 18.00, declared safe 8/9, cleared 13/9; Sand Street Crossing (Charlton – Woolwich Dockyard), 18.15 (50 yards from line), cleared 8/9; Brockley 18.30, cleared 11/9; Sydenham 18.30, cleared 18.00 8/9; South Bermondsey 18.30, cleared 13/9; Beddington Lane (single line) 20.45, cleared 8/9; Clapham – Brixton/East Brixton 20.56, South London (SL) Line cleared 07.55 8/9, Eastern Section 9/9; Chipstead – Kingswood 21.40, cleared 9/9; Hackbridge 22.19, cleared 23.50; Wallington 22.19, cleared 24.00 7–8/9; Crystal Palace LL – Bromley Junction/Norwood Junction 23.25, cleared Bromley Junction 01.05 8/9, Norwood Junction 18.50 12/9; Angerstein Wharf, cleared 18/9; Kempton Park 00.48, cleared 8/9; Elmstead Woods – Chislehurst 04.45, cleared 07.40 9/9; North Kent East Junction 05.50, cleared 9/9; Blackheath Tunnel 05.52, cleared 11.10 9/9; Rotherhithe Road 06.00, cleared 16/9; Lee Junction 07.40, cleared 10/9; Queens Road, Battersea 07.50, cleared 16.50; Lewisham Junction 09.00, cleared 11.00 9/9; Hackbridge – Mitcham Junction 09.30, cleared 10.50; Longhedge Junction 12.22, cleared 17.30; Stewarts Lane 13.50, cleared 17.30; Worcester Park – Stoneleigh 18.30; Hampton Wick 23.10, cleared 06.00 9/9; Queens Road, Peckham, cleared 17/9.

On the morning of Monday 9 September, the situation was dire.

GW: General Restriction on all traffic for Poplar, and on all except Government priority for Paddington, Smithfield, Victoria & Albert Docks, South Lambeth,[16] Acton, Park Royal, West Ealing and Brentford. Also stops placed on loading coal for all SR (Eastern and Central Section) stations, as well as for LT&S via Acton.

LMS: Steam passenger service restored east of Barking. Shuttle LPTB electric service Upminster – East Ham. Steam services west of Barking restored gradually during ensuing week, but damage at Stepney and Fenchurch Street held up through services until 17/9.

General Restriction, including coal, on freight traffic for LT&S Section via Western Division, and on all traffic to Grays, Purfleet, Canning Town and Poplar (LNW and Midland Depots). Later in day, Restrictions extended to Haydon Square, City and Commercial Road Depots, Upton Park and Victoria & Albert Docks.

LNE: General Restrictions on Acceptance of all goods, including coal and priority traffic, to SR via GN main line, also on loading (except Government priority and perishables) for King's Cross. Goods services north and south of Thames via ELR and MWL suspended at request of SR. Also General Restriction on all traffic via Whitemoor for East London.

'Fog service' instituted on Chingford and Enfield lines, but Platform 1 at Liverpool Street now clear.

SR: Unable to accept any traffic for Hither Green from LMS or LNE via MWL. Eastern, Central and Western Sections in London unable to accept freight from LMS or LNE via MWL or via Feltham. To other Companies, only Government Priority and perishables and traffic via London Bridge from Eastern Section. Traffic for Bricklayers Arms and to certain other stations from there not accepted until 11/9. Traffic for Eastern Section via Reading and vice-versa only by prior arrangement. Later in day, SR could accept limited amount of priority traffic for Hither Green or Herne Hill via MWL by prior arrangement. These Restrictions remained in force for several days. Several other lines closed for a period owing to suspected DAB. No passenger trains into London nearer than outer suburbs.

9/9/40

GW: Old Oak Common 02.30: Fifty IB fell on goods sidings, passenger yard and Up Carriage line. Six wagons burning and Down Main line fouled by these wagons.

Perivale: UXB reported, presumably blocking Birmingham line.

West Drayton 21.15 9/9: DAB suspected on Relief line and all traffic diverted to Main lines.

LMS: East Ham: Both Local and both Steam lines blocked by HE during the night.

Homerton 02.00: Fire at adjacent Berger's Paint Factory fouling Down line to Broad Street. nwr 05.45.

Broad Street 02.15: HE fell on line adjacent to Broad Street No. 1 signal-box, affecting all lines. Bomb penetrated to LMS Electrical Department's air raid shelter below ground and it was feared that several men were trapped in the shelter. All electric trains reversing at Dalston. One staff killed, four injured. Lines restored Broad Street – Skinner Street 14.00, but platforms still blocked for steam service. Reopened 16/9.

Dalston 03.15: HE fell close to Dalston No. 1 Box, blocking all lines. No. 2 lines cleared 12/9, No. 1 lines 23/9.

Euston: 03.45: Bomb fell on No.2 Box, damaging instruments, wires, etc. No. 3 Box also damaged. Trains being worked into and out of Euston at caution.[17] One staff injured. nwr 05.35.

Haggerston: HE on line. Lines already closed from Dalston. No. 2 lines restored after 3½ hours, No. 1 lines after 15 hours.

LNE: Liverpool Street 00.10: DAB exploded in Sun Street Passage, damaging two trains standing in Platforms 1 and 2 and blocking No. 3 with debris. Also IB fell on Main Line arcade, setting fire to 20 yards of woodwork and rubberoid. Platform No. 3 restored 9/9, No. 2 17.20 11/9.

Burdett Road: Two arches collapsed, carrying railway over northern approach to Rotherhithe Tunnel, so no trains on Stratford – Fenchurch Street line. Reported safe 11/9.

Goodman's Yard (Royal Mint Street North): Warehouse on fire from IB. Bomb crater discovered in Up Slow line and Fenchurch Street trains terminated at Stepney. Lines cleared 13.50.

Stratford, CME's Works: Damage by fire to main working shops – not serious. Slow lines likely to be out of use for some days owing to damaged arches. (No further details).

Temple Mills: HE damaged locomotive servicing area.

King's Cross: HE fell on Main Locomotive Shed and Stores building, damaging several locomotives,[18] blowing out three lines, demolishing breakdown van and one side of Shed wall and roof over two roads. Water main burst, but alternative water column available. Coaling plant and telephones out of action. Glass in Suburban Shed all blown out, and LMS dividing wall demolished. "Engines can still be got out." Five railwaymen injured, not thought seriously.

Manor Park 22.00: Bomb near goods train blew wagons over all lines. Local lines cleared 06.43, remainder 17.25 10/9.

SR: Loco Junction, Vauxhall 06.15: Up and Down Through and Up Main Local lines blocked owing to bomb crater. Up and Down Through reopened 18.50.

Battersea Yard early morning: HE fell on the Main lines opposite Battersea Power House. Bridge archway supporting these lines demolished and Down Engine line blocked by debris. Eastern Section Main Lines and Metropolitan Lines out of use. Battersea Wharf branch sidings reopened 11/9.

Barnes – Barnes Bridge and Barnes – Mortlake 08.35: One DAB 100 yards from Mortlake station and another on line to Barnes Bridge. Traffic terminated at Richmond or Chiswick, thence LPTB buses. nwr 11/9.

Other UXB: Tulse Hill – Peckham Rye 00.20, cleared 06.30; Windmill Bridge Junction, Croydon 01.48, cleared 04.35; New Cross – St Johns 07.00, cleared 11.40; Queens Road, Battersea 09.50, cleared 11/9; East Putney – Southfields 18.15, cleared 20.30; Crofton Park – Nunhead 18.30, cleared 10/9; Eltham Well Hall 18.30, cleared 10/9; Honor Oak – Nunhead, cleared 13/9; Walworth Road – Camberwell, cleared 12/9; Plumstead – Marsh Siding, cleared 12/9; Stewarts Lane – Longhedge Junction (affecting Central and Eastern Sections), cleared 17.28 11/9.

The raids of 9–10 September were heavy, killing 322 people (including 200 in a shelter in West Ham and 75 in one in Southwark). Two conflagrations occurred in the City and one from Stepney to Minories and there were five major and 24 serious fires. Important public buildings affected included Somerset House, Royal Courts of Justice and Greenwich Naval College.

Sir E. Missenden (General Manager, SR) was evidently able to be quite up-beat in his statement (slightly paraphrased) to the REC of 11.55 on 10 September.[19] "The position this morning so far as traffic working is concerned was very much better. On the Western Division, there are still no services operating between Clapham Junction and Waterloo, but all main line services are being terminated and starting at Clapham Junction. Transport between that place and Waterloo is being afforded by Tube and bus services. It may be said that having regard to conditions, communications between London, Southampton, Portsmouth and the West of England are satisfactory. There is as yet no through service between Reading and Twickenham, but a bus service is covering Ascot – Virginia Water – Twickenham. Other suburban services are working in as far as Richmond, Chiswick and Clapham Junction … On the Central Division, both long distance and suburban services into Victoria are practically normal. On the Eastern Division, there are no services operating to and from Victoria, Charing Cross and London Bridge, but Cannon Street, which has now been reopened, and Holborn Viaduct are working to their maximum capacity. Long distance and suburban services are being operated to and from these stations, and are giving a moderately adequate service. From Cannon Street 10 separate suburban services are being operated. Holborn Viaduct are dealing with trains which are normally dealt with at stations which are closed, and in addition extra services are being worked to and from Blackfriars to overcome the discontinuance of services from other stations. In each Division there are certain branches over which it is not possible to run a service owing to unexploded bombs, but these are unimportant … The closest co-operation is in force with the LPTB outside London, and connecting services are being given with the Southern Company's trains at Richmond, Wimbledon and Balham."

10/9/40

GW: West Brompton (WLER): Bomb 100 yards south of station. Traffic suspended, then SLW instituted 15/9.

Subway Junction: Retaining wall damaged. Repaired by 14/9.

LMS: Haydon Square Goods 04.35: HE on depot started serious fires. Grain warehouse and dry bond gutted. Loading banks and shed on HL and small warehouse destroyed. Horse cartage vehicles and equipment badly damaged. LT&S Down Through lines reopened 19.55 9/9, Up Through line late morning 10/9.

Thames Wharf Goods 10.00: Two DAB exploded, damaging sidings. Further DAB found, and working stopped until 21/9.

West Kensington Depot 10.00: Crater in yard and two wagons smashed. Yard closed until 11.45 11/9.

Highgate Road – Junction Road 17.30: UXB affected T&H lines. nwr 15.00 11/9.

Upton Park – Plaistow 22.10: UXB on line, stopping all traffic.

LNE: Fenchurch Street 03.30: IB set fire to roof, booking-hall and Swan Street bridge. Station closed.

Burdett Road: UXB on track. Service Stratford – Fenchurch Street suspended.

Shadwell: All lines blocked in night by HE.

Tidal Basin: Station severely damaged by fire in night.

Bethnal Green: Footbridge over railway damaged by HE.

Bow Junction: HE in night broke glass of signalbox. Only Local lines usable Coburn Road – Stratford. nwr 16.25.

Manor Park: All lines blocked.

Marylebone 23.35: HE damaged tracks in passenger station yard, smashed two wagons and burst water-main. Four UXB in station and goods yards. All services suspended. Passenger trains terminated Wembley Hill, with buses provided from there to Wembley Park. nwr 11.35 11/9.

SR: Charing Cross 00.25: Bomb fell through Platform 2 onto roadway beneath Platforms 3–6. Platform 1 also suspected unsafe. LPTB District Lines blocked by debris and water. No damage to signalling, but signalman seriously injured. Platforms 1, 4–6 available 14.35, with restricted service. nwr 22/9.

Gipsy Hill – Crystal Palace LL 01.00: HE damaged tracks, telecom and LCC sewer. nwr not until 15.45 24/9.

Mottingham 01.55: HE outside SR property covered goods sidings with debris and interfered with working.

Nine Elms Goods 03.00: Empties shed set alight; Granary and wharf wall damaged by HE. A number of DAB found later, so all traffic in and out of Depot suspended until 12.00 11/9. Bomb exploded inside one shed, wrecking 12 wagons and rendering shed unsafe.

Cannon Street: Station glass shattered.

Nine Elms Loco Shed 23.40: HE on shed, causing fire but extinguished by staff. Several locomotives[20] damaged. No casualties. Further damage caused by exploding DAB.

UXB: Longhedge Junction 00.12, cleared 11/9; Queens Road, Battersea 00.15 – station closed, cleared 11/9; Honor Oak – Nunhead 08.35, cleared 10.20; Mortlake – Barnes Bridge 08.36, cleared 10/9; Victoria, Grosvenor Road Bridge 20.57, cleared 00.40 11/9; East Putney – Southfields 18.15, cleared 20.40; Kidbrooke – Eltham Well Hall, cleared 12/9; Loughborough Junction – Canterbury Road Junction, cleared 15.45 18/9; Brockley, cleared 11/9; Kidbrooke– Eltham Well Hall; New Cross Gate – Brockley.

On the night of 10/11 September, 172 people were killed, with three conflagrations in the city and five major and nine serious fires. The Science Museum, two hospitals and the Caledonian Cattle and Smithfield Markets were hit.

General Restrictions extended to Willesden – SR Central Section traffic. Also on LNE, stoppage of all traffic to Marylebone and King's Cross Goods. SR still unable to accept virtually any cross-London traffic, and GWR – Eastern Section only by prior arrangement.

11/9/40

GW: Royal Oak 16.25: UXB between H&C and Empty Carriage lines. Hammersmith service suspended until 12.15 14/9.

Brompton & Fulham Depot (WLER) 06.45: UXB found and depot closed until 10.30 22/9.

LMS: St Pancras 16.12: Signalling, also empty coaches, damaged by AA shell. Platforms 1 and 2 out of use, and trains working from 18.30 on fast lines only, with points operated by hand. nwr 13.00 12/9.

Maiden Lane 16.20: Two UXB in embankment near bridge over LNER.

Bromley: Shuttle service instituted Barking – Bromley by steam trains at 30 minute intervals. Control telephone lines restored at Gas Factory Junction.

Devons Road 21.00: HE in yard, blocking four roads and derailing several wagons.

St Pancras 21.45: Wagon hit by IB burnt out. nwr 23.00.

SR: Victoria (Central) – Battersea Park 09.30: DAB exploded, damaging Down Local line and both lines Victoria – Stewarts Lane; cleared by 18.05.

Parks Bridge Junction – Hither Green 16.00: All lines blocked by debris. Not cleared completely until 15.30 26/9.

Deptford Wharf 16.00: Lines destroyed at entrance and Wharf isolated. Much damage to plant. Not clear until 23/9.

Hither Green 17.40: DAB exploded in subway, injuring PW Inspector and four other people.

Hither Green Sidings: Yard and Loco Shed closed owing to fires in wagons and detonation of two wagons carrying explosives.

Nine Elms Yard: Sidings and wagons in Top Yard damaged by HE.

Bickley 21.20: Down Local line blocked until 12/9.

Holborn LL – Snow Hill 23.25: MWL closed by debris and unsafe wall; not reopened until 16.00 18/9.

Additional UXB: Metropolitan Junction, cleared 16/9; Gipsy Hill – West Norwood, cleared 12/9; Eltham Well Hall, cleared 18/9; Deptford Wharf – Docks, cleared 18/9; Lewisham – Ladywell, cleared 16/9; Charlton – Woolwich Dockyard, cleared 16/9; Lewisham (Nunhead line), cleared 16/9; Herne Hill – Brixton, cleared 12/9; Hither Green station, cleared 16/9; Lordship Lane, cleared 13/9; Waterloo & City (on LPTB District Line above), cleared 12/9.

The night raid of 11/12 September was very heavy – and lasted over nine hours from 20.20. Including some on 11/9, deaths were 356. The GPO Central Telegraph Office was hit and a UXB was left threatening St Paul's Cathedral.

12/9/40

GW: Royal Oak (H&C) 15.30: Further UXB found. Station closed until 12.15 14/9.

Lillie Bridge (WLER) 22.00: HE damaged gas mains and lifted tracks. Up line and Nos 3, 4 and 5 sidings blocked, also GW refuge line. All locking out, so no access to GW or LMS yards at Warwick Road. UXB on District Line. LMS electric trains suspended. SLW from 15/9.

LMS: Little Ilford 00.20: UXB near No. 3 Goods Box, affecting only entrance to sidings.

Wandsworth Road Goods 04.00: Two HE in yard burst water main, damaged traverser and derailed three wagons.

Barking 04.25: Bomb on station, affecting all lines. After UXB at Grays removed 12.25, services restored Bromley – Shoeburyness and Tilbury – Grays.

Kew Bridge: UXB on track between Lionel Road and Great West Road bridges. All lines affected.

Willesden 07.25: UXB on bank. Services over Fast lines towards Sudbury suspended, but available for passenger trains from 10.15. nwr at 19.00, but another DAB precluded access to Heinz Siding until it exploded 20.55.

Camden 09.02: UXB two feet from the Up Fast near Primrose Hill Tunnel. Services diverted from Fast to Slow lines. nwr 20.45 13/9.

LMS resumed 20-minute service terminating at Leman Street from 15.30, after colour-light signalling restored from Gas Factory Junction 15.05.

Dagenham 16.30: Bomb on station, affecting all lines, with debris on Up Through and signalbox.

Kilburn High Road 21.50: IB set fire to station and staircase. nwr 22.15!

LNE: Marylebone 00.15: IB fell in Goods and Passenger yards. Another UXB found in coal road. Traffic allowed no nearer than 100 yards.

Grange Hill 04.45: HE exploded at Ilford end of tunnel and DAB suspected on track. Buses substituted Grange Hill – Chigwell. nwr 14.15.

SR: Brixton – Herne Hill 03.10: Lines blocked by crater in track. Cleared 13/9.

Blackheath 04.05: Crater in cutting and DAB on top of tunnel. nwr 21.00 16/9.

Charlton 04.35: Both Greenwich lines blocked by HE.

Crystal Palace LL: Station offices and portion of platform bridge damaged. Lines to Gipsy Hill closed. Reopened to Bromley Junction, Norwood 13.50. Down line from Gipsy Hill re-opened 24/9.

Penge West: Station building and Up platform damaged. All lines closed for a few hours.

Lee 03.00: Both lines blocked by damage, until 10.00.

London Bridge – North Kent East Junction: Nos 1 and 2 lines damaged, preventing traffic running to London Bridge and Cannon Street. Cleared 13/9.

Lower Sydenham – New Beckenham: Both lines damaged. Cleared 13/9.

Kent House – Beckenham Junction: Bridge 48 damaged.

Bickley Junction: HE damaged Up side wall.

Other UXB: Waterloo & City Line 07.00, cleared 19.00; Loco Junction – Nine Elms Junction, cleared 15/9; New Beckenham – Clock House/Beckenham Junction 06.00, cleared 13/9; Parks Bridge Junction – Hither Green, cleared 26/9;[21] Hither Green Sidings and Loco, cleared 13/9; Catford Bridge – Lower Sydenham, cleared 13/9; Merton Abbey – Tooting, cleared 16/9; Lewisham – Blackheath, cleared 13/9; New Cross – St Johns (all lines), cleared 12.00 13/9; Blackheath – Charlton; Hinchley Wood, cleared 13/9.

Fewer than 100 tons of bombs were dropped on the night of 12/13 and only 125 tons on 13/14. Fires were limited, but 394 people died in all. The Imperial War Museum was hit and Battersea Power Station (245,000 kW) was put out of action for three days.

13/9/40

GW: Very extensive Restrictions, including most coal, also general traffic via Gloucester and via Crewe and to LT&S via Acton.

West Brompton (WLER) 22.30: Seventy feet of wall blown onto lines and station roof damaged.

North Acton – East Acton (E&SB): DAB near Up side at North Acton. HE damaged Ducane Road Bridge at East Acton. nwr 09.00 15/9 and 09.12 14/9 respectively. Meanwhile LPTB trains suspended Wood Lane – Ealing Broadway owing to unsafe bridge.

LMS: Brompton & Fulham (WLER) 12.40: Bomb on Rolls-Royce premises threw debris onto shunting neck and yard. LMS stables burnt out but horses saved.

Canonbury 12.35: IB damaged cable from sub-station, interrupting electric services into Broad Street and Euston until 15.00 16/9.

LNE: General Restriction of all traffic for SR via GN line, all for King's Cross Goods (lifted 14/9) or Marylebone Goods (until further notice), and still on all via Whitemoor for East London and SR.

Bishopsgate: Hydraulic power disabled.

Temple Mills Sidings 00.05: HE in Down Yard fouled main lines and burst water-main. Some main and suburban trains cancelled. Down Goods lines blocked. Up Main clear 01.30, Down 05.00.

SR: Much traffic, also from SR, stopped, especially over MWL. Bricklayers Arms Goods still out of operation.

Queen's Road, Battersea: Damage to bridge put all Central and Western Section lines out of commission. Windsor lines and Central Section Up Main line, Carriage Sidings and Down Local cleared same day.

Battersea Park 07.26: Station and bridge damaged. All lines blocked by debris, but cleared by 11.40.

Blackheath – Angerstein Junction 08.30: Lines in tunnel damaged by DAB. Cleared 16.19.

Coulsdon – Earlswood 14.25: Both lines blocked. Up line cleared 18.00, Down 20.35.

Queens Road, Peckham – Old Kent Road Junction 22.45: HE blocked both lines. Cleared by 18.00 18/9.

Gipsy Hill: HE damaged goods yard and footbridge.

Beckenham Junction: HE damaged goods yard.

Other UXB: East Dulwich, cleared 13.30 13/9; Stewarts Lane – Longhedge Junction, cleared 12.40 13/9; Beckenham Junction, cleared 14.50 13/9; Stewarts Lane Loco, found to have exploded 13/9; Cambria Junction (SL Line), cleared 14/9; Hayes, cleared 16/9; Streatham Hill, cleared 16/9; Balham, cleared 20/9; Camberwell, cleared 18.00 13/9; South Bermondsey – Old Kent Road Junction, cleared 12.25 23/9.

14/9/40 (Saturday)

GW: Kensington, Addison Road (WLR) 11.25: DAB exploded, disturbing platform and affecting electric lines. Kensington – Willesden service substituted by buses. Freight suspended pending examination. nwr again 18.25.

South Lambeth Goods 16.00: HE damaged track, roofs, doors and windows. Considerable further damage done on 15/9. Working not much affected, as WLER already blocked.

Lillie Bridge: Further HE during night damaged main WLER line and sidings. Services still suspended, until 09.00 15/9.

LMS: Kentish Town 00.10: UXB between Loco Shed and Junction. Up and Down lines closed and trains diverted via HL line. 'Bomb' later found to be an AA shell. nwr 19.20.

Camden Yard 05.30: Down line damaged by bomb through Chalk Farm station roof. Yardmaster's office and station buildings damaged. Station closed and trains diverted via Hampstead Road Junction. nwr 13.30 14/9.

LNE: Bow Junction: Signal-box burnt out during night by IB. All lines clear but trains being worked by TIW/HSW. Block restored Coborn Road – Stratford Bridge Boxes during day. Signalbox reopened 15.40 16/10, but still not working junction.

London Fields: IB fell on 02.36 Liverpool Street – Chingford local train, but fire soon put out by guard.

SR: Clapham Junction 'A' Box 00.18*: Several HE fell near signalbox, some not exploding. Large bomb on the middle sidings broke crown of arch over passenger subway, damaging Up Windsor and Kensington lines. Two HE within 50 yards of it but 'A' Box unscathed. All Windsor and WLER lines closed, also Down Main Through line, but these lines restored same day. DAB fell at Platform 5, and went off on 16/9.[22] Up Windsor Local line and West London arrival and departure roads not normal 1/10. As three arches had to be reconstructed, Windsor Local line not restored until 15.40 25/10, West London lines not repaired until 11.00 1/1/41.

*From Lt.Col. Mount's Report (22/9): Clapham Junction 'A' Box just missed when two large bombs fell just 50 yards north, doing terrific damage to neighbouring houses. Third bomb in vicinity fallen in middle siding, breaking crown of [subway] arch and shattering two piers. Up Windsor and Kensington (WLER) arrival and departure lines affected. Lt Jones with 20 carpenters and 20 mates of 158 Company RE timbering three arches with baulks, to support the rails. Notwithstanding this heavy underpinning, it was deemed necessary to fill in the arches with grouted sand and heavy concrete walling, although this would require occupation of the lines for four days.

London Bridge – New Cross Gate 01.30: Fire in arches under fork of Up SL line, so all Central Section lines temporarily closed. Current cut off to Holborn and London Bridge until 13.20.

West Dulwich 01.30: Alleyn Park Road bridge damaged and both lines cut.[23]*

*From Lt.Col. Mount's Report (22/11): Bridge 50ft span of girders with cast iron piers each side. Bomb destroyed both the main girders and cross girders. Although on Chatham main line, bridge required three weeks to repair, but no urgency as Penge Tunnel blocked next day (see below). Trestling erected in roadway and temporary joist bridge constructed there, which allowed double line of traffic to pass, slowly. The old main girders erected on ends of the trestles as parapet girders. New bridge later fabricated, of standard type – in spite of objections of Dulwich College Estates, "who tried to use some archaic nonsense of Victorian legislation to insist on the restoration of cast iron panelling in accordance with their belief in maintaining the particular ambience of the old Dulwich Village district." New bridge required about 100 tons of steel, allowing release of 45 tons Victorian scrap.[24]

Wimbledon 06.25: Station closed owing to DAB between the Up Tooting and Down Local lines, 100 yards from 'A' Box. Platforms 1–3 in use later in day. All cleared early 16/9.

Victoria (Central) 07.45: DAB between Platforms 12 and 13. Station closed until 08.32.

Victoria (Eastern): Current off, so 30-minute steam service run to Herne Hill.

Westcombe Park 05.00: Station glass and electric train damaged by HE. Telecom cut.

Lewisham – Mid-Kent line 06.00: DAB exploded, closing both lines.

Nine Elms Loco Shed 09.30: Several HE (including AA shell) hit depot. Much damage to Shed. Five locomotives damaged

Richmond – St Margaret's 09.30: Both lines damaged by HE. Cleared 14.40.

Battersea area c. 16.00: Main girder of Russell Street Bridge (Victoria lines over Waterloo lines) hit by two HE, cutting Down Main and Up Local Victoria lines. Restored 17/9. Bomb on gas-holder and other HE resulted in following blockages: Stewarts Lane – Longhedge Junction (two lines) – clear 18.05; Factory Junction – Longhedge Junction – clear 18.30; Queen's Road – Loco Junction – clear 18.10; Factory Junction – Stewarts Lane – clear 17.00. Access temporarily blocked to Battersea Yard and Stewarts Lane Loco. Pouparts Junction: DAB on Down Local line – set off 17.00 19/9 (see below)

Victoria (Eastern) 17.20: Three bridges between Grosvenor Road and Factory Junction hit and all lines blocked. [Not clear for how long, but probably only a few hours].

Other UXB: Hampton – Fulwell, cleared 14/9; Earlsfield – Wimbledon, cleared 14/9; Brentford – Kew Bridge, cleared 14/9; Crystal Palace HL, cleared 28/9; Peckham Rye, cleared 18/9; Eden Park – West Wickham, cleared 14/9; Nine Elms Loco 09.30, cleared 16/9; Balham – Streatham Hill 11.00, cleared 21/9.

On the fateful day 15 September, when the Luftwaffe launched two massive daylight raids against London but were roundly defeated by the RAF, their bombers were over London 12.00–12.45 and 14.45–15.15. They did relatively little harm, although 52 people were killed. By now the railways were experiencing extensive accumulations of freight traffic, and all lines had made arrangements for extensive Sunday working to reduce them.

15/9/40 (Sunday)
GW: Pouparts Bridge (Latchmere Junction – Longhedge Junction) 14.05: Bomb hit bridge, and Down lines expected to be out for some days. Up lines "free as far as GWR is concerned". Also two DAB near Latchmere Junction (see also SR below), but not cleared until 11.00 22/9.
LMS: Upton Park 15.00: Bomb damaged bridge and stairway to Down

Local platform. Station closed and all lines blocked. LPTB trains terminated Barking. nwr 17.00 17/9.

Plaistow – Upton Park 23.10: Bomb fell alongside 13.02 Shoeburyness – Leman Street local train. Locomotive derailed and crew and two other staff injured. UXB in sidings, removed 11.15 16/9. Services to/from Leman Street suspended (Fenchurch Street was still closed from 8/9). nwr 09.35 17/9.

Barking – Ripple Lane 15.00: Bombs near line. Driver of goods train injured. Two wagons in yard set on fire. No trains east of Barking. Buses substituted.

Plaistow 23.10: DAB found, precluding shunting in and out of sidings.

LNE: Leyton 03.20: Bomb close to station, blocking lines with debris.

Highgate, Park Junction 22.30: Suburban train derailed, blocking Down line.

New Cross – Surrey Docks (EL Line): Closed owing to DAB.

SR: West London Junction 12.30 (see GW above): Bombs fell on Bridges 11 and 12, carrying Up and Down Through and Local Windsor lines. Clapham Junction – West London line No.6, West London Sidings and WLER line also affected. Windsor lines closed. Up Windsor Local line reopened 16.40 17/9, for steam only. Fully repaired by 1/10, but on 2/10 reported that Up and Down Windsor Through lines still closed.[25]

Birkbeck 12.36: DAB fell. Two exploded at 20.05, blocking both lines. Beckenham Junction – Crystal Palace service suspended. Cleared 16.00 29/9.

Victoria (Eastern) 13.00: Enemy plane fell[26] in forecourt, causing fire, which was extinguished 13.30. Shops and restaurant damaged.

Sydenham – Penge West 14.55: Two or three HE. Main lines and Down Crystal Palace line blocked. Down Local and Up Main reopened 14.00 17/9, the rest clear by 13.30 20/9.

Penge East 15.00*: One HE in tunnel mouth and one on each platform, damaged platforms, put both lines out and cut telecom. Another bomb* fell through the tunnel roof a quarter mile inside. Not all normal until 9/10.

*From Lt.Col. Mount's Report: "Heavy bomb fell about 60ft from centre line of Penge Tunnel where only 20ft of cover. Concussion from explosion caused crown of arch to collapse over 35ft and width 16ft. Soil continued to fall through into tunnel until a hole showed at ground level above. Unable to commence restoration work for several days by DAB in vicinity. When this disposed of, mechanical excavator taken to site and about 2,000 cubic yards of soil removed from above tunnel. New arch then constructed, the soil removed from inside tunnel and line reopened for traffic 9/10, 24 days after the damage.

Bricklayers Arms Branch 22.30: Both lines damaged at Bridge 506. Clear 18.55 18/9, except Up line North Kent West Junction. South Bermondsey station damaged.

Clapham – East Brixton 23.00: Both SL lines blocked by HE. Cleared by 18/9.

Cannon Street 02.50: Station closed, owing to roof damage from bomb exploding on river bank. Platforms 4–8 clear by 16/9. Platform 1 in use again 10.00 24/9.

Crystal Palace HL: IB on coaching stock. One coach burnt.

Other UXB: Birkbeck 12.26 (two), cleared 26/9; Hither Green 13.00, cleared 18.25; Barnehurst 13.42; Charlton (two UXB), cleared 16/9; Loughborough Junction – Camberwell, cleared 16/9.

A fairly major attack was made again in the night of 15/16 September, and the casualties in 48 hours were 230 killed and 496 seriously injured. Two major and 10 serious fires were caused and both Guy's and St Thomas's Hospitals were hit, also the Tate Gallery. Some of the railway damage was quite serious.

16/9/40
GW: Southall West Junction 02.30: Bomb damaged Up running loop from Hayes, and seriously damaged Crow Catchpole's Sidings, also Glede Siding slightly. Loop reopened 12.30.

East Acton (E&SB) 04.00: DAB in embankment. LPTB service from Wood Lane suspended.

Westbourne Park 21.20: Bombs on western end of station, blocking Relief lines. Traffic stopped, but Main lines clear 23.30. Bomb on platform damaged Up Relief line, so Down Relief used for Up empty stock working. nwr 14.40 17/9, except Up Relief platform not in use after dark.

LMS: Harlesden, Acton Canal Wharf (N&SWJ) 01.05: Bomb crater blocking both lines. At 02.50 reported bomb had fallen on swimming-bath and thrown debris on line but trains could pass with caution. At 03.50 DAB was found right beside lines, so closed again, also loop from Neasden Sidings. nwr 16.30 18/9.

Leyton – Leytonstone 19.55: IB blocked lines until 00.30 17/9.

Wanstead Park 21.30: Lines blocked by UXB. nwr 03.40 17/9.

Victoria Park 23.00: HE blocked all lines. One staff injured. nwr 12.00 17/9.

Homerton 23.45: Bomb exploded near Digby Road Bridge, blocking both lines. SLW on Up from 17.00 20/9. nwr 17.45 23/9.

LNE: Temple Mills, Loughton Yard 02.10: Bombs damaged 200 yards of five sidings and 25 wagons, also windows of coaches in carriage sidings, telecom and electric cables.

East Smithfield 11.30: DAB found.

Canning Town 11.30: DAB found.

Kilburn & Brondesbury 03.40*: Underbridge carrying four Metropolitan Line and two LNER tracks over Kilburn High Road badly damaged by HE. All LPTB services suspended – LNER services already suspended since 10/9. Bridge not restored until 15.00 22/9, with SLW Canfield Place – Neasden.

*From Lt.Col. Mount's Report (26/9): This serious incident affected primarily the LPTB, whose double-line Down bridge in centre was destroyed and all Metropolitan Line trains had to run over Up lines. Segment also blown out of arch carrying Up LNER line. This was supported by emergency girders of steel joists and reopened 20.25 22/9, with SpR owing to cracked piers and arches each side. Evidently morale of repair men raised by posting an armed guard at site, who's "gun was able to go into action when the enemy came over to take photographs the day after the attack."

Marylebone [time?]: Bomb made crater in circulating area. Considerable damage to station buildings. Station closed. Four passengers and six staff injured. Restricted working from 07.30 17/9. Platforms 3 and 4 restored 20/9.

Leyton – Snaresbrook: Lines damaged and services suspended. nwr on 17/9.

Stratford Market: IB in yard caused fires. nwr 18/9.

Ilford 21.47: All lines blocked by adjacent fires. nwr 05.40 17/9.

Forest Gate 22.00: Local lines blocked by debris of arcade. Station closed. Three craters in section, but trains working on Fast lines. nwr 12.30 17/9.

Bethnal Green 22.22: Down Local line damaged. nwr 10.45 17/9.

SR: Angerstein Wharf: During night following damage done: Shell-Mex filling shed damaged, Nos 1 and 2 roads out; weigh-bridge blown out; telecom cut; tank-car damaged and derailed; BP Oil lead badly damaged; Gas Co's bridge, wall and road approach damaged; Nos 1 and 2 main roads. LCC and Cripples Sidings buckled. Three tank-cars and three wagons derailed. All (except LPTB Siding) reported normal 7/10, but meanwhile further incidents occurred – see below. Not all cleared until 12/10.

SR: London Bridge – Bricklayers Arms Junction and North Kent West Junction 00.00: Closed after HE fell on lines a quarter mile north of South Bermondsey. South Bermondsey station also hit. Damage minor, and Nos 1 and 2 Up and Down lines on Eastern Section available from 13.00. Bricklayers Arms branch reopened 18.55, except Bricklayers Arms Junction – North Kent West Junction not cleared until 16.00 27/9.

Brixton 00.15: Station extensively damaged by fire. Bridge damaged, but lines clear 14.00.

Metropolitan Junction 00.40: HE blocked lines to Blackfriars and Ewer Street, until 06.10. Ewer Street Depot damaged; reopened 3/10.

Hayes 00.50: Offices and shops at station badly damaged, and station closed. Reopened 19/9.

Whitton Junction – Feltham Junction 01.00: DAB blocked lines, but exploded 03.50 harmlessly.

Stewarts Lane 01.30: Bomb exploded in builders' yard, causing damage to track, wagons and signalling. All lines blocked with debris and line to LMS Yard damaged. DAB in mileage yard – cleared later in day. Lines to Factory Junction and Longhedge Junction cleared 18/9. Rest cleared by 20/9.

Queen's Road – Loco Junction 01.35: Damage sustained by Down and Up Main Local lines near the bridge carrying the Central Section lines over Western Section at west end of Queen's Road station. Lines cleared 18/9.

Petts Wood – Orpington 03.30: HE blocked all lines. Clear 06.55 18/9.

Anerley – Penge West 04.20: Five bomb craters, blocking all four lines, also DAB. All lines clear 18/9.

Vauxhall – Waterloo 09.15: Up Main Local line damaged. Clear 12.20 17/9.

Ladywell – Catford Bridge 23.00: HE damaged both lines.

Eden Park – Elmer's End 11.28: HE damaged both lines. nwr 14.15 17/9.

Swanley – St Mary Cray 15.00: HE damaged both lines.

Bricklayers Arms Junction 16.30: HE damaged arch on Up Local line. nwr 18/9

Clapham Junction 18.00: DAB from 14/9 exploded in Platform 5*, forming crater in track and blowing out buildings and blocking Up and Down Main Local and Up Main Through with debris. Down Main Through lifted and completely blocked. Windsor lines obstructed, also Down side cables cut. Main Local lines cleared 18/9. Station reopened 19/9.

Other UXB: East Croydon (Up Local line) 00.55, cleared 17/9; Tulse Hill – Streatham Hill 01.07, cleared 16/9; Tulse Hill (Herne Hill line, two UXB) 01.40, cleared 19/9 and 2/10; St Helier – Sutton Common 03.15, clear 15.20; Tadworth – Tattenham Corner 03.50, clear 06.45; Barnehurst – Bexleyheath; Brockley, cleared 17/9; Clapham – East Brixton (SL Line), cleared 18/9; Penge East, cleared 24/9; Deptford, cleared 17/9; Upper Sydenham (2) 08.00, cleared 24/9.

* From Lt.Col. Mount's Report (22/9): DAB hit Platform 5 platform and formed crater in track, blowing out portion of station building, but line made ready for traffic within 24 hours. However, another DAB dropped at same time on Down Local at Pouparts Junction. This was not detonated until 17.00 19/9 – second attempt by BDS working continuously. (They had meanwhile placed two wagon rakes as screen). Big gang at work. Main lines opened at 09.00 on 19/9, Local lines next day.

A fairly heavy attack was made on the night of 16/17 September, in two waves. Deaths were 221, and three major and 21 serious fires were caused. The Tate Gallery and St Pancras Hospital were hit. Many parts of inner South London were now without gas, owing to accumulated damage. Obviously the Blitz was bringing the railways in the London area to near standstill. The GWR had a long list of stations on all Companies' lines unable to receive traffic. The LMSR reported that mining had been stopped at many collieries due to shortage of empty wagons. All inter-Company interchange of freight with SR in London area stopped, except GWR – Western Section. "Limited" working of traffic by alternative SR routes in operation, but traffic could not be received or forwarded at a number of SR stations and depots because traffic facilities were out of use.

17/9/40

GW: Chelsea Gas Works (WLER) 11.40: DAB exploded, necessitating SLW Lillie Bridge – Chelsea. Repaired by 14.15 18/9.

Shepherds Bush (H&C Line) 21.16: UXB which exploded in early morning, covered track with debris. Shuttle service introduced Latimer Road – Edgware Road.

Shepherds Bush (WLR) 22.23: UXB on depot, suspending work.

Wood Lane (E&SB): Power station damaged. Services on LPTB Central London Line suspended until 17.30 18/9.

Victoria & Albert Dock Goods: Further damage done to offices, warehouses and stables.

LMS: Poplar 'B' Goods: Warehouse destroyed and other buildings heavily damaged.

Broad Street 01.15: Five coaches damaged by fire due to IB.

Bow Goods 02.20: UXB in yard suspended working until 05.00 19/9.

Dagenham 04.20: Up Local line blocked by debris, but cleared by 06.00.

LNE: Temple Mills – Lea Bridge 21.34: Down Goods line blocked by masonry. nwr 18/9.

Stratford Market: Fires in yard. nwr 19/9.

King's Cross, Belle Isle 23.50: HE on wall dividing Goods Yard from Down Passenger lines. Debris blocked Down Main, but cleared by 01.50. Down slow buckled, but reopened 07.20. Belle Isle Box damaged, also porters' room on the HL. One staff injured. nwr 15.50 18/9, but King's Cross Telephone Exchange out until 18.00.

SR: Selhurst 00.30: Inspection Shed damaged.

London Bridge – New Cross Gate 22.00: All lines closed for examination, also five other routes. Damage found near Lindsey Street and all not declared clear until 23/9.

Chislehurst 22.30: HE blocked all lines. nwr 03.30 18/9.

Honor Oak Park 23.22: HE caused blockage of all lines. Down Local and Up Main cleared 15.00 19/9.

Bricklayers Arms Depot: 'L' Shed and Stables damaged by fire from IB.

UXB: Streatham Junction South – Mitcham Junction (bomb sandbagged 19/9 then trains run past at caution); St Mary Cray ("magnetic mine"), cleared 18/9.

A heavy attack was made in the night of 17/18 September, for nine hours, which killed 256 people and caused six major and 10 serious fires, especially in the Docks. Also, major department stores in Oxford Street were struck.

18/9/40

GW: Uxbridge Road (WLR) 06.39: DAB exploded at station near signal-box. All lines blocked.

LMS: Dalston Junction 01.10: Debris on roof of station.

Kentish Town 03.20: DAB blocked Cattle Dock Sidings. nwr 10.00 20/9.

Dalston Junction – Mildmay Park 04.55: Debris from bombed buildings blocked Nos 2 Up and Down (electric) lines. Lines blocked to Canonbury until 14.30, to Broad Street until 16.00. Electric trains terminating at Camden Town, thence steam to Broad Street. nwr 17.00.

Bow Junction – Gas Factory Junction 06.50: Both lines blocked by crater. nwr 12.30 21/9.

Somers Town 19.30: Heavy bomb in Euston Road demolished front wall and damaged roof and offices of Goods Station. Nine staff injured.

Euston House 21.15: Structural damage.

Willesden 22.20: Numerous IB blocked all lines until 22.50. One wagon destroyed, another damaged at Goods station. Kitchen car damaged in 'A' Sidings.

Plaistow 22.35: HE caused considerable damage to station. Services suspended until 14.10 19/9.

Queen's Park 23.23: Numerous IB on lines. Electric lines clear later in day. Fast lines clear 12.30 19/9

LNE: Stratford, Bow Junction 05.15: HE struck bridge over River Lea. Both Fenchurch Street and Fast lines blocked. Down Fast restored 06.15. All clear 18/9, except Down Fenchurch Street line. nwr 12.30 21/9.

Stratford, Loughton Branch Junction 05.20: Main and Goods lines "destroyed" – but restored same day! "Damage at Loughton Branch Junction will enhance difficulties at Temple Mills. Other London Yards still congested".

Wood Street – Highams Park 21.22: Both lines damaged by HE. Bus service Wood Street – Chingford, then SLW from 09.55. nwr 12.00 19/9.

Bruce Grove: 22.37 Liverpool Street – Enfield Town local train damaged by blast from nearby HE. Many passengers suffered shock and mild injury. Forster Road underbridge made unsafe, so trains shuttled Enfield – White Hart Lane and Seven Sisters – Liverpool Street. nwr 07.00 19/9.

Lea Bridge – Temple Mills: Up Main and Goods lines blocked by crater. SLW on Down Main until 08.35 19/9.

Coborn Road: Crater in Up Through line, but nwr 10.15 19/9.

Stepney East: Slow lines blocked by debris from blast nearby, but nwr 08.35 19/9.

Custom House: Track damaged, for several hours. (Lines closed anyway)

Other UXB: East Smithfield; Canning Town; Leman Street; Fenchurch Street.

SR: New Eltham 04.55: Both lines damaged by HE. Down line clear 09.00, Up line 15.00 20/9.

Eltham Well Hall 04.55: Station damaged by HE. Down line cleared 09.00. nwr 15.00 20/9.

Barnehurst/Perry Street – Fork Junction 08.00: HE damaged both lines. Cleared by 17.20 20/9.

Nunhead 12.30: Down line damaged. Cleared 17.55.

Forest Hill – Sydenham: HE blocked all lines. Cleared 03.30 19/9.

Nine Elms 22.30: Compressor house damaged.

Mortlake – North Sheen: Fitzgerald Road Bridge damaged.

UXB: Clapham Junction – Wandsworth Town; Charlton – Woolwich Dockyard; Deptford, cleared 25/9; Brockley Lane (in LNE Yard), cleared 24/9; Parks Bridge Junction (Lewisham loop), cleared 25/9; Ladywell – Catford Bridge, cleared 20/9; Battersea Yard, cleared 24/9; Anerley – Penge West, cleared 20/9; North Sheen – Mortlake, cleared 19/9; Clapham Junction – Earlsfield, cleared 19/9.

Overnight London suffered an even heavier attack on 18/19 September, with 339 tons of HE, which killed 495 people; 31 serious fires were started; County Hall, the Inner Temple and the Wallace Collection were bombed.

19/9/40

GW: Paddington 20.42: AA shell fell through roof of platform 5 and then a coach of 22.10 Down Postal before bursting on track. Two men in Lamp Room injured by debris.

LMS: Leyton 01.00: HE near viaduct caused masonry to block lines. SLW on Up line from 15.30. Down line not reopened until 16.45 27/10.

Camden Town – Chalk Farm 05.00: DAB exploded, blocking all lines. nwr 08.00.

Broad Street 07.45: UXLM blocked all lines and station closed. nwr 17.05.

Kensal Rise 08.00: Station buildings damaged.

Plaistow 10.35: HE damaged station. nwr 14.10 – nevertheless!

Burdett Road 22.00: HE through station roof, damaging arcade and passimeter. Both lines blocked. Down line clear 13.30 20/9, then SLW. nwr 23/9.

Old Ford (Poplar branch) 23.30: HE blocked both lines.

LNE: Stratford Loco Yard: Unexploded 2,000-lb parachute mine near Works. Removed 03.20

SR: Ladywell Loop: Blocked by debris, cleared 21/9.

Charing Cross 21.25: HE fell on Nos 3 and 4 platforms, penetrating to cinema below. Coach in train at Platform 6 wrecked. Platforms 1 and 6 also closed temporarily owing to falling glass. Most of station glass broken, but wiring prevented large pieces falling. Station not fully reopened until 10.00 11/10.

Waterloo – Vauxhall: Down Through line blocked at Arch 120a.

Windmill Bridge Junction, Croydon: Local line blocked. Cleared 11.35 24/9.

Penge West – Anerley: All lines blocked, until 08.10 20/9.

Other UXB: Petts Wood (UXLM), cleared 20/9 (after stations

evacuated for a few hours on 19/9); Bricklayers Arms ('J' section), cleared 23/9; Blackheath, cleared 19/9; Tulse Hill (near sub-station), cleared 20/9.

The transport situation in the London area was becoming grave. Since 8/9 many severe Freight Operating Restrictions had been brought into force, attempting to minimise the congestion that had developed in the London area, also to divert freight traffic normally routed through London. To quote from an LMSR Memorandum of 19/9: "The most serious difficulty at the present time is in the working of traffic for the Central and Eastern Sections of the SR. All the normal routes to the Central Section are closed and for some days we have not been able to work any traffic to the SE&C Eastern Section via the normal London routes. Commencing last night, however, it has been possible to work a few trains from Brent (Midland) to Herne Hill, Bricklayers Arms and Blackheath via the MWL.

On the LMSR, Haydon Square was out of use, probably for a long time, owing to serious damage caused on 10/9. At Poplar, very serious damage was caused to the LMS and GW Companies' properties at Poplar 'A' on 7/9, in addition the East Quay was damaged and the coal tips and overhead crane were out of action. The damage at Poplar 'B' was so bad that the Depot had been closed. At Homerton, a bomb damaged the Broad Street end of the bridge on 16/9, totally blocking Up and Down lines. This meant that no traffic could be conveyed from the Western Division to the GE Section of the LNER via Victoria Park and Temple Mills, or to the Tilbury Section via Bow, or to the depots east of Homerton such as Old Ford, Devons Road, Lea Cut, etc. At Leyton, a bomb had dropped on the bridge that day, blocking both lines, so no traffic could be worked over the Tottenham & Forest Gate line onto the Tilbury Section. The West London line was also obstructed."

The LNER would have reported in precisely the same terms. On 14/9, they had 12,224 wagons on hand in their London yards and only 5,058 had been moved in the previous 24 hours (a Friday). Of course this was only the beginning. Such blockages and consequent interruptions and diversions of traffic were to recur relentlessly during the ensuing eight weeks or so, and then less continuously until the climax of the Blitz in May 1941. However, the Railways, like everyone else, soon became adept at finding ways of dealing with the situations as they arose.

The night raid on 19/20 September was almost as heavy, but only 178 people were killed and one major and two serious fires were caused. Lambeth Palace was hit.

20/9/40
GW: East Acton – Wood Lane (E&SB) 23.00: HE near line and LPTB trains terminated at Wood Lane until 23.50.
Old Oak Common West Box 23.00: Windows smashed.
LMS: Leyton – Leytonstone 00.35: Down line blocked by HE. Up line already cut, so all traffic stopped. Local trains terminating at Leyton.
Hendon – Silkstream Junction 00.45: Goods lines closed owing to UXB. Bomb exploded 09.00. nwr 14.40 21/9.
Upton Park 06.00: UXLM at station. Cleared 17.55.
Hendon, Welsh Harp Junction 15.20: Slow lines blocked by DAB. Clear 14.40 21/9.
Old Ford 22.30: Lines now blocked by three UXB. Down line clear 10.00, Up 11.00 21/9.
Willesden Carriage Sidings 22.50: Fire in Control Office and Mitre Bridge Carriage Shed. Three coaches damaged. UXB on No. 2 line.
LNE: Stratford, overnight (19/20): HE fell in Carriage Sidings near Erecting Shop, causing little damage, but a man broke a leg while taking cover. Two HE exploded in New Suburban Yard, causing slight damage – nwr later on 20/9. At Cambridge Yard (Temple Mills), four roads cut, three wagons derailed and hump work stopped, until 06.30

21/9. At Channelsea Sidings land-mine made large crater on No. 26 road. Carriages blocked in and several destroyed. Stratford Central Junction Box damaged but still working. One staff injured. nwr 23/9.
New Barnet 01.45: UXB forced diversions via Hertford 01.45–02.55, and again 03.15–04.25 when crater found beside line.
King's Cross Passenger Station 21.42: AA shell exploded outside refreshment bar, killing two passengers and injuring 27.
Bow Junction, Stratford 23.15: HE exploded on LMS Poplar line near overbridge carrying LNER, cutting telecom Bridge Junction – Coborn Road. SLW instituted on Up line from 07.07 20/9. nwr 12.30 21/9.
SR: Herne Hill: Signalbox damaged by HE and signalman injured. All lines affected, but Fast lines clear 08.00 21/9. nwr 16.30 23/9.
Waterloo 21.15: Station closed owing to fires in vicinity, until 23.30.
Blackfriars – Elephant & Castle (Pocock Street/Hill Street Bridges) 21.55*: HE struck arches, cutting Through lines. Local lines thought unsafe and traffic off MWL suspended until lines cleared 08.40 21/9. However, further extensive bridge damage done in later raids (see below). Down Through line not reopened until 26/12/40, Up Through line not until 11.15 10/2/41!
*From Lt.Col. Mount's Report (22/11): Bomb fell on wide abutment pier [of the Blackfriars – Loughborough Junction four-track line on high viaduct]. Arch (30/35ft span) over Pocock Street and adjacent arch smashed, leaving one track suspended. The adjacent track was rendered unsafe; the third track, provided with centring, retained traffic; the fourth track not affected. 158 Company RE put in steel trestle each side of pier in four days and Down Main carried over it (15 mph) by weigh beams. Thereafter buttresses built to strengthen adjacent pier. Trestling and weigh beams later replaced by pre-cast concrete slabs encasing the joists. A second destroyed arch span bridged by second-hand girders; concrete cross-slabs added to carry ballasted track. Two lines were always available at this site.
London Bridge 21.55: Traction current cut, owing to IB on roof of station. Restored in 1¼ hours.
Charing Cross – Waterloo 22.16: Up lines blocked at Belvedere Road Bridge.
Victoria (Eastern and Central) 22.16: Station closed owing to failure of power signalling. Restored in three hours.
Clapham Junction – Battersea Park: DAB exploded, causing damage. Clear 21/9.
Catford: Bridge 567 damaged – lines blocked, presumably.
Angerstein Wharf: Considerable damage done.
Syon Lane – Brentford: Wires and cables damaged.
Other UXB: Balham – Wandsworth Common, cleared 21/9; Crofton Park – Bellingham, cleared 20/9; Catford Bridge – Ladywell, cleared 20/9; Ravensbourne, cleared 21/9; Windmill Bridge Junction, Croydon (Local lines), cleared 24/9.
Most cross-London freight routes not working, except MWL to Eastern Section.

At last the night raid on 20/21 September was not severe, although 185 people were killed and one major and seven serious fires were caused. Stepney Power Station (104,000 kW) was put out of action and the Naval College and Maritime Museum at Greenwich were hit.

21/9/40 (Saturday)
GW: Park Royal – Perivale 09.40: DAB forced closure of lines until 12.00.
LMS: Canonbury – Dalston 06.28: All traffic stopped owing to UXLM. Buses provided Willesden – Canonbury and Dalston – Broad Street. nwr 11.45.
LNE: London Fields 03.56: Windows smashed at station and in train. Station closed until 07.05. Lines not affected.
Clapton: Land mine 30 yards from line. Debris cleared 13.05.
South Woodford: Land mine 10 yards from line. Debris cleared 16.00.

Stratford Market: Signalbox damaged. Debris on shunting spur, but only minor delay caused.

IB at Holloway, Ashburton Grove, Chingford and South Woodford caused temporary dislocations.

SR: Welling: Dover Road Bridge damaged.

UXB: Woolwich Arsenal 08.38, detonated 12.35; Beckenham Junction – Shortlands 09.10, cleared 13.00; New Eltham, cleared 22/9; Angerstein Wharf, cleared 24/9; Greenwich – Maze Hill, cleared 25/9; Queens Road, Peckham, cleared 21/9; Deptford, cleared 25/9.

A similar attack was made in the night of 21/22 September. Deaths were 116; fires were five major, six serious and considerable damage was done in the Docks, also at Kennington Oval Gas Works.

22/9/40 (Sunday)

LMS: Broad Street 01.34: HE exploded in Appold Street, affecting all lines and interfering with sub-station and telephone switchboard.

Camden Goods 01.45: Set on fire by IB. All traffic to/from Euston stopped. Also DAB in embankment at Camden No. 2 end of Empty Carriage Line. Princes Road stables on fire, but horses safely evacuated. Fires out by 03.40. nwr 04.30.

Haggerston 01.50: Three HE on line at rear of Acton Mews. One archway completely destroyed and water main burst. Power cables and telecom cut. All rail traffic into Broad Street suspended. From 06.15 buses run Broad Street – Dalston Junction, where all electric services reversed. No. 2 lines reopened 12.50, No. 1 lines 16.50.

Bow (NLR): HE damaged both lines, also access restricted in/out Bow Common Gas Works.

Hackney, Graham Road Box 23.55: DAB blocked lines. Down line reopened 15.05 22/9, but bomb exploded 14.35 23/9, killing one man of the BDS and Up line was obstructed with his remains until 16.08.

LNE: Angel Road 06.50: Explosion of AA shell damaged 14 wagons.

SR: Crofton Park 03.00: Signalbox damaged.

Waterloo – Vauxhall 05.30: All lines closed owing to another (small) bomb damaging Bridge 117 (Juxon Street). Only Main Local lines reopened 16.00 23/9. Both Main Through lines restored 25/9.

Nine Elms 20.10: HE through roof of Empties Shed and on cart road. Five road motor vehicles damaged.

Clapham Junction (Western Section) 20.13: Services interrupted owing to loss of signal current, until 21.30.

Tooting: SM's house damaged.

Beckenham Hill: Bridge 484 damaged.

UXB: Sidcup – Albany Park (two mines, 03.07 and 04.50), one cleared 26/9 and service resumed, other 5/10; Abbey Wood – Belvedere 06.55, cleared 07.55; Raynes Park – Malden: exploded, nwr from 19.07 22/9; Nunhead (UXLM, affecting Catford – Lewisham line), cleared 22/9.

The attack on the night of 22/23 September was moderate, with 127 deaths, four major and three serious fires; many factories, also Woolwich Arsenal affected again. Restrictions of freight traffic reported were becoming even more comprehensive, owing to cumulative air raid damage.

23/9/40

LMS: Devons Road 01.22: HE damaged track in Loco Yard and caused power failure to coaling plant. nwr 11.00.

Leytonstone 22.40: Station on fire from IB, and lines closed for an hour.

SR: Catford Bridge – Lower Sydenham 00.02: HE cut telecom and power cables. nwr 08.20.

Norbiton 00.25: Station buildings damaged.

Waterloo sub-station 00.30: HE caused damage, killed two staff; two Home Guard and porter injured. Cables damaged, affecting signalling to Clapham Junction.

London Bridge – Bricklayers Arms/South Bermondsey; New Cross Gate – Norwood Junction: All lines now clear, but at South Bermondsey HE damage in station approach necessitated temporary closure of station. Lewisham Junction; clear later in day.

UXB: Catford Bridge – Lower Sydenham, cleared 08.20; Blackheath – Kidbrooke, cleared 11.10; Upper Sydenham, cleared 24/9.

A heavier attack occurred in the night of 23/24 September, with over 250 tons of HE dropped, 217 killed, and four major and 13 serious fires. The Homeopathic and St Bartholomew's Hospitals were hit.

24/9/40

GW: Kensington, Addison Road South Box (WLER) 01.50: HE blocked lines with debris. SLW on Down line 07.30 25/9.

Paddington 21.30: HE in Passenger Yard demolished shunters' cabin. Platforms 7–12 out of use and certain trains cancelled. Damage to point motors, track circuits and power cables. Canal wall cracked. Up Main and Relief lines re-opened 25/9, but Down Carriage Siding still out of use.

Brentford Dock: HE and IB caused extensive damage.

LMS: Kentish Town 01.00: HE on Somers Town low-level line damaged wagons. Up and Down Local lines closed. nwr 06.45.

East Ham 03.15: HE on Up Through, blocking all lines. Trains terminated at Barking and buses substituted. Main lines clear 13.40.

Upton Park – Plaistow 05.45: "Several bombs dropped on running lines. Lines in order 06.45"[27]

Barking 05.45: IB on station. One staff injured.

Junction Road: DAB on Down side between LL lines, so HL lines blocked and traffic passed by LL. nwr 16.35 29/9.

Bow Junction – Hackney (Victoria Park) Junction 06.20: HE damaged Up line and entrance to Fairfield Sidings. nwr 08.00 25/9.

Dagenham – Elm Park 21.05: Bomb crater between steam lines and adjacent factory on fire. Electric lines disabled. nwr on steam lines 11.25, electric lines 13.25 25/9.

Upminster – East Horndon 21.15: HE fell on Up line and locomotive of 20.14 Shoeburyness – Barking fell into crater, derailing three coaches. None of the 17 passengers hurt. Lines blocked and telecom Barking – Upminster cut. Down line clear 17.00 25/9, Up line 16.30 26/9.

Hampstead Road Junction – Kentish Town Junction (NLR) 21.45: HE in Haven Street cut electricity supply. Electric trains diverted over Hampstead branch (via Gospel Oak). nwr 02.30 25/9.

Willesden: Fires reported in North and South Carriage Sheds, also in Sudbury Basin which was closed 04.25–05.40. Lines to Sudbury Junction from New Hump blocked from 04.30. Forty wagons and three sleeping-cars burnt out.

LNE: Wood Green 00.00: HE badly damaged a suburban set in carriage sidings.

Goodmayes: Two suburban sets damaged by fire started by IB.

Chadwell Heath – Romford: Down Local line damaged by HE. nwr 12.00.

Hackney Downs: DAB damaged bridge and station closed. Trains running and passengers allowed to alight or interchange. nwr 25/9.

Farringdon Street: Goods station damaged by HE, preventing traffic in/out of yard. nwr 22.00.

Stratford: Old Ford Bridge 'completely destroyed'. Up Fenchurch Street line damaged near Bow Junction Box. Temporary bridge provided during same day (!) for traffic to/from Liverpool Street, two lines by 15.30, four lines by 19.00. Subway between Merton Street and Loco Depot damaged. Up and Down Goods lines blocked Chobham Farm Junction – Loughton Branch Junction, until 11.05 only, also Up lines from latter to High Meads. LNER Gas House damaged by fire. Telecom out of use extensively, and with Shenfield

Control seriously disorganised.

Abbey Mills Lower Junction: Owing to further damage there and at Albert Dock Junction and Custom House, trains on North Woolwich branch terminating at Stratford Market.

Newbury Park: Signalling damaged by HE. Cleared same day.

SR: Wandsworth Common 00.18: HE on Down side buildings, killing Station Foreman, also body of clerk found in wreckage next day. Main lines cleared 08.45, Local lines 18.42.

Brentford 05.07: Down platform and HT cables damaged. Both lines blocked, but cleared by 09.45.

Vauxhall 21.25: HE damaged the Milk Arch, but traffic not affected as all suspended already.

Nunhead – Crofton Park: Blocked by UXB – not cleared until 30/9.

The next night attack on 24/25 September was again quite heavy, with 250 tons of HE dropped, killing 259 people. There were three conflagrations (all in Holborn), four major and 13 serious fires. The Inner Temple Hall and nearby GPO Telephone House were seriously damaged. St Pancras and University Hospitals, County Hall, St Margaret's Church (Westminster) and Queen's Hall were hit. Three factories in the Acton/Harlesden area and one in Bermondsey were destroyed.

25/9/40

GW: Kensington, West London Junction (WLR) 01.50: All lines blocked. nwr 07.20.

Warwick Road Coal Yard (WLER) 14.05: HE damaged track and DAB blocked access to LPTB Sidings, until 29/9.

Uxbridge Road (WLR) 23.25: Station damaged by HE, crater blocked lines. Addison Road – Latimer Road H&C service suspended.

Ealing Broadway: HE on LPTB section, so E&SB and District services suspended until 09.30 26/9.

GW&GC: South Ruislip 23.30: HE on embankment undermined all lines except Down Relief. 22.36 High Wycombe – Marylebone LNE local train ran into crater. Locomotive and first coach derailed. No casualties. Down lines and Up Main cleared 26/9, Up Relief 13.00 27/9, then nwr.

LMS: St Pancras Goods 03.00: HE and IB damaged water mains and hydraulics, also several wagons.

South Hampstead 03.45: IB cut traction current, but restored in one hour.

Wembley 04.25: A rail blown from elsewhere blocked all lines until 05.25.

Dalston, Kingsland Road 09.00: UXB – Depot closed until 10.30 5/10.

Willesden Junction 17.30: Sheet Repair Shops on fire.

Acton Canal Wharf 22.45: HE threw debris over lines. Cleared 02.50 26/9.

Cricklewood 23.30: HE near station. Cables severed by suspected DAB. Lines declared safe 20.45 26/9.

Kentish Town Junction – Hampstead Road Junction: UXB on Up lines and Down also affected.

LNE: Finchley Central 21.05: Two HE near signalbox. Current supply cut off and steam trains substituted to High Barnet, for some hours on 26/9.

SR: Queen's Road – West London Junction 00.50: HE damaged track and all lines closed. Main Local lines reopened 10.25, but other lines unusable due to damage to Juxon Street Bridge (see above).

Queen's Road: Electricity Department transformer house damaged. Signal current interrupted at Loco Junction, Queen's Road and West London Junction. Traffic stopped Waterloo – Clapham Junction Main Local lines restored 10.45; Through lines and Up Windsor Through line restored 26/9.

Charing Cross 01.08: Signalbox set on fire and all communications severed. All trains diverted to Cannon Street. (nwr must have been quite soon, as this incident not mentioned in other records!)

Chiswick 01.40: IB destroyed by fire oil merchant's building in yard.

Tooting: Land-mine fell nearby and both lines cut.

Waterloo 01.50: Roof over No. 2 Deck and No. 12 platform damaged by oil-bomb. 02.00: HE made large crater in North Sidings, damaging four roads, coaches and wagons. Woman killed in shelter. 02.10: Coach in Platform 3 damaged by oil-bomb. The Up and Down Through lines were reopened as soon as 16.00!

Blackfriars 02.00: HE outside station damaged front and interior including roof. Station closed and all traffic suspended, until 07.00 29/9.

Nunhead 02.15: Bomb on Down platform damaged both lines. Up line restored 08.20, Down 17.20.

Pouparts Junction – Longhedge Junction 08.48: Lines blocked until 17.40.

UXB: Wandsworth Town 08.54, cleared 11.10; New Cross Gate: DAB of 22/9 in St James's Church cleared – traffic had been passing meanwhile; Nunhead – Peckham Rye 10.30, cleared 26/9.

On 25/26 September there was a heavy raid for a third night, with 260 tons of HE, 315 people killed and 14 serious fires, but no noteworthy buildings affected – not so on the railways.

26/9/40

GW: Old Oak Common 00.20: Bomb in Carriage Yard blocked 19 roads. Several DAB also.

Westbourne Park 01.17: IB in Alfred Road Sidings damaged empty coaches.

Acton Yard 03.55: HE cut five roads and damaged wagons.

Wood Lane (E&SB) 05.12: Damage by HE closed LPTB service to Ealing Broadway, until 09.30 SLW. nwr 15.15.

GW&GC: Ruislip Gardens 23.55: Up line unsafe, so SLW on Down until 16.40 27/9, then SpR.

LMS: Willesden Wagon Shops 00.10: HE bomb made large crater and injured two men.

Acton Central 01.10: HE damaged electricity supply and Down lines. DAB suspected, so all traffic suspended.

Watling Street Junction 02.45: IB cut all telecom and Block. Gas main set on fire. All traffic suspended. Up Fast clear 04.35, other lines 05.10.

Kentish Town Junction 04.30: Lines blocked by UXB. Down line clear 09.15, Up line 17.45.

Gunnersbury – Kew Gardens 05.29: HE holed Thames Road Bridge, blocking Richmond service.

Kentish Town 21.40: HE caused large hole in Highgate Incline [onto T&H line], also on archway under NLR line 150 yards on Willesden side of Kentish Town signalbox (NLR), which was damaged. DAB about 20 yards from Down platform at Kentish Town West station. Station and lines closed. nwr under SpR 27/9. (Six weeks later, on 7/11, the archway over a pub that had been damaged at the time was found to be affected and so SLW was reintroduced Kentish Town West – Kentish Town Junction).

Camden 21.30: Four HE caused considerable damage in Yard, also to electric lines Chalk Farm Junction – Kentish Town Junction. Many wagons were derailed, water and gas mains damaged, and wires brought down. The Loco Shed and clerks' canteen also damaged. UXB found on Hay line at 04.00 cleared 08.00. All lines to/from Euston and Broad Street blocked. Euston lines cleared midnight, Broad Street 15.15 27/9.

Harringay Park 23.00: DAB exploded, blocking all lines including single line from LNER. Main lines cleared 01.00, branch 14.00 27/9.

LNE: Canfield Place, Finchley Road 03.00: Signalbox destroyed by HE and lines damaged. Trains to/from Marylebone suspended, until 15.30, then run at 5 mph.

Crouch End, Alexandra Park Branch 10.20: UXLM found 200 yards from line. Trains suspended until 27/9, then 10 mph SpR.

Maryland Point 09.40: HE damaged station and debris blocked Through lines, so trains run on Local lines until cleared 27/9.

Finsbury Park 23.30: UXLM near station. All traffic stopped. Trains reversed at Wood Green. nwr 14.00 27/9.

SR: Old Kent Road Junction 01.15: All lines affected. Block, HT cables and a bridge damaged. nwr 12.50.

Kew Gardens – Gunnersbury 01.30: Both lines blocked. Cleared by 18.20.

Clapham Junction Yard 02.14: Coaches and sidings damaged by IB.

Cambria Junction 02.58: Signalbox damaged by oil-bomb and lines affected. nwr on SL 15.30, however.

Herne Hill Sorting Sidings 04.30: Signalbox and sidings damaged and wagons derailed. Two locomotives damaged.[28] Also DAB close to lines – cleared 26/9, and one in sidings. nwr after DAB cleared 16.45 7/10.

Loughborough Junction – Herne Hill 05.14*: All lines, including SL, blocked by direct hit at Hinton Road/Ridgway Road/Belinda Road Bridges. Holborn services diverted to Victoria. nwr not until 8/1/41.

*From Lt.Col. Mount's Reports: In one of enemy's deliberate attacks on neighbourhood of this important junction, heavy bomb fell between two viaducts. Two railways cross here, one over the other and over a road, namely SL and Catford Loop (four tracks) over main City lines (ex-LC&D) Holborn – Herne Hill; both lines on important through freight routes. One of the viaducts needed immediate attention, and one line supported with timber trestle in two days. The SR Company's own staff erected an old girder between a new column and existing abutment, using cross-girders from the Alleyn Park Road bridge (see 14/9/40 above). The other viaduct relatively little damaged at time, but hot weather in summer 1941 caused expansion pressure on outside curve (adjacent to crater) and longitudinal cracking occurred through four arches. Therefore, service girders were introduced, ready to tie up with rails right across viaduct, also clamps across the cracking; ends of piers stiffened and underpinned as necessary.

Chiswick – Kew Bridge 07.00: Both lines blocked. Restored by 16.20.

Camberwell 09.30: Local lines blocked. All lines, including Through lines blocked previously, cleared by 15.50.

Cannon Street – Metropolitan Junction 10.15: Both lines cut and steam trains run through Metropolitan Sidings, until 17.00 when one line repaired. Up line repaired and all nwr not until 3/10.

UXB: Richmond – Kew Gardens 06.30, cleared 20.10; Herne Hill Sorting Sidings (two, one cleared same day, one 7/12).

For a fourth consecutive night (26/27 September), there was quite a heavy raid, which killed 258 people and caused one major and eight serious fires. The Old Palace Yard and St Stephen's Hall at Westminster were hit, also two suburban hospitals.

The GWR and LMSR were now giving a longer than ever list of General Restrictions, including 50% of normal Goods and all Coal. LNER Restriction of 8/9 of traffic via MWL to SR remained, but goods service to Thames Wharf restored. SR freight traffic in London area now almost at a standstill, with all traffic to/from other Companies via MWL stopped. On 28/9, all Cross-London freight to/from the SR was stopped.

27/9/40

GW: Park Royal 01.15: HE at Hanger Lane bridge set fire to freight train.

Southall – Friars Junction 01.45: Failure of colour-light signalling necessitated TIW until 02.45. nwr 28/9.

Royal Oak (H&C) 01.50: Up line damaged at Portobello Bridge. Cleared 06.30.

North Acton (E&SB): HE on line, but traffic not affected as line already out of use.

Brentford Town Goods: DAB exploded, holding up working until 3/10.

LMS: St Pancras, Islip Street Junction – Camden Road old station 21.20: HE near Goods line, also DAB, so all traffic stopped on Goods line until bomb cleared 16.15 28/9.

Euston – Camden 21.30: HE fell between Up Fast and Up Slow, blocking both. Down lines declared safe at 04.45 28/9. nwr 10.45.

Barking 21.55: DAB between Up Local line and East lay-by. Up District Line trains diverted to No. 3 line and Down trains to No. 1 line. nwr 06.00 28/9.

Brondesbury 22.15: HE on bridge, blocking both lines, but only until 23.30.

Cricklewood – Dudding Hill (N&SWJ) 23.30: HE blocked both lines and cut water-main in Carriage Sidings. DAB at Taylor's Lane Bridge (south of Neasden Junction) exploded later and blocked the N&SWJ line there as well. Down line clear 06.00 29/9, Up line 15.10 30/9.

Cricklewood/Brent Sidings 23.30: DAB 50 yards north of Cricklewood Junction and HE 20 yards further on. DAB exploded 01.45 29/9 and all lines blocked except Down Goods. Up Local and Goods lines reopened 12.00, Down Fast 17.00 30/9, Down Local 15.50, Up Fast 16.40 2/10.

Broad Street – Dalston Junction 23.55: HE blocked all lines. No. 1 lines cleared 02.00, No. 2 lines 12.00 28/9.

Falcon Lane Yard, Clapham Junction: HE damaged wagons.

LNE: Hillgrove Road Tunnel (South Hampstead) 00.00: HE near end of tunnel blocked Marylebone – Neasden lines*.

*From Lt.Col. Mount's Report (2/ 7/10): A 500 kilo bomb fell on two houses on Carlton Hill, blowing in abutment walling and making hole 30 x 10ft in tunnel roof 8–10ft below. (The two houses fell into 60ft crater, two occupants killed.) Tunnel therefore blocked by mass of debris, but access made through a vent. With two excavators and five compressors, shattered masonry cleared and start made on rebuilding arch. Expected to reopen line into Marylebone in a week, but at 23.45 on 1/10 another 500 kilo bomb in garden of St John & St Elizabeth Hospital, Grove End Road penetrated 23ft to tunnel (600 yards nearer Marylebone), where it exploded, destroying area 30 x 30ft, filling tunnel with 1,000 cubic yards debris. Repairs to first breach relatively easy and tunnel roof not reconstructed, but at second site roof had to be made good. However, at hospital access confined to nine-foot gap and wide shaft had to be sunk 23ft deep, a much more difficult undertaking in confined space and wet weather making ground unstable. By 21/11 only SLW possible owing to limited clearances, but complete reconstruction for double-line working achieved three weeks later. In meantime, temporary Up and Down platforms erected on GC Section at Neasden, so incoming passengers could change there onto LPTB trains. Platforms were built by RCC RE troops, beginning 5/10 and station soon in use, being employed until Marylebone reopened.

SR: Streatham Hill 03.48: Large fire damaged booking-hall, bookstall and some coaches.

Surbiton – Hampton Court Junction 04.00: All lines blocked. Up and Down Local clear 08.40. 10.45: DAB found between Through lines, so all closed again. Lines of coal wagons placed on both 11.40 28/9, allowing use of Local lines.

Longhedge Junction – Clapham Junction 05.30: Both lines blocked. Cleared 17.30.

Clapham – Wandsworth Road 05.30: Crater in track formation.

Clapham Junction – Earlsfield 05.40: All lines blocked. Empty electric train damaged. Local lines cleared 11.25, Through lines 18.15.

Clapham Junction – Wandsworth Town 05.40: Up Local and Through lines blocked. Up Through cleared 10.15, Up Local 16.00.

East Brixton 09.15: Slow lines damaged, but clear 14.05.

Victoria 09.30: HE on Eastern Up Main, another in Carriage Sidings affecting Down Relief, another on Central Up Through (already closed). All signalling disabled. Also damage at Grosvenor Road. All lines blocked, but Central lines restored 12.10; Eastern Down and Up Main lines clear 17.00. Buses provided to Kent House, later 20-minute shuttle service to Herne Hill.

Nine Elms 09.30: About six HE (plus IB) fell, doing extensive damage in Central, Empties and Albert Yards, sidings, etc. 'A' and 'B' Sheds damaged. South Viaduct Box demolished. Depot unusable.

Canterbury Road Junction – Loughborough Junction/Cambria Junction 09.40: All lines blocked at Belinda Road/ Coldharbour Lane. HE fell on pier of brick viaduct blowing out much of the arches of the two double lines converging here. Canterbury Road Junction – Loughborough Junction clear 16.20. For other lines timber trestles and weigh beams erected temporarily. Then new arches built, with help of RE troops. nwr over temporary structure 08.35 7/10.

Woolwich Arsenal – Woolwich Dockyard 18.50: Unnoticed DAB exploded, blocking both lines. Cleared by 02.20 28/9.

Surbiton 22.30: Station buildings damaged by AA shell. Points affected, so temporary HSW on Down Local line.

Elephant & Castle: Platform damaged.

Mitcham: Depot damaged.

UXB: Herne Hill Up Carriage Sidings, cleared 16.50 6/10; Grosvenor Road Carriage Sidings, coaches moved away, bomb cleared 4/10.

The raid on the night of 27/28 September was rather less severe, 177 people being killed and there were five major and eight serious fires. The following night London had a heavy night raid again, with 252 killed and one major and seven serious fires. The Central and the West Middlesex Hospitals were hit.

28/9/40 (Saturday)

GW: Westbourne Park 01.10: DAB between Portobello Sidings Nos 1 and 2. Exploded 10.30, damaging sidings and blocking access to marshalling yard.

LMS: Kentish Town 01.30: Six lines blocked – but clear 03.50.
04.20: UXB in Spring Lane stables, so evacuated until bomb removed 12.00 29/9.
Camden Town 04.25: Arch damaged and both lines blocked, but nwr 14.55!
Upton Park 06.15: Electric lines blocked, but clear by 11.25.
Upper Holloway 08.30: Several UXB at station. Lines closed until 14.30 29/9.
Willesden 23.35: IB set fire to 'B' Carriage Sidings, Lodging House and Loco yard, but brought under control by midnight.
Old Kew Junction 23.55: HE blocked lines to Feltham (see SR).

SR: Battersea Wharf 02.00: Goods Shed and Nos 4–6 roads damaged, also Walton's Banana Store and many empty wagons.
Abbey Wood – Belvedere 02.05: Both lines blocked, but cleared by 13.15.
Waterloo (Eastern) – Metropolitan Junction 02.20: All lines blocked at Joan Street arches.
Windmill Bridge Junction, Croydon 21.50: All lines blocked by DAB, which exploded 04.15 29/9. Through lines clear 09.00, nwr 17.05 29/9.
Denmark Hill 22.00: Both Eastern Section lines blocked; cleared 13.00 29/9.
Old Kew Junction 23.30: Both lines blocked, but clear 15.50 29/9.
Streatham Hill 23.35: Down side buildings badly damaged, Up side less so. Signalbox and carriage washing machine damaged. One passenger injured. Both lines blocked. nwr 14.50 29/9.
Twickenham – Strawberry Hill 23.50: Both lines blocked, but clear 13.15 29/9.
UXB: Mitcham – Beddington Lane 08.12, cleared 10.10; Streatham Hill, cleared 28/9; Streatham Hill – Leigham Junction, cleared 28/9; West Norwood – Gipsy Hill, cleared 28/9; Eltham Well Hall, cleared 28/9; Nunhead, cleared 28/9.

29/9/40 (Sunday)

GW: Acton c. 00.30: HE badly damaged Main lines and put Relief lines out of alignment. Further HE at London end of station damaged Yard lines and severed connections with NLR.

Cables destroyed and retaining wall damaged. Train of meat wagons set on fire on Acton Loop and several wagons fouled the Up Relief line. DAB suspected Acton West – Ealing Broadway. nwr 16.00 30/9.
North Acton 01.30: HE fell on Goods line – already closed. nwr 17.00 1/10.
Park Royal 01.30: Warehouse damaged by fire.

GW&GC Ruislip & Ickenham 03.30: Damage done to track and walls.

LMS: Brent Sidings 00.15: IB set fire to wagons in Nos 4–6 roads.
Harlesden 00.35: HE blocked both electric lines. Not reopened until 18.00 6/10.
Fenchurch Street – Bromley 07.50: DAB forced stop on all trains at Bromley.
Willesden No. 7 23.10: HE in field near track damaged Block. Trains delayed until 00.32, then Up Fast and Down Slow blocked "until Charge man arrived". Wagons burnt. nwr 03.00 30/9.
Upper Holloway 23.35: IB set fire to station and offices.

LNE: Finsbury Park 21.35: HE nearby damaged bridge at north end of station. Traffic suspended until 22.40, then Down Slow Nos 1 and 2, Up Main and Up Slow reinstated (5 mph SpR). Down Fast reinstated 23.09, two remaining lines 02.00. nwr 07.55 30/9.

SR: Kew Gardens – Gunnersbury 00.30: Up line blocked. nwr 05.15.
Chiswick 00.45: Station damaged by fire.
Mortlake – North Sheen 01.55: Crater found and both lines blocked, but clear 15.20!
Hounslow 02.27: Both lines flooded after HE broke water main.
Purley – Purley Oaks 03.40: Down and Up Local lines blocked. Clear 17.45.
Metropolitan Junction 04.00: All lines blocked by debris from adjoining buildings, but cleared by 09.00, except Ewer Street line not clear until 3/10.
Hackbridge – Mitcham Junction 22.53: Both lines blocked. nwr 08.08 30/9.
UXB: Mortlake – North Sheen (two) 01.55, cleared 15.20; Hounslow (two) bombs screened and freight trains (with volunteer crews) allowed to pass, cleared 12.55 3/10.

On 29/30 September, London had a rather lighter night attack, in which 145 were killed and there were only two serious fires, but Willesden Power Station, Stonebridge Park (128,750 kW) was hit and put of action for three days. A UXB threatened St Paul's Cathedral, again

30/9/40

GW: Acton 22.40: Subsidence in Down Main (from damage of 29/9). Repaired by 15.00 1/10.
Hanwell & Elthorne 23.30: Track damaged.
Ladbroke Grove: Carriage Sheds damaged.
North Acton: Track and platform wall damaged.

LMS: Willesden 20.05: Passenger stock in sidings set on fire by IB, also Goods LL lines blocked. 15 coaches and eight wagons extensively damaged.
Stonebridge Park Power Station 20.50: Generating stopped owing to bursting of reservoir by heavy bomb.[29] All electric services interrupted until 21.40. Temporary steam service already running Queen's Park – Wembley due to damage at Harlesden was extended Euston – Watford Junction during this interruption.

LNE: King's Cross 01.30: Three wagons derailed at north end of Gas Works Tunnel, blocking Down Main No. 2 and Down Slow.
Stratford early morning: Small crater found in Up Main. SLW until 11.00. nwr 16.00 1/10.
Shadwell: HE made two craters in Up Slow and brought cables down. Service to Fenchurch Street suspended.

SR: Twickenham – St Margaret's 00.45: Down line blocked, but clear 09.50.
Gipsy Hill – Crystal Palace LL 01.00: Both lines blocked by debris. SLW 16.00 1/10.

Nine Elms Locomotive Shed 01.55: Direct hit at west end of Shed by HE virtually destroyed T14 4-6-0 No 458. RE Construction troops used to help clear up mess.[30]

Carshalton – Sutton 05.00: Down line damaged, clear by 10.00.

Blackfriars 08.10: UXB fell through empty EMU in No. 1 Bay, then bridge girder into Thames.

West Wickham – Elmer's End 23.05: Both lines blocked, until 07.30 1/10.

UXB: Hounslow (New Goods Yard); Eltham Well Hall 08.30, exploded 12.55; Nine Elms 'H' Shed 12.00, requiring closure of Up and Down Main Local lines, until cleared 1/10.

London had a fairly heavy night attack 30/9–1/10, but with only one serious fire and no notable incident, although 221 people were killed. On the night of 1 October, London was attacked only between 20.10 and 23.10, albeit quite heavily and 143 people were killed. There were two serious fires and the Tower of London was hit.

For the next week, attacks were fairly minor, but many incidents were reported on the railways, some of which caused extensive disruption.

1/10/40

GW: Latchmere Junction (WLER) in night: Tracks slewed, and DAB closed both lines. All lines not reopened until 14.00 9/10.

Brentford Town Goods: UXB reported.

Paddington, Albert Road Depot 22.45: HE damaged warehouse, lorry, trailers and containers.

LMS: Leytonstone 06.30: DAB found on platform, so both lines closed and buses substituted Leyton – Wanstead Park. nwr 4/10.

Finchley Road Goods Yard 21.10: HE opposite signalbox blocked Up and Down Hampstead Junction lines. 00.05: Reported up to four girders at Willesden end of Hampstead Tunnel fallen on the electric (NL) lines. Down line clear 19.30 5/10. Up line not cleared until 15.15 5/1/41 – and only for freight.

LNE: Temple Mills New Suburban Yard in night: HE damaged four roads and derailed 20 wagons. nwr 17.30 2/10.

Stratford Loco 20.24: HE fell between Nos 6 and 7 roads, blocking entrance to Loco Shed. End of Shed blown out and fires started. Two staff injured. Eleven locomotives damaged. All cleared by 3/10.

Stratford Market 22.00: Factory hit and debris blocked both lines. Clear by 10.30 2/10.

Harringay 23.30: HE at south end of station caused extensive damage to lines. DAB found 04.00 2/10, so all lines except Up Slow blocked. nwr 14.30 2/10.

Marylebone, St Johns Wood Tunnel 23.45*: HE penetrated roof of tunnel, blocking both lines with debris. Marylebone Passenger and Goods closed, but some traffic being dealt with at Wembley Stadium. Marylebone station was not reopened until 20.00 25/11. [*See Report under 27/9, above].

SR: Worcester Park 02.40: Sidings damaged.

Malden – Raynes Park 03.00: Local lines damaged, so all blocked, but cleared by 15.20.

Surbiton – Hampton Court Junction: Both Main Through lines blocked. Clear 13.30 2/10.

Bromley South – Bickley 06.50: All lines blocked by damage, until 15.45.

Battersea Park: HE severely damaged Road Motor Repair Shop and offices, and 18 vehicles.

East Croydon – South Croydon 22.20: Down relief line blocked, but cleared 16.25 2/10, although Down Main declared unsafe until 3/10.

UXB: Norbiton – Malden, lines slewed by DAB, which was sandbagged and made safe 13.30 6/10, then detonated 8/10; Shepperton cleared 6/10; Sunbury – Shepperton, cleared 8/10.

2/10/40

GW: All Yards in London at a standstill.

Mitre Bridge Junction (WLR) 07.46: DAB exploded in Milk Dock.

LMS: Willesden Junction 00.15: Main lines blocked (until 01.12) and Nos 8 -13 sidings damaged, also wagons.

Harringay Park – Crouch Hill 01.05: Whiteman's Road Bridge (LNER over T&H) damaged by HE. Both lines blocked – but nwr by 07.55.

Canonbury – Dalston Western Junction 01.45: HE blocked both lines. No details as phones cut. Steam lines restored 02.15, electric 16.20.

Commercial Road 04.50: Loaded wagon burnt.

Willesden HL 05.20: EMU ran into debris. Track and conductor rail severely damaged. Services suspended, but only until 10.15.

Islip Street Junction – St Paul's Road Junction, St Pancras 06.25: HE blocked Goods lines, but nwr by 09.20.

Stonebridge Park 09.02: DAB exploded, severely damaging Carriage Shed and six coaches.

Sudbury Sidings 06.45: DAB exploded in carriage sidings, damaging 20 wagons. nwr 10.00.

LNE: Stratford Western Junction 00.40: HE on track blocked Down Through and Up and Down Local lines. Cleared by 07.45.

Harringay 00.55: Wall of viaduct cracked and track damaged. All (five Up and two Down) lines blocked. Reopened in stages 06.55–14.40.

King's Cross Goods: DAB interfering with loading.

SR: General restriction on all traffic via West London line now also.

Streatham Common substation 00.33: Hit by HE and destroyed by fire. No traction current Thornton Heath – Balham or Mitcham Junction – Tulse Hill. Electric trains steam-hauled through Streatham area until current restored 07.45. Streatham Common – Streatham North and South Junctions cleared same day. All normal 3/10.

Nunhead – Brockley Lane 01.00: Down line blocked. nwr 08.00.

West London Junction 01.52: Up Windsor Local line and signalbox damaged. Line cleared 08.55.

Peckham Rye 15.09: HE damaged two six-car EMU's. One man killed and eight injured. Signalling cables cut, so no colourlights at Victoria, with Central Section trains terminating at Clapham Junction until 18.12 and both SL lines closed until 16.50. DAB by 'B' Box, cleared 3/10.

UXB: Chessington North – Chessington South, not cleared until 10.15 11/10.

Since 7/9, many main SR lines were reported closed for examination. On 2/10, this included Waterloo – Vauxhall 02.00 for up to six hours

3/10/40

GW: Southall: HE demolished Acid Store and damaged Goods offices and shed, and shunters' cabin. Damage also at Roof Metalling shed and Loco shed. Crater in railway allotments.

Park Royal Goods 04.00: HE on north side loading platform. Roof damaged and motor vehicles destroyed. Two loaded wagons damaged.

St Quintin Park (WLR) 03.52: Oil-bomb set fire to station, which was completely gutted. All lines blocked, until 16.30. Station closed permanently.[31]

LMS: Stonebridge Park New Carriage Depot 00.05: Several UXB. Cleared 12.00 – except one exploded 11.40, causing much damage.

Cricklewood Junction 14.30: Down lines blocked by AA shell explosion, until 18.25.

LNE: General Restrictions draconian, including all traffic to London, GW and SR.

North Harrow (Met & GC) 00.50: HE and oil-bomb damaged points, signalling and conductor rails, blocking entry to goods yard at Harrow North Junction. Traction current cut off and Met trains suspended until 04.55 4/10. Main lines clear by 04.45 4/10.

Enfield Lock 04.40: HE blocked Up and Down Main lines and Up Loop. Trains diverted via Seven Sisters and Churchbury, with buses provided Enfield Lock – Waltham Cross. Normal 16.45 3/10, but telecom London – Cambridge not restored until 11.00 4/10.

Wembley Hill – Neasden North Junction 05.00: HE cut both Main and Loop lines. Lines cleared by 12.20 but SLW over Up Loop until nwr 13.40.

Temple Mills, Loughton Yard in evening: HE damaged five roads and derailed 10 wagons. Not all cleared until 8/10.

Silvertown 20.20: Tunnel damaged by HE, blocking North Woolwich lines.

SR: Beckenham Junction 05.58: Two coaches badly damaged by HE. Traction current cut off to Crystal Palace LL until 08.24. DAB reported, so all lines blocked and bus services provided, until cleared 18.35 8/10.

Angerstein Wharf 23.00: HE damaged various sidings and 17 wagons.

Beddington Lane – Mitcham: Single line blocked by damage. Normal 09.30 4/10.

4/10/40

GW: East Acton (E&SB): Station damaged by blast.

GW&GC: Ruislip – Northolt West Junction 22.00: HE cut telecom, so TIW until 12.25 5/10.

LMS: Acton Central – South Acton 14.45: DAB nearby demolished plate-layer's cottage and damaged underbridge. Lines blocked and trains terminated Acton Central. Down line cleared 16.00, Up line 18.00.

Euston (Stanhope Street) 14.45: HE near No. 2 Box affected all lines until 15.00. Signalling damaged on Up Loop, Down Carriage Sidings and Nos 7 and 11 platform lines. nwr 20.25.

Kew East Junction 20.30: HE nearby damaged signalbox.

Cricklewood 21.50: UXB exploded in New Wharf Sidings. Running lines not affected.

Willesden 22.25: Several HE made craters in Sudbury Sidings area (High and Low Level). Wagons damaged in 'G' Sidings and Brent South End Nos 2, 3 and 7 roads in Sudbury Basin cut. Sudbury Middle Sidings out of use. 06.20 (5/10): Crater found in New line and No. 20 (Engine) road. Block out at Brent Junction No. 7 Box. Main and LL Goods lines restored by 23.20, HL Goods by midnight. As a consequence of all this, all traffic blocked back until 05.00 6/10. Block working at Brent No. 7 not restored until 11.10 6/10.

Neasden Junction – Harlesden (N&SWJ) 22.40: HE badly damaged Craven Park Road Bridge. Lines damaged and flooded. Traffic suspended. nwr 08.30 5/10.

LNE: North Harrow (Met&GC) 15.50: DAB found at north end of goods yard, south of station. Station evacuated. LNE and LPTB services suspended. Buses substituted Wembley Park – Pinner, until 18.40. Goods yard clear 04.45, nwr 18.25 5/10.

Wood Street 16.00: DAB exploded, damaging both lines. Buses substituted Hoe Street – Wood Street. nwr 14.20 5/10.

Crews Hill 20.30: HE blocked both lines. Shuttle service instituted Hertford North – Crews Hill, with buses on to Gordon Hill. nwr 09.15 5/10.

Spitalfields 20.50: Bomb crater behind No. 4 road. Five wagons, brake van and a loco damaged.

Neasden North Junction 22.00: Bridge over River Brent damaged and Down Slow out of use Neasden North – Wembley Hill. nwr 17.10 5/10.

SR: Mitcham Junction 01.10: All lines blocked. Buses provided until cleared 09.30.

Balham Intermediate Box 19.23: Lines blocked by barrage balloon (BB), which dragged its lorry onto the railway! Local lines clear 20.45, Main lines 00.15 5/10.

Addiscombe 20.50: Signalbox and carriage shed damaged.

Thornton Heath – Selhurst 21.15: HE blocked Main lines. Down Main cleared 09.00, Up Main 14.45 6/10.

5/10/40 (Saturday)

LMS: Cricklewood Carriage Sidings 03.55: HE between Nos 12 and 13 roads derailed coaches in No. 10 road and damaged Nos 10–15 roads and the carriage shed.

Wanstead Park – Woodgrange Park 05.00: Debris from adjacent bombed houses blocked lines. Buses substituted Wanstead Park – East Ham. nwr 11.45.

Willesden Junction (New) – Harlesden 06.55: Electric lines blocked by debris.

Poplar 11.35: HE cut Nos 6–11 roads and derailed four wagons.

Upper Holloway 23.35: HE and oil-bomb in Down line at west end of station, but damage slight. SLW to Junction Road until 10.25 6/10.

Silkstream Junction – Mill Hill 22.12: Lines closed when HE fell, but craters found between Up Fast and Down Slow had not damaged track, so traffic resumed 00.15 6/10.

Haydon Square 23.30: HE fell through bridge on line into Depot, cutting it off. nwr 20.00 9/10.

LNE: Gidea Park 15.15: HE damaged sidings.

Wood Green 22.45: HE fell just north of station. 02.10 6/10: Another on Down Slow line. Down Enfield and Down Goods lines also blocked; 5 mph SpR on other lines. Down Enfield line cleared 19.00 6/10, nwr on remainder 09.30 7/10.

Many telephone lines down in Eastern Section and connection with Shenfield Control difficult.

Royal Mint Street (LNE&LMS) 23.40: Gas and water mains cut by HE in GN Yard. Warehouse damaged and all hydraulics out of use, rendering depot inoperative.

6/10/40 (Sunday)

LNE: Chigwell: HE blocked lines and cut telecom. Buses substituted, until 10.35.

Gidea Park 01.14: HE damaged Local line platform and all lines blocked until 06.15, then SLW. UXB near goods yard. All lines clear later in day, but colour-light signalling remained inoperative.

SR: Purley Oaks in night: Station roof damaged.

Catford – Bellingham 00.18: One HE fell on Down side embankment, four on Up side. Lines not blocked, but telecom cut Nunhead – Bellingham, until 07.30.

Woolwich Dockyard 04.10: Station roof damaged.

Woolwich Arsenal 04.30: HE exploded on Up platform, damaging station and blocking both lines by debris. TIW until telecom restored 07.30. nwr 12.00.

UXB: Angerstein Wharf 04.45 (sunk below river bed), not cleared until 2/11; Bricklayers Arms Shed (in 50,000-ton coal stack, where bomb left until coal used up).

7/10/40

GW: Old Oak Common 20.40: Bombs on No. 19 road burst water mains, other roads damaged, also 19 coaches. Restored 8/10.

Westbourne Park 20.20: Fire bomb on Up Goods road to Subway Junction damaged station extensively. HE on Mouse Hole Tunnel underbridge made five-foot crater in track and badly damaged two wagons and Hill-Evans Store. 20.45: Another HE near Mileage Yard damaged Foreman's cabin, also lorries. nwr 11.00 9/10.

Acton 20.40: HE blocked Up and Down Main and Relief lines. Down Main cleared 21.00. Up Main traffic diverted via Park Royal until 22.05, at 5 mph. Lines cleared by 11.15 8/10.

Paddington 22.22: IB caused damage to No.1 weighbridge siding.

LMS: Homerton 23.35: HE in Mill's coal siding blocked both lines until 01.00 8/10.

Camden 23.45: Up and Down Slow and Up Fast damaged – but clear in 30 minutes.

LNE: Bow Creek 10.30: Three HE damaged buildings and weighbridge in yard. Three LNER clerks and one other person injured.

Mill Hill East 20.30: Crater found in track 100 yards northward. Goods service from Finchley suspended. Normal 15.25 8/10.

Enfield Lock – Waltham Cross 05.03: HE blocked both lines. Trains diverted via Churchbury, with shuttle Stratford – Waltham Cross. Up line cleared 07.40 for SLW. nwr 12.25 8/10.

Woodford: Down line fouled by debris from HE on embankment. Up line clear, but DAB also on Down side. nwr 09.00 8/10.

On 7 October SR reported difficulty being experienced with exchange traffic. Both WLR and ELR lines closed. GWR unable to accept LNE and LMS traffic, except Government traffic by special trains via Basingstoke, an alternative route to those closed. Secondary alternative routes being utilised, via Staines, Winchester Cheesehill, or Templecombe.

SR: New Cross Gate – Brockley 14.10: UXB damaged Up Main, so all lines closed. UXB cleared 12.35 16/10, but other lines must have been reopened long before..

Belmont 20.55: HE on Down line 200 yards north. Both lines blocked. Buses provided Sutton – Epsom Downs until Up line clear, then SLW until Down line clear 12.35 8/10.

Charlton – Woolwich Dockyard 21.05: Both lines blocked. Down clear 10.20 8/10, Up line not cleared until 16.30 18/11.

Grove Park – Sundridge Park 22.40: Both lines blocked. Clear 05.25 8/10.

On the night of 7/8 October, London again had a moderately heavy raid, in which 169 died and three serious fires were caused.

8/10/40

LMS: Broad Street 03.00: Debris from bombs in vicinity blocked all lines until 04.15.

South Hampstead – Kilburn High Road 20.35: HE fell on freight train and caused crater 60 x 15 ft. All steam lines blocked and trains terminated at Willesden Junction. Slow lines reopened 12.00, Fast lines 19.00 9/10. nwr 10.45 10/10.

Thames Wharf Goods: Track and buildings damaged.

LNE: Bishopsgate 03.00: HE damaged hydraulic mains and hoists; basement damaged by water. Mess rooms,18 vehicles and five trailers destroyed by bombs that fell through arches. DAB outside main entrance. Bishopsgate South Box damaged but workable. Four staff and seven other people injured. Depot closed. Daytime work resumed 9/10, but without roof. Hoist restored 11/10. Black-out precautions not restored, so no night work, until 22/10.

Stratford, Chobham Farm Junction 19.35: HE damaged signalbox and two signalmen injured. Tracks not affected, but telecom interrupted to Loughton Branch Junction, necessitating TIW.

Finsbury Park 20.40: HE fell on lavatory at north end of platforms 7 – 8 while 20.20 local ex-King's Cross standing at No. 8. Three coaches damaged. Seven persons killed, others injured. Up lines and Down Main and Goods lines still workable. No. 1 Down Slow reopened 08.00 9/10 and all normal by 10/10.

Willesden Green – Dollis Hill (Met.) 21.00: LNE lines damaged.

King's Cross Goods 22.02: At Camley Street coal drop, IB damaged gantry and injured two men.

SR: West Croydon – Waddon 04.15: Both lines blocked. Clear 12.30.

Charing Cross 08.48: Oil and HE bombs on station, damaging track, signalling, roof and girders, also an eight-car EMU (ex-07.47 from Hayes). At least four people (two staff) killed and 19 injured, some on Hungerford Footbridge. Station closed and special buses provided to London Bridge, until Platforms 4 and 5 reopened 10.00 11/10. Using a standard steel trestle, placed in position by 158 RCC RE, to shore up the damaged girders at the south end and the footbridge.[32] Platforms 3 and 6 restored 18/10, but No. 2 not restored until 18/11, No. 1 not until 15.00 7/1/41. (All LPTB services through Charing Cross were also suspended until 16.10 9/10).

Bricklayers Arms Goods 09.10: HE fell in 'F' Outwards Shed, damaging also sidings and wagons. Four staff killed.

Eltham Well Hall – Kidbrooke 11.50: Up line blocked until 14.50.

Motspur Park 20.34: HE near line covered tracks with debris. Both lines closed until 22.10. Station closed until 06.00 9/10.

Chislehurst Junction – St Mary Cray 20.55: Up Chislehurst Loop blocked. Cleared 01.25, for steam trains.

Victoria 21.15: Station closed, owing to gas main ignited on Grosvenor Road Bridge. Eastern Section reopened 22.00, Central Section 22.45. Meanwhile Central Section trains terminated Clapham Junction, but only one train on Eastern Section affected, being diverted to Cannon Street.

Bickley Junction – Petts Wood Junction 21.38: Up line blocked, also Down line 22.04. Both cleared 01.15 9/10.

London received quite a heavy night attack on 8/9 October, with 113 killed; one conflagration (at LEP Transport Ltd, Chiswick), one major and five serious fires. London Docks, Stepney were hit, also St Matthew's Hospital, Shoreditch. There was some bombing of London by day also on 9–11 October.

9/10/40

LMS: Poplar 06.25: HE fell on East Quay. Wagons and track damaged, also lock gates.

Barking – East Ham 11.35: HE blocked electric lines and Kentish Town branch lines. Cleared in stages by 17.10.

St Pancras Junction 21.43: HE destroyed west departure lines. Two locomotives damaged.[33]

Somers Town Goods 21.45: HE fell in HL and penetrated to LL, damaging two wagons, two carts and weighbridge.

Willesden No. 6 – Kensal Green 23.20: Crater found near Up City (electric) line.

LNE: Stratford Works, in night: Two HE fell on Foundry. Damage to roof of Pattern and Element Shops, also windows and doors of Cell Repair Shop. Foundry closed.

Seven Sisters – Hackney Downs: Telecom damaged.

Noel Park – Wood Green: Telecom damaged.

Hadley Wood North Tunnel 01.05: Bomb on roadway nearby made tunnel unsafe, so trains diverted via Hertford until 05.45, then run at caution.

Devonshire Street 01.30: Coal wharf set on fire. Up Through line blocked until 03.00.

Forest Gate Junction 14.55: HE struck Balmoral Road Bridge, damaging wall and bursting water main. Down Local line blocked.

King's Cross, York Way 20.30: HE demolished boundary wall, burst gas main and damaged 10 road vehicles, also SM's office on York Road platform.

SR: Deptford Wharf 15.40: Sidings damaged.

Crystal Palace LL – Bromley Junction 19.35: Victoria – West Croydon EMU ran onto a dead section and two motor cars caught fire.

Elmer's End – Clock House 20.00: Both lines damaged. Down cleared 15.40 11/10, Up 16.55 13/10.

Malden – Berrylands 20.34: All lines blocked. Down Local reopened (for steam) 10.00 11/10, remainder on 12/10.

Elmer's End – Woodside 21.45: Both lines damaged. Down line clear 15.40 11/10, Up (for steam) 16.45 12/10.

Victoria 22.25: HE struck Platform 16, damaging Platforms 15–17 and buildings. At least three EMU damaged, including Brighton Belle unit, also three vans. Another HE extensively damaged station forecourt. 26 people injured. "Mail on platform blown to pieces". Grosvenor Hotel also severely damaged. Platforms 16 and 17 out of use, but "station will open for morning services". Not all normal until 1/11.

Woodside: HE damaged station.

Elmer's End – Eden Park: Lines blocked by debris. Down line clear 15.40 11/10.

Clapham Junction – Wandsworth Common 22.31, also Clapham Junction (Western Section) 22.40: All lines closed for clearance of IB, but only until 22.55!

UXB: Birkbeck 05.50, exploded 14.30, but no damage done to

lines; Elmer's End – Eden Park 20.34, cleared 09.50 10/10; Teddington – Hampton Wick, screened 17/10; Bickley – Petts Wood, detonated 15/12.

There was quite a severe attack again on 9/10 October, with 190 killed, and two serious fires. The Royal Courts of Justice and St Paul's Cathedral were affected. Collapse of 130ft of a main sewer (serving 400,000 people) at St John's Wood meant that untreated sewage had to be allowed into the Grand Union Canal for several months.

10/10/40
GW: Hayes & Harlington 20.30: HE near Down Main blocked line with debris. Cleared 21.50 (5 mph).

Castle Bar Park 20.35: HE blocked both lines. Line clear 16.10 11/10, then TIW at 5 mph. 06.00 11/10: Owing to subsidence SLW reinstated on Greenford South Loop until 11.15.

Wood Lane – East Acton (E&SB) 22.00: Crater in track, damaging GW line and LPTB conductor rail. nwr 11/10.

LMS: Devons Road 05.40: HE destroyed Foreman's cabin and derailed many wagons. Access to carriage sidings blocked. Field sidings damaged. Driver and fireman of shunting loco, also one other staff, killed.

Willesden 07.35: UXB found and lines blocked. Bomb exploded 10.15 blocking City Goods lines. Up lines restored 13.25, Down lines 18.00.

Dagenham Dock 09.15: HE in Ripple Lane Up Sidings damaged Nos 4–6 roads.

Devons Road 12.00: DAB in coal yard. "Instructed by Police to leave it for four days." Clear 14.30 16/10.

Queen's Park – Willesden 20.40: Several HE in vicinity of stations broke windows, also those of Willesden Nos 4 and 5 Boxes and HL Box. Windows broken in stock of 20.25 Willesden – Euston empty train. nwr by 21.10!

St Ann's Road – South Tottenham 20.55: Both lines blocked by damage to LNE bridge on Enfield line. nwr 08.00 11/10.

Hendon – Silkstream Junction 21.20: Up and Down Fast lines damaged. nwr 15.05 11/10.

Kentish Town 21.35: HE demolished Engine Shed Box, blocking Fast and Goods lines. Lines restored in stages 00.45–11.25 11/10. Bomb through roof of No. 2 Shed at Loco Depot damaged five locomotives, killed a steam-raiser and injured six other staff.

Dudding Hill – Acton Wells Junction 21.35: Bridge damaged and both lines blocked. Down line clear 19.30 11/10, Up not until 17.00 27/10.

Willesden 22.10: UXB damaged Up LL Goods line between No. 4 Box and platform. Removed 12.00 19/10.

Willesden Loco 22.20: HE cut water, gas and electricity supplies at Stephenson Street.

Old Oak Junction 23.50: HE in vicinity and IB damaged and blocked both lines towards Acton. nwr 01.45 11/10.

LNE: Finsbury Park 21.18: Four HE fell. One near No. 1 Box damaged Down Canonbury line, also five brake vans, 13 wagons and a locomotive. Cleared 10.00 11/10, but Ashburton Grove and East Goods Yards closed by UXB, and there were others.

Wembley Park (Met&GC) 21.55: HE fell north of station, derailing an LPTB train. Crater formed in Up LNE line and debris covered LPTB lines towards Harrow-on-the-Hill. Down line also damaged. Expresses diverted to GW&GC route. Suburban services covered by Met trains from Harrow, with buses Harrow – Wembley Park. SLW on Down line introduced 09.00 11/10, with shuttle service on Met line.

Seven Sisters 23.00: Lines from Stamford Hill and to West Green blocked. Normal 10.30 11/10.

Churchbury Loop: Both lines out at Edmonton Junction.

Devonshire Street 23.00: East Box damaged but workable. Down Through line blocked until midnight, Up Through until 00.45 11/10.

Lea Bridge 23.30: Two HE made signalbox unworkable. Up Main

line blocked until 00.50 11/10. Lea Bridge Curve out of use because points damaged. SLW Copper Mill Junction – Temple Mills North, until nwr 10.30 11/10.

SR: Surbiton – Hampton Court Junction 06.50: HE damaged three of four lines. Two wheels at rear of 05.53 Guildford – Waterloo EMU derailed – no casualties. Down and Up Local and Down Hampton Court lines reopened 17.15, Up Main Through cleared 19.00.

Ewer Street 19.59: Direct hit on Depot by HE caused extensive damage to buildings and to No. 1 road. Debris thrown onto running lines and HT cables severed. Locomotive[34] damaged. Signalling out of action at London Bridge (Central and Eastern), Borough Market Junction, Cannon Street, Holborn, Metropolitan Junction and Blackfriars, so all lines closed. Signalling restored by 04.45, except at Borough Market and Metropolitan Junctions and Moorgate, where not restored until 18.15 11/10. Several of the lines to Blackfriars and Charing Cross damaged, also threatened by a DAB until removed 14.15 11/10. Local lines Charing Cross – Waterloo Eastern not reopened until 18.00 18/10.

St Mary Cray Junction 20.23: HE nearby damaged junction and broke windows of 17.39 express Dover Priory – Victoria. Both lines blocked until 22.00.

Feltham Junction 20.35–50: HE on embankment damaged vehicles of 19.30 empty van train Clapham Junction – Surbiton. HT and signalling cables severed.

Victoria – Victoria Junction (Eastern) 21.43: All lines closed until 21.59 for clearance of IB, and to Battersea Park until 22.20 for examination.

London Bridge (Central) 21.50: Damage to cables stopped all trains until 02.40 11/10.

West Croydon 22.00: Two HE exploded, one on Down, one on Up platform, blocking both lines. 21.30 EMU Epsom Downs – Forest Hill hit; motorman, soldier and girl badly injured; in all six staff and three passengers injured. Station closed, until London platform and Wimbledon bay reopened 10.15 11/10. Down line clear 17.15 11/10. Up line clear 06.00 12/10.

Clapham Junction – Wandsworth Town 22.45: All lines blocked. Normal by 16.20 11/10.

Nine Elms Yard 23.30: Sidings and wagons damaged.

All signalling failed 20.25 London Bridge, Borough Market Junction, Cannon Street, Metropolitan Junction and Blackfriars. Trains terminated at St Johns.

UXB: Clock House – Elmer's End, cleared 17.45 11/10.

The night raid was similar on 10/11 October, with 200 killed and one major and four serious fires.

11/10/40
GW: Brentford Branch 00.05: Crater near track. Down line slewed. SLW from 07.45 and passenger service suspended until 15.45 11/10 (at 5 mph).

West Drayton, Dawley Box 20.25: HE fell near signalbox. Lines found to be clear 21.18, but Block cut, so TIW Hayes – West Drayton East until 13.07 12/10.

Viaduct Junction – Uxbridge Road (WLR) 23.00: Block and telecom damaged and DAB suspected, so all lines closed for 70 minutes.

LMS: Poplar 20.25: Two HE and suspected DAB in Field Sidings near No. 15 road. Twenty wagons derailed.

Shepherds Bush Yard (WLR) 21.30: HE fell on Target 74 goods train, also damaged Block and telecom.

Bushey & Oxhey 23.20: HE in coal yard damaged several wagons and station roof.

LNE: King's Cross Goods: UXB required closure of Outwards Shed.

Chadwell Heath – Goodmayes 19.55: HE blocked Up Local line. Cleared 08.05 12/10.

SR: All exchange traffic stopped Feltham – Neasden/Brent, Battersea – Brent via Barnes, also via Staines Loop.

Victoria (Eastern) 20.07: HE in Hudson Place damaged veranda at front of station, Royal Waiting Room and Platforms 1 and 2. Lines not affected.

Kent House – Penge East 20.25: Both lines blocked by damage. Clear by 06.45 12/10.

Belmont 20.30: Direct hit by HE on station house and booking office. Down platform and both lines blocked by debris. One passenger and a clerk severely injured. Cleared 14.55 12/10.

Chislehurst Junction – St Mary Cray Junction 20.55: Down Loop blocked, also current off Bickley – St Mary Cray for 70 minutes. nwr 12.30 12/10.

Kingston 21.00: HE fell in goods yard, demolishing Goods office and shed, also damaging some lorries. No casualties. Running lines not affected.

Waterloo 21.50: HE fell on track on Vauxhall side of bridge over Westminster Bridge Road, causing large crater which penetrated arch and cut both Main Through and Local lines. All lines closed until daylight, then Windsor side reopened 07.50. Up Main Local restored 12.20 14/10, Down Main Through 12.05 15/10.

Hampton Court Junction – Hinchley Wood 21.50: Down line blocked by HE, until 15.30 12/10.

Purley – Purley Oaks 21.50: Up Local line blocked. Cleared 12.05 12/10.

Waterloo (Eastern) 22.05: HE through roof onto Down Local line damaged Platforms A and B. Station closed and trains run on Through lines. Station reopened 07.30 12/10, also Up Local and Main lines. Down Local and Up Through cleared (for steam trains only) 11.20 12/10.

Shortlands – Bromley South: Debris blocked lines until 12/10.

UXB: Stewarts Lane, Midland Yard 07.30: UXLM, all adjacent running lines closed, but later found to be only a parachute flare and nwr 10.53; Twickenham – St Margaret's 08.30, screen of loaded coal wagons put on Up Local at 10.00 and trains worked on Up Through and Down lines, cleared 16/10; Forest Hill 13.40, cleared 20.05 20/10; Point Pleasant Junction – East Putney 16.45, Down line also Down Windsor Local line closed, bomb detonated 15.30 11/11; Syon Lane 20.00, one line probably clear 16.15 16/10, but UXB not removed until 15.40 1/12.

A rather shorter and lighter night raid on 11/12 October killed 108 people and caused just one serious fire, but the southern approach to Blackwall Tunnel was blocked, and Queen Mary's Hospital and the Convent of the Sacred Heart at Roehampton were hit.

12/10/40 (Saturday)

GW: Shepherds Bush, Sterne Street (E&SB) 02.01: HE in coal wharf. Gas and water mains burst, and horses trapped in stables. Service restored Ealing Broadway – Shepherds Bush 11.30 13/10.

Smithfield Depot 04.15: DAB exploded, closing entrance from Farringdon Street. Reopened later in day.

Kensington, Addison Road (WLR) 09.20: DAB between North Box and Richmond Road Bridge. All lines closed, until 10.00 only.

Brentford Branch 20.30: HE demolished Trumper's Lane Bridge at Southall. Debris blocked both lines. Down clear 18.00 13/10. SLW (15 mph SpR) until 16.10 14/10. nwr 16.30 17/10.

Uxbridge Road (WLR) 20.40: HE damaged overbridge. All traffic stopped until restored under TIW 18.00 13/10. SLW from daybreak.

Westbourne Park 22.00: HE near-miss blocked Goods lines with debris and signalling damaged. Down line cleared 23.00, signalling restored 23.58. Up Goods restored 17.00 13/10.

Old Oak Common: HE on top of bank smashed many windows in Loco Sheds.

LMS: Devons Road 01.45: UX AA shell outside shunters' cabin displaced track and blocked access to Carriage Shed.

Highgate Road – Gospel Oak 11.45: DAB required evacuation of Highgate Road Box. Passenger, but not Goods, trains on HL line suspended. nwr not until 15.00 2/11.

Queen's Park Tunnel, Kensal Green 19.35: Penetrated by HE, blocking Up electric line. Steam trains substituted, until cleared 10.30 27/10.

Dagenham, near Ford's Bridge 20.30: HE damaged Block and telecom; also made crater at Slip level-crossing over Ripple Lane and filling with water. The 19.02 local train from Tilbury returned to Dagenham Dock wrong line. All lines affected, so shuttle introduced Tilbury – Dagenham Dock, with buses Barking – Dagenham Dock. Two lines clear 12.25 13/10, other two 16.00 16/10.

LNE: Finsbury Park, Clarence Yard 20.25: HE blocked four Down Goods and Carriage lines. Damage to Inspector's office and Shunters' cabin, also to suburban stock in Western Sidings and 25 wagons of meat (Farringdon traffic). Two railwaymen injured. Clear 18.00 13/10.

SR: Sidcup – New Eltham 00.40: Both lines blocked, but clear 16.35.

Catford – Crofton Park 16.55: HE blocked both lines. Clear 11.15 13/10.

Blackfriars/Metropolitan Junction/Borough Market area 19.57: Several HE affected working. nwr by 06.05 13/10.

Nine Elms 20.00: HE made crater in Central Yard, derailing and damaging 22 wagons, also points and crossings damaged.

South Bermondsey 20.30: Up SL line blocked, after crater reported in Up side. SLW over Down line.

Barnes 21.17: Station and East Box badly damaged by HE, also 17.00 LNE special freight East Goods Yard – Feltham waiting in loop. Signalman, Station Foreman and driver and fireman of goods train injured, also one passenger killed and one injured at station. Lines cleared 18.30 13/10.

The night raid on the Saturday/Sunday was moderate, with one major and one serious fire and some damage at the National Gallery, War Office and Tooting Grove Hospital. Two nasty incidents occurred on the LPTB, about 40 people being killed at Bounds Green and eight at Praed Street. Bombs also fell in London during the day.

13/10/40 (Sunday)

GW: Perivale 20.40: HE near signalbox broke windows and cut telecom to Greenford East Loop, necessitating TIW.

North Acton (E&SB) 22.30: All Block out to Viaduct Junction. TIW until nwr 06.30 14/10.

Paddington 23.00: HE in Praed Street blasted GWR Hotel and Offices.

LMS: Accident at Sudbury Junction and enemy damage at various points in London area forced a stop on all freight to London stations and to all sections of SR. Meat traffic from Scotland being sent by LNER.

Dalston Western Junction – Shoreditch 13.58: HE blocked all lines. Poplar lines clear 11.00 15/10, No. 2 Down lines 12.00 21/10, No. 2 Up lines 21.55 25/10.

Hampstead Heath 20.15: IB set fire to two wagons, but lines all right. 21.20: Both lines blocked by HE. Up line clear 17.00 17/10, but owing to further damage on 19/10 Down line not restored until 17.40 7/11.

Kentish Town Loco 20.45: HE broke 6-in. water main, damaged turntable and extinguished lighting at Shed and Control offices.

LNE: London Fields – Cambridge Heath 22.00: Local lines cut by HE. Traffic worked over Fast Lines, until nwr 18.30 16/10.

Spitalfields 22.40: HE fell on Top and Lower Yards. Lamp and Mess rooms destroyed by fire. One Home Guard seriously injured. All work stopped, but nwr 14/10, except hoist still out of use.

South Woodford 23.45: HE badly damaged booking-office and blocked both lines. One porter and one other staff injured; two other casualties believed under wreckage. Trains run

Liverpool Street – South Woodford and Woodford – Ongar, with buses in between. nwr 15.00.

SR: Lee – Mottingham 13.00: Both lines blocked. Down line restored 21.00, Up 15.30 14/10.

Hither Green Sidings 13.05: HE in Yard damaged Nos 6 – 8 roads, also derailed and damaged 33 wagons, which blocked three further roads.

St Helier 13.10: HE fell at entrance to goods yard, damaging station glass.

Chipstead 20.00: HE smashed windows at station and signalbox.

Barnes – Mortlake 21.35: Two HE damaged signalbox and killed a woman at White Hart Lane Crossing. Railway cottages and fog-man's hut also damaged. Lines cleared for steam trains 08.45, normal 21.05 14/10.

Clapham Junction – Wandsworth Town 23.25: All lines blocked. Down Local clear 14.30 14/10. Failure of pneumatic power disabled points worked by Clapham Junction 'A' and 'B' Boxes, until 09.15 14/10. Up Through line clear 13.00 18/10, Down line not until 16.10 29/10. All lines clear only at 10.40 30/10.

A fairly severe night attack was suffered on 13/14 October, with four serious fires. Over the two nights 264 people had been killed, including one of the worst individual incidents of all in London when 154 people were killed or drowned in a basement shelter in Stoke Newington.

14/10/40

GW: West Brompton (WLER) 01.20: IB fires gutted station and all lines blocked. Traffic normal 10.00, but station remained closed.[35]

Park Royal Trading Estate: Fire in adjacent premises spread to GW Goods Salvage Depot.

Smithfield Goods 21.20: HE damaged lifts at east end, turntable, goods platform, several cabins and stores and one wagon. One person injured. No traffic in or out during night. nwr 15/10.

LMS: Highgate Road Junction 00.50: HE damaged two roads in coal wharf.

West Thurrock Junction 01.14: HE nearby cut all telecom and blocked Upminster single line. Buses substituted Grays – Upminster. nwr 08.42 15/10.

Gospel Oak 20.10: HE at side of line east of station. Line already closed for passengers since 12/10 so now for goods.

Highbury & Islington 20.15: Station set on fire and badly damaged. Electric lines blocked until 09.55 15/10.

Woodgrange Park – Wanstead Park 20.25: Wall of viaduct badly damaged and both lines blocked with debris. Buses substituted Leytonstone – Woodgrange Park. Clear 14.30 15/10.

Kentish Town 21.00: IB damaged coaches in Cattle Dock Sidings. 21.20: 20.10 GPO Mail St Pancras – Derby hit by IB and one van near rear damaged. Up Passenger line blocked until 14.30 15/10.

Hackney Wick, Carpenters Road bridge 21.20: HE fell in sidings.

Upper Holloway 21.39: Large crater formed in Down sidings, leaving only Nos 1 and 2 and Down Reception lines available.

Plaistow – Bromley 22.20: Several HE on lines. LPTB services suspended Upton Park – Bromley; steam trains substituted. nwr 17.10 15/10.

Skinner Street – Broad Street 22.30: IB caused fire under arches, which collapsed forming a 20ft crater. Primrose Street bridge destroyed and all lines except No. 1 blocked. "No trains to Broad Street for several days." In fact, it was four weeks.

LNE: Holloway 19.32: HE in cattle pens and sidings. One staff injured. 20.50: Bomb on Up Coal line adjacent to Star Brush factory sidings demolished 12 wagons, two being blown over onto Star Brush ARP shelter; a number of casualties feared. Also five wagons derailed on Up Coal line and debris blocked Up Slow and Up Goods lines. One passenger and one staff injured in 19.30 Hertford North – King's Cross local, which was passing; another passenger train perhaps involved. Up Main, Goods, Coal and Slow lines cleared 16.30 15/10. Up Goods line not clear until 11.20 22/10.

Chingford – Highams Park 21.43: Both lines cut at country end Highams Park station. Buses substituted Wood Street – Chingford.

Tufnell Park Yard: Stables, roadway and some track damaged.

SR: Selhurst Sidings 01.00: HE on Cleaning and Inspection Sheds. Six sidings and some electric stock damaged. Nos 5 and 6 sidings not restored until 3/4/41, rest not until 6/9/41.

Bricklayers Arms 19.40: HE on 'B' side damaged two sidings and derailed 14 wagons. 22.52: Further bombs on 'J' section damaged three sidings. Dividing wall collapsed on Loco Depot, burying six locomotives. Mobile crane damaged by fire.

Wandsworth Common 20.21: HE fell on Up Local lines. All lines blocked by debris. No current. All Up trains reversed Balham. Local lines clear 16.15 16/10 and used also for main line trains. Up Local subsided again, and until restored 08.35 17/10, trains reversed Balham, locals at Wandsworth Common and Streatham Hill – but see 15/10.

London Bridge (Eastern) 20.23: Several HE fell. 17.10 Hastings – Cannon Street express ran into crater on No. 1 Up line at the station, locomotive[36] being derailed. Passengers detrained. No casualties. All lines to North Kent East Junction closed, but Nos 2 and 3 Down lines cleared by 05.25 and current restored at 06.00 15/10. Locomotive removed 18.05 15/10 but DAB suspected in debris under engine. Declared safe eventually 19.15 15/10, and No. 2 Up platform line reopened 05.24 16/10.

London Bridge (Central) 20.23: Heavy bomb made 50-ft crater in arches where tracks fan out near signalbox at south end. All lines blocked to Bricklayers Arms Junction, but Down and Up Through lines restored for steam working by 21.00 15/10. All lines except Central Section Down Slow and Down Local lines (and Eastern Section No. 1 Up line) clear by 16/10. Down Local cleared 15.15 18/10. No. 1 Up line not restored until 29/10, Down Through 13.40 31/10, Up Through 10.55 4/11. Platform 18 and Central Section generally not working normally until 14.30 28/2/41.

Loco Junction, Vauxhall 22.19: All traffic suspended until 22.43, "owing to signalman having evacuated Box, because of fire in nearby Nine Elms Gas Works." Several sheds at Nine Elms Goods damaged.

Kew Bridge – Brentford 22.45: Both lines cut by HE. Clear 16.15 16/10.

Plumstead – Abbey Wood 22.57: Both lines cut by HE, but clear 15.50 15/10.

Waterloo 23.30: IB fell on various parts of the station. A van in Dock road and electric train in Platform 4 set on fire, but all fires put out by 23.45. At 23.39 it was reported that all lines were closed until 00.45, due to "signalmen having evacuated Box owing to enemy action".

Wimbledon – Merton Park 23.45: HE at 'B' Box. Debris blocked lines and telecom to Mitcham. Soon clear.

Overnight 14/15 October, there was another heavy raid, in which 240 people were killed and there were one major and 24 serious fires. A number of factories were destroyed and public utilities damaged. Bombs seriously damaged Hillingdon and St Stephen's Hospitals, Church House (Westminster), Kensington Palace and St James's Church, Piccadilly. A particularly bad incident occurred on the Underground, when a bomb penetrated down to the platforms at Balham where over 500 people were sheltering and 75 were killed, mainly by drowning.

Some enemy aircraft attacked London in daylight on 15 October. There followed a particularly heavy attack on the night of 15/16 October, which resulted in 430 deaths (over half in three bad shelter incidents, at Kennington Park and Morley College,

Lambeth and at Lady Owen's School, Finsbury), with six major and nine serious fires. Numerous Key Points in the Docks and elsewhere were affected: St Pancras Power Station (49,000 kW) was hit by HE including a parachute-mine and put out of action for 10 days; three Gas Works were set on fire; three very large water-mains (the Enfield Loop of the New River) were broken, affecting the supply to 17 Boroughs, and the Fleet Sewer was fractured flooding the railways between King's Cross and Farringdon; extensive damage was done to Broadcasting House; the London Jewish Hospital, the Natural History Museum and Earls Court Exhibition Hall were hit.

15/10/40

GW: Chelsea & Fulham (WLER) 02.40: Explosion in the Wandsworth Gas Works blew out windows of signalbox. Traffic blocked back until 07.00 and even then only under TIW from Latchmere Junction, owing to damage to telecom. Lines clear 07.30. Sidings Nos 5–7 at Chelsea Dock damaged.

South Lambeth Goods: HE blocked Nos 5–10 roads. No. 8 warehouse and four hydraulic cranes disabled. Two locomotives[37] damaged. Eight road vehicles and some stock damaged by fire. Repairs put in hand directly and Depot working to 60–70% of capacity at 06.00 16/10, but rail access not restored until 22/10.

Paddington 04.00: Hotel damaged and water supply failed.

Smithfield Goods Depot resumed normal working, but owing to further damage to MWL in night 15–16/10 the Depot was closed again and traffic dealt with at Paddington. Access not restored to Smithfield until 25/10.

Latchmere Junction (WLER) 19.30: Collision between two trains blocked all lines. Cleared to Longhedge Junction 07.30 16/10, but line to SR (Western Section) remained blocked on account of DAB.

Clapham Junction (WLER) 22.20: HE nearby damaged No. 2 Branch to SR and several buildings.

Hayes & Harlington 23.00: HE in embankment damaged Foreman's office at Creosote Works. nwr 02.35 16/10.

LMS: King's Cross Tunnel (St Paul's Road Passenger Junction – St Pancras Tunnel Box) 00.24: HE exploded at mouth of tunnel and both lines blocked. nwr 16.00 19/10.

Dock Junction – Cambridge Street 00.24: Another HE caused deep crater in Fast lines. Passenger trains run on Goods lines, until Down Fast cleared 02.05. nwr 05.45.

Haverstock Hill – Carlton Road Junction 00.35: HE fell through road overbridge, blocking Passenger lines. Traffic worked over Goods lines. Fast lines clear by 14.30.

Camden Town 01.00: Lines closed owing to UXB, until 11.00.

Camden Town, Hampstead Road Junction Box 04.15: HE blocked running lines and damaged sidings, also buildings in Maiden Lane Yard.

Dalston 11.32: UXB found, interfering with repairs under way on blocked lines. Cleared 19.10.

Queen's Park 19.45*: Heavy bomb in contractor's stable off south side of line. Earth and brick debris were projected onto Down Fast line 100 yards in front of 19.30 Euston – Inverness express, approaching at 20 mph on account of the Red Warning in force. Locomotive[38] ran into debris and overturned to right and following brake-van and 1st-class sleeping-car were derailed; the remaining 11 coaches were not derailed or damaged. Fireman buried in coal in tender and severely injured, being finally released only after an arm amputated. The driver was not hurt, nor were any other staff or passengers. The Up Fast and Down Slow Lines were also blocked. 21.25: HE near Harvist Road to the north side opposite Queen's Park station blasted retaining-wall onto track, blocking both electric lines with 25 tons of debris. Up electric line to Euston completely blocked by heavy debris and some thrown onto island platform. 23.12: HE beside line burst water-main. Electric lines blocked by flooding. Roof of substation blown off,

leaving no power or lighting. 01.30 16/10: Further HE made large crater in Down Fast line in rear of derailed coaches of Inverness express. 02.00 16/10: Further bomb damaged No. 2 Box and electric lines blocked with more debris. One staff injured. Down Slow Line reopened for traffic 22.50 16/10, but Up Fast, occupied by breakdown cranes, not clear until 16.30 17/10. Crater in rear of derailed train filled in and Down Fast clear 18/10. Meantime practically normal service of steam passenger trains in/out Euston worked over Slow lines, also Camden freight. Clearance work slow as tunnel restrictions prevented use of cranes. North of station, where Bakerloo and LMS trains shared only two electric lines, Up line was blocked by recent damage to Kensal Green Tunnel and was not repaired until 04.45 21/10.. Meanwhile, restricted single-line LMS electric service worked over Down line Kilburn – Willesden, Bakerloo trains reversing at Queen's Park, until nwr 09.30 26/10.

Leytonstone – Walthamstow 21.05: Lines blocked by debris nwr 03.00 16/10.

Chalk Farm 21.30: Down NLR electric line blown away. Forty yards of Down platform demolished. Up electric line blown out.

Gunnersbury 21.40: HE fell on track, but lines restored 00.45 16/10.

Kentish Town 23.15: IB in Cattle Dock Sidings set fire to coaches.

Kentish Town Junction – Maiden Lane Junction 23.15: Five HE destroyed No. 1 NLR lines. Repaired by 15.30 16/10.

Cricklewood Junction – Watling Street Junction 23.30: Large crater made between Up Fast and Down Local lines; both Fast lines blocked. Up Goods line clear 09.10, all four passenger lines by 16.30 16/10.

Brent Sorting Sidings 23.30: HE between Nos 5 and 6 sidings, another on adjacent Gas Works.

Broad Street – Shoreditch 23.45: HE blew out No. 2 Down line and damaged No. 2 Up. Several rails displaced and telecom cut. (Lines already blocked by previous damage).

Poplar 'A': HE damaged warehouse, three sidings and wall.

Poplar 'B': damage to girders, offices, two turntables, lock gates and 50-ton crane.

LNE: Finsbury Park 01.40: HE blew out all windows of No. 1 Box. Weighbridge at Highbury Vale Sidings damaged, but all running lines clear.

Gordon Hill – Enfield Chase 03.40: Two DAB fell on bank. One exploded 11.12, the other 13.05 – damaging track. Up line clear 13.40 and traffic restored 16.35 (15 mph), but from 09.40 embankment slip where crater filled earlier necessitated SLW.

Goodmayes: Nos 9 and 10 roads in Upper Yard blown out. Nos 1 and 2 roads blocked by derailed wagons, also No.3 road and Up Through line flooded by burst water-main. Up Through restored 06.00 16/10.

Spitalfields: HE between Coal and Up Goods roads, causing damage. Electric hoist working by 18.00, but gas and water supplies still cut off.

Bishopsgate: HE fell in Cheshire Street stables, killing five horses and injuring 15.

Stratford 10.30: HE in Cooks' (private) sidings damaged five wagons and Loop Junction line. Engine road also blocked, so impossible to work engines into Shed. Crater found in coal stack of Shop Engine road. Stacks collapsed and track blown out. Points and stock damaged at Chobham Farm. Later all roads into Carriage Sidings found to be damaged, with 18 vehicles wrecked and 28 others damaged. Vacuum-cleaning plant and plant house badly damaged. Local Crane Shop and dormitory roof damaged.

Ilford 22.20: Oil bomb made crater, damaging track, signalling, platform and windows. Up and Down lines reopened 12.00 16/10.

Forest Gate: Debris thrown on tracks. Clear 12.00 16/10.

SR (Western Section):

Clapham Junction – West London Junction 00.44: All Windsor lines cut, also lines to Latchmere and Longhedge Junctions. 'A' Box made unusable and two signalmen injured. Signals on Main line set to 'automatic'. Clapham Junction – Latchmere Junction not reopened until 15.00 24/10. All Windsor lines not clear until 16.05 31/10.

Vauxhall – Queens Road, Battersea: Damage to Arch 42 closed Local and Main lines, until 15.40. UXB suspected.

Nine Elms Goods 01.08: HE damaged 'A' and 'B' Sheds.

Waterloo 09.16: A bomb pierced the arch near Lambeth Road Bridge, causing damage to all lines except Up Windsor and Down Main Local. Six people sheltering in the archway were killed and seven injured. 08.35 EMU ex-Shepperton stopped a few yards from crater – and no one hurt. Waterloo closed, but reopened 16.15 – using only Up Windsor and Down Main Local lines. Both Main Through and Up Main Local reopened same day. That evening, at 20.55 HE exploded on concourse at the end of Platforms 3 and 4. EMU standing at platform struck, and its only two passengers slightly injured. Platforms 1–10 put out of use. Up Windsor, both Main Through and both Main Local lines clear 19.00 17/10. Down Windsor lines reopened 09.20 19/10. Nos 1, 2, 9 and 10 restored 09.45 17/10, Nos 3, 6, 7 and 8 by 17.00 17/10. All platforms not fully in use until 15.20 26/10. Down Windsor Local and Up Main Relief lines not restored until 11.20 24/12.

Southfields – Wimbledon Park 19.55: District Line train to Wimbledon struck by HE, damaged and derailed. HT cables cut and Down line also blocked. Nine passengers injured. District Line shuttle service Wimbledon – East Putney on Up line, with buses on to Putney Bridge. Down line clear 13.15 16/10.

Durnsford Road (Wimbledon) Power Station 21.15*: HE struck, felling the west chimney stack and putting half the boilers out of action. Eight staff injured. Current supply of Western Section suburban area cut off. Limited alternative supplies obtained immediately, and plant partially restored during 16/10.

*SR Report: "This attack was potentially serious. Improvised repairs made to damaged equipment. By good fortune and remarkably good work of Chief Electrical Engineer and his staff, difficulties caused much less than expected. Certainly, electrification enabled arrangement of emergency services from stations not designed for terminal working – impracticable with steam traction."

That night many lines were closed for examination. After several HE fell beyond the railway near 'C' Box, Clapham Junction station was closed 20.00 until declared clear at 08.10 next morning. At Vauxhall, all Main lines and Up Windsor Local and Through lines were closed 20.50 and reopened 13.10 next day.

SR (Central and Eastern Sections):

London Bridge 10.04: UXB, cleared 19.15. Arches under Central Section station thought unsafe and all lines closed for much of day. In evening Down Main line remained closed owing to seriously damaged arch.

Charlton – Woolwich Dockyard 20.15: Lines blocked by debris from Bridge 585 and other buildings. nwr 10.20 16/10.

Falconwood 20.55: Station damaged.

Balham 22.25: Down and Up Main lines blocked. nwr 12.10 16/10.

Herne Hill 22.45: Up Local line damaged. Station and two road vehicles damaged. Line cleared 11.05 16/10.

New Wandsworth Goods – Wandsworth Common 23.17: HE fell on track and all lines blocked. Local lines reopened 11.05 16/10, Main lines 16.25 19/10.

Stewarts Lane Carriage Shed 23.24: HE damaged roof and started fire. Four vehicles destroyed.

Battersea Wharf: Damage done to crane and grab.

UXB: Streatham Common Goods Yard; Woolwich Dockyard, both cleared 16/10.

With General Restrictions of Freight Movement as great as ever, especially in the London area, the railways suffered many further serious incidents.

GW: Southall West – Dolphin 00.15: Down main line "uncertain". Traffic diverted to Down Relief, until 02.45.

Greenford 21.30: Goods depot damaged. TIW in operation to Northolt. nwr 14.00 17/10.

LMS: St Pancras 01.10: Land-mine exploded in Goods Yard, causing extensive damage. 12 wagons derailed. One goods guard seriously injured.

Becontree 01.10: All lines blocked by two HE. Steam lines clear 14.15 16/10, electric lines 17.00 17/10.

Chalk Farm 02.55: DAB exploded in coal yard, damaging wall. Mechanical horse and van blown into road.

Leytonstone 03.20: DA land-mine exploded, practically demolishing the station. Buses substituted Walthamstow – Woodgrange Park. Down line clear 12.30, Up 15.30 17/10.

St Pancras 03.20: DA land-mine fell at end of platform 1 and exploded 05.23. Extensive damage done, including to water and gas mains. Station closed and trains worked to/ from Kentish Town only, until morning 21/10.

Gospel Oak: HE very close to No. 2 Box put out all Block and telecom, but trains able to pass.

Dalston 13.10: UXLM found, cleared 19/10.

LNE: King's Cross – Farringdon 03.35: HE penetrated Clerkenwell Tunnel. Metropolitan and MWL blocked by water from burst sewer. Three patrolmen trapped by gas and water. nwr 08.30 18/10.

Aldersgate 03.52: Two DAB close to signalbox. Lines to Moorgate closed, LMSR and LNER passenger services not restored until after the war.

Thames Wharf: HE in night damaged a wagon, weigh-house, road and water-tank; an oil-bomb caused further damage.

New Cross Depot: Evacuated because of DAB. Signalling destroyed at Canal Junction. ELR lines closed until 5/11.

Chigwell 05.45: 05.34 local train Woodford – Ilford ran into crater. Locomotive turned over. Several coaches derailed. No casualties (!). Both lines blocked. Normal 17.35.

Hackney Downs 05.50: UXB suspected. Trains suspended or diverted, until clear 15.25.

Chadwell Heath 11.15: All lines closed owing to UXLM. Buses substituted Goodmayes – Romford, with trains reversing at each. Certain trains diverted via Bishops Stortford and Witham, also via Cambridge, Bury St Edmunds and Ipswich. nwr 13.00 17/10.

Enfield Chase 05.00: Two DAB very close to line. One exploded 11.12, other 13.05, damaging track. Shuttle services run to/from Grange Park and Enfield Chase, with buses between. 09.40: Embankment slip necessitated SLW.

SR: Deptford Wharf: Outward road blocked. Cleared 19/10.

New Cross Gate: Damage done to sidings and wagons.

North Kent East Junc: Track circuits and signalling damaged by HE.

Victoria 00.02: Two HE fell on Grosvenor Road Bridge.[39] Up Main Eastern line torn up and Up Relief blocked with debris. Central Section lines found clear. Shuttle services put on Victoria – Clapham Junction half-hourly, Victoria – Peckham Rye hourly. Eastern Section all clear at Elizabeth Bridge 15.30 20/10. However, a later report stated: "Down Main clear 12.00 29/10. Up Main slewed into Down Main and used for Up traffic from 13.05 30/10." Up Relief not restored until 08.00, Up Main 16.00 17/11.

Streatham Junction – Tooting 01.00: Both lines blocked by HE. nwr 16.00.

Waterloo – Vauxhall 01.30: Damage to Arch 79 put out Up Windsor Local line (already blocked). Not repaired until 07.20 8/2/41.

Bricklayers Arms Loco 02.00: Shed roof and water tank damaged, also oil store set on fire.

Bricklayers Arms Goods 02.00: Roof and stables demolished. SR cottages damaged, but no casualties. Mechanical horse and three trailers damaged, also four wagons in No. 3 road of 'J' Yard.

Balham 04.00: Main lines blocked. Clear 10.10 17/10.

Tulse Hill – Streatham 04.05: Conductor rails damaged. Current supply cut, precluding electric working into Victoria from Streatham Hill or Streatham Common. Lines cleared by 10.05 (to Wimbledon 16.00)

Kingston 05.40: HE damaged veranda and waiting-rooms.

Orpington – Chelsfield 13.10: Both lines blocked. Clear 14.45 17/10.

Wandsworth Common 20.21: All lines blocked by damage. Local lines clear 16.15 17/10.

Berrylands – Malden 20.45: Up local and Through lines blocked. Cleared by 15.10 17/10.

Elmer's End – Woodside 22.40: Both lines blocked, due to subsidence of repaired crater. nwr 12.20 17/10.

Bexley – Crayford 23.20: Both lines blocked. Bomb derailed a conflat. Porter flung off Crayford platform and injured. Cleared 18.00 17/10.

UXB: West Sutton 08.15, cleared 14.50 26/10; Clapham Junction (Kensington line) 22.30, cleared 15.20 24/10; New Cross Gate (ELR Line) – two bombs, one cleared 15.45 22/10, other detonated 17.10 26/10.

Another bad night raid occurred on 16/17 October, which caused only two serious fires but killed no less than 600 people. Farnborough (Kent) and Friern Barnet Hospitals were hit. Serious industrial damage was done, especially at the Regents Canal, Royal Victoria (where the PLA engine sheds were damaged) and Surrey Commercial Docks.

17/10/40

GW: Castle Bar Park: Subsidence from incident of 10/10 necessitated closure of one line and SLW.

Brentford Branch 00.30: Down line damaged. SLW, until nwr 16.20.

Park Royal Trading Estate 01.40: HE on crossing at entrance to Estate, damaging both lines. SLW until nwr on 18/10.

LMS: Gunnersbury – Richmond 00.12: Telecom cut and LMS trains terminated at South Acton, until 07.20 18/10.

Kilburn High Road 08.30: Down Slow blocked by subsidence of earlier crater. Repaired 19.30.

Bromley 21.00: HE set fire to adjacent warehouse and debris thrown across all lines, so current off 21.35–21.55. Some steam locals run over electric lines East Ham – Campbell Road Junction Full electric service from 12.45 21/10, with SLW Barking – Dagenham. nwr 06.40 18/10.

Willesden No. 5 – Sudbury Junction 21.15: Telecom cut, necessitating TIW temporarily.

LNE: Cuffley 06.45: DAB fell at north end of goods yard. Exploded 21/10, damaging both lines, two sidings and telecom. nwr 15.00 22/10.

Enfield Lock: DAB near station. Passenger trains suspended and freight passed through at extreme caution. Buses substituted Brimsdown – Waltham Cross. Main line trains diverted via Churchbury Loop. nwr 15.00 22/10.

Stratford, Bridge Junction: UXB closed lines until removed 09.45 18/10.

SR (Central and Eastern Sections):

Blackfriars Junction and Ewer Street 02.27: HE struck Blackfriars Road Bridge*. Another HE exploded at Barclay & Fry's adjoining Ewer Street Depot, damaging Blackfriars Goods office and a locomotive. Shunter injured. Depots and all lines closed. Signalling out of action London Bridge – Holborn, until 10.50. Local lines clear 18.00, but Charing Cross not available for suburban trains. Blackfriars station reopened 22/10, nwr 08.25 23/10.

*From Lt.Col. Mount's Report: The Blackfriars Road Bridge has 100ft span carrying four lines leading to Charing Cross Station, with two lattice and one plate girder. Three tracks run between the lattice girders, the fourth (Up Through) between a lattice girder and the plate girder; a double conduit LPTB tramway runs underneath on Blackfriars Road. Heavy bomb destroyed part of western abutment under outer lattice girder, the end being left hanging. Adjacent arch also partly destroyed, putting three lines out of action. Girder itself practically undamaged and is being supported by small timber trestle in roadway. A Contractor and section of 158 RCC (RE) are doing work. The end of girder will be supported by steel trestling from the pavement and steel weighbeams will carry the tracks over the damaged arches onto nearest sound brick pier. Further damage occurred at 09.50 25/10 (see below).

Wandsworth Common – New Wandsworth Goods 05.15: Up Local line blocked again, owing to subsidence of previously filled crater. Clear 08.35 18/10. Main lines restored 16.25, but occupied by Engineers from 18.00.

Slades Green 14.00: DAB exploded, damaging station premises, Railway Institute and a brakevan.

London Bridge 14.30 (see 14-15/10 above): Further serious damage to archways found, so all Central Section lines closed again. No. 1 Up line cleared 15.30 18/10. Up SL line reopened 08.00 21/10.

Bellingham 16.30: Both lines blocked. Signalbox damaged. Signalman and a fireman injured. Clear 15.30 18/10.

New Cross Gate 19.35*: HE and IB on road overbridge. Station buildings and shops set on fire. Crater on Down side of arch of bridge. Road vehicle fell on line, blocking Down lines. Traction current interrupted. Station foreman and a guard of shuttle service train injured. Station closed, until 15.00 18/10. Shuttle service to London Bridge restored 15.00 18/10. Up Local line restored 18/10, Down Through 20.20 20/10, but Down Local not clear until 11.45 25/1/41.

*Lt.Col. Mount reported: 500 kilo bomb fell in roadway immediately over railway. Road blocked two days. Booking-office demolished. SR provided temporary joists for carrying road cables across cavity. One abutment badly shattered. Two military trestles erected by 158 Company in two days.

Crystal Palace LL 19.45: All lines blocked at Tunnel Junction. Platforms 1–4 and station roof damaged. Some services run 19/10. nwr 20/10.

Abbey Wood – Belvedere 22.04: Both lines blocked. Clear 11.00 18/10.

Lee – Mottingham 22.05: Both lines blocked. Down clear 12.00, Up 15.50 18/10.

Canterbury Road Junction – Cambria Junction 22.55: Both lines blocked. Clear 10.45 18/10.

Maze Hill 23.35: Both lines blocked by several HE. Telecom destroyed. 09.45 18/10: DAB exploded in Up Carriage Sidings. Extensive damage to station buildings, carriage shed, berthing sidings. One coach destroyed, three other sets damaged. Another destroyed seven wagons of coal. No casualties.

SR (Western Section):

Point Pleasant Junction – Putney 19.50: Up and Down Through and Up Local lines blocked. Clear 12.50 18/10.

Raynes Park – Malden 20.17: Down Local line blocked. Clear 09.05 18/10.

Surbiton – Wimbledon and Richmond – Feltham, Cannon Street – London Bridge 20.30: Signal current supply failed. Emergency diesel generators operating from 07.15 18/10.

Durnsford Road 22.20: HE damaged roof of Inspection Shed, tracks and coaches. Through lines clear 15.10 21/10.

Norwood Loco Shed 23.40: HE shattered glass.

Parks Bridge Junction – Hither Green 23.45: Main and Lewisham lines blocked. Main lines reopened for steam 15.30, electric 17.50 18/10. Lewisham lines reopened for electric trains 13.30 19/10.

Hither Green 23.45: Telecom cut 'A' Box to Sidings 'C', Petts Wood Junction, Orpington 'B', Bickley Station and Bickley Junction Boxes. All restored by 10.00 18/10.

UXB: Bromley North – Sundridge Park 03.21(UXLM), cleared 18/10; Slades Green Electric Shops 11.10, cleared 23/10; Nine Elms Goods 11.15, discredited 17.05 23/10; New Cross Gate (two bombs in yard); Maze Hill, cleared 2/11.

London had yet another heavy night attack on 17/18 October. 324 people were killed, but there were no serious fires. The Colonial Office, Horse Guards and Treasury were hit. Only a few enemy planes attacked London overnight 18/19 October, but a very heavy raid began the next evening.

18/10/40

GW: Hayes & Harlington 21.49: Six HE in Gramophone Co.'s sidings. Glass at station damaged, also in front coaches of an empty stock train. Telecom and sidings extensively damaged, wagons derailed.

LMS: Harrow & Wealdstone 21.30: Oil-bomb in goods yard caused fire and minor damage.

LNE: Chigwell, in night: HE on Up platform blocked lines with debris. Lines soon reopened with TIW. Block restored 19/10.

Seven Sisters – West Green: Traffic suspended owing to DAB. Buses substituted.

Canning Town – Tidal Basin: Lines blocked overnight by debris, but traffic being worked into Thames Wharf and Silvertown. Clear 14.30 22/10.

SR: Angerstein Wharf in night: DAB exploded, damaging Nos 4–8 roads and 16 wagons.

Clapham Junction – Wandsworth Town: Down Windsor Local and Up Windsor Through lines blocked by DAB nearby. Kensington lines open for goods and parcels only. Cleared 13.00.

Chessington South 02.45: Sidings damaged.

Clapham Junction – Earlsfield 14.55: Another DAB exploded, blocking all lines. Through lines clear 11.35 19/10.

London Bridge: Up Through line (Eastern Section) cut.

Selsdon 20.15: Both lines blocked. Empty three-car EMU damaged and motorman injured. Down line cleared 02.05, Up 10.35 19/10.

Hinchley Wood – Claygate 20.45: Lines blocked by HE. Clear 11.52 19/10.

Sydenham – Crystal Palace LL 22.10: Both lines blocked. Cleared 08.00 19/10.

UXB: West Sutton

19/10/40 (Saturday)

GW: Friars Junction, Acton 20.00: HE damaged signalbox and signalman injured. Trunk telegraph and signal lighting failed as far as Southall. Traffic blocked until 22.00, when all restored except Relief lines. Normal 13.10 20/10.

North Acton, Victoria Road Bridge 21.30: HE made bridge unsafe, so trains suspended until declared safe 11.50 20/10.

LMS: Willesden HL Sidings 01.25: HE damaged Nos 1–3, 6 and 12 'D' sidings and derailed 11 wagons.

Upper Holloway 19.30: HE damaged Up platform and footbridge, blocking both lines. Ticket collector injured. nwr 12.00 22/10.

Acton Wells Junction 19.50: HE on viaduct cut telecom. TIW introduced temporarily.

St Pancras 20.10: HE in LNE Camley Street coal bays damaged Cambridge Street Box.

Canonbury 20.28: HE blocked and damaged all lines with debris. No. 1 Down line clear 17.00 22/10, No. 2 lines 17.00 25/10, No. 1 Up and nwr 09.00 1/11.

Euston 20.35: IB set fire to roof of Great Hall. Roofs of Arrival side and of offices in Drummond Street and west wing of Euston Hotel damaged by HE that exploded in roadway between Platforms 2 and 3. Debris derailed several coaches of 'Down Postal'. Nos 1, 2, 3 and 6 platform lines also Nos 4 and 5 platform lines (electrified) put out of use. Electric workings suspended. Platform 7 used for steam trains. Platform 6 restored 21/10, Nos 4 and 5 on 24/10, and

remainder late on 27/10.

Hampstead Heath 21.45: Direct hit by HE on station, which was demolished and debris blocked both lines. Two Home Guard injured. nwr 15.30 20/10, but station closed for some time.

West Ham 22.30: HE cut cables at Abbey Mills Upper Junction. Current off Upton Park – Bow Road. Buses substituted Upton Park – Whitechapel. nwr 14.00 20/10.

West Kensington Goods: Warehouse damaged.

Kew Gardens – Richmond: HE cut lines (see SR). Trains reversed at Gunnersbury.

LNE: Beckton: HE damaged three sidings.

SR (Western Section):

Earlsfield – Wimbledon 20.25: All lines blocked by HE on Through lines near Durnsford Road. Fell just behind 19.59 EMU Waterloo – Hampton Court, derailing two rear coaches. One passenger killed; guard and six passengers injured. Traction and signal current failed. Local lines cleared 16.15 20/10, Through lines 15.10 21/10.

Waterloo 20.30: Struck by several HE. One fell in Waterloo Road outside the Wellington Hotel, one in York Road, one on a taxi outside (driver and three passengers burnt to death), one on the General Offices and one on the east side booking-office. Altogether "50–60 cases were dealt with at the station, some fatal." All roof glass down, also covered way to Eastern station. Station closed 22.15, with all lines blocked. Reopened 07.30 20/10 – but it is not clear if any services were restored – or what lines open. Down Through line not restored until 12.25 29/10, Up Through 16.00 17/11. Down and Up Local lines not reopened for electric trains until 12.30 17/2/41. Signalling power supplies failed Metropolitan Junction – Cannon Street, Borough Market Junction and Blackfriars.

Barnes Bridge – Chiswick 22.10: Both lines blocked. Clear 07.30 22/10.

Pouparts Junction – Longhedge Junction 22.10: Both lines blocked. Cleared 14.00 20/10.

Kew Gardens/North Sheen – Richmond 22.15: Both lines blocked. Cleared 16.00 20/10.

Wimbledon area 22.25: Traction and signalling current off over wide area. Restored 16.15 20/10.

SR (Eastern and Central Sections):

Dartford Loop and Bexleyheath lines: Traction current off. Steam trains substituted, until supply restored 14.45 20/10.

New Cross – St Johns 01.30: HE fell on Through lines, damaging Local lines also. Down Local line clear 21.15 (steam only), Up Local and Down Through 20.24 20/10. Down Local clear for electric trains and Up Local for steam and electric trains 12.00 21/10. Down Through line clear 15.00 24/10, Up Through 16.00 25/10 20/10.

Waterloo (Eastern) 19.35: All lines damaged 60 yards west of station, which was damaged and foreman injured. Up and Down Local lines cleared 21/10, Up Through 14.25 24/10. Signal current failed, but restored by 17.20 21/10. Down Through line not cleared until 16.30 24/11.

London Bridge (Eastern) 19.41: Signalling current supply cut on all SE lines inwards and out to St John's, until 21.44. Signalling restored in stages by 03.10 20/10.

Eltham Well Hall 19.46: Both lines blocked. Cleared by 15.45 20/10.

Streatham – Mitcham Junction 20.00: Both lines blocked. nwr 06.30 20/10.

New Cross – St John's 20.00: All lines affected, but Down Local clear for steam trains. Blacksmith's shop and roof damaged. Down Local clear for electric trains and Up Local for all 12.00 21/10. Down Through clear 15.00 24/10, Up Through 16.00 25/10.

Eardley Sidings 20.08: Many coach windows smashed.

Rotherhithe Road 21.00: Down line and shunting-neck damaged. Signalbox and locomotive[40] damaged. Signalman, also driver, fireman and guard injured. Down line not cleared until 15.45 21/11.

Mitcham Junction – Hackbridge 21.10: Both lines blocked. nwr 05.25 20/10.

New Cross – North Kent East Junction 21.20: HE blocked all lines. Some lines clear 20.24 20/10, remainder 16.30 21/10.

Bricklayers Arms 21.20: Sidings Nos 10–14 of 'B' section damaged and 12 wagons derailed. Not restored until 28/11.

Victoria (Eastern) 22.10: Certain platform lines damaged, but "working not further affected". All cleared 15.30 20/10.

Dartford – Bexleyheath: Cables damaged. Steam trains substituted, until 14.45 20/10.

London suffered severely once again on the night of 19/20 October, with 274 deaths, three major and 11 serious fires. Westminster Abbey, Westminster School, The Royal Mint, and four hospitals (St Bartholomew's, Mile End, East Ham Memorial and West Park, Epsom) were hit.

20/10/40 (Sunday)

GW: Latimer Road (H&C) 22.20 and 23.45: UXB near bridge over WLR Viaduct Junction – Uxbridge Road. LPTB trains reversed at Ladbroke Grove. Service Latimer Road – Uxbridge Road suspended. (See also 21/10).

Kensington Addison Road (WLR) 18.00: Three HE fell between Kensington Middle and South Boxes. Buildings extensively damaged and all lines blocked. Down 'West Coast Postal' (diverted from Euston) was damaged and had to be cancelled.[41] Two guards (one SR) injured. Lines cleared by 15.50 22/10.

Lillie Bridge (WLER) 23.29: HE near Philbeach Exhibition Hall blew up rails and damaged wagons. nwr 28/10.

LMS: Willesden New Sidings 01.18: Three HE destroyed No. 12 siding and No. 31 overbridge damaged.

Upminster 19.55: HE fell on Up side embankment, affecting all lines.

Kentish Town, Mortimer Street Junction 20.30: Oil bomb on Down lines.

Becontree – Upney: HE fell on electric lines, resulting in several craters. LPTB electric services suspended from Barking and temporary LMS steam service introduced through to Pitsea and Tilbury.

West End Sidings, West Hampstead 22.20: Two craters made by HE. Bridge damaged, also Nos 1–3 arrival and Nos 1–8 departure lines; 20 wagons derailed.

Willesden Junction 23.15: Wagon on fire.

LNE: Royal Mint Street in night: Roof of Depot offices damaged.

Beckton in night: Three roads in yard damaged by HE.

Neasden Loco Shed 04.15: HE blocked exits. Coal road clear and engines being worked out of back of depot.

Wood Street, Walthamstow 20.00: Two roads in carriage sidings damaged, also Block and telecom. Water-mains burst. Clear 22/10.

Bow Road 21.26: Footbridge brought down. Debris on both lines.

Enfield Lock 22.15: HE fell on Up line, but Down usable. nwr 15.45 21/10.

SR: Waterloo Depot (W&C) 01.35: Nos 6 and 7 sidings damaged. Clear 23/10.

Angerstein Wharf 02.30: Weighbridge, road and offices damaged.

Norwood Junction 03.30: Sidings and stores damaged.

Hounslow: HE in yard badly damaged goods shed and passenger station.

Barnes 12.20: DAB in East Yard exploded, damaging sidings and derailing 10 wagons.

New Cross – St John's 13.30: DAB exploded, affecting all lines except Lewisham Loops. Restored 18.15.

Eltham Well Hall 13.35: HE on Up side approach damaged station and railway cottages.

Camberwell – Loughborough Junction 20.40: All lines blocked at Gordon Grove Bridge*. Through lines cleared (for electric

trains only) 15.55 21/10, restored for steam trains 08.55 28/10. Up Local line clear 15.30 1/11. Down Local cleared to Canterbury Road Junction (for steam trains) 14.30 5/11.

*From Lt.Col. Mount's Report: Two arches under two tracks down. Structure under other two tracks cracked and supported by centring. Pier being constructed to take weigh-beams 58ft overall. Existing arches will then have three rings added, centring gradually struck as work proceeds. Possible to keep two tracks in traffic. In August 1941, he reported that after long period of inactivity a contract placed for carrying both lines on girders and reinforced concrete slabs, the military steel trestles acting as piers on the Up line being replaced by concrete.

Crystal Palace LL – Bromley Junction 21.20: Both lines blocked. Cleared 08.45 21/10.

Kingswood – Tadworth 21.20: HE blocked lines. Cleared 19.00 21/10.

Longhedge Junction – Latchmere Junction/Pouparts Junction 22.55: Both lines blocked. Cleared 17.00 21/10.

UXB: Tooting, cleared 14/11.

A further heavy attack was made on London on the night of 20/21 October. Fatalities were 283, with 12 major fires – notably at Surrey Docks. Raids on London were then quite minor between 21/22 and 24/25 October.

21/10/40

General Restrictions on Freight traffic were now as widespread as ever.

GW: Viaduct Junction (WLR) 05.00: DAB exploded, blocking all lines. Up loop to Uxbridge Road also severed – and was never reopened.[42] Up Main reopened 15.20.

LMS: South Kenton 00.20: All lines blocked until 01.20.

Euston 22.45: Wall beside No. 1 platform damaged.

LNE: Tottenham West – South Tottenham 02.35: HE blocked Up line and made Down unsafe. Services suspended Palace Gates – Stratford until cleared 14.45.

King's Cross Goods: Outwards section closed owing to UXB. Traffic handled at Inwards section.

Chingford: Station closed and staff evacuated, owing to UXB. Buses substituted.

Chigwell: UXB on track. Lines closed. Shuttle service run from Ilford, with buses on to Woodford.

Park Junction, Highgate 20.05: HE on lines, also DAB present, so branch services suspended until 08.50 22/10.

Abbey Mills Lower Junction: All traffic stopped for sewer repairs, until 22/10.

Cranley Gardens 21.00: UXB near south of station. Trains substituted by buses.

SR: Merton Abbey – Merton Park 09.10: Goods-only line blocked. Cleared 23/10.

Haydons Road: Station damaged.

Herne Hill 14.30: Station closed and traffic suspended while UXB dealt with, until 15.10, then again 15.30–15.55 for detonation. No damage done.

Deptford Wharf: Traffic ex-ships being regulated, owing to damage to vessels alongside.

22/10/40

GW: Latchmere Junction – Clapham Junction (Western Section): Traffic suspended until 23/10 owing to damage to arches.

Wood Lane (E&SB) 19.58: Lines blocked by debris. GWR reopened 23/10.

Kensington Addison Road (WLR) 20.42: HE in Howard Street near station caused fire from burst gas main. All traffic and work stopped.

Westbourne Park – Old Oak Common East Junction 21.30: HE blocked Relief and Down Goods lines. Some services cancelled. Cleared 11.45 23/10.

West London Yard: HE on cart road to Barlby Road shed, also crater by shunters' cabin.

LMS: Junction Road 07.30: HL lines closed by UXB, until cleared 10.00 23/10.

SR: St Helier – Sutton Common 19.35: Debris on track, telecom cut.
Hither Green Yard 21.30: Sidings damaged.

23/10/40

LMS: Maiden Lane – Maiden Lane Junction 18.45: Three HE fell, in St Pancras Yard, Maiden Lane Yard and on NLR Maiden Lane Junction – St Pancras Junction Boxes. The last penetrated the arches carrying NLR over Midland lines, so all lines blocked. Five railwaymen killed and five injured. No. 1 Down and No. 2 Up NLR lines cleared by 15.30 24/10. NLR freight trains run over No. 2 Down, along No. 3 Siding then out at York Road. No. 2 Down restored 15.30 25/10 and through working over NLR to Docks resumed on 26/10. No. 1 Up line reopened 09.00 1/11. Midland Fast lines reopened 14.45 24/10.

*From Inspector's Report: Damage considerable and widespread, affecting many buildings, signals, telegraph wires etc. Electric conductor rails also disturbed over some distance. St Pancras Junction Box badly damaged, although frame remained intact. Five railwaymen killed (three enginemen, Traffic Inspector and Head Shunter), and two injured. 40ft crater in middle of south (electric) pair of running lines. Another crater of 50ft on north side in Maiden Lane Sidings, bomb penetrating bridge onto No. 8 road of St Pancras Goods Sidings, destroying wagons. Third bomb fell alongside engine[43] standing near Maiden Lane Box which was seriously damaged. Bomb also blew out girder and bridge decking immediately above passenger main lines [Midland] but sparing Goods lines; empty stock train damaged. Bridge decking and filling cleared away through crater into wagons standing underneath. First Up NLR freight train about to be handled through No. 3 St Pancras Siding.

LNE: King's Cross Loco 19.58: HE damaged a locomotive[44] and slightly damaged foreman's office.
Chadwell Heath – Romford 21.45: HE cut telecom. Lines blocked by debris, but nwr 23.25.

SR: London Bridge 19.45: An oil-bomb fell through roof of Platforms 11 and 12, blocking Platforms 10 and 11 with debris. One passenger injured. Partial restoration 10.00 25/10.

24/10/40

GW: Hayes & Harlington 14.45: HE on main road bridge at station. Windows broken, but rail traffic still running.
Acton 20.30: A number of HE and IB fell between Middle and East Boxes. Damage at several sidings, buildings and retaining wall, also wagons. Down Main line cut until 22.40, Up Relief until 08.15, Goods line 09.55 25/10. Acton East Box temporarily out of commission.

LMS: Barking 05.00: Crater in goods yard. Failure of lighting.
Harlesden 20.15: Signalbox damaged. One staff injured.

LNE: Liverpool Street – Bethnal Green 15.00: No trains run on Through lines until 17.50, while UXB beside line being removed.
Lea Bridge Junction – Channelsea Junction 21.45: HE nearby cut telecom. nwr 22.50.

SR: Exchange traffic with LMS via Battersea, Barnes and Brent now running, after clearance of UXB of 16/10 at Clapham Junction, which freed one Up and one Down line to Putney.
Clapham Junc 15.18: Detonation of DAB damaged two coaches.
Belvedere – Erith 22.14: Both lines blocked near Pembroke Crossing. Cleared 11.10 25/10.

On 25 October, the enemy was unusually active by day and about 70 planes visited London in the morning and 30 in the afternoon, before quite a heavy attack in the evening. Fatalities were 35 by day and 99 by night. Six serious and 43 medium fires occurred and significant damage was done.

25/10/40

GW: North Acton 13.30: HE near crossover, blocking Ealing – East Acton (E&SB) line. Debris fell on Birmingham lines, where TIW introduced from 15.50 for local railcar service. Main line trains diverted via West Ealing – Greenford. nwr 16.00 29/10.

Ealing Broadway 13.30: HE smashed glass at signalbox. Three LPTB trains damaged.
Old Oak Common Carriage Yard 15.00: HE demolished corner of Depot Master's office, broke gas and water mains, also severely damaged new Painting and Lifting Shops and three coaches. Telephone exchange badly damaged. Debris on Main lines. Two staff injured. TIW on Carriage lines from 15.50, until nwr 01.08 26/10.

GW&GC: Ruislip Gardens: Telecom damaged.

LMS: Devons Road – Bow 13.23: Both lines blocked by damage. nwr 14.45 26/10.
Barking 20.35: HE fell on LPTB lines. Service suspended to Upney, until restored 17.07 28/10.[45]
Brent Loaded Sidings 21.15: HE damaged track and wagons. Roads Nos 33–39 out of use.
West Hampstead 21.15: Wagon fire and damage at Cadbury's warehouse. Coal stack on fire at West End Lane.
Haggerston 21.55: Damage to arches blocked all four lines. No. 2 Up and Down clear 10.00 2/11. No. 1 lines remained blocked until 12/2/42.

LNE: Bethnal Green 00.10: HE nearby damaged signalbox and Timekeeper's office.
Fairlop – Barkingside 07.30: UXB in Up line and both lines damaged. Trains diverted via Ilford. Bomb exploded 10.54, producing crater in Up line, so SLW until nwr 12.00.
Beckton 10.35: Two HE fell near Tramways Crossing, badly damaging track, but this was restored by 14.30!

SR: Lewisham – Blackheath 09.09: Both lines blocked owing to damage to Plough Lane Bridge. Using steel trestles temporarily, lines not reopened until 16.00 7/11; permanent reconstruction completed 3/41.
Eastern Section Suburban Area 09.09–09.35: HT cables cut, so no supply for North Kent to Gravesend, Blackheath or Dartford Loop lines. Normal on 28/10.
Herne Hill Sorting Sidings 09.55: HE damaged Nos 6, 7 and 8 sidings. Clear 15.00 27/10.
Waterloo Eastern – Metropolitan Junction 09.50: Both Through lines blocked by further damage to Blackfriars Road Bridge*.

*From report by Lt.Col. Mount: Subsequent to damage of 16/10, another bomb on 25/10 hit centre of Up Main span, blowing out web of main plate girder. Some tramcars were bunched under bridge: two completely wrecked and three others less seriously damaged (mainly glass). Five drivers and conductors killed; two of Bridge Repair Contractor's men missing and two injured, also two men of 158 RCC and two SR staff seriously injured. Timber trestling provided at once to carry end of lattice girder, which had sunk 13 inches. Pressure piling then resorted to found two steel trestles, which were subsequently erected by 158 RCC to enable lift to be completed. Two other trestles erected either side of tram tracks to support the girder now damaged. 40ft weigh-beam carried by trestles now supports six temporary cross-girders to other main girder. Upon this Up Main line opened on 17/11, permitting extension of shuttle service, Charing Cross – Cannon Street. Down Main opened 25/11.

Catford 15.15: Both lines blocked. Station, platform, subway and a passing train damaged. One passenger injured. Down line clear 15.20 26/10, Up line 16.10 27/10.
Petts Wood – Orpington 19.45: Local lines blocked. HE struck carriage shed opposite 'A' Box. Coaches and 'A' Box damaged. Local lines clear 17.15 27/10. 18.36 EMU Cannon Street – Sevenoaks damaged, with three people killed and four injured.
Sanderstead 20.30: Both lines blocked. Cleared 15.45 26/10.
Mitcham Junction – Mitcham/Streatham Junction South 21.20: All lines blocked. Clear 12.35 26/10.
London Bridge – Spa Road 21.52: HE damaged arches. On Eastern side, No. 1 Up and Nos 1, 2 and 3 Down lines blocked. Down lines cleared 09.10 26/10, Up 16.20 27/10. On Central side, Down Local line blocked, and not cleared until 29/10.
UXB: Battersea Yard 09.15, declared safe 30/10.

A moderate night attack on London in the night of 25/26 October killed 93 people (including some during day); 50 people died while sheltering in the Druid Street railway arches near London Bridge (see above). Six serious fires were caused.

26/10/40 (Saturday)

GW: Latimer Road: DAB (of 21/10) exploded, damaging bridge.

LMS: Dagenham – Barking: HE fell on track, blocking all lines. LPTB District Line trains stopped at Barking, and a shuttle service run Dagenham – Upminster with buses Barking – Dagenham. Steam shuttle service ran Pitsea – Dagenham. Steam lines clear 17.20 27/10, electric lines 17.07 28/10.

LNE: Chorley Wood – Chalfont & Latimer (Met&GC) 20.10: Both lines blocked. Traffic suspended until 07.15 27/10.

New Southgate 23.40: HE including oil-bombs near station damaged SM's house and coal office, also telecom.

SR: Merton Park – Merton Abbey Goods 00.10: Both lines blocked. Clear 12.10.

Brentford – Syon Lane, in night: HE damaged Brentford station, cutting cables and telecom.

Petts Wood – Orpington 15.19: Windows of 14.08 EMU Victoria – Orpington broken. Three passengers injured. [Trains bombed at same place two days running!]

West Dulwich 19.40: Abutment of bridge damaged.

Bexleyheath 20.50: IB set fire to waiting-room. Porter and passenger injured. Lines closed until 21.50. Cleared on 27/10.

New Beckenham – Beckenham Junction 21.15: Both lines blocked. Clear 09.50 27/10.

Holborn Viaduct 21.55: Blast smashed station glass.

North Dulwich – Tulse Hill 22.20: Both lines blocked. Clear 11.20 27/10.

UXB: Battersea Yard on arrival roads and Central Section Through lines, Carriage line also out of use, all cleared 29/10; West London Junction, removed; Loco Junction, removed; Coulsdon North, one on Quarry lines, cleared 13.55 27/10, another on station approach road, cleared 16.00 9/11.

On the night of 26/27 October, a moderately severe attack lasting over 12 hours was made on London: 164 people were killed, and one major and two serious fires started. Croydon (Waddon) Power Station (90,000 kW) was disabled and three hospitals hit.

Only minor raids were made between 27/28 October and 7/8 November, except for a moderate raid on the night of 1/2 November, although aircraft bombed London sometimes in daylight.

27/10/40 (Sunday)

LMS: Woodgrange Park: IB on track. One person injured.

LNE: Woodford 00.37: HE on Up and Down lines. Two empty trains in sidings badly damaged, also new road bridge on London side of station. Buses provided from 05.35 South Woodford – Woodford, but rail service normal from 07.30.

South Tottenham – Black Horse Road 21.40: HE fell on bridge, damaging both lines. Down line clear 09.00, Up line 14.45 28/10.

Beckton: UXB stopped traffic until 16.00 8/11.

SR: Sydenham Hill 00.45: Station windows smashed.

Honor Oak 01.00: Station damaged.

Waterloo 04.18: Track damaged and all trains blocked back to Clapham Junction. In morning, steam services resumed, with Main Through and Windsor lines clear at 07.30. Electric services resumed later. Local lines reopened 16.00 28/10. 'B' Sidings not reopened until 11.50 26/11.

St Helier 19.45: Lines blocked by debris.

Malden 19.50: HE in goods yard burst water-main, causing much flooding. Traction and signalling current cut off until 20.35/22.55 respectively, with all lines Malden – Surbiton closed in meantime. Both lines Malden – Norbiton blocked, until 17.00 28/10.

Worcester Park 20.10: Station glass smashed.

28/10/40

LNE: Bishopsgate Goods 23.50: HE on No. 10 road penetrated No. 32 arch.

SR: Nine Elms Goods 01.18: Damage done to Vauxhall Cake Co. (Hay Yard), Empties Shed, loading banks and 18 horse-vans. At Albert Road Yard, buffers, rails, wagons and 10 horse-vans damaged.

Gloucester Road Junction – Norwood Fork Junction 21.30: Damage blocked both East Croydon and both Selhurst lines. nwr 14.12 29/10.

29/10/40

LNE: Snaresbrook 00.25: HE in goods yard made large crater and cut water-mains. nwr 16.00.

SR: Mitcham Junction 00.15: Station damaged and all lines blocked, but nwr 16.00.

Nine Elms 01.18: HE extensively damaged premises in Hay and Albert Road Yards, and Empties Shed.

Streatham Hill – Balham 00.25: Both lines blocked, but Down cleared 01.25.

East Croydon – South Croydon: Both Local lines blocked 00.55, cleared 15.00. Both Main lines blocked 01.15; Up Main clear 15.00, Down lines 16.30 30/10. Up Through not clear until 12.50 2/11.

Norbury 01.20: All Main and Local lines blocked, but Main lines clear 06.15. Station closed, with Down side station approach destroyed, Middle and Up platform approaches damaged. Local lines reopened 09.10. Down platform reopened 09.45 30/10.

Waterloo (W&C) 11.02: Boiler plant damaged.

Charing Cross – Waterloo 11.10: Engineers' lobby at Belvedere Road damaged, also slope to Hungerford Bridge.

Welling – Bexleyheath 12.53: Both lines blocked, but Up cleared 14.40, Down 16.20 30/10.

Beckenham Junction 13.18: Cattle dock damaged.

North Kent West Junction 13.30: HE damaged bridge. Lines to Bricklayers Arms blocked, also Down line from North Kent East and Bricklayers Arms Junctions. Not cleared until 5/11. At Rotherhithe Road Carriage Sheds, No. 8 road, Electric Shop and 30 coaches damaged; 8 staff injured.

Bricklayers Arms Goods 13.35: Inwards and Outwards roads blocked. Depot closed. Not clear until 15.00 5/11.

South Bermondsey 13.35: Station closed, until 30/10.

London Bridge – North Kent East/Bricklayers Arms Junctions 13.38: HE near Spa Road caused total failure of telecom and signalling. Central Section lines blocked. All lines closed until 16.50, then TIW on Eastern Section. Some lines clear 29/10. Signalling restored 30–31/10. Central Section Down Main clear 12.40 31/10, Up Through 10.55 4/11.

Petts Wood – Petts Wood Junction 16.00: All lines blocked. Up Local restored 11.00, Down 18.40 31/10, Down Through 16.30 1/11, Up Through 12.50 2/11.

Gloucester Road Junction – Norwood Fork Junction 21.30: Blockages by HE of East Croydon Spur lines, also Spur lines Gloucester Road Junction – Selhurst. One Up line soon clear, but all lines clear and nwr not until 07.50 1/11.

Norwood Yard: IB considerably damaged three EMU outside Carriage Shed.

East Croydon Goods: Crater in coal yard.

New Cross Gate 22.00: HE extensively damaged points, crossings and sidings. ELR (LPTB) service suspended, but inward goods traffic on it being accepted.

UXB: Nine Elms (Nine Elms Lane/Wandsworth Road), cleared 12/11; Catford Bridge – Ladywell, new DAB protected by sandbag screen and trains passing, cleared 1/11; Southfields – Wimbledon Park, cleared 16.30 9/11.

30/10/40

LMS: Mill Hill – Elstree 19.47: HE falling on Slow lines blocked all and cut telecom. Later, trains passing on Up Fast, Up and Down Fast and Down Slow cleared 21.37 30/10.

LNE: Brent North Junction – Neasden South Junction 00.10: HE between Up LNE and Down Metropolitan lines damaged track and cut wires, then a further bomb fell between Down Main line and Up Sidings. Traffic worked through sidings.

SR: Southfields 11.15: UXB found, lines closed and LPTB service suspended, until 22.00 9/11.

Grove Park 22.05: Coach damaged by IB.

31/10/40

LMS: Dalston Eastern – Western Junctions 19.35: HE nearby, Up line blocked by debris. SLW until nwr 10.30 1/11.

LNE: Seven Sisters – Bruce Grove: UXB beside line. Services suspended, and shuttles provided White Hart Lane – Enfield and Liverpool Street – Palace Gates. Buses provided White Hart Lane – Seven Sisters. nwr 09.30 1/11.

SR: Hither Green 'A', Grove Park and Bromley North 01.30: Signals failed, until 05.15.

New Cross – St John's 12.25: Sewer burst, flooding all lines. Local lines clear 04.46, Down Through 07.48, Up Through 14.30 2/11.

November 1940

1/11/40

LMS: Commercial Road 19.30: HE fell on cart road, No. 3 Bond and mess room. Working in/out of yard suspended.

Upney – Becontree 19.35: All four lines damaged. Steam lines clear 20.05, Electric lines 17.10 2/11.

LNE (Met&GC): Harrow-on-the-Hill – Pinner 06.20: HE fell on Down line; wagon damaged. SLW over Up line until 09.45.

Temple Mills 19.20: HE in Down Yard disabled Hump; 20 yards of hump line and 150 yards of sidings damaged. One man killed and five injured (three seriously). Hump restored 12.15 2/11. nwr 4/11.

West Ham 11.30: HE fell in coal depot. Craters in No. 2 road and cart road. Two tenant's employees injured.

SR: Blackfriars Junction 03.40: Bridge near Ewer Street Depot damaged, blocking rail entrance and Down line Blackfriars Junction – Metropolitan Junction. Line cleared 07.45.

West Wickham 19.28: HE on platforms and track, blocking both lines. Down side demolished and Up side damaged. Two staff and four passengers injured. Station closed; reopened 12.35 3/11. Both lines to Hayes blocked by crater, cleared 17.00 2/11 (steam). Crater in bank on line from Eden Park. nwr 12.00 3/11.

UXB: Lee – Mottingham 13.30, trains passing, cleared 14/11; Selhurst 14.30, trains passing, cleared 12.00 25/11; Thornton Heath 19.40, trains passing, cleared 3/11.

Moderate raids during the night of 1/2 November killed 92 people and caused one serious fire.

2/11/40 (Saturday)

LMS: West End Lane 20.25: Passenger services suspended by UXB; not removed until 17.00 14/11.

SR: Ravensbourne – Shortlands 10.20: HE on Up side blocked both lines. 09.31 EMU Holborn Viaduct – Sevenoaks was damaged, guard and one passenger injured. Up line cleared 12.33.

UXB: Abbey Wood – Plumstead 11.40, screened; cleared 5/11.

3/11/40 (Sunday)

LNE: Hornsey 14.00: HE damaged footbridge to Loco Shed. One passenger injured. Up Slow, Up Goods and Reception lines to Ferme Park and Up Engine line all blocked. Up Slow clear 15.15 4/11, Up Goods and No. 5 Reception lines 13.20 5/11. UXB removed 8/11,[46] but Up Coal, three Reception lines and Engine line remained blocked. Reception roads were not repaired for a long time, so operations at Ferme Park very much hampered. nwr not until 17/11.

4/11/40

SR: Purley – Purley Oaks 06.30: Up Local line blocked by subsidence of filled crater from bomb of 11/10. Cleared 11.25.

Malden – Raynes Park 13.15: Up Local line blocked by subsidence of filled crater from bomb of 1/10. Cleared 15.15.

Brentford – Kew Bridge 19.20: Both lines blocked. Sidings at Brentford Goods damaged – cleared 16.20 5/11.

Chelsfield 19.25: Both lines blocked. Bomb struck footbridge, which then fell across 18.00 EMU Cannon Street – Sevenoaks, damaging two coaches and killing one passenger. Sub-station and Up platform also damaged. Clear 12.00 7/11.

Barnehurst 19.40: Both lines blocked. Up cleared 22.20, Down 09.05 5/11.

Blackheath 20.05: Both lines blocked. Down platform damaged and one passenger injured. Cleared 15.30 5/11.

UXB: Brentford 19.40, cleared 5/11; Blackheath 20.05, in garden of station-house, but freight trains passing, cleared 8/11.

5/11/40

LMS: Willesden 07.30: Sidings damaged, two wagons destroyed.

LNE: Leytonstone 20.40: HE damaged three wagons and blocked Down line. SLW until 09.35 6/11.

SR: Hampton Court Junction – Surbiton/Thames Ditton 00.05: Up Local and Branch lines blocked. Main Local lines cleared 10.45, Branch 15.00.

Clapham 04.30: Two HE in goods yard, damaging neck of three sidings and coal trader's lorry.

Queens Road, Battersea 05.00: Damage to bridge and platform.

Victoria – Brixton 04.48: HE blocked all lines, also Wandsworth Road – Clapham, but lines cleared by 12.00.

Catford Bridge – Ladywell 09.13: Lines blocked by subsidence of crater from bomb of 18/10. Cleared 11.15.

Streatham Common South – Mitcham Junction 11.30: Both lines blocked by HE. Cleared 11.05 6/11.

6/11/40

GW: Shepherds Bush (E&SB) 04.35: HE in McFarlane Road caused fire in arches towards Wood Lane, but services already suspended since 21/10.

Hanwell & Elthorne 01.35: One track put out of alignment. nwr 10/11.

Westbourne Park 07.30: DAB near Railway property west of Golborne Road Bridge. Up Goods and Down Carriage lines closed, and Relief lines closed to passenger trains; SpR of 5 mph on Main lines. DAB screened on 9/11, removed 15.00 13/11. nwr (except Up Goods) 21.00 9/11.

Royal Oak 18.55: HE fell between westbound H&C and Down Carriage lines, opposite sub-station. Westbound line badly damaged, also eastbound platform. Debris blocked Up Main and Relief and Down H&C lines. Coaches on Down Carriage line damaged. Porter's room demolished and porter injured. Steam locals terminated at Ealing Broadway. Up Main clear 23.45. Down Carriage line restored 16.40 7/11. All except westbound H&C clear on 8/11. H&C lines restored 11/11, but Royal Oak station remained closed until 12.30 16/11.

LMS: Queen's Park 02.45: HE caused retaining-wall at south end of station to fall on Up electric line. SLW for electrics Kilburn – Willesden Junction. Local steam services stopping at all stations. Shuttle steam service Euston – Willesden Junction. Buses substituted Queen's Park – Willesden Junction, with LPTB Bakerloo Line trains reversing at each, until 15.45 6/11. Normal 17.25 9/11.

Brent Sidings 07.30: Damage and derailment in Nos 22 and 23 roads.

Acton Central 21.16: HE threw debris on Down line, damaging Up conductor rail. All services stopped, until 14.40 7/11. Later, electric trains terminated at South Acton, with buses provided on to Willesden. SLW over Down line for freight only.

LNE: Willesden Green 20.50: HE near signalbox blocked all lines, including LPTB – but LNE lines already out of use due to damage at Wellington Tunnel on 27/9.

Hornsey 23.55: Two HE fell near station. One locomotive damaged and telecom cut.

Ferme Park Up Siding 23.58: HE in No. 10 road damaged two wagons, control office, signalbox and Block.

SR: Strawberry Hill – Shacklegate Junction: Both lines blocked and current cut to Fulwell Junction. Up line clear 11.20, Down 14.07 7/11.

Fulwell – Hampton 00.01: Down line blocked by HE. Clear 15.20 7/11.

Waddon Marsh 00.07: HE blocked private siding of Standard Steel & Metal Propeller Co. Running lines closed until 07.03.

Waddon 04.00: Station damaged.

Nine Elms, Brunswick Road 04.00: HE damaged six motor trailers and one tractor. Blacksmith's and Fitter's Shops damaged, also General Office, Carpenter's Shop and 'A' Shed.

Esher 04.30: HE blocked both Down lines. Clear 11.35 7/11.

Haydons Road 20.00: HE blocked both lines. Clear 08.25 7/11.

Wandsworth Town – Point Pleasant Junction 20.23: HE blocked all lines. Down Local line clear 11.35, Down and Up Through 12.30 7/11, Up Local 09.45 9/11. DAB near loop to East Putney, cleared 11/11.

7/11/40

GW: Hammersmith Coal Depot 21.10: Buildings damaged.

Latimer Road (H&C): HE damaged booking-hall. UXB also, so line closed, until removed 15/11.

Ruislip (GW&GC) 21.15: HE half mile north of station cut telecom to Denham. Seven wagons damaged. TIW, until 15.25 8/11.

Castle Bar 22.40: Due to subsidence of filled crater, locomotive[47] of 19.45 goods West Drayton – Greenford overturned and damaged. Both lines blocked. Up line cleared 23.45, then SLW until 07.00 8/11. nwr 15.50 8/11, but later found to be a new crater, so both lines closed again and buses substituted Ealing – Greenford. nwr finally 08.20 10/11.

LMS: Kentish Town – Kentish Town Junction 12.00: Arch damaged on 22/9 gave way and Down line blocked. SLW until nwr 13.00 13/11.

Kensal Green 19.20: HE fell through roof of tunnel, burst a main and blocked Slow lines by flooding. Trains diverted to Fast lines. nwr 20.10 21/11.

St Pancras 21.13: Three HE fell. One on Platform 1 penetrated to the LL, one in booking-hall damaged roof, one on main approach road in front of station. IB set fire to 4th – 6th floors of Hotel. Fires extinguished by 02.40 8/11. Nos 1, 2 and 3 platforms out of use until 11/11. One passenger and three staff killed, eight staff injured. Passenger stock damaged. Passenger services reversed at Kentish Town.

Kew Gardens – Gunnersbury 21.30: HE made large crater in Down line. SLW, freight only. nwr 07.20 8/11.

LNE: Clapton Junction – Hall Farm Junction 19.45: HE blocked lines. Reduced service provided Chingford – Liverpool Street via Tottenham – presumably reversing there.

Copper Mills Junction – Lea Bridge Junction 20.00: HE damaged Up Main and Goods lines. SLW over Down line Lea Bridge Junction – Copper Mills Junction, until 11.30 8/11. Normal at Hall Farm Junction 13.50 8/11. Up Goods line Copper Mills – Lea Bridge clear 9/11.

Wembley Hill 23.10: HE near station blocked Up Loop, Blind Lane Box – Wembley Hill. Up stopping trains run from Main line to south end and backed into Up platform. nwr 16.00 8/11.

SR (Western Section):

Fulwell – Hampton 00.01: Down line blocked by damage. nwr 15.25.

Vauxhall – Loco Junction 20.52: Down and Up Main Local lines blocked by HE. Windows broken on 20.27 electric Waterloo – Portsmouth & Southsea, but no casualties. Up line cleared 12.35 8/11. Down Main Local clear 15.35 10/11.

Kew Gardens – Richmond/Gunnersbury 21.15 (see also LMS above): All lines blocked by HE. Up line clear 01.22 (for goods), all traffic 07.20 8/11.

Nine Elms (Albert Road) 23.02: HE damaged 'B' Shed, also buildings adjacent to main line. UXB, screened 9/11, cleared 14.30 12/11.

SR (Central and Eastern Sections):

Streatham 02.50: Station house damaged.

London Bridge 19.36: Several HE fell in the area. One exploded on Artillery Street arches of Nos 1–3 Down (Eastern) lines. All lines blocked with debris. Signal current failed over much of SE Suburban area, being restored at 03.25 8/11. All Central lines, and Eastern Nos 1 and 2 Up and No. 3 Down cleared 08.35 8/11. No. 2 Down Eastern line not cleared until 16.30 24/11. No. 1 Down line not cleared until 11.55 1/2/41*.

*Report of Lt.Col. Mount: At Artillery Street bridge, large bomb fell alongside one pier, forming 50ft crater in very bad ground. Bridge and viaduct carries main approach (12 tracks) to London Bridge. Lattice girder (84ft span) concerned carries two Down lines. Pier and adjacent arches badly shaken and foundations drawn towards crater, causing serious settlement. Pier alone represents 550 tons masonry. Support of girder completed in two days by 158 RCC (RE), but subsequent settlement necessitated resort to pressure piling. Adjacent arches needed heavy timbering, as large cracks revealed movement outward.

Two arches of same viaduct (Crucifix Lane) also hit and demolished 29/10. Four tracks knocked out but with centring on one and weigh-beams on the other, two tracks reopened. For Up Local line, permanent reconstruction necessary, a two months' job, but Traffic Department not pressing for the fourth line.

Bricklayers Arms Goods 19.40–21.45: At intervals, HE on and near depot damaged four sidings, roof of 'F' Shed, Empties office, one coach, seven wagons and one road vehicle. Traders' and SR huts in 'D' Shed demolished. (A UXB just 30ft from 'N' Section was not discovered until 11 April 1945, when the Section was closed for 2½ days while bomb removed!).

Selsdon – Sanderstead 20.00: Up line blocked by HE, until 20.55.

Bexleyheath – Barnehurst 20.45: Both lines blocked by HE. Clear 11.00 8/11.

Deptford – Greenwich 20.45: Both lines blocked by HE, until 10.54 8/11.

Queen's Road – Peckham Rye 21.00: Both lines blocked by HE. Clear 09.30 8/11.

Canterbury Road Junction – Loughborough Junction 21.13: Both lines blocked by HE damaging arch and retaining wall. Down line clear 11.30 8/11, Up clear 14.00 9/11.

Windmill Bridge Junction 21.48: Down and Up Through and Down Relief lines blocked by HE, until 08.20 8/11.

East Croydon Goods 21.40: Sidings damaged, also Selhurst – Norwood Fork Junction.

Brockley 21.55: HE blocked all lines. Up Main line cleared 08.55 8/11, and used by Down trains until Down Main line cleared 15.53 8/11. Down Local line restored 16.00 17/11.

Abbey Wood – Belvedere 23.30: Both lines blocked by HE. Clear 11.00 8/11.

UXB: Streatham Hill – Balham 10.45, cleared 11.45; Catford Bridge – Lower Sydenham 17.00, cleared 16.00 8/11.

London suffered quite a heavy raid on the night of 7/8 November, albeit with only two serious fires and 176 people killed.

8/11/40

GW: Latchmere Road Bridge (WLER): UXB in night blocked all lines to South Lambeth etc. On 9/11 found to have exploded.

LMS: Caledonian Road & Barnsbury 00.45: HE in goods depot. Telecom cut, so TIW York Road – Barnsbury.

Dalston Western Junction 19.45: Much debris from adjacent buildings blocking lines. Electric trains terminating Canonbury.

Broad Street freight temporarily cancelled. No. 2 lines cleared 21.10, then freight run at caution. No. 1 line restored 14.30 14/11.

Serious damage had now been done to arches at several points Broad Street – Dalston Junction (see also 13, 14 and 25/10). The succession of viaducts carried two double-lines, Nos 1 and 2, only No. 2 being electrified. Consequently, Broad Street Station (already cut off for short periods on eight occasions) was completely isolated 14.00 13/10–16.00 11/11. No. 1 lines were seriously damaged at many points and not completely restored until 14/2/42, although limited goods traffic was seen many months earlier. Meanwhile, Haggerston station had closed 6/5/40, Shoreditch 4/10/40 when the steam-worked local service Broad Street – Finsbury Park LNER and beyond was suspended. The Broad Street – Poplar service survived until 14/5/44.

    Brent Sidings 23.30: HE fell on wagon of girders, derailing wagon and damaging sidings. No interference to traffic.

LNE: Beckton: Traffic suspended while cavity caused by UXB of 27/10 filled. nwr 16.00.

    Canning Town: Up and Down Goods lines damaged. Clear 10.45 9/11.

    Caledonian Road Coal Depot 00.20: HE damaged tracks, shed and a wagon.

    Finsbury Park 04.20: HE near Up Canonbury line blocked it with debris. nwr 11.00.

    Hackney Downs – Clapton 19.15: Both lines blocked and telecom cut. Trains diverted via Stratford. No service at Clapton. Special service from 06.00 9/11. nwr 11.30 9/11.

SR: Norwood Yard: Closed early 8/11, owing to damage to sidings in night.

    Catford Bridge – Ladywell 18.32: Lines blocked. nwr 12.00 9/11.

    North Kent East Junction 19.15: HE damaged three arches, blocking No. 1 Up and No. 2 Down lines, also HT cable cut. Signalling and points disabled until 01.00 9/11. Traction current cut, until 21.20, also Herne Hill – Beckenham Junction until 21.50. No. 2 Down restored 15.30 10/12, No. 1 Up 15.30 24/1/41.

    Loughborough Junction 19.23*: Two HE blocked all lines. Station buildings, arch and sub-station damaged. Main lines clear 12.15 10/11. Both lines to Cambria Road Junction clear 12.15 9/11, to Canterbury Road Junction 16.00 9/11 for steam, for electrics on 10/11. Down line to Herne Hill clear (for steam trains) not until 23/12, Up line and platform not open until 6/1/41.

*From Lt.Col. Mount's Reports: 500 kilo bomb demolished half of viaduct for three spans on Holborn – Herne Hill route. Both lines and platform between blocked, the arches completely shattered – "obviously another of several deliberate attacks". Cost will be up to £15.000. Damage is just short of junction, the other lines remaining open; substation not hit. By 5/2/41 the three shattered arches under Down line shored up with timbering and traffic now passing at 5 mph – four weeks earlier than expected. Arches were later reconstructed in concrete, the Up line being carried over three arches through temporary RSJ spans supported on concrete buttresses, with a central pier of military steel trestling. Concrete piers eventually provided with concrete flat-top spans.

    Falconwood – Welling 19.30: HE blocked both lines and damaged HT cables. Clear 16.05 9/11.

    Victoria 20.38: Station lighting and signalling failed. Restored (with diesel emergency set) 08.32 in Central, 12.50 Eastern Section 9/11.

    Norwood Yard 21.15: HE damaged Nos 9–11 sidings. Clear 11/11. Up Yard closed owing to damaged sidings.

    Windmill Bridge Junction: Down Relief line damaged, cleared 08.20 9/11.

    Nine Elms 'B' Shed (not in use) damaged again.

    Brockley: Down Local line damaged, cleared 15.55 9/11.

    Petts Wood – Orpington 21.45: Up Through line blocked. Clear 09.40 9/11

    Woodmansterne 21.50: Telecom cut by HE near station.

    UXB: St Mary Cray – Swanley 10.45, sand-bagged and trains allowed past, exploded 22/11; Nine Elms 'C' Shed, Goods Depot closed, clear 14/11; Loughborough Junction – Canterbury Road Junction, clear 9/11; Latchmere Junction, found exploded 9/11.

One or two planes came over London in daytime – but were remarkably 'lucky'.

9/11/40 (Saturday)

GW: Brentford Dock: Two HE damaged Cripple Sidings and forced SLW until 11/11.

LMS: West Kensington Goods: HE damaged siding and mess room.

    Stanmore – Belmont 08.00: UXB suspended service from Harrow, until cleared 11.00.

LNE: King's Cross Goods 10.30: HE caused extensive damage to Main Offices, Outwards Shed, Motor Garage, Invoicing and Counting offices, Granary and Midland Shed. Damage also to roof and windows of other buildings, several wagons and motor vehicles. 24 staff and four others killed, 103 staff and one other injured. "Working retarded". No 'nwr' given.

    High Meads, Stratford 18.46: HE fell on Engine Repair Shop. Coaches damaged and derailed. No casualties or interruption of traffic.

    Sudbury Hill 19.45: HE at London end damaged sidings, shunting neck and signalling.

    General Restrictions now put on all goods (except Government priority) by LNER (GN line) to SR.

SR: Mottingham 05.00: HE damaged sidings and buffers. Two wagons derailed.

    Malden Manor – Tolworth 05.55: HE cut both lines and damaged telecom, but clear by 12.15.

    Raynes Park 16.30: HE in Aston Road slightly damaged 15.56 EMU Teddington – Waterloo, also the signalbox.

    UXB: Norwood Yard 16.30, exploded 18/11 but no interference with working.

London received quite a heavy attack again on the night of 10/11 November. There was one conflagration (in the City), one major and two serious fires; 139 people were killed. The Evelina Hospital, Southwark and Highgate Hospital were hit. A few planes bombed London in daylight on 11 November, very few that night, and on the 12th there was a fairly minor attack – which however killed 108 people, many of them in a bad incident when Sloane Square Underground station received a direct hit at 21.50. There were a few incidents on the next night, then on the night of 14/15 November – for the first time since early August – not one enemy aircraft came over London. Instead, hundreds raided Coventry.

10/11/40 (Sunday)

GW: Old Oak Common East – Ladbroke Grove 22.25: Oil Gas Works damaged. Debris on Up and Down Main caused signal failure, so TIW until 00.50, then nwr 09.00 11/11.

LNE: Shadwell – Stepney East 18.00: Crack found in archway, so Slow lines closed. Normal (with 10 mph SpR) 11.30 12/11.

    Bethnal Green 21.50: Through and Local lines damaged by HE and Suburban lines blocked by debris. At Spitalfields, gantry brought down and wall damaged. Two coaches of an empty stock train from Liverpool Street were damaged. Guard, messenger-lad and fire-lighter injured. Spitalfields Yardmaster's office damaged and Assistant Yardmaster injured. Telecom to Cambridge Control and Liverpool Street cut. Access to Spitalfields Goods was blocked, and power and telecom failed. Most of the very busy Liverpool Street traffic was stopped. Much effort and ingenuity was applied: Shenfield, Gidea Park, Ilford and Loughton trains diverted to Fenchurch Street, Southend passengers changing at Shenfield; Enfield line trains reversed at Hackney Downs; Chingford, Hertford and Cambridge main-line trains run into Liverpool Street, but only the short Platforms 1–4 could be used; Clacton and Colchester main-line trains diverted via Lea Bridge to gain access to these platforms. Nevertheless, all lines were usable 15.00 11/11, except Down Through clear 14.55 12/11. Signalling was clear by 14/11. All a remarkable achievement.

Ilford 22.20: HE in goods yard smashed windows in 21.40 local Liverpool Street – Southend, which was terminated Gidea Park with one passenger injured. Two road motors, wagons and shunter's hut damaged, but all except one siding working 11/11.

SR: Tulse Hill 02.15: HE damaged station platforms, bridge and shops.

Brockley 18.45: Up Local line blocked. Clear 10.30 11/11.

Penge West 19.45: Down Local line blocked. Clear 09.10 11/11.

Bromley South 19.35: All lines blocked. Up Local clear 21.25. Down Local 09.05, Up Through 11.40 11/11, Down Through 11.40 12/11, then nwr.

Epsom Downs 19.48: Platforms 3–8 blocked by HE. Station closed, as Platforms 1 and 2 not electrified. Platforms 3 and 4 cleared 10.55 11/11 and station reopened. Remainder cleared by 18.00 16/11.

Mitcham Junction – Hackbridge 20.15: Down line blocked. Clear 04.55 11/11.

Queen's Road, Battersea 20.45: Through lines blocked by damage. Cleared 11/11 and 12/11.

Windmill Bridge Junction 20.49: Main and Down Relief lines blocked. Down Main clear 11.35 11/11. All clear (except Down Main – Down Relief connection) 12/11.

Nine Elms 21.00: HE fell on 'J' Shed, damaging roof and a wagon.

Waterloo 21.00: Station closed until 22.10, owing to fire in Waterloo Road.

Chiswick – Kew Bridge 21.55: Both lines blocked. Clear 08.40 11/11.

Wandsworth Town – Clapham Junction 21.20: Up lines blocked by damage. Up Through clear 00.30, Up Local 10.40 11/11.

Battersea Yard: HE damaged Arrival and Departure roads. Cleared 07.35 11/11.

UXB: Wandsworth Town – Clapham Junction 21.20, trains passing, cleared 07.40 11/11; Sidcup, trains allowed past from 11/11; Queen's Road, Battersea – bomb screened 11/11 and trains allowed to pass, Through lines clear 12/11; West Sutton, trains passing, cleared 18/11; Kenley, trains passing, but found exploded 11/11.

11/11/40

The list of General Restrictions on goods traffic now longer than ever, and for a few weeks all coal (including block – 'Convoy' – trains) to SR 'Generally Restricted', either by the GN line, Banbury or Neasden.

LNE: Ponders End: Down line closed by UXB until 00.30 11/11.

SR: Battersea Yard: HE in night damaged arrival and departure lines at Stewarts Lane Depot. Also culvert under Engine Incline and adjoining sidings damaged, not repaired until 6/5/41.

Riddlesdown – Upper Warlingham 07.09: Down line blocked, until 12.30.

UXB: Belmont 19.51, both lines closed, but found exploded 12/11.

12/11/40

GW: Wood Lane (E&SB) 21.30: HE damaged MacFarlane Road Bridge and track, but line already closed from an earlier incident. HE also extensively damaged houses on GWR Housing Estate. H&C also closed from Latimer Road owing to damage to arches.

LMS: Upminster East – West Thurrock Junction 22.10: HE on embankment south of bridge over road cut telecom. PMW instituted for single line.

SR: London Bridge – North Kent East Junction 08.30: Subsidence at damage site of 8/11 blocked No. 2 Up line, but line clear 16.20.

Victoria (Central and Eastern) 10.28: All signalling and points failed, but restored by 11.45.

Brockley – Honor Oak Park 19.15: HE caused failure of signalling

and telecom. Block resumed 16.05 13/11.

Feltham Yard 19.40: HE blocked Up Reception lines. Nos 1 and 2 lines reopened 22.00, the rest during13/11.

Brockley – Honor Oak Park 19.53: Up lines, also Block, blocked after craters on Up side damaged retaining wall. Windows broken on 19.03 Down EMU from London Bridge. Up Main clear 20.55, Down Main and Up Local 12.00 13/11.

Vauxhall – Loco Junction 20.10: Up and Down Main Local and Down Main Through lines blocked by damage to arch. All lines closed for examination 21.15–00.45. Down Main Through clear 15.00 13/11, Down and Up Local 14.50 15/11.

Angerstein Wharf 21.10: Various sidings damaged, also a locomotive.[48] Nos 1 and 2 sidings and access to certain private sidings and wharf cleared 14/11. Draw roads clear 12.00 16/11. No. 4 road and LPTB Siding clear 16.35 21/11.

New Cross Gate 23.48: HE damaged offices and shops at station.

UXB: Grove Park 20.00, Up Through line blocked, bomb discredited 10.15 13/11. Smitham goods yard, trains allowed to pass, cleared 23/11.

13/11/40

GW: Paddington Goods 00.00: HE damaged many cartage vehicles.

LNE: Bush Hill Park 03.38: HE damaged both lines at country end. Craters made in Down line and goods yard entrance. Several tracks blown out and UXB suspected in yard. Train service introduced at 20-minute intervals: Liverpool Street – Lower Edmonton, thence buses to Enfield Town. nwr 16.00.

Ponders End 08.50: DAB found 16 yards from Down line. SLW instituted to Brimsdown.

Tottenham 11.05: DAB exploded, damaging Goods offices.

King's Cross Goods 18.28: HE damaged walls, cables, three motors and two trolleys.

SR: New Cross 00.15: Station windows broken by HE in Yard on Down side.

Gipsy Hill – West Norwood 01.32: Both lines blocked by damage to retaining wall. Clear 16.00 15/11.

UXB: Clapham Junction Yard – AA shell, removed 22/11.

14/11/40

LMS: Willesden 00.40: HE damaged Wagon Shops Yard.

SR: Barnehurst 21.15: Land-mine blew in doors of sub-station and smashed glass of station shops and offices.

UXB: Barnehurst – Bexleyheath, trains passing, discredited 09.30 15/11.

The reprieve given to London was very brief. On the night of 15/16 November, the Luftwaffe attacked the capital in greater strength than at any time since 7 September: 358 bombers, 414 tons of HE and over 41,000 IB over nearly 12 hours from 17.30, although they 'only' killed 142 people and caused three major and 19 serious fires. Important buildings hit included Westminster Abbey, Westminster School, the National Portrait Gallery, Wellington Barracks and four hospitals (Queen Charlotte's Hammersmith, Princess Louise Kensington, Friern Barnet and Whipps Cross).

There followed two weeks with only minor diversionary attacks or none at all on London.

15/11/40

GW: Park Royal: Salvage Department premises destroyed by fire and small shed in yard damaged.

Old Oak Common – Westbourne Park 19.50: Two HE on adjacent property damaged West London Carriage Sheds, Shunters' and Inspectors' Stores and Signalling Cabins. Many carriage windows broken. Five staff injured. However, the running lines were clear in 15 minutes.

LMS: West End Lane 23.12: Station badly damaged by HE. Up line blocked, cleared 16.45 16/11.

St Pancras Goods 22.30: IB in warehouse caused injury to one staff and four Home Guard.

LNE: Cranley Gardens 02.45: HE damaged station.

Waltham Cross 22.10: Signalbox badly damaged by HE, but lines clear.

Enfield Town 22.29: Land-mine in town centre caused extensive damage at station, loco shed and other buildings, also two stabled trains.

West Finchley 23.37: Lines blocked by HE. Clear 20/11.

Temple Mills 23.45: HE damaged Up Goods line between North and South Boxes, also Hump. Wires and coal yard ground-frame damaged. Two oil tanks set on fire and 4,000 gallons burnt. Normal at midnight, but shunting suspended until 06.00 16/11 in case of fire.

Canfield Place – Kilburn 23.52: LNE also Met Lines damaged by HE at (former) Lords station.

SR: Spa Road 05.00: Owing to fire in adjacent premises, Nos 2 and 3 Up lines blocked until 08.35.

Chiswick 23.55: IB set fire to timber yard. Conductor rails and cables damaged. Clear 10.30 16/11.

Hounslow Junction – Feltham Junction 23.59: Crater in formation.

UXB: Hampton – Fulwell, UXLM, made harmless 12.19 16/11.

16/11/40 (Saturday)

GW: Acton West 00.15: HE blocked Down Main line. Clear 11.10.

Hanwell – Southall 01.15: UXB found just west of viaduct. Services suspended for a while. Cleared 16.30 20/11.

Kensington Addison Road (WLR) 02.40: Bay road blocked and platform damaged. J. Lyons' shed damaged.

Castle Bar Park: During night HE wrecked experimental wireless mast,[49] so damaged set returned to Marconi Co.

Hayes & Harlington early morning: Two HE and one UXB in sidings. Trains passing, but four goods roads damaged and working suspended. Clear 20/11.

North Pole Junction (WLR) – Old Oak Common East Junction 19.10: HE damaged telecom, requiring TIW. No damage to track. nwr 18.08 17/11.

West London Carriage Sidings 19.10: HE on allotments near Mitre Bridge damaged ARP office and stores, Smith's shop and Fitting shop.

Mitre Bridge Junction – North Pole Junction (WLR) 19.25: Telecom cut, requiring TIW. nwr 17/11.

LMS: Euston: Nos 14 and 15 platform lines put out of use, also No. 18 line. No. 14 reopened on 17/11, No. 15 not until 15.45 24/11.

Willesden – Stonebridge Park 00.10: IB through roof of carriage caused fire, but extinguished and train proceeded.

Willesden HL Sidings 00.40: Sidings damaged, causing much dis-location. Cleared 16.15.

Willesden Loco.: HE on New Shed. "Extent of damage not known." (Not serious).

Acton Branch 00.47: Both lines blocked. nwr 16.55.

North Wembley 01.00: UXB found between Fast lines. Cleared 11.00.

Kensal Green Junction 01.00: Up and Down Hampstead Junction and City Goods lines blocked. City lines clear 12.40, other lines 16.45.

Kensal Rise 01.05: UXB exploded in bank, damaging retaining wall, leaving it leaning towards Up line. Both lines blocked. Clear 16.45.

Brent Junction 01.35: HE put five sidings out of use, derailed 20 wagons and blocked Slow lines. nwr 12.30.

Leyton 02.00: HE in goods yard damaged motor vehicles, sidings etc.

St Pancras 02.15: HE fell on No. 6 platform line, fracturing base of cast-iron support column. Platforms 1, 2, 6 and 7 out of use. Certain trains terminated Kentish Town.

Sudbury Junction – North Wembley 02.20: HE fell between Up and Down Fast lines, blocking all, but Slow lines reopened 04.20, Fast lines 11.00.

Brent Sidings 04.20: IB fires destroyed wagons.

Stonebridge Park 05.03: Fires started in Carriage Sidings.

Kentish Town Junction 18.15: IB on line and signalman injured

trying to extinguish them. All lines blocked briefly.

Highgate Road 18.30: IB near signalbox put instruments out, so box closed.

Kentish Town Loco 18.30: IB set fire to Paint Shop and Road Motor Shed. Two men injured.

Gospel Oak 22.30: HE on station and track near signalbox caused much damage. All lines blocked. Signalman injured. nwr 10.40 17/11.

LNE: Winchmore Hill 02.45: HE damaged station and garage in goods yard.

Crouch End 04.30: Crater found in line. Service suspended. Up line clear 07.45, then SLW until Down clear 09.45.

New Southgate 08.30: UXB exploded in No. 4 siding, Engineer's Yard. SM killed; two ARP workers and two platelayers seriously injured. Wires cut, so TIW Cemetery Box – New Southgate until 09.25 17/11. nwr 12.00 21/11.

Gidea Park 22.10: Two land-mines in vicinity. Brake van of 08.05 freight Whitemoor – Goodmayes damaged by blast and guard injured. Many windows broken in spare stock in sidings. Junction out of use, until 17/11.

Maryland 23.10: Land-mine fell at end of station, but damage relatively slight.

Rectory Road: Station buildings damaged.

SR: Purley – Purley Oaks 00.07: Crater in formation and HT cable cut.

St John's 00.50: Cables damaged and track-circuits out. Restored 13.22.

Syon Lane 00.55: Lines already blocked by DAB now blocked by damage. Cleared 16.15 17/11.

Clapham Junction 02.00: No. 3 West London siding damaged and locomotive[50] and van derailed. Clear 11.15.

Battersea Park 03.40: HE on Local lines blocked all lines. Main lines clear 08.30, SL lines 09.30. Slow lines clear 16.15 18/11.

Blackfriars 06.50: Extensive fires caused by IB in Paper Warehouse and New Shed. One wagon destroyed and two damaged. Current to Holborn cut until 09.30.

New Cross – St John's 08.35: All lines blocked, but nwr 12.35 17/11.

Nine Elms 19.21: HE fell on cattle-loading bay. Various sidings and engine road on Up side damaged, with 15 wagons damaged or derailed. Engine road and sidings clear 17.00 22/11. Cattle bay not restored until 12/12.

Strawberry Hill: Damage at EMU Depot.

UXB: Feltham, found exploded 17/11.

Damage at Bricklayers Arms and Battersea Yards limits working and non-urgent traffic being regulated.

Telephone problems on SR worse than ever. Severance of Redhill Control lines to suburban stations necessitating transmission via Deepdene and Waterloo, so further congestion.

17/11/40 (Sunday)

GW: Southall West Junction 06.15: HE blocked all lines and damaged telecom. Normal by 11.15.

LMS: West Kensington Goods: Damage to buildings.

SR: Nine Elms 20.27: HE damaged roof of Loco Shed and No. 25 road. Premises of S.W. Stone Co. (on SR property) damaged.

UXB: Kenley – Whyteleafe 10.55, trains passing, made safe 20/11.

18/11/40

SR: Feltham Yard 02.57: Land-mine extensively damaged general office, sidings and wagons, and wrecked telephone exchange, also Hump signalbox and shunters' cabin on Up side. Eight staff and two soldiers injured. No. 1 Down Sorting Sidings not clear until 23/11.

Wimbledon – Mitcham Junction 03.45: Single line blocked, but clear 08.30. At Mitcham Junction, goods shed, offices and staff accommodation damaged.

Earlsfield 21.20: Up Through line closed by embankment slip. Reopened 08.20 19/11, but closed again by DAB 18.00, until daylight 20/11. Reopened 08.20 20/11, but closed again 18.00 until daylight 21/11.

19/11/40
LNE: Silvertown 09.05: UXB found on PLA property on Down side, so SLW on Up.
SR: Kenley 15.00: UXB, but trains passing. Found exploded later in day.

20/11/40
SR: Wandsworth Town – Point Pleasant Junction 15.00: Subsidence of Up Local line, from damage of 10/11. Restored 16.30.
Coulsdon South – Earlswood/Merstham 20.53: All lines blocked by debris. Lines restored in stages 00.25–16.55 21/11.

21/11/40
LMS: Harringay Park – St Anne's Road (T&H) 11.40: UXB; not removed until 16.30 27/11, but Up line closed for only two days.
SR: Honor Oak 05.50: HE caused damage to station and telecom.

23/11/40 (Saturday)
LMS: Euston 06.45: HE in station derailed two carriages. nwr 16.15.
Willesden (Brent Junction – No. 7 Box) 08.25: HE damaged Up and Down Slow and Down Fast. Fast line clear 10.10, Slow lines 18.30 24/11. Down Slow closed again 07.00 25/11 for Engineers.
LNE: Leyton 07.00 and Temple Mills 07.15: HE damaged lines in Engineer's Yard, also new LPTB Sheds at Hainault.
SR: Malden Manor – Tolworth 02.15: Loco of freight derailed by crater in Down line. Re-railed and lines clear 15.45 24/11.
Lewisham Junction – Parks Bridge Junction 06.19: HE fell on bridge. Main lines blocked and all telecom cut to east and south. Up line cleared 07.35, Down 09.10. Telecom and signals restored in stages to 13.00, but signalling still out at Grove Park.

26/11/40
SR: Streatham Hill 19.40: HE damaged footbridge and blocked lines, until 00.15 27/11.

The next heavy raid on London occurred on the night of 29/30 November, when 130 people were killed and one major and 12 serious fires resulted. A number of factories and works were struck, also Queen Mary's Hospital, Roehampton and the West Middlesex Hospital.

There then followed 10 days of relative peace while the Luftwaffe attended in force elsewhere. No planes at all came over London on some nights, until the next major raid on 8 December.

29/11/40
GW: Ealing Broadway 22.15: HE severed telecom and smashed windows of train.
Brentford: HE damaged station and signalbox.
LNE: Stepney 22.45: HE damaged signalbox.
SR: Kent House – Beckenham Junction 19.20: All lines blocked by HE, also a DAB. Down Main clear 11.55, Up Main 14.00 30/11.
Twickenham – Whitton 19.35: Both lines blocked. 20.05: Goods shed considerably damaged by fire, but extinguished 21.35. nwr not until 13.00 3/12.
Brentford 19.50: IB badly damaged a wagon.
Strawberry Hill 21.00: Both lines blocked. IB damaged electric stock in sidings. nwr 17.20 30/11.
Feltham Yard 22.05: Nos 6–9 Departure roads blocked. Clear 16.30 30/11.
Hither Green – Lee 22.10: Both lines blocked by damage. Not cleared until 16.00 3/12.
Sunbury 22.20: Both lines blocked. HE on Up platform completely demolished all Up side buildings. Signalman and porter injured.
Hampton – Fulwell 23.00: Both lines blocked by damage and UXB. Repaired 2/12, but remained closed until UXB discredited 4/12.

30/11/40 (Saturday)
SR: Hampton Court Junction – Hinchley Wood 00.00: Down line blocked. Clear 16.15.
Battersea Wharf 19.00: Nos 5 and 6 roads blocked, until 23.30.
Malden – Norbiton 20.35: Both lines blocked. Clear 08.30 1/12.
Teddington – Shacklegate Junction 21.20: Both lines blocked. Clear 13.30.
Teddington – Hampton Wick 21.20: All lines blocked, until 07.00 1/12.
UXB: Syon Lane, screened and trains passing from 11/12, defused 28/12; Hampton – Fulwell (two); Strawberry Hill, made safe 1/12.

December 1940

1/12/40 (Sunday)
SR: Richmond – North Sheen/Kew Gardens 23.59: All lines damaged by debris. nwr 01.55 and 06.00 respectively 2/12.
UXB: Teddington 12.38, in adjacent gardens, cleared 15.45 2/12.

3/12/40
LMS: Queen's Park 22.07: HE damaged Down Electric line and station premises. Five passengers killed and two (also two staff) injured. Debris blocking all lines, but not for long. Fast lines clear 22.58, Down Slow 23.20, and Up Slow clear 02.45, Up Electric 06.15. nwr 16.05 4/12.
SR: Feltham 14.20: Two HE fell in Yard. Two Down Departure lines and sidings damaged.

4/12/40
GW: Westbourne Park, Old Mileage Yard: UXB exploded, damaging wall.

5/12/40
SR: West Croydon 18.53: Pullman car in siding damaged by IB.

London next had a very heavy raid on the night of 8/9 December for nearly 12 hours. Deaths were 250; fires, nine major and 24 serious. Serious damage was done at many factories, in the Docks and again to Broadcasting House.[51] Important buildings hit included: House of Commons, St Stephen's Hall, Westminster Abbey, New Horticultural Hall and the National Gallery; the Royal Mint and the PLA Building; Royal Naval College, Greenwich and seven hospitals (mostly suburban).

After that raid there followed another relatively quiet period of nearly three weeks, again while the enemy heavily bombed provincial cities.

8–9/12/40 (Sunday – Monday)
GW: West Ealing 01.40 8/12: UXLM 200 yards from railway, so trains diverted via Greenford and Hanwell Loops, with shuttle service Ealing Broadway – Paddington, and buses West Ealing – Ealing/Hanwell. Cleared 11.55 9/12.
LMS: Caledonian Road & Barnsbury 19.20: HE fell on 18.50 EMU Broad Street – Watford. Four passengers and one staff killed, seven passengers and a guard injured. All lines closed, but nwr 15.30 9/12.
Woodgrange Park 21.00: HE fell in sidings, damaging Nos 3 and 4 roads. Block failed.
Dalston Junction: HE fell on line near Ridley Road, blocking Poplar line. Trains terminated Victoria Park, thence buses to Dalston Junction. Freight for GE Section cancelled. nwr 16.00 9/12.
LNE: Fenchurch Street – Leman Street: Signal gantry at Leman Street demolished and Camber Street Bridge damaged. LNE trains suspended, LMS trains reversed Stepney East, until 10/12. nwr 12/12.
Marylebone 19.15: HE fell far end Nos 1 and 2 platforms. Offices and two coaches damaged. Trains worked from Platforms 3 and 4, until nwr 09.45 9/12.

Stratford 21.20:[52] HE fell in High Meads Carriage Sidings. 30ft crater formed. Two empty stock trains damaged and three coaches set on fire. 12 vehicles damaged and some destroyed. Crater and debris blocking six roads.

East Smithfield 22.00: Top floor of warehouse set on fire and track damaged. HE also fell on old unused building in Goodman's Yard, Leman Street.

Bruce Grove – Seven Sisters 21.10: Up line blown out. SLW on Down, until 11.37 9/12.

Stratford Market 22.45: HE blocked Main and Goods lines. Station damaged, with lines flooded by burst water-main. LNE Printing Works damaged. Trains terminated Stratford LL, until nwr 12.00 9/12.

King's Cross – Farringdon 02.10: Met and MWL closed owing to unsafe buildings adjacent, until 12.15 9/12.

Abbey Mills Lower Junction: Signalbox and signalling damaged. Down Passenger line blocked until 18.00 9/12.

Silvertown: Wagons damaged.

Ilford 02.40 (9/12): Wagons damaged.

Stoke Newington, Manor Road Sidings: UXB exploded nearby, damaging track.

SR (Western Section):

Hampton Court 22.15: Seven electric coaches burnt out and three steam coaches damaged. Station closed owing to fires on platforms and in sidings.

Waterloo 22.45*: Large bomb fell on approach road, opposite Victory Arch, forming 70 ft crater and penetrating to W&C tunnels below. General Manager's offices, dining-room and Stores Department buildings in York Road set on fire and damaged by IB and HE.

02.00 (9/12): Arches by west abutment of Westminster Bridge Road bridge damaged, blocking Up Windsor line. Also at Arches 199/198 HE damaged all lines, and blocked No. 1 South siding and Nos 2 and 3 Down sidings with coaches stabled in them. Signal supply failed, owing to damage to cables in Windsor Lines sidings. UXB also suspected. All trains terminated at Clapham Junction until morning 9/12. The approach lines restored in stages: Up and Down Windsor and Up Main Relief lines clear 16.00 (9/12), but Platforms 1–7 remained out of use; the Main Through lines reopened 16.30 10/12, but the Main Local lines not clear until 11.00 16/12. In meantime, by manipulating routes over the many crossings in the approaches to Waterloo it was possible to work most services. Nos 1 and 2 lay-by sidings not repaired until 07.20 22/2/41.

Bank – Waterloo 23.12*: Both W&C lines blocked, due to HE that fell through tunnel. Services not restored until 06.30 3/3/41.[53] Nos 1 and 2 North Sidings not restored until 04.00 2/12/41. 27/12: 50ft of Down tube and 21ft of Up tube collapsed.

Vauxhall 23.20: Windsor lines blocked by debris. Windsor Through and Up Main Relief clear 17.00. All lines clear 07.05 9/12.

*From Lt.Col. Mount's Report: W&C running tunnels in brick construction with cover of 25ft. Abutment probably destroyed, also pier between tunnels. Water-mains fractured and water flowed down to bottom of slope under river (about 35ft), completely flooding both tunnels with 4½ million gallons. (The floodgate proposed at Waterloo end of tunnel – nearer the station – would have prevented the flooding).

The contractors (Robinson & Cole) employed two mobile excavators working down through crater, also pumping plant with eight-inch pipes installed to dispose of water. Subsequently, 50ft of Down tube collapsed and required replacing by 'cut and cover' construction. Length of 21ft of Up tube collapsed as well, and further 12ft of old construction so badly damaged that necessary to rebuild. Skilled men from Mowlem & Co. superintended actual work, but contractors assisted with labour and loan of two excavators and pile driver. Two new tubes constructed and inverts completed rapidly, work being carried out uninterruptedly under conditions prevailing, to allow earliest resumption of traffic. However, work expected to take six weeks, in the event took three to four months.

SR (Central and Eastern Sections):

Walworth Road 20.24: Portions of an enemy plane fell on the track, so Up Local line closed for its removal, until 22.35.

Blackheath – Kidbrooke 20.50: Kidbrooke Box, both lines and empty train damaged. All telecom cut Blackheath – St Johns. 02.00 (9/12): HE at Blackheath blocked both lines, but nwr 08.40.

Bricklayers Arms Goods 21.44: Numerous IB caused extensive fires in 'S' and 'G' Sections, also damage in 'K' Section to Paper shed, four tractors and one motor.

Holborn Viaduct – Loughborough Junction 22.39: All lines closed owing to fires near railway, until 03.45 9/12. Minor damage done.

London Bridge 22.40: Roof of two coaches in 20.15 ex-London Bridge circular electric service damaged by IB. Signal and traction current failed. 00.01:[54] UXLM fell (on parachute) on top of main Central Section signalbox, and everybody evacuated. All Central and Eastern traffic had to be stopped to avoid vibration. Navy could not defuse it until daylight. They achieved this at 12.55 – to everyone's relief – and Eastern Section traffic resumed 14.00. Most Central Section lines also restored, but closed again 21.45 overnight. Up Local and SL lines restored by evening 10/12.

Brixton – Herne Hill 22.48: Fires on and near railway forced closure until midnight.

Hither Green Sidings 23.00: Wagon and contents set on fire.

St John's 23.02: Signalbox windows smashed.

Southwark Park Road Bridge 23.15: All lines affected by damage to arches, but not too serious. Most lines were clear by 13.30 9/12. Only Down (Central) Local and No. 1 Eastern lines closed, until 15.30 10/12.

Cannon Street 01.30(9/12): BB landed on roof of station.

Anerley 04.40: Driver reported two craters in Up Main. All lines blocked. Local lines clear 10.00, Main lines clear 14.50.

Camberwell 09.50: All lines blocked due to fire at old station, until clear 12.45.

12/12/40

LNE: Plaistow & West Ham Depot 12.05: HE in coal yard damaged stacking-ground. One person injured.

15/12/40 (Sunday)

GW: Westbourne Park (New Mileage Yard): Heavy UXB still being excavated, as it has slipped down to a new bed. Yard work being interfered with.

19/12/40

SR: Communications severely disrupted in evening on many Eastern Section lines by fallen BB cables.

On 21 December there was no concerted raid, but a single plane, probably guided by the accurate Y-Verfahren equipment, made a pin-point attack in the early evening on Victoria station with one massive (2,500 kg) bomb.

21/12/40 (Saturday)

LNE: King's Cross Loco 00.55: AA shell exploded, severely injuring a driver, but doing only minor damage.

SR: Victoria* 18.52:[55] Large 'LM' made 30ft crater on Down side 100 yards from Central signalbox. Station closed 19.00. All four Eastern tracks cut and two Central tracks distorted.

*From Engineer's Report: Main Eastern and Central Sections signal and telephone cable routes destroyed on either side, breaking 60 cables (containing 1,500 cores) and 13 joint boxes. Ten point-machines seriously damaged. Fourteen shunt signals damaged. Down Starting Signal bridge blown into street. At Central signalbox all windows and frames shattered, also glass panels of power frame. Most cells of point and describer batteries broken. Telephone switchboards, train-describer apparatus and indicator lamps of frame broken, also indication glasses. No structural damage to signalbox (built to 'ARP' standard), although all surrounding buildings seriously affected, including Imperial Airways Building, staff lobbies and turntable. Two staff killed, eight staff and two other people injured. One locomotive damaged.[56] On 22/12, emergency supply connected to Battersea Park Box from supply feeding West London Junction, and shuttle service to Waterloo put on to relieve congestion at Clapham Junction. For daylight working only, Central Main lines cleared 07.30 23/12, Local lines 17.00 24/12; all Eastern Section clear 07.30 24/12, normal 25/12. From 24/12, many signal engineers from SR, Westinghouse and Royal Corps of Signals worked throughout all week-ends,[57] also 13 hours per day in signalbox when possible during hours of darkness. 100-pair telephone cable restored 26/12. Repair on Central side given preference as main cable route on Eastern side buried in debris, but emergency feeder connected for continued operation of point-battery in Eastern Box. All cables repaired on Central side by 1/1/41, point machines and shunt signals 17.00 5/1. On Eastern side, 80% of repairs complete 8/1, enabling signals and TC southward, remaining signals 9/1.

22/12/40 (Sunday)
LNE: Wood Street: Station buildings damaged.

23/12/40
LNE: Stepney – Salmons Lane Junction 07.45: Signalling and TC cut. LMS services interrupted only until 08.20. LNE trains Ilford – Fenchurch Street cancelled. nwr late on 24/12.

Neasden 19.50: Four HE fell, damaging PW Inspector's office, lamp-man's cabin and telecom. Windows broken in Ambulance Train No. 18 and in South Box. Extensive damage done also to LPTB yard and plant.

Stratford Market 20.30: HE fell on the Market, blocking Nos 1 and 2 departure lines. Goods lines also blocked until 23.35. nwr 16.00 24/12.

SR: Loughborough Junction 19.45: IB damaged roof of Foreman's office.

Crystal Palace HL 19.50: Berthed coach damaged by IB.

New Cross Gate 20.30: Down Local and Main lines blocked by HE near South Box. Down trains diverted via Peckham Rye and Streatham Common. Shuttle service London Bridge – New Cross Gate. Clear 12.00 24/12.

On the night of 27/28 December,[58] London suffered a moderate attack of relatively short duration. 141 people were killed and there were five serious fires; two hospitals were hit.

27/12/40
LMS: Silkstream Junction 21.00: Large crater found between Up Fast and Down Slow lines – but no damage to lines. Block failed, but trains running from 21.50. Block repaired 09.00 28/12.

LNE: Bow Junction – Coborn Road 20.27: HE in vicinity affected signalling and Block. Windows broken in an empty stock train from Liverpool Street. nwr 08.30 28/12.

Spitalfields Goods 20.55: Two wagons damaged by AA shell.

Northumberland Park 21.38: Station buildings damaged and signalbox windows broken.

Silver Street 22.15: HE in vicinity broke station windows.

Surrey Docks, Canal Junction (ELR) 19.36: Crater in track blocked line to New Cross Gate, until 17.30 29/12.

SR: Southwark Park Road – North Kent East Junction 18.50: Large crater in No. 2 Up and Down lines (already blocked), also (until 22.30) Down line from Rotherhithe Road Yard blocked. IB caused failure of all signal and traction current in area, until restored 10.40 28/12. All trains reversed at Peckham Rye, Forest Hill or Crystal Palace. No. 2 Down and No. 2 Up clear 16.20 29/12.

Lewisham sub-station 18.58: Supply cables cut by IB, isolating Park's Bridge Junction – New Cross until 12.18 28/12.

Ladywell – Lewisham 19.45: Both lines and telecom blocked. Lines cleared 09.30 28/12, but with TIW.

Beckenham Junction – Shortlands 19.45: Failure of signalling, so HSW until 15.45 28/12.

North Dulwich – Tulse Hill 19.50*: North end of Knights Hill Tunnel penetrated by HE, and debris run into by 18.30 EMU London Bridge – London Bridge, which came to a stand inside the tunnel. Motorman trapped and evidently died

instantly. Guard slightly injured, but no passengers hurt. Seven coaches moved away by a locomotive, but leading coach was left embedded. Both lines blocked, also coal depot. Lines not reopened until 14.00 10/3/41.

*From Lt.Col. Mount's Report: Heavy bomb fell short distance inside portal. Cover was 23ft and a crater of 50ft formed in bad clay; 40ft of tunnel arch destroyed nearly to rail level. Robinson & Cole provided two drag-line excavators and worked from the top. Weather very bad and a slip occurred, but excellent progress made. Traffic expected to run in four weeks. In spite of unexpected complications, new arch of concrete built with three feet of filling on top including debris, as necessary weight to prevent distortion.

Crofton Park, about 20.00: Station damaged.

New Cross 20.15: All main and ELR lines blocked by damage at London end of station. Through and Up Local lines clear 17.00 28/12. Down Local and ELR lines cleared 17.30 29/12.

Penge East 20.50: HE fell between station and tunnel, displacing sidings and damaging signalling.

Honor Oak Park 21.30: HE damaged bridge abutment, station buildings and platforms.

Bricklayers Arms Goods: 100 IB, widespread in yards. Fitters' shop and wagon damaged and lorries of coal burnt.

Rotherhithe Road Carriage Sidings: Timber shed damaged by fire.

New Cross Gate: CME's Store badly damaged by fire.

28/12/40 (Saturday)
LMS: Poplar 11.00: UXB put two sidings out of use. Cleared 7/2/41.

The night of 29/30 December was that of the infamous Second Great Fire of London, when just 136 enemy bombers in a little over three hours overwhelmed the Fire Services, so causing six enormous conflagrations (four in the City, two just across in Southwark), together with 28 major and 52 serious fires. Low water in the Thames prevented use of fire-boats and combined with broken mains to force the abandonment of many fires, in spite of fire-fighting reinforcements from up to 150 miles away. The death toll was only 163, but the damage done was immense. Apart from the destruction of large areas of the Square Mile, numerous factories and dock installations in the East End were destroyed or severely damaged. Buildings of special interest involved included nine important hospitals, County Hall, the Guildhall, the Tower of London and Westminster City Hall. The Central Telegraph Office and several telephone exchanges in the City were destroyed, and all telecommunication between London and the South-East was interrupted. Great damage was also done more upstream and at the Surrey Commercial Docks. Water supplies were severely restricted for a week.

29/12/40 (Sunday)
GW: Wood Lane (E&SB) 19.25: Station and other buildings on fire. nwr 07.44 30/12.

Smithfield: MWL blocked, so traffic being dealt with at Alfred Road (Paddington).

LMS: Dalston Junction 18.33: UXB near signalbox. Lines closed and Broad Street trains terminated at Canonbury, Poplar trains at Hackney. Damage also prevented working to Worship Street and Shoreditch Goods, also to LNE at Victoria Park. Eight coaches damaged in sidings. UXB cleared 03.45 30/12.

Broad Street Goods: Warehouse on fire, wagons damaged. Whitecross Street Depot badly damaged.

Skinner Street, near Broad Street: Several alarms earlier in evening. Traffic finally stopped 20.30, with electric trains terminating at Dalston Junction.

Haydon Square 22.55: Warehouse fell on tracks, blocking entrance to depot. Running lines not affected, but owing to damage near Fenchurch Street, Haydon Square, Commercial Road and City Goods stations closed at least until 2/1/41.

Peckham Coal Depot: Damaged and closed.

LNE: Bishopsgate Goods 17.25: UXLM 200 yards away, so 5 mph SpR imposed Bethnal Green – East London Junction.

Spitalfields: Telecom and Control circuits out. Wagons damaged. Hoist disabled until 4/1/41. Three staff injured.

Liverpool Street: IB on west side set fire to roof and Hotel. Trains stopped until 18.40, when fire extinguished. Water shortage forced locomotives to take water elsewhere. Heavy delays.

East London Junction: Hydraulic hoist failed. Trains to SR reversed at Liverpool Street. Restored 2/1/41.

Devonshire Street – Liverpool Street 20.31: Fires blocked all lines, but restored 21.37.

Fenchurch Street 19.15: HE fell outside signalbox, putting all points and signals out. Debris strewn all over lines. Signalman injured. Station closed. LMS trains terminated at Bromley-by-Bow for transfer to LPTB electric service or buses. Ilford service suspended. 20.21: HE fell on railway bridge at corner of Chamber Street and Mansell Street, causing fire. LMS trains resumed 12.00 31/12, but with manual operation of points and signals. Ilford service and nwr morning 6/1, but some points and signals still being worked manually.

Finsbury Park – Harringay 19.19: Broken rail in Down Goods line. Repaired 11.10 30/12.

Gas Factory Junction 20.10: Power to signalbox cut. Restored to Christian Street Junction 31/12.

Stepney, Victoria Junction: TC and signals out.

Bethnal Green 20.40: Hut on fire and lines occupied by Fire Brigade, although Local lines freed 20.46, Through lines 21.37.

Ferme Park 20.50: Down Slow line damaged by AA shell.

Royal Mint Street North 21.30: HE and IB set fire to depot, putting it out of use. Warehouse and granary destroyed, along with 18 loaded, 11 empty wagons and 10 road vehicles. Offices and loading-bank under granary badly damaged. Goodman's Yard buildings damaged and debris thrown on lines. At Royal Mint Street East, warehouse (badly damaged on 8/9) further damaged and put out of use. Beehive Depot, Whitecross Street destroyed by fire.

Farringdon: MWL closed owing to fires and damaged buildings nearby.

Communications generally difficult because telephone lines cut.

SR (Western Section):

Waterloo 18.30: Stores offices in York Road severely damaged by fire, but extinguished by 02.00. 19.30: UXB at end of Platform 11. Station closed and signalbox evacuated, but UXB proved to be an UX AA shell. Main telephone and Block cables affected*. 19.50: Large fire near station, so all traffic stopped, trains reversing at Wimbledon or Clapham Junction. HE also blocked Main Through lines at site of old 'B' Box. 22.55: Down Main Through line damaged, also signalling. Emergency GPO telephone line brought into use Waterloo – Woking. Main Local lines reopened 16.15 30/12. Signalling still out of use on 30/12, but trains resumed on Windsor lines from 16.00, with HSW in meantime. Up Main Through reopened 15.10 1/1/41. Platforms 10 and 11 not clear until 11.00 4/1/41. Signalling not restored to Platforms 1–12 until 17.40 5/1/41. Down Main Through line not clear until 19.45 3/2/41.

West London Junction 20.40: Main Through lines blocked by damage to Bridge 14 (over WLER) next to carriage-washing plant. Down line clear by 14.40 30/12. Up Main Through line not clear until 16.40 26/1/41.

Waterloo – Vauxhall 22.20: Up and Down Main Through lines blocked by damage to Arches 200-201. Up line clear 15.10 1/1/41, Down line 07.45 3/1.

* – "Affected" is a gross understatement. From a report to the MoWT: The cable arch at Waterloo crossed under all tracks between platform ends and the signalbox, conveying a large number of cables. HE severed and threw into disorder 27 cables together with eight subsidiaries. Almost all

signalling and communications put out of use, although during 30/12 certain connections were made to allow signalling to Platforms 17 and 21. However, all cables (containing 1,400 cores) required new lengths let in. Twenty cable jointers and mates were collected from the LPTB, Callender's Cables, the Royal Corps of Signals and from the SR, and set to work: two joints per core in each cable, and before jointing each one correctly identified by Railway staff. As jointing progressed, points previously operated by Hand Signalmen were brought under power. Meanwhile, telephone circuits became available progressively. In all some 2,800 joints were made, 1,500 of these (paper-insulated) on telephone cables, and 60 lead sleeves wiped to encase the finished joints. The bulk was completed by 17.00 5/1/41, the whole 15.00 6/1. All work was carried out 24 hours a day, without regard to Air Raid Warnings.

SR (Central Section):

London Bridge 19.00*: All Central Section (also Eastern LL) lines blocked. Station premises and General Offices (Central Section) badly damaged by fire,[59] which engulfed several trains. Station closed and staff evacuated. Flames spread to Eastern Section and LL station still on fire at 06.00 30/12, but trains still run through HL. Lifts to Underground destroyed by fire. Platforms 8–13 clear 15.30 1/1/41, Nos 14 and 15 16.00 2/1/41. No. 17 not clear until 14/1/41.

*From Lt.Col. Mount's Reports: Station roof and buildings over concourse destroyed by fire and damage estimated about £500,000. Platforms and signalling not affected and roof over platforms left practically intact. Fire not due to IB that landed in station itself, which were dealt with by staff, but to fires started in adjoining St Thomas' Street and Guy's Hospital, and to failure of water pressure. Concrete roofing over concourse soon built to provide accommodation for return of evacuated staff. Fire-fighting trains and other measures[60] would be introduced, [as was done nationally], to prevent such a fire disaster occurring again.

New Cross Gate – Surrey Docks 20.00: Lines blocked by damage, also UXB – removed 22.15. Clear from Down side at New Cross Gate 1/1/41, but nwr not until 14/3/41.

Denmark Hill – Peckham Rye 20.00: Lines blocked by explosion of DAB. Up Catford Loop line clear (for steam) 15.00 30/12, Down line 15.00 31/12. SL lines remained blocked by UXB, screened from 31/12 but not removed until 11/4/41. Electric services restored 13.50 2/1/41.

Clapham Junction – New Wandsworth Goods 20.02: All lines blocked by debris. Local lines clear 01.00, remainder 10.15 30/12.

London Bridge – New Cross Gate 20.30: Bridge timbers damaged by fire. Masonry on line from adjacent buildings on fire.

Latchmere Junction – Clapham Junction 'B' 20.40: Both lines blocked at Bridge 14. Not cleared until 14/1/41.

SR (Eastern Section):

Bricklayers Arms Goods 12.20: UXB in cart road, 'J' section. Roads roped off and bomb removed 15.00 15/1/41.

Elephant & Castle – Walworth Road 18.30: All lines blocked. Through lines clear 05.45, Local lines 08.30 30/12. Shuttle then run Holborn Viaduct – Victoria.

Bricklayers Arms Junction, Bridge 509 19.30: Down Local and both Main lines blocked by one HE. Another blocked six main lines and 'In' and 'Out' Bricklayers Arms lines by damage to ELR line underbridge. 20.00: Spur lines, Up Local and Branch lines cut, also Bridge EL54 and junction of EL lines from Up side. Down Local reopened 15.00, 'In' and 'Out' lines by 16.30 1/1/41. Other lines slewed so that one also available for Up direction. Three wagons of 17.15 goods Brent – Bricklayers Arms derailed on Arrival road. Up Branch clear 16.45 5/1/41, Spur lines 12.30 11/1/41. Down Through line not clear until 16.20 26/1. Up Local and Through lines not reopened until 15.00 2/2/41, when all lines clear London Bridge – New Cross Gate.

Blackfriars – Holborn Viaduct 19.30–21.00: Owing to surrounding fires and blockage by fire-fighting equipment, all lines blocked until 02.20. Current restored 06.50. Up Local line closed until 14.35 30/12.

Lewisham – Blackheath 19.30: Crater and debris blocked both lines, but clear 21.30.

Spa Road – North Kent East Junction 19.45: Nos 1 and 2 Up and No. 3 Down lines blocked by crater. Reopening delayed by UXB – removed 3/1/41. No. 3 Down line clear 15.25 5/1/41, No. 1 Up on 7/1/41.

Blackfriars – Elephant & Castle 20.00: Power cables cut, so signalling out.

Elephant & Castle – Loughborough Junction: Down Through and both Local lines blocked by debris and damage. Clear 09.35 30/12.

Bricklayers Arms Goods 20.12: HE at country end of 'K' Shed damaged Police Office and Electricians' Shop. Several lines affected. Two brake vans, 59 wagons and 11 containers in 'L' section damaged. Goods station closed during 30/12.

Blackfriars Goods 20.30: HE struck 'B' Bond, demolishing building and wall.

Crofton Park – Catford 20.30: Both lines blown out. Clear 16.45 30/12, then shuttle run Nunhead – Shortlands.

Tulse Hill – Herne Hill: Two UXB sandbagged. Trains allowed past (at caution) from 14.00 2/1.

From SR Chief Engineer's Report: In London, especially on SE Section, traffic brought virtually to standstill for several days at least. Overnight 29–30/12 situation was: Traction current off between Charing Cross, Cannon Street, London Bridge, Bermondsey and Lewisham sub-station 19.00–05.50, to enable fires in vicinity to be tackled. Trains terminated New Cross, Eltham Well Hall, Blackheath or Maze Hill. Charing Cross, Cannon Street, London Bridge (HL), Holborn and Blackfriars Stations closed. London Bridge (Central and LL) closed, as station premises and headquarters offices badly damaged. Waterloo (Western) closed, owing to large fire in rubber factory in Westminster Bridge Road near signalbox: all trains terminated short of Waterloo until evening service, which ran from Platforms 16 – 21 and over Windsor Lines to Queen's Road. Subsequently, after discovery of UXB at Peckham Rye, Blackfriars and Holborn Stations closed. Also UXB at Spa Road forced diversion to other routes [presumably Victoria] of all Eastern Section trains to London Bridge, Cannon Street and Charing Cross, but 40% service run morning 30/12. Peckham Rye UXB screened and trains allowed to Blackfriars and Holborn afternoon 2/1/41. Spa Road UXB, deemed dangerous and holding up repair work to Nos 1 and 2 Up and No. 3 Down lines, removed 3/1/41 by BDS. Clearance of debris from London Bridge (Central) premises and platforms took until 1/1/41 before even 25% service reinstated.

Effect on freight working serious. LNER reported at 20.45 29/12 that owing to buildings adjacent to MWL on fire and unsafe, all traffic to/from SR via Blackfriars Bridge suspended, until 11.00 30/12. Bricklayers Arms Depot out of action throughout Monday 30/12, so traffic between other Railways and SR largely suspended until at least 12.00 30/12 or else widely diverted. Nevertheless, total wagons exchanged between SR and other Railways during 24 hours 16.00 29/12–16.00 30/12 still 2,332 (!), compared to 3,196 during same period in previous week. That underlines how great was the freight traffic moving even on Sundays.

30/12/40

SR: Norbury – Thornton Heath 05.20: UXB 60ft from Up side.
Peckham Rye Junction 07.25: UXB 100 yards from Down side. All traffic stopped.
West London Junction 10.00: UXB hole on Down Windsor Through line. Trains reversed Point Pleasant Junction (not Clapham Junction, as trains would have to pass over the UXB). Later found to be exploded AA shell, so line handed back 14.40.

31/12/40

LMS: Knights Hill Coal Depot: Closed (for two to three weeks) owing to damage in night.

SR: Waterloo – Vauxhall 12.30: UXB found in Hercules Road. Main Local lines closed, Screened by wagons in sidings, removed 08.30 4/1. Also: Brakevan and wagon loaded with heavy beam accidentally pushed into crater on Down Main Through line! – recovered 14.30.

Nine Elms Goods. After the raid of the night of 10/11 September 1940, a view in North Yard westwards towards Nine Elms Gas Works, showing the effect of one of many bombs that fell that night.

Between Vauxhall and Loco Junction. A view westwards, dated 13 September 1940, of recent bridge damage, probably of the Windsor Lines. Gasholders of Nine Elms Gas Works are right ahead and Battersea Power Station beyond.

Bricklayers Arms 'L' Shed. Clearing up the mess on 7 October 1940, three weeks after the raid of 17 September. Bricklayers Arms Goods was a large complex and the photograph shows just two of the 13 bays of the Outwards Shed.

Belinda Road Bridge, East Brixton. In a daylight attack on 27 September 1940, a bomb blew out much of the arches carrying the two double lines converging at Canterbury Road Junction. As soldiers assist with clearance, passengers look out from a train that evidently was still able to pass.

Victoria. The News Cinema on the Central Section side, after a bomb had exploded close by on Platform 16 at 10.25pm on 9 October 1940.

Nine Elms Goods. The shattered interior of one of the Sheds, 15 October 1940.

Durnsford Road Power Station, Wimbledon. The loading bank the day after half this large and important plant (including one of its massive chimneys) was destroyed at 9.15pm on 15 October 1940.

Blackfriars Road Bridge. The mess in Blackfriars Road two days after the Luftwaffe landed a heavy bomb, at 2.27am on 17 October 1940, smack on the major bridge carrying the main lines into Charing Cross.

Loughborough Junction. Devastation after two bombs struck the island platform at the London end at 7.25pm on 8 November 1940. The loop lines from Canterbury Road Junction had been on viaduct in the foreground and took some time to restore.

Waterloo. The big hole made by HE near the Victory Arch at 10.45pm on 8 December 1940 as it dropped through to the W&C below. (No one is to be seen).

London Bridge (Central). The Great Fire Raid of 29/30 December 1940 was not confined to the City. Fire also engulfed London Bridge Station across the river. The intensity of incendiary bombing on a Sunday night with few people around and a lack of water resulted in the complete destruction of the main buildings of the ex-LB&SC terminus. The view is northward from Great Maze Pond across St Thomas's Street to Joiner Street. Behind the two helmeted wardens is all that remained of the main offices, which had once been a hotel. It was very many years before anything else was built on this bomb-site.

Victoria (Eastern) Signalbox. As seen the next day, at about 7pm on 21 December 1940 a lone raider dropped a very large bomb right in the centre of the station throat, putting both signalboxes out of use; even more damage was done to the Central Section Box.

Victoria. Scores of railwaymen and soldiers hasten to restore normality just outside the station, the day after the precision bombing of 21 December 1940 which destroyed the signalling for some days.

South Lambeth Goods.
A general view of
damage on the
morning after the raid
of 15/16 October 1940.
Nevertheless, the
depot was working at
two-thirds capacity
that day.

Old Oak Common
Carriage Depot.
Damage to the Painting
and Lifting Shops after
a raid in daylight (3pm)
on 25 October 1940.

Royal Oak (H&C) Station. Eastward view on the island platform after the raid of 6/7 November 1940, showing a shattered Down H&C line and damaged stock (including a restaurant car) on the Down Carriage line. Note that the sign refers to a service to Addison Road, which had ceased just three weeks before. Not surprisingly, Royal Oak remained closed for another ten days.

Stonebridge Park
Carriage Sheds. The
consequence of a DAB
that did go off, at 9am
on 2 October 1940. The
corridor coach visible
appears to be one of
the earlier LMS
saloons.

Another view of
Stonebridge Park
Carriage Sheds on 2
October 1940 with an
ex-LNWR 'Oerlikon'
electric set.

St Pancras. The shell of a non-corridor coach on a train at Platform 1, after a parachute-mine had exploded at 1.10am on 16 October 1940, closing the terminus for five days.

St Pancras. A view inward on Platform 4, as on 16 October 1940, with debris and damaged coaches of a local train.

Queens Park. Scene on 16 October 1940, the day after the 19.30 sleeping-car express Euston to Inverness came to grief by running into debris in the dark just after HE had fallen beside the railway. The tender is being lifted, the engine – still in steam – having already been set upright.

Opposite top Goodmayes. View eastwards down the Ipswich main line, the day after several bombs were dropped on the station and yards at 9.30pm on 5 September 1940, doing considerably more damage than is evident from this photograph, including derailment of a Down Southend train in the debris. Men are hard at work restoring the bombed Main lines, while an Up local (headed by N7 0-6-2T No. 2635) stands at the Up Slow line platform.

Opposite North Woolwich. The very badly damaged terminus, after the raid of 7 September 1940.

Above North Woolwich. The remains of the Goods and Parcels offices at North Woolwich after the heavy raid of 7 September 1940, which put the Station and Pier out of action for many weeks, as well as the line from Stratford.

Liverpool Street, West side. A glimpse of the damage done at Platforms 1 and 2 in the night of 8/9 September 1940. Up above is Broad Street LMSR Station.

Custom House. A typical scene of 8 September 1940, eastward after the big raid of the day before, which resulted in closure of the Stratford – North Woolwich line for at least two weeks for goods and eight weeks for passengers.

Goodman's Yard, ex-GER. View towards Fenchurch Street Station; the firemen are trying to save the contents of wagons on fire beside a massive warehouse, after the raid in the night of 9/10 September 1940.

As above, but 50 yards further east. Sightseers looking at something fascinating and on fire below the Goods warehouse, after the raid in the night of 9/10 September 1940. The bridge carried the 1935 Fenchurch Street signalbox.

Liverpool Street. Wreckage of local trains in Platforms 1 and 2 after a DAB exploded at about midnight on 9/10 September 1940.

Bow Junction. After the raid of 13/14 September 1940, Evershed's Paper Works is destroyed beside the GE main line, but the fire-fighters haven't given up. Bow Junction Box, seen in left distance, was also burnt out.

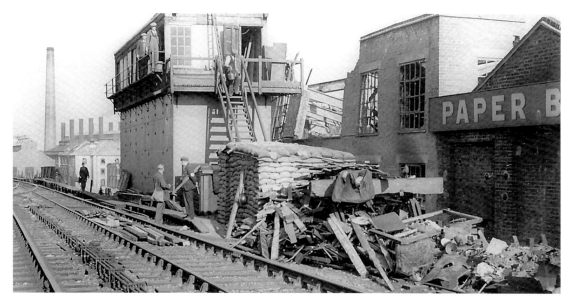

Bow Junction Signalbox. This important signalbox, which controlled the junction of the main lines through Stratford into Liverpool Street and Fenchurch Street, was photographed apparently in use 11 days after being gutted in the raid of 13/14 September 1940 and subjected in the meantime to further bombing close by.

Kilburn & Brondesbury. A view towards London of the damage done at 3.40am on 16 September 1940 to the bridge over Kilburn High Road carrying the four-track LPTB Metropolitan/Bakerloo lines parallel to the two-track LNER line into Marylebone.

Bush Hill Park. The station was thoroughly bombed at 3.40am on 13 November 1940. The scene shows two rather unhappy women perhaps waiting for the substitute bus to Enfield Town.

St John's Wood Tunnel. A view on 7 October 1940, probably from Loudon Road at Carlton Hill, of clearance work in progress on the tunnel on the lines into Marylebone, following its penetration by a bomb at midnight 26/27 September 1940. Note that debris is being hauled up to street level as well as being put into railway wagons.

Finsbury Park. Southward view next day of Down Platforms 8, 9 and 10 after bombs struck at 9.20pm on 10 October 1940. These single line platforms (Nos. 2, 3, 6-9 at Finsbury Park) were useful for dashing from one train to another in the rush-hour.

Seven Sisters. A scene in Seven Sisters Road the day after a bomb exploded at 11pm on 10 October 1940 beside the overbridge carrying the LNER Enfield line just south of Seven Sisters station.

Neasden. A view towards London, taken on 16 October 1940 – just 11 days after work began on its construction – of the Up temporary wooden platform built by RE troops beside the LNER line immediately east of Neasden South Junction and next to the LPTB Neasden station. The LNER lines into Marylebone had been well and truly blocked by the bombing of St John's Wood Tunnel, so these platforms for some weeks allowed passengers to change into LPTB services for London. The view shows an Up LNER train receding and an LPTB Bakerloo Line train for Stanmore approaching.

Above Woodford after a bomb at 00.37 on 27 October 1940 struck the railway south of the station on the Epping line, damaging empty coaches and Broadmead Road bridge. The new bridge looks remarkably like the North Circular Road, but the photograph is labelled 'Broadmead Road', which is just to the north.

Hornsey. Two bombs fell at the north end of the station in a daylight raid (2pm) on 3 November 1940. This is the northernmost crater, with dozens of men beavering away to restore the lines: Up Slow (nearest to Hornsey Up Goods Box), Up Goods and Up Reception (for Ferme Park Up Yards).

Waterloo. Accessing the W&C tunnel from the hole near the Victory Arch, January 1941.

1941 – The Heavy Bombing Continues

January 1941

After the Great Fire raid of 29/30 December, the enemy did not return in force for about two weeks, although scattered Luftwaffe aircraft visited on several nights (60 on the night of 9/10 January) and in daytime on 5 and 7 January, but with minimal effect.

1/1/41

LNE: Silvertown Tunnel 10.18: Reopened (after damage of 7–8/9/40), and trains resumed from North Woolwich, but at 06.30 (2/1) water in tunnel forced service to be curtailed again at Custom House!

SR: Tulse Hill – Herne Hill 20.00: Two UXB found – from 29/12. On 30/12 at 12.05 they were incorrectly reported as having exploded and traffic was resumed. However, on orders of the Regional Commissioner it was interrupted again 18.50. One UXB sand-bagged 1/1/41 and traffic passing (5 mph), then removed 3/1/41. The other bomb had exploded.

5/1/41 (Sunday)

GW: North Pole Junction – Old Oak Common East: Several fires from IB. Block failed. One staff injured. nwr 15.30 6/1.

LMS: Acton Wells Junction 19.15: Fall of IB interrupted electric service, until 20.28.

Mitre Bridge Junction – North Pole Junction (WLR) 19.18: HE on track buckled rails, and all lines blocked. Lines clear by 15.35 6/1.

Cricklewood: UXLM in Exeter Road 400 yards from railway. All trains started/terminated Hendon. Shuttle service provided St Pancras – West Hampstead, thence buses to Hendon. Working stopped in Brent Sidings South End, and Cricklewood Down and Carriage Sidings.

LNE: Romford 21.45: HE damaged Main lines. Traffic run on Local lines. nwr 11.35 6/1.

Chobham Farm Junction 23.00: Debris blocked all Main and Goods lines and Reception line. Down Main line clear 00.10, Up Main 04.15, Reception line 16.30 6/1. Nos 1–6 Carriage roads affected, five coaches demolished and three damaged.

SR: Waterloo 21.36: HE fell between General Offices, platforms and York Road. LPTB booking-hall blocked by debris, but clear by morning. Offices extensively damaged. Platform 21 blocked with debris, and Platforms 19 and 20 owing to danger of falling glass, until 15.20 6/1.

Streatham Hill 14.45: Empty stock train machine-gunned, windows broken.

6/1/41

LMS: Somers Town Goods in night: Three HE damaged Nos 1–6 HL and Nos 9 and 10 LL roads, also offices, gateways and several wagons damaged. Depot closed until daylight.

7/1/41

SR: Clapham Junction 13.00: Many IB, but all dealt with by staff. Coach burned on 12.51 EMU Victoria – Coulsdon North at station.

Sutton 13.32: Lines to Cheam and St Helier blocked by numerous IB, only until 13.50. No damage done. Some electric trains substituted by steam trains.

Orpington 15.35: HE destroyed LMS van and damaged two other wagons.

9/1/41

SR: Maze Hill 23.50: Carriage sidings damaged by IB.

10/1/41

GW: West Ealing 02.00: UXB between Engineer's Yard and No. 1 Loop exploded 05.55, causing much damage. Up Main clear 09.08, Down Main 16.05, Up Relief 18.30, Loops 11.00 11/1. Up local services terminated Southall and Down trains at Ealing Broadway, with buses provided in between. Freight traffic gravely disrupted.

Shepherds Bush Goods Yard: IB set fire to coal dump.

LNE: Spitalfields 00.50: HE caused failure of hydraulics. Run on half pressure until 02.30. nwr 09.30.

The night of 11–12 January saw the next attack on London in some force (about 160 planes), although restricted to about three hours. The 105 deaths that night included 84 in railway station incidents (57 at Bank,[61] six at Green Park and 43 outside Liverpool Street). Fires included three major and 10 serious. Lambeth and St Thomas's Hospitals and the Old Bailey were hit. The enemy attacked London again on the following night, although less heavily and for under three hours. 106 people were killed, and eight serious fires started. Several factories were damaged, including Woolwich Arsenal.

11/1/41 (Saturday)

GW: Wood Lane 19.15: IB caused many fires in depots. H&C service Hammersmith – Paddington suspended until 21.00, then Hammersmith – Ladbroke Grove only. Westbourne Park – Paddington not reopened until 12.05 13/1.

LMS: Maiden Lane Junction 19.36: Many IB, including in St Pancras Sidings and Maiden Lane Yard, causing some damage, but nwr by 20.00!

LNE: Holloway South Up Box 19.50: UXB on Up Main, so all traffic to King's Cross stopped. Trains terminated Finsbury Park, and no traffic to/from King's Cross Goods, Farringdon or SR. 11.25 12/1: Bomb thought to have exploded below ground, and trains recommenced to King's Cross, with four of seven lines in use, allowing working freight to SR. On 12/1 Down Main and Down Slow No. 1 lines still blocked by UXB, and Alexandra Palace service suspended until morning of 17/1. Working over MWL disorganised. nwr not until 15.20 16/1, when Military reported bomb had indeed exploded. Traffic restored briefly, then Down Main closed until 16.20 17/1 to allow repairs.

Noel Park 19.10: HE off railway damaged Down platform and caused gas escape. All trains stopped. Up line clear 12.20, nwr 14.00 12/1.

Liverpool Street 20.10: HE in Bishopsgate blew in east side. Debris blocked Platforms 16 – 18. Fire seriously damaged Railway Offices in Hamilton House, also East Side booking-office, cloak-room, snack bar and shops, all rendered unusable next day. Ticket Collector killed; six staff and 12 passengers injured.[62] Locomotive and first coach of 20.48 to Southend damaged, but no passengers in train. All platforms except No. 18 and 60ft of No. 17 usable on 12/1.

Seven Sisters 21.10: Crater on Down line, Up line blocked also. Buses substituted Hackney Downs – Edmonton. Liverpool Street – Enfield service run via Clapton, Angel Road and Lower Edmonton, also on 12/1. Special buses provided Hackney Downs – Lower Edmonton. Shuttles run Palace Gates – Seven Sisters and Stratford – North Woolwich. Enfield lines and one line to Palace Gates reopened 16.00 13/1. nwr Liverpool Street – Enfield 17.30.

White Hart Lane 21.25: Crater in Up Goods line and Reception line blown out. Subsequent crater in goods yard on Down side damaged seven wagons and blocked lines. Local services adjusted as above. Up line restored 16.30 12/1. nwr 17.30 13/1.

Leman Street: IB came through booking-office roof and damaged offices.

SR: Blackfriars Goods 19.30: Offices damaged by HE nearby.

Chessington North – Chessington South 19.51: Both lines blocked by HE. Clear by 15.45 12/1.

Bank (W&C) 19.57: Blast from aerial torpedo in LPTB subway damaged ventilator fan and signal relay panel. [Very serious damage was done at LPTB station].

Elmer's End – Eden Park 20.00: Lines blocked by UXB, until 14.25 30/1. Buses substituted.

Blackfriars 21.15: HE on Bay Platforms 1 and 2 and on Loop Platforms 3 and 4. Signals and two EMU damaged. Local and Through lines clear 23.45. Steam working resumed 10.30 12/1. Platforms 3 and 4 restored for trains to Holborn

Viaduct 12/1, but station not reopened until 06.10 19/1.

Putney – Barnes: "Small object with wires attached on track. Removed by BDO, but nature unknown"! Lines reopened 22.45.

Waterloo 20.45: News Theatre and a bookstall damaged by fire, also one coach of EMU in Platform 14. No trains to/from Clapham Junction until 01.45 12/1, while lines checked.

Rotherhithe Road: C&W Oil Store damaged by fire. Carriage Lighting Shops gutted and eight coaches damaged – by a fire not discovered until 05.58 12/1! Gas mains broken and two vans damaged.

Nine Elms: Fire damaged 'A', 'B' and 'C' Sheds, canteen and four road vehicles in Albert Yard.

[On 11 and 12/1, many minor stoppages of under two hours reported, also failures of Block].

12/1/41 (Sunday)

GW: Royal Oak 19.15: AA shell exploded, damaging track and conductor rail. Three passengers suffering from shock. Trains stopped. H&C service suspended Paddington – Hammersmith until 21.00; in morning (13/1) resumed west of Westbourne Park. nwr 11.45 13/1.

LMS: Plaistow – West Ham 20.00: Exploding AA shell made crater in Down Through line and Up Local also blocked. LPTB electric trains terminated Bromley and Upton Park, with buses provided between. Down Through line clear 09.00 13/1.

Barking 20.20: Block instruments failed at Barking West and at East and West Ham.

Upney – Becontree 20.30: HE blew out all lines. Electric cables cut and live electric rail thrown across footbridge. Fenchurch Street trains terminated Barking, Up trains at Upminster. Tilbury services terminated Grays. LPTB service suspended East Ham – Upminster, but restored morning 13/1 Barking – Dagenham. Up Through line clear 18.30 13/1, Down Through 16.00 14/1; Electric lines 18.30 15/1, then nwr.

LNE: East Smithfield: IB in night set fire to wagons of flour.

Royal Mint Street: Cartwright Street stables damaged by IB.

Liverpool Street – Stratford: Telecom cut, but restored by 14/1.

Temple Mills Lane bridge 00.45: UXB exploded in bank. Down Goods line blocked by debris. Lines blocked High Meads – Loughton Branch Junction, until nwr 03.00 13/1.

North Woolwich 19.30: IB caused extensive fires. Guards' room, Foreman's room and Ladies' waiting-room burnt out. Two coal stacks and two wagons burnt. Trains suspended until 22.00 [only!].

King's Cross Goods 19.33: Buildings and six wagons damaged.

Harold Wood 20.40: Two craters at country end near Up Through line. Clear 15.00 13/1, but signalling still out. Colour-lights out, so TIW Gidea Park – Brentwood. Shenfield Control lines affected. nwr 22.30 14/1.

Stratford 22.00: Many IB caused fires in Main Office buildings and Print Works, but extinguished by staff. CME's Erecting Shop and Chemical Lab destroyed by fire. Telecom and Control circuits down.

Leyton – Loughton Branch Junction 22.30: Crater in Down Main and Up line shifted. Shuttle service (15-minute) provided Loughton – Epping. SLW Leyton – Chobham Farm Junction in morning (13/1).

SR: Maze Hill – Westcombe Park 19.55: Both lines blocked. Clear 12.05 13/1. Nos 1 and 2 roads in sidings damaged and two vans derailed. Windows of coaches damaged.

Welling 19.55: IB set fire to station buildings on Up side. Slight damage also at Sidcup station. IB caused Block failure Sidcup – New Eltham, Welling – Eltham Well Hall and Plumstead – Abbey Wood. All restored by 11.00 13/1.

After 12 January there were few significant raids for nearly two months, mainly thanks to weather conditions. There were quite minor raids on the evening of 29 January, the nights of 15/16, 17/18, 19/20, 20/21, 21/22, 26/27 February, 1/2, 3/4 and 4/5

March, and in daylight on 31 January (28 people killed) and 3 February.

13/1/41
LNE: Stratford 00.45: DAB exploded and debris blocked Down Goods line until 08.00.

19/1/41 (Sunday)
SR: Elmer's End 22.35: Lines blocked and station damaged. nwr 12.20 20/1.

Brentford – Syon Lane 22.40: Both lines blocked by HE. Down line clear 14.00, Up 16.00 20/1.

30/1/41
LMS: Brent Junction (Sudbury – Willesden No. 7) 15.55: HE near line stopped traffic – but only until 16.16.

Camden 16.05: IB on line, but extinguished by staff and traffic interrupted only 15 minutes.

Hornchurch – Elm Park 16.06: HE alongside blocked Up Through line with debris.

LNE: King's Cross Goods: HE in car park and another near mess-room – in previous bomb crater. Nine cars damaged, five seriously. One staff killed, five injured.

Angel Road – Pickett's Lock 15.23: HE blocked Up Main and both Goods lines. Main line clear 16.00. nwr 14.45 31/1.

31/1/41
SR: Streatham Hill 14.25: Machine-gunning smashed windows of empty stock in washing-plant.

February 1941

3/2/41
LMS: Willesden Junction 23.00: IB caused damage to Time Office on North Circular Road.

5/2/41
SR: South Croydon – Purley Oaks 11.47: UXB. Screened 15.45 and Local lines reopened. Removed 13.20 18/2.

9/2/41 (Sunday)
LNE: Goodmayes Yard 20.30: No. 1 Reception road damaged. nwr 10.30 10/2.

13/2/41
LMS: Hendon 20.00: Blast[63] broke signalbox windows.

14/2/41
SR: Borough Market Junction 21.35: HE blocked Down and Up Through and Up Local lines until 22.59, Down Local until 01.52 15/2. Roof and windows of signalbox and points damaged. All trains over Up Local to Metropolitan Junction stopped until 11.00 15/2.

15/2/41 (Saturday)
SR: Woolwich Arsenal – Plumstead 20.45: Both lines blocked; 30ft of retaining wall damaged. nwr 13.35 16/2.

17/2/41
LNE: Neasden 20.00: Coal yard sidings damaged. Repaired 10.10 18/2.
Ilford 21.42: Signalbox damaged, but lines blocked only to 21.52.
SR: Mitcham – Mitcham Junction 19.50: HE blocked both lines. Damage to cables caused traction power failure on Down line Tulse Hill – Mitcham Junction and on Sutton lines until 21.35. Down line clear for steam trains 23.24. nwr 09.05 18/2.

Earlsfield – Wimbledon 21.30: HE blocked all lines. Trains diverted via East Putney. Through lines clear 11.35, Local lines 17.00 (daylight only) 18/2. nwr 19/2.

London Bridge 22.25: HE on Central Section concourse near entrance to Platforms 20 and 21. Bomb fell through to Stainer Street public shelter below, killing 60 people and injuring 70 (50 seriously). Staff shelter also damaged, and five staff seriously injured (one, a Ticket Collector, dying later). EMU damaged by debris. Platforms 20 and 21 closed, until 15.30 18/2. UXB fell 04.12 near same spot. Platforms 15 and 16 closed 18/2 for clearing debris.

18/2/41
SR: Coombe Road – Bingham Road: UXB; trains passing, not cleared until 16.00 27/2.

19/2/41
LMS: West End Lane (NLR) 21.55: HE on Up platform damaged 30 yards of coping. Up electric trains diverted via Camden. Up line reopened for freight at 00.05; electric services restored next morning (20/2) but not calling at West End Lane until 10.00 24/2.

West Hampstead 22.03: HE on shunting neck and wharf.

SR: Clapham Junction – Earlsfield 21.36: IB on Up side damaged gas pipes, so all lines closed and trains diverted via East Putney. Local lines reopened 22.00, Through lines 22.15.

20/2/41
LNE: Marylebone – Canfield Place: Bomb in night about 200 yards from London end of Hampstead Tunnel, damaging brickwork. SpR imposed. Nevertheless, at 10.05 21/2, one coach of 09.50 express Marylebone – Manchester derailed. SLW, until 16.30.

SR: Raynes Park – Malden 13.00: UXB; screened, but found on 3/3 to have exploded.

26/2/41
LMS: East Ham 23.30: UXLM 200 yards from station. All traffic stopped, and trains terminated at Barking, Upton Park and Plaistow. Mine removed 11.35 27/2, and LPTB District Line service resumed 12.00.

The next severe attack on London occurred on the night of 8/9 March. The Luftwaffe were now concentrating their attacks into shorter durations of four to five hours, and 125 bombers this night caused only one serious fire but killed 212 people. Buckingham Palace, also the Café de Paris (with heavy casualties), were hit as were St Thomas's and St George's-in-the-East Hospitals. Moreover, the Germans followed on with another raid the following night with 94 bombers.

8/3/41 (Saturday)
LMS: St Paul's Road Junction – St Pancras Box: Up lines blocked. All traffic suspended until 22.10, then 23.10–00.30 9/3.

Haggerston 21.20: IB on line extinguished by 21.35, but current off. All Down trains cancelled. Up trains terminated Dalston Junction. Current restored 02.30. nwr in morning.

South Bromley/Bromley 21.40: Clutton Street (Poplar Branch) overbridge damaged. IB and adjacent fires stopped all traffic on LT&S until 22.30.

Broad Street: HE in LNE yard at Liverpool Street (see below) severed all GPO normal and emergency lines to LMS switchboard.

Haydon Square Goods: Depot closed after UXB went through viaduct into arches. Reopened 11/3.

Broad Street Goods 23.10: HE in yard damaged telecom, mess-room and other offices. All freight cancelled. One staff injured. nwr 03.00 9/3.

West Ham 22.30: UXB near Upper Mills Box. Steam trains terminated Barking, LPTB at Plaistow and Bromley. Buses in between, but nwr 23.00.

Harringay Park (T&H) 22.40: Signalbox damaged by HE nearby.

Plaistow 23.30: HE damaged sub-station wall and all lines. LPTB Lines reopened 00.10 9/3, LMS steam lines 11.15 11/3.

LNE: Farringdon – Aldersgate 21.15: Debris on tracks and signalling failure blocked MWL and to Smithfield. Resumed with HSW 11.10 9/3.

Liverpool Street 21.30: HE damaged West Platform Box. All traffic at Platforms 1–6 suspended until 02.05, then working resumed only from Platforms 1–3 and 6. Five staff killed, three seriously injured (including driver and fireman), also three other people. DAB fell and exploded 9/3. Three ambulance vans destroyed, two damaged. West side reopened 12.25 10/3. Loco Siding cleared 11/3.

Spitalfields 21.35: HE damaged hoist and other equipment.

Shadwell 21.45: Sutton Street arch damaged. Station closed.[64] Stepney East – Leman Street blocked, with Main and Down Slow lines blown out, also lines blocked to Haydon Square and Commercial Road LMS Depots. Passenger trains terminated Stepney East. Down Slow cleared 14.00 10/3. nwr not until 06.00 17/3.

Loughton Branch Junction 22.00: Up Goods blown out, Down Goods line damaged. Down Main also blocked, so SLW over Up Main to Chobham Farm Junction. nwr 17.15 9/3.

SR: Borough Market Junction 20.20: HE damaged signalbox and HT cables, stopping traffic. Restored to London Bridge 21.07, Cannon Street 00.32 9/3.

Battersea Yard 20.20: HE damaged shed roof and verandah, and LMS brakevan.

Woodside – Addiscombe/Bingham Road 20.30: All lines blocked. Cleared by 16.35 9/3.

Waterloo – Vauxhall 21.00: Traffic suspended, owing to damage to Arches 118, 119 and 120A. Windsor Through lines cleared 09.40, Local lines 14.50, Down Windsor Local 17.00 9/3. Down Main Through line cleared by 09.10, Up Main and Up Relief 15.15 10/3.

Bricklayers Arms Goods 21.00: Several HE fell. Damage done to 'L' section No. 5 road and building, Nos 3 and 4 roads in 'C' section; Nos 2 and 5 roads in 'D' section, where wall fell in roadway and 10 wagons derailed. Lines cut at Mercers Crossing, cleared by 01.30. 'C' and 'L' Sheds working 17.00 9/3.

Nine Elms 21.10: HE damaged two sidings and some wagons. 'B' Box demolished. Sidings repaired 16.00 14/3.

Cannon Street 21.26: Blast from HE nearby damaged glass in roof, buildings and carriage windows. Station closed. Platforms 5–8 reopened 17.00 9/3, Nos 1–4 and all lines 16.00 10/3.

Herne Hill Sorting Sidings 21.55: Three HE in Down sidings damaged Nos 3, 6 and 8 roads and derailed two wagons. HE in Up sidings damaged No. 2 road and derailed three wagons. Clear 17.40 9/3.

Old Kent Road – South Bermondsey 22.47: SL lines blocked. Clear 11.30 9/3.

UXB: Purley, removed 11/3; Stewarts Lane 20.00, removed 17/3.

9/3/41 (Sunday)

LMS: Broad Street 01.10: Two UXB, one between wall and No. 1 Bay, the other between Nos 5 and 6 Bays. The first exploded later, damaging dock and cart road; no damage from second. (No. 1 Bay already closed by previous damage). Only one line available to/from station. Owing to UXB in Sun Street also, station closed, but reopened 11.10 10/3.

Commercial Road Goods: UXB went through No. 3 arch to LL, so no traffic over Hooper Street branch. HE blew out two arrival roads. nwr 12.00 10/3, but damage to arches at junction forced closure of all lines into Fenchurch Street until 11/3.

Devons Road 10.00: Crater in yard. nwr 09.35 10/3.

St Pancras 22.30: IB on station and sidings. Two coaches damaged.

LNE: Liverpool Street 01.15: UXB forced closure of Platforms 7 – 12. Loco office and carriage-cleaning premises evacuated. Owing to UXB in Broad Street, all entrances from street closed, but opened later on East side. 07.30: DAB exploded, killing three parcels porters and a fireman. Platform 1 closed after another UXB found in Broad Street Goods Yard. All entrances closed, again except on East side.

North Woolwich 22.00: HE struck No. 2 road as 21.51 local from Stratford arriving, and locomotive partly derailed. Arcade between platforms brought down and booking-office damaged. Spare carriage in sidings damaged by another HE. Porter injured. Trains terminated at Silvertown, and buses provided to/from North Woolwich. Platform 3 and restricted service available from 08.50 10/3. nwr 17.00 16/3.

Ponders End – Pickett's Lock: Telecom cut, so TIW until 10.00 10/3.

King's Cross Metropolitan 22.24: HE damaged Down Widened Line and both Metropolitan lines blocked by crater. Platforms and station roof badly damaged, also one LPTB train. Traction and telecom cables cut. Two staff killed; two staff and one passenger injured. All MWL traffic suspended until temporary signalling arrangements enabled reopening 15.15 10/3, for LNE traffic only. LMS traffic blocked by clamping of points at King's Cross Metropolitan.

10/3/41

GW: Smithfield: Traffic being dealt with at Acton and Paddington New Yard.

LMS: Broad Street 11.54: UXB (see above) exploded, slightly injuring 19 staff and damaging brickwork of Platforms 1 and 2, temporarily putting them out of use. In Dogs Yard cartage vehicle and wooden dock damaged. "Nos 1 and 2 Bays will be out of use indefinitely and No. 5 for two weeks."

SR: Whitton Junction 02.40: Signalbox damaged, wires brought down. 03.00 12/3: UXB found, but all passenger trains allowed past (at 5 mph). Bomb removed 15/3.

On 14 March, the SR gave a list of lines still out of use: Metropolitan Junction, outwards line from Ewer Street since 19/9/40; Selhurst Carriage Inspection Sheds, Nos 1–6 roads since 14/10/40; Stewarts Lane, Incline Road since 16/11/40; Waterloo, Westminster Bridge Road Nos 1 and 2 sidings since 8/12/40; Denmark Hill – Peckham Rye, Down and Up SL lines since 29/12/40.

After 9/10 March London enjoyed a few peaceful nights until 15/16 March, while Clydeside and Merseyside were plastered. The capital then suffered a moderate raid by 94 aircraft, which was poorly targeted and only about 50 people were killed, again on 18/19 March similarly. Then, with better weather, came a very heavy raid on London, 'The Wednesday' 19/20 March. This was about the worst raid yet, affecting principally the Docks and the East End. No less than 751 people were killed, and there were three conflagrations (two in Poplar and one in Greenwich), 12 major and 56 serious fires. Numerous factories and works were destroyed or severely damaged; Docks warehouses and installations were destroyed on both sides of the river, seven Gas Works were damaged (Bromley-by-Bow and Bow Common Lane, badly); sewerage was seriously compromised at Abbey Mills pumping station and at the Northern Outfall (Beckton), with the result that sewage from three million people was discharged into the Thames untreated for nearly three weeks. Damage was done to the Royal Naval College and Miller General Hospital at Greenwich, also two other hospitals.

15/3/41 (Saturday)

GW: South Lambeth 22.00: Fragments from HE on Battersea Gas Works (see SR) damaged water tower.

LNE: Lea Bridge 22.08: HE cut telecom to Temple Mills, so TIW. Station buildings damaged, also arches of Lammas Road Bridge damaged and flooded. nwr 11.45 16/3.

SR: Kidbrooke 21.00: Signalbox windows smashed, station buildings damaged, track flooded. 22.03: Block failure to Eltham Well Hall.

Peckham Rye 21.55: Station buildings set alight and badly damaged. Windows of trains in sheds broken. Emergency exit siding blocked. All lines closed until fires extinguished by 23.15. 23.00: UXB found by Nunhead line, but trains passing, removed 22/3.

Catford Bridge – Lower Sydenham 22.05: Both lines blocked by HE. Cleared by 12.00 16/3.

Hither Green – Grove Park 22.10: All lines blocked by HE. Cleared by 00.55 16/3.

Battersea Park Junction – Pouparts Junction 22.13: Down Local line closed until 22.58 owing to fire in Battersea Gas Works. All Down trains run over Down Through line.

Rotherhithe Road 22.15: HE in Carriage Sidings. Damage done to Transport Department office, cleaners' lobby, three PW Dept lobbies, passenger stock and four sidings. Two staff severely injured. Normal 16.00 16/3.

London Bridge – Bricklayers Arms Junction 22.17: Down and Up Through and Down Local lines blocked, and other lines closed until 23.55 for examination. Through lines clear 16.40, Local 17.15 16/3.

Blackfriars – Elephant & Castle 22.17: HE nearby caused TC failure, so HSW until 23.18.

19/3/41

LMS: Plaistow 21.20: Numerous fires started. Breakdown train, CME's stores, glassman's warehouse and many wagons set on fire, but all extinguished by staff. Signalbox damaged. Electric sub-station on fire, but extinguished by Fire Brigade. Lines closed for examination in daylight. Shuttle service run Barking – Upton Park and Plaistow – Aldgate East. Normal electric service by 15.00 21/3.

Bromley: Signalbox badly damaged and two staff injured.

Highbury & Islington 21.22: Three HE fell on line towards Canonbury. Liverpool Road Bridge brought down onto track, also 100ft of retaining wall. No. 1 Down line blown across No. 2 Up line and all lines blocked. Up electric trains terminated Camden Town, Down trains at Canonbury; buses provided between. No. 1 lines already out of use since 13/10/40 and not restored until 17.50 10/11.

Devons Road 21.30: IB set fire to Loco Shed and many wagons, also oil wharf. No water available. Yard closed. Up line clear 09.20 20/3, Down line 16.00 21/3.

Wanstead Park 22.15: UXB on Cobbold Road Bridge. Bomb exploded 01.50, damaging lines and bridge. Down trains terminated Leytonstone. Down line clear 10.15 20/3, then SLW. Up line not reopened until 6/7.

LNE: New Barnet 00.36: HE near line damaged South Box and some coaches. Two staff injured. nwr 13.10.

Stepney East 03.30: Up and Down lines damaged and entrance to yard blocked. 27 wagons derailed. Gas main cut. Shuttle service in operation.

Shadwell: Station on fire.

Stratford Market: Fires stopped all traffic. Three warehouses destroyed, seven others damaged. One staff injured. nwr not until 6/4.

Stratford Western Junction: All lines blocked, Up Though by fallen gantry. Various buildings damaged. ARP van and two coaches destroyed. Through and Fenchurch Street lines clear early 20/3, but Local lines not until 11.15 22/3. (Fenchurch Street station not reopened until 06.00 24/3).

Custom House 21.30: Fires from IB damaged station and stopped all traffic.

Chobham Farm Junction: Crater blocked both Main lines. Signalbox and wires damaged. nwr 08.45.

Poplar and East India Docks 21.00: Two warehouses, also Millwall Junction Box destroyed; other buildings and four sidings damaged. Nine rail vehicles destroyed, 15 damaged. Dock working stopped.

Victoria & Albert Dock: Two sidings and roadway damaged. All work stopped.

Beckton: HE in Gas Works Sidings damaged station and signalbox. Lines blocked and no traffic in/out sidings. Alternative way into Gas Sidings opened 24/3, but nwr not until 13.30 29/3.

Coborn Road 21.10: 21.00 express Liverpool Street – Ipswich set on fire. Passengers conveyed by special train to Stratford. Passengers for later trains taken by bus to Stratford. Two coaches left to burn out.

Canning Town – Tidal Basin: Goods lines blocked by masonry. Debris also on Main lines. Cleared 10.30 20/3. Tidal Basin station badly damaged.

Northumberland Park – Angel Road: Down Main line blown out. Up Main usable at caution. Clear 11.55 20/3, but Block out until 21/3.

Clapton – Copper Mill Junction: Adjacent fires forced temporary closure of Up Main line.

Loughton Branch Junction: Signalbox badly damaged and Block cut. Train standing nearby also damaged.

Temple Mills Yard: Several roads damaged. Working to/from Loco Depot continued with great difficulty. Wagon Shop on fire and two wagons burnt. In Yard, 25 wagons damaged or derailed. Wagons re-railed and normal goods working evening 20/3, but three roads still unusable. Down side normal 16.00 21/3.

Buckhurst Hill 21.30: Station buildings, signalbox and wires damaged by HE.

Ilford: Station buildings damaged. Windows smashed in East and West Boxes. UXB in Ley Street Goods, removed 31/3.

Gas Factory Junction: Down line blown and Up disturbed and blocked. Wall, two coaches and signals damaged. Up line restored 16.00 20/3. nwr 24/3.

Lea Bridge – Temple Mills: Debris from exploded DAB blocked Up line.

Thames Wharf Yard: One siding, 54 wagons and 10 brakevans damaged.

Silvertown: Two wagons damaged.

SR: Blackheath 20.30: Nos 4–12 sidings and many wagons damaged by HE. Clear 24/3.

Maze Hill – Westcombe Park 21.30: Both lines blocked. In Green Lane Sidings, four coaches damaged and one on fire. nwr 12.30 20/3.

New Cross area 21.40: HE caused power failure London Bridge – St John's/New Cross Gate. All trains terminated St John's or New Cross Gate. Power restored 23.20, but not for signalling, so trains to/from Eastern Section termini signalled by telephone. At New Cross Gate, blast damaged windows of 24 coaches in Up sidings with two compartments gutted. Roof and windows of Yard Box damaged. Superstructure and instruments of East London (LPTB) Up Box damaged. Roof and windows of Bricklayers Arms Junction and Deptford Lift-Bridge Boxes damaged. Block from London Bridge also cut.

Bricklayers Arms Goods 21.40: Roofs of 'F' and 'L' Sheds damaged by IB. In 'C' section, three sidings damaged and two wagons derailed, but restored by 14.30 20/3. In 'B' section, two loaded wagons damaged. In order 14.30 20/3.

Deptford Wharf: Two cranes damaged by HE and one on fire. Wall of Upper Dock and water-mains damaged. Lines slewed. nwr 11.00 20/3.

Lee 21.45: Nos 2–4 sidings damaged, also two wagons and a container. Clear 17.00 21/3.

Eltham Well Hall: No. 6 siding and a wagon damaged. Repaired by 26/3.

Angerstein Wharf 22.30: Offices burnt out, weighbridge office damaged, also some wagons. Branch reopened 20/3.

North Kent East Junction 23.30: No. 2 Up and Down lines blocked by damage to arches. nwr 24/3.

UXB: Lewisham – Nunhead 22.00, detonated 19.58 20/3; Rotherhithe Road Bridge, removed 25/3.

Lines closed overnight for examination included: London Bridge – North Kent East Junction; Lewisham – Nunhead; Old Kent Road Junction – Queen's Road, Peckham until 08.00 21/3; New Cross – Deptford Wharf until 11.50 21/3.

The situation was evidently pretty chaotic in East London. There can have been little traffic moving on the railways before 21 March. The lines between Liverpool Street and Stratford were probably obstructed overnight. "All trains onto North London line stopped owing to bridge damage between Highbury and Barnsbury, and no trains over North London line eastward owing to damage at Gas Factory Junction."

20/3/41

LMS: Woodgrange Park 00.01: HE struck Romford Road Bridge, blocking all lines with debris. Shuttle service provided Barking – Woodgrange Park, thence buses on to Leytonstone. Clear 10.15.

West Ham, Avenue Junction: Much debris thrown onto lines. (Lines already closed).

Hackney 01.30: HE hit bridge over Mare Street, making it unsafe. Signalbox on bridge badly damaged and signalman severely injured. All lines blocked, but normal by 14.30!

Bow 02.00: Station on fire.

Barking – Campbell Road Junction 03.50: No current for signalling or points. "Mobile diesel set sent to Upton Park for generation, but this can't be done until stretch examined by Electrician's Department, which will take two to three hours."

Ripple Lane 21.15: Windows and locking of No. 2 Box damaged. Freight trains backed into sidings at No. 1 Box.

Victoria Park: Station buildings damaged.

Poplar: Station buildings and lines damaged, also 20 wagons and six brake-vans.

Owing to damage at Highbury, it was impractical to work trains to Broad Street, Poplar or Victoria Dock. The only access to Tilbury Docks was via Forest Gate and with SLW from Wanstead Park – for freight only.

SR: Deptford Wharf: Lift and Bridge Box damaged.

North Kent West – North Kent East Junctions 01.50: Both lines and Relief line blocked, also UXB (removed 26/3). No. 2 Down line cleared by 17.30. No. 2 Up line reopened 17.25 21/3, but closed again 14.30 22/3 and opened 24/3 for business services only until 25/3. nwr 15.10 27/3. 'In' and Relief lines clear 16.00 27/3 and Relief line used as 'Out' line until normal 'Out' line cleared 29/3.

Clapham Junction – Wandsworth Town 04.30: Down Local line blocked, but clear 07.55. Carriage Sidings Nos 48, 49 and 52 damaged by HE, but restored 16.45.

Brockley Lane – Lewisham 19.58: UXB exploded, blocking both lines at Breakspeare Road Bridge. Up line clear 16.20 21/3, Down line 06.00 24/3.

Bromley North 21.10: Blast blew out windows of signalbox, some coaches and covered way. All signalling and telecom down; restored 13.30 21/3.

Eltham Well Hall – Eltham Park: UX AA shell, removed 24/3.

West Wickham – Hayes: UXB, removed 22/3.

Crystal Palace HL branch: Service suspended, owing to cables being cut by explosion at Brockley Lane (see above). nwr 14.00 21/3.

On 20 March, there was still a complete blockage at Highbury & Islington on the NLR, but traffic was working to Victoria Docks by other routes. Trains for Broad Street were diverted via Harringay, Ferme Park and Canonbury (!). No. 2 Down line (only) was open for freight from 17.00 21/3–07.00 22/3, then 15.00 22/3–08.00 23/3. On the MWL, traffic from the LNER (GN line) to New Cross was suspended, and to Hither Green and Herne Hill diverted to other routes.

On 21 March, GWR traffic for Victoria & Albert Dock was being dealt with at Paddington and Acton (outwards), St Ervan's Road (Portobello Sidings) (inwards); traffic for shipment from Poplar was being barged from Brentford. The LNER was running limited freight traffic from the GN Section to Royal Mint Street and Poplar Docks, and to the GW and SR via Canonbury and Kingsland (Dalston).

After this holocaust there was another comparatively quiet period for five weeks, helped by bad weather and the Luftwaffe having turned its attention elsewhere, especially to the West Coast Ports, although there were occasionally some sorties over London.

26/3/41

GW: West Ealing 12.30: Goods depot machine-gunned from the air, but no damage done or casualties.

SR: London Bridge – North Kent East Junction: No. 1 Up and No. 3 Down lines damaged by crater made during removal of UXB. Cleared 22.15 26/3.

8/4/41

LMS: Thames Haven Branch, in night: HE damaged track and telecom, blocking single line. One Workmen's train cancelled. nwr 16.15.

10/4/41

LNE: Burdett Road: Station badly damaged, and closed – permanently.

SR: Bricklayers Arms Goods 03.20: Offices and roof of 'L' Shed damaged by HE and cart road blocked.

11/4/41

SR: Denmark Hill – Peckham Rye 11.30: UXB removed, but Down and Up SL lines still awaiting repair.

The night of 16/17 April became the occasion of the worst attack ever on London. Some 685 bombers (some making up to three sorties) dropped 890 tons of HE and 151,230 IB, in a raid lasting seven hours from 20.50. The Concentration Point embraced the Docks on either side of the Thames, causing eight major and 41 serious fires – with several massive explosions. Key Points affected amounted to 53, including 33 factories and works: Grove Road Power Station, Marylebone (75,000 kW) was disabled; damage to holders and mains reduced gas pressure in South London to a very low level; numerous major water mains and trunk telephone lines were severed. Important public buildings hit included the City Temple, the Admiralty, Houses of Parliament (Commons chamber burnt out), Royal Courts of Justice and Westminster County Court, National Gallery, Somerset House – and an UXB penetrated the roof and floor of St Paul's Cathedral. Ten hospitals were hit: Westminster, Chelsea, Fulham, St Pancras, St Thomas's, Mayday and Fever at Croydon, Queen Mary's Sidcup, St Nicolas's Plumstead, Warlingham Park. Casualties were 1,179 killed and 2,233 seriously injured. Railway damage and disruption was proportional.

16–17/4/41 (two 24-hour periods combined here)

GW: South Lambeth Goods: Damaged by fire. Steam lines clear 17.38 17/4.

Paddington 02.40: Parachute mine on roadway at Departure side caused extensive damage to buildings, some property being demolished: booking-office, waiting-rooms, also HQ offices, porters' room and Hotel damaged. Roof over Departure carriage-road brought down and roadway blocked with debris. One locomotive[65] was damaged. On Platform 11 side, AA shell damaged arch, girder, garage, Parcels Office and stables. Platform 1 closed, but trains continued to use other lines. Some cancellation of morning local trains. Six staff and 10 others killed, 34 staff and 60 others injured.

West Brompton (WLER) 03.00: Buildings (already closed) and Approach Road further damaged. Goods buildings damaged. Two people killed. WLER blocked.

Further details from General Manager's Report: Destroyed or seriously damaged: Post Office, Boot's, Lyon's and Wyman's stalls, Urgent Parcels office, Stationmaster's office, No. 2 Booking-office, Waiting-room and Buffet, Season Ticket office, Enquiry office. Paddington Borough Council, also Army Pioneer Corps, sent rescue parties to assist. Only a few early morning trains cancelled, otherwise normal service run. Tobacco kiosk on Lawn used as Temporary Booking-office. Platform 1 line used for four days for wagons collecting debris.

LMS: Upney 23.10: Loco and first coach of 22.30 Fenchurch Street – Shoeburyness derailed in crater on Down Through. SLW from 00.45 (17/4) on Down Local. Train taken on to Hornchurch by locomotive of 20.08 freight Shoeburyness – Little Ilford.

Elm Park – Dagenham 00.30: HE exploded on LPTB train on Up Local line near Rom Valley bridge, throwing debris over all lines. Block and telecom cut. This and Upney blockage necessitated diversion of Southend steam services via Tilbury. Shuttle steam service run Pitsea – Hornchurch; LPTB electric service Barking – City, with buses Hornchurch – Barking. nwr 18.00 20/4.

Brondesbury Park 00.45: Station buildings, but not lines, damaged by HE nearby. Station closed 05.30.

Dagenham Dock 00.57: HE damaged Goods offices, wagons and signalbox, causing complete failure of Block and telecom.

Dagenham Dock Sidings 02.00: UXLM exploded. Two sidings blown out and about 30 wagons derailed/damaged.

Broad Street 03.00: HE through No. 2 line into stables below. Platform and line damaged and several horses killed.

West Hampstead 03.00: Signalbox windows smashed.

St Pancras Junction 03.00: Signalbox windows smashed, injuring signalman.

West End Lane 03.30: Up and Down lines blocked by debris. Block and telecom cut. Working resumed 04.15 under caution, but station closed at 05.30, until 11.30.

Upminster – Hornchurch 03.50: All lines affected. SLW over Down Local Barking – Dagenham from 05.40. Steam lines clear 16.05 18/4. nwr 19.15 20/4. LPTB services suspended on 18/4; resumed Barking – Dagenham 14.25 21/4 (see below).

Haggerston 04.30: Underbridge and signalbox damaged by blast. Fire on track cut telecom and blocked all lines. One staff injured. Trains terminated at Dalston, thence buses to Broad Street. No. 2 Down line clear 11.45 (freight only on single line), No. 2 Up line 18.00 18/4. No passenger trains from Broad Street until No. 1 lines clear 16.10 12/5.

Chalk Farm 05.00: Station buildings and Inspectors' and shunters' cabins damaged by blast.

Old Ford: Several HE in yard during night. Seven loaded carts and several wagons damaged. Fifteen Outwards roads damaged. Yard blocked.

Walworth Road Depot: Damaged by fire.

St Pancras Goods: Offices damaged.

LNE: King's Cross in night: HE fell in Milk Yard, causing damage to several outbuildings.

Farringdon Street Goods overnight: Offices and new HL Depot destroyed by fire, warehouses seriously damaged and contents destroyed. LL blocked by debris and water. Hydraulics and power supplies failed. Two wagons and 12 cartage vehicles destroyed. Depot closed. Once cleared, LL can be used, but much traffic being transferred to King's Cross and Tufnell Park. LL Depot reopened 12/5 – and then only for potato traffic.

MWL 03.45: Closed by damage and fires in adjacent buildings, until 16.25 17/4.

Royal Mint Street: Stables and East Smithfield Depot damaged by blast

Stratford 00.15: HE on line in Triangle Junctions. Signalboxes, offices and shed at Carpenters Road damaged, also no less than 170 coaches in Channelsea Sidings damaged. nwr 08.00!

Bishopsgate Goods 02.40: HE and IB on warehouse (No. 7 bank) caused extensive damage. Traffic stopped 03.45. Fires under control by 06.00. ELR line traffic to SR restricted until 13.00, owing to loss of pressure in hoist.

Marylebone 03.16: Goods warehouse totally gutted by fire from IB and HE. All interior equipment destroyed, also at least 80 cartage vehicles. Two staff injured. Traffic into Goods Depot stopped from 04.20, but running lines still clear. Temporary platform being constructed at Barge Sidings; in a few days this will allow restricted amount of shed traffic

to be handled. Meanwhile, use being made of emergency facilities at Neasden and old Wembley Exhibition station.

SR, Western Section:

Waterloo – Vauxhall – Clapham Junction: Waterloo: 22.30: Bombs falling around, so all stopped for examination until 22.45. 23.00: Station closed and all traffic to Clapham Junction stopped owing to HE on tracks near Vauxhall. In Necropolis Sidings one coach wrecked and three burnt out; one staff injured. 00.05: Explosion of HE in United Dairies Depot damaged front of Vauxhall station, refreshment room and Parcels office; parapet blown off on Windsor Line side, throwing debris over Windsor lines. 01.00: Six Waterloo – Clapham Junction lines now blocked by several HE at six places, including Wandsworth Road Bridge. Only Up and Down Main Local lines left in use. 01.00: Queen's Road: All lines blocked, but Main Line side clear by 03.55, Windsor Lines an hour later. Windows of Queen's Road Box smashed. 01.30: Waterloo signalbox and substation windows smashed. Apparatus apparently in order, but reported at 04.55 18/4 that no lights or power, so HSW in operation. 03.00: HE in Down Windsor Local line opposite Field's candle factory cut traction cables, so no current to Clapham Junction. Down Windsor Through and Local and Up Windsor lines also blocked. HE also fell in night near the site of 'D' Box, blocking the Up and Down Windsor and Down Through lines. Other bombs damaged the Salamanca Street bridge at 0.95 miles from the terminus and at Miles Street (Vauxhall) at 1.6 miles, each affecting principally the Windsor Lines.

Access to terminus available for steam trains from 12.00 17/4. Up Windsor Local line clear 12.20, Down and Up Main Local lines (daylight only) 15.00 18/4 and first train out of Waterloo left at 16.07. However, signalling still out of order and TBW operated, until 22–23/4. Through lines restored for electric trains 14.45 20/4, but not used as no current. Eight trains/hour being run on Local line; on 21/4 12 trains/hour, but although signalling and tracks were in order as far as site of old 'B' Box, not so on to Loco Junction.

Between Waterloo and Clapham Junction, Up and Down Main Through clear 12.50 20/4, Down Windsor Local was cleared 10.30 22/4, Down and Up Windsor and Up Windsor Through in places by 10.30 22/4. However, repairs to adjacent lines and to arches also problems with signalling meant that Up Windsor Local not fully reopened until 05.00 3/5, Down Windsor Through 05.30 3/5, Down Windsor Local 07.30 6/5, Up Windsor Through 08.00 7/5.

However, on **18/4**, Earlsfield 16.05: All lines closed to Clapham Junction owing to DAB found six feet from Up Main Through line, and lines out of alignment. Therefore shuttle service run Waterloo – Clapham Junction, with electric trains running on to Earlsfield to reverse. Buses provided Clapham Junction – Wimbledon. Then at 17.10, another UXB reported 50 yards from Down side. Steam trains run via East Putney to Clapham Junction (Windsor side), shunting there via yard onto Up Main Local to continue to Waterloo! On **19/4**, screen of wagons placed on Down Through line and then Local lines reopened 15.15. Main Through lines at Earlsfield not clear until 09.30 25/4, after UXB removed 16.05 24/4.

Nine Elms Locomotive Shed and Fitters' Shed: Damaged by HE. Two locos overturned.[66]

Nine Elms Yard: About 12 HE fell, mainly in Up side yard. Sixteen sidings and 26 wagons damaged, also several road vehicles and cranes as well as many buildings, various points, crossings and two water mains. Body of Driver Towers and presumed remains of Fireman Humphrey discovered and removed in afternoon of 17/4. All sidings back in use by 28/4.

East Putney: Station buildings damaged. Lines blocked towards Southfields. LPTB services (15 mph) resumed 13.00 18/4, in spite of UXB on top of West Hill Tunnel. UXB was removed 16.30 24/4, then nwr 10.00 25/4.

Waterloo & City Line 09.00: Closed by current failure. Buses substituted until 07.45 18/4, when current obtained from LPTB. (Trains were also suspended 15.30–17.30 19/4 while Navy swept Thames for mines!)

SR, Central Section:

Waddon 22.55: Station buildings damaged.

Anerley 23.15: Station windows and ceilings damaged by blast

Belmont 23.50: Goods siding damaged by HE. Repaired 16.45.

St Helier: Station buildings damaged. Both lines slewed by UXLM. nwr 14.55 19/4.

Sydenham: Station buildings damaged.

East Brixton – Clapham: Both lines damaged. Not cleared until 16.30 1/5. Down platform at East Brixton damaged.

London Bridge (Central) – New Cross Gate: Large crater in Down and Up Local lines. All lines blocked, but all cleared by 15.00 17/4.

Brockley – Honor Oak Park 00.20: Vesta Road Bridge hit. Debris from crater and water blocked all lines. Clear 12.45.

North Dulwich – Tulse Hill: Debris on track and fencing damaged.

Eardley Sidings: Damage to three Pullman cars, old W&C stock, 23 coaches and railway housing.

Victoria, Grosvenor Road Sidings 01.00: Extensive damage to Carriage Sidings and Shed etc., 10 coaches, 12 electric coaches and seven Pullmans.

Battersea Yard 01.40: Gasometer in Queen's Road blown up, causing signalbox, shunters' cabin and staff lobbies to be wrecked. A signalman, a guard and another person injured.

Streatham Junction South – Mitcham Common 02.10: Both lines blocked by damage, but clear by 12.30.

Shepherds Lane (Clapham – Brixton) 02.05: Signalbox demolished and arches damaged. Signalman killed. SL lines reopened (5 mph) 16.30 30/4.

Crystal Palace LL – Birkbeck 02.30: Stations and signalboxes damaged.

Old Kent Road Junction – South Bermondsey 04.35: Lines blocked at underbridge, but clear 18.45.

SR, Eastern Section:

Camberwell Box – Loughborough Junction 21.10: All lines blocked. Arch No. 111 (Hinton Road Bridge) collapsed, retaining wall damaged. All lines clear 10.00 18/4.

Herne Hill – Loughborough Junction 21.40: Both lines blocked by debris. Current failed. Down line clear 11.00 17/4, Up 18.00 18/4.

Herne Hill – Brixton 21.40: Telecom failed, but lines clear 08.30.

Catford Bridge 23.00: Signalbox damaged.

Beckenham Junction – Kent House 23.15: HE on Down lines, so all lines blocked. Failure of telecom. Coaching stock damaged in Mid-Kent sidings at Beckenham Junction. Fast and Up Slow lines clear 07.05. At 12.15 Down Slow still blocked (clear 12.00 18/4), but other lines clear and traffic working up to Herne Hill, albeit by TIW in some sections. nwr 17.00 18/4.

Bromley South 23.30: All lines blocked by debris from adjacent house, but clear 12.15.

Kent House: Station buildings damaged.

Crofton Park – Catford: Both lines blocked, 40-ft crater. Up line cleared 12.25, but Down train still running via Herne Hill. Down line clear and nwr 10.00 20/4.

Elephant & Castle: Station buildings and platforms damaged. Owing to damage to arch in night, Down and Up Through lines blocked. Lines also blocked by damage or debris at three bridges towards Camberwell. All lines except Down Through clear by 12.00. Down Through opened 5/5 in conjunction with single line at Southwark Street Bridge.

Walworth Road Depot: Roofs thrown onto Down Through line. 50 yards of depot burnt out, wagons and signalbox damaged by fire.

Ravensbourne – Shortlands 00.30: Station buildings at both damaged, also Shortlands Box at 03.00. All lines blocked, also telecom Shortlands Junction – Bromley South. Lines clear 12.15 17/4, telecom restored 15.27 18/4, but with TBW on Up to Ravensbourne.

Loughborough Junction – Cambria Junction 01.12*: Both lines blocked by damage to arch of viaduct, but Up lines clear 16.15. Down line not reopened until 14.00 14/5.

*From Lt.Col. Mount's Report: Heavy bomb fell alongside corner of one abutment of Padfield Street bridge, making big crater undermining foundations. Before reopening for traffic, girder first supported by timber trestling, secondly by steel stanchion on timber and concrete. As abutment cracked it needed permanent reconstruction and work soon commenced.

Beckenham Hill 02.15: Station buildings damaged.

Blackfriars Junction 02.13: Signalbox burnt out, as no water available and Fire Brigade slow to arrive. Replaced by temporary box with frame of limited capacity. A permanent box was not opened until 11/8/46.

Holborn Viaduct 02.30: Offices and Carriage Examiners' lobby damaged. UXLM in Ludgate Circus stopped all traffic from Blackfriars.

Bickley Junction 03.00: Down Slow line and telecom damaged. Current off, but nwr 07.35.

Victoria (Eastern) 05.15: UXB between Down Main and Down Relief lines, so screen placed on Relief line to allow working of Central Section. Lines open to Battersea Park 11.15, but no current until after DAB screened, when emergency generator installed. Victoria (Central) operating by 12.30, with signalling from 15.15. Until then, trains reversing at Clapham Junction, SL trains at Forest Hill. On 20/4, UXB removed 12.45, then both Relief and Up Main lines reopened, but Down Main remained blocked by damage until 18.35, then nwr.

SE Lines:

Lower Sydenham – New Beckenham 21.44: Both lines blocked by portion of crashed aircraft, which was cleared 22.30 by RAF. 05.00: Crater found in track and lines damaged, but nwr 19.15.

Slades Green – Dartford 22.00: Both lines blocked. Six wagons of ammunition on fire. Signalbox, hut and cottages damaged. nwr 14.20.

Belvedere 22.40: Both lines blocked. Two coaches derailed. Station buildings unsafe and platforms unusable. Lines reopened 13.00 18/4, but trains not stopping at Belvedere.

Petts Wood Junction 22.40: Signalbox damaged by fire from IB. Up Through line closed until 02.50.

Sidcup – Albany Park: Debris on track and wires broken.

Southwark Park Junction – New Cross: Nos 1 and 2 Down and Nos 2 and 3 Up lines blocked by damage. No. 2 Down and Nos 2 and 3 Up clear 18/4, No. 1 Down 15.19 28/4. No signals working, as diesel generator cannot be used owing to DAB.

Bricklayers Arms Goods: Two HE and oil-bomb burnt out 'K' Shed. Several other HE did much damage elsewhere in yards. Four horse-vans destroyed and seven damaged, also several wagons.

Hither Green: Damage to signalbox, offices, telecom and wagons. One LNER staff injured in Hither Green Sidings.

Eden Park – West Wickham: Both lines blocked at two points. Clear 09.45.

Grove Park – Sundridge Park 00.18: HE blocked both lines and cut telecom to Bromley North, but clear 16.35.

London Bridge (Eastern) 00.20: Old Divisional Office damaged by HE in Tooley Street. Station closed until 01.05. 05.14: Eastern Section booking-hall under Platforms 6 and 7 damaged by fire. 06.00: UXB in Station Approach, so station closed under strict orders from Military. Meanwhile, trains reversing at Forest Hill. At 16.35 Regional

Commissioner says Central Section can be reopened, but on east side Up Local to Borough Market Junction must be blocked and SpR on Up Through line. Central Section station closed also, owing to UXB in Station Approach. Bomb screened, removed 10.00 21/4.

Cannon Street: Station closed owing to UXB on London Bridge Station Approach.

Coombe Road – Bingham Road 01.30: Both lines blocked, until 07.30.

Grove Park – Elmstead Woods 01.45: All lines blocked by HE. Through lines clear 14.40, Up Local 17.40. Down Local clear 16.00 18/4, but Grove Park – Bromley North trains not running, while Orpington trains terminated in Branch platform at Grove Park.

Charing Cross 02.45: Station Hotel, platforms and four empty coaches damaged by land-mine and fire. Wooden extension to Platforms 1–6 and steps to signalbox burnt out. Four trains set on fire. One Hotel staff injured. UXLM suspected, so station closed. Platform 1 reopened (seven coaches only) 18/4, No. 4 04.40 21/4, No. 3 24/5, but Platform 6 not reopened (six coaches only) until 6/5, fully on 18/5, No. 2 18.38 18/5 and No. 5 18.00 1/6**.

**From Report: Roof at Charing Cross had been "well covered in and the timber platform extensions onto the bridge were covered with thin concrete slabs as protection against fire. The signalbox roof was also hit by IB, but the steel protection saved the structure and IB that landed on verandah were kicked onto the track by the signalman."

Rotherhithe Road 03.00: Signalbox burnt out. Bricklayers Arms lines blocked by debris, cleared 17.00.

West Wickham – Hayes 03.30: Two HE in yard and lines blocked by debris. Down line clear 07.30 18/4, Up line 16.40 19/4. nwr 18.00 23/4.

Woodside – Selsdon: All telecom cut.

Addiscombe 03.55: Windows of EMU smashed.

Blackheath 04.00: Current and telecom failed on Bexleyheath line.

UXB: Charing Cross 02.45, UXLM on No. 1 line, made harmless 15.45; Victoria (Eastern), all lines blocked, screened 17/4, removed 12.45 20/4; St Helier 07.00, UXLM; Holborn – Blackfriars 04.05, UXLM, made harmless 09.13, another UXLM in Ludgate Circus 04.12, made safe 09.13; New Cross Gate – Brockley 04.37, UXLM, made harmless 11.05; Longhedge Junction – Stewarts Lane 07.00, screened and freight passing 18/4, then wagon screen placed allowing traffic on Eastern and Central Lines, bomb removed 22/4; East Putney – Southfields (West Hill Tunnel) 12.35, District Line service suspended 18.55 18/4, then run with 15 mph SpR; Sanderstead 18.00 (18/4), small bomb so BDO allowed trains to pass, removed 16.15 23/4.

On the morning of 17 April, there was of course extensive general disruption in the London area. Holborn Viaduct, Blackfriars, Cannon Street, Waterloo, Charing Cross, Victoria and London Bridge were all closed. "It is possible that Victoria may reopen later in the morning". (London Bridge reopened on afternoon of 17/4, but by access from Denman Street). There was no traction current to Charing Cross or Cannon Street, or Hither Green – Blackheath, and no signal current at Charing Cross, Holborn Viaduct, London Bridge – Metropolitan Junction, or Victoria – where HSW was in operation on the Central Section when reopened at 10.45, with a UXB screened. The W&C was not running. All freight exchange routes were closed, except LMS/GW – Central Section, also Willesden/Brent/Neasden – Feltham. On the MWL, no exchange possible on 17/4 and very restricted on 18/4, but two extra trains were run to Central Section via Harringay and Gospel Oak.

On 18 April, the SR reported that "in the London area serious interference with services continues, but position is improving. At London Bridge (Eastern Section), traction and

signalling current was restored by 11.00, and Cannon Street had 25% normal service, London Bridge normal service. Signalling restored Bricklayers Arms Junction and Brockley only at 20.35. Between Waterloo and Clapham Junction, the Main Local lines (the only lines open) were not available to passenger trains during darkness, owing to weakness of adjacent lines, and signalling only partly restored 21/4. Further UXB Earlsfield – Clapham Junction was screened 19/4 and removed 16.05 24/4; Up Through line remained shut owing to damage. nwr 09.30 25/4.

Matters were exacerbated by an even worse raid on the night of 19/20 April (21.15–04.15), by 748 bombers (many in double sorties). They dropped 1,026 tons of HE and 153,000 IB, again concentrating on the Docks areas. They killed 1,208 people (including 92 in a shelter in Shoreditch) and caused two major and 11 serious fires. Some 46 factories and works were affected (five badly); the Gas Works at Union Street, Stratford and at Beckton were severely damaged and two holders were blown up at Kensal Green Works. Damage to Waterloo Bridge forced its closure for 10 days.

19–20/4/41 (Saturday – Sunday, combined)

GW: West London Carriage Depot 22.35: Large fire damaged buildings and stopped all traffic to Paddington.

Old Oak Halt 23.15 UXLM blocked Birmingham main line and LPTB Central Line. 06.15 20/4 Friars Junction – Acton: Another UXLM fell in night 30 yards from lines, near path to Carter Patterson's Yard and affecting LMS lines. Main lines clear (SpR 2 mph) 09.20.

Victoria & Albert Docks Goods: Offices, warehouses, stables and six wagons damaged by fire.

LMS: Devons Road Loco Shed 06.35: UXB discovered in yard 200 yards from running lines.

Plaistow: Goods office and several wagons damaged.

Barking East – Dagenham 21.50: Closed for examination, and 20.14 Shoeburyness – Fenchurch Street held at Dagenham until 01.30. Through clear 00.50, Local lines 01.20 20/4.

Hatch End 21.50: IB caused closure of lines, but electric services resumed 22.12 and main-line trains 22.52.

Euston 22.10: IB started fires in Electrical Engineer's Repair Shop and Road Vehicle office, but in hand by 23.30. Lines closed at No. 2 Box until 22.30, but traffic otherwise unaffected.

Mildmay Park:[67] HE made small crater on No. 2 Up line. Conductor rail on Up side overturned. Passenger trains terminated Canonbury, as electric lines blocked. nwr 14.00.

Upminster Bridge 00.40: Station damaged and lines closed, but nwr from 02.30.

Ripple Lane 02.45: Barking By-pass Bridge damaged, but traffic continued.

Dunloe Street, Shoreditch: HE blocked all four lines. 03.00 special freight Willesden – Broad Street ran into crater on No. 2 (electric) line and tender derailed. Lines blocked by 30 yards of collapsed retaining wall. Two staff injured. Down No. 2 line clear 16.40 20/4, No. 2 Up 16.30 21/4 for freight trains only. Passenger services into Broad Street had been terminated at Dalston or Canonbury as necessary since 04.30 17/4 and did not resume until morning of 24/4.

Dagenham 03.25: HE made small crater on Up Through line. All lines blocked, but only until 05.00.

Little Ilford No. 1 Box 03.50: HE on adjacent houses broke windows of signalbox and threw debris on Loop. All roads in East Ham Electric Sidings covered with debris and several electric trains damaged by blast. Sufficient passenger stock available for 20-minute service on this Sunday (20/4). East Ham Loop line closed.

Homerton 04.50: HE made nine-foot crater and blew out 60ft of track. Block and telecom cut. Lines blocked – but nwr by 12.15 20/4!

East Ham 08.00: UXLM closed all four lines until removed 12.00. District Line service suspended Upton Park – Barking.

Highgate New Station (LPTB) 21.20: Portal of northbound tunnel demolished. Restricted LPTB Northern Line service restored on Up line 20/4.

Bow Junction – Devonshire Street 21.45: IB fell in compartment of 21.01 Shenfield – Liverpool Street, but damage not serious and train continued at 22.22.

Hoe Street – Wood Street 22.17: 21.45 Liverpool Street – Chingford damaged by HE. One engineman and three passengers injured. Overline bridge damaged, debris on line. nwr midnight 19–20/4 – but see Wood Street, below.

Highgate, Wellington Sidings 22.20: HE damaged eight feet of north end Highgate Tunnel, blocking LPTB lines, until 23.20, then LPTB trains run on Up line (15 mph).

Bow Junction – Stratford Bridge Box 22.45: HE nearby threw debris on line, but traffic continued, at extreme caution.

Thames Wharf – Custom House 22.45: All lines blocked. One staff injured, another at Bow Creek Wharf.

Spitalfields: Siding and two wagons damaged. Signalbox unworkable.

Mile End: Goods siding damaged.

Blackwall: Three warehouses damaged by fire.

Abbey Gate Junction[68] – Abbey Mills Lower Junction: Lines blown out, wires cut. nwr 14.00 20/4.

Bow Road: Three arches of bridge damaged and unsafe. Fenchurch Street trains terminated at Ilford. nwr not until 5/5.

Ilford in night: UXB blocked Main lines, removed 15.40 24/4.

Tidal Basin: UXB stopped North Woolwich service.

Wood Street: UXLM fell 50 yards from station. All trains stopped. Buses provided Hoe Street – Chingford. nwr 12.45 20/4.

Custom House, in night: Station offices damaged. Up line lifted, Down broken at Tidal Basin. nwr not until morning of 7/5.

Stratford 01.15: Two HE damaged Boiler Shop.

Enfield Chase 01.30: HE put Down line out of alignment. SLW, but buses provided Enfield Chase – Gordon Hill. nwr 09.20.

Bishopsgate 02.15: Wall of bridge damaged, also eight wagons and 17 cartage vehicles. All running lines blocked by debris. Suburban lines clear 05.45, Local 06.50, Main 11.00.

Bethnal Green 02.25: Signalbox badly damaged. One staff injured. Also UXLM stopped working, removed 15.30.

Stratford East – Maryland 02.25: Through lines blocked by debris.

Chadwell Heath 02.30: HE blocked all lines. Signalbox and the booking-office wrecked. 100 yards of Up Through platform, also arcade blown out. One staff injured. Local lines clear 06.30, Through lines 18.00; Up platform restored later.

Stratford Western Junction 04.10: All lines blown out. Up Through clear 07.20, Down Through and Local lines (5 mph) 16.30 21/4.

ELR Line 19.40: UXB near Thames Tunnel. All traffic blocked, until removed 05.35 21/4, when line reopened for steam traffic only 18.00 4/6, only at night until 23/6.

SR (Central Section):

New Cross Gate 21.40: All signals and TC failed, restored 01.15.

Norwood Fork Junction 22.53: HE blocked Down Relief lines, also two craters on each side in Norwood Yard, where various sidings and 33 wagons damaged or derailed. Running lines cleared 06.50 20/4. All wagons and debris cleared 22/4, except eight sidings on Up side out of use until 18.00 23/4.

Brockley 23.48: BB fell on and blocked all lines. Cleared 02.45.

Eardley Sidings: 32 coaches machine-gunned and holed.

Balham Intermediate Box: Main lines blocked by damage from HE on Up side. Clear 17.00.

West Croydon: Station walls damaged by HE off SR property on Down side.

Streatham Hill 03.55: HE damaged Electric Car Sheds and stock. Both lines blocked by crater, clear 17.50.

Peckham Rye 04.10: Locomotive[69] of empty stock train fell into crater and derailed. Catford Loop lines blocked. Locomotive re-railed 18.30 20/4, lines clear 12.00 21/4.

SR (Eastern Section):

LC&D Lines:

Blackfriars Junction 22.15: Signalbox badly damaged. Two signalmen killed, also four other men killed and five shunters and one Engineer's staff injured. All lines blocked.

Blackfriars Goods 22.15: HE damaged Goods Offices on HL and LL, also 'A' and 'B' Bonds. Five road vehicles and 12 wagons damaged. Company's stables badly blasted. Damage done also to Nos 1 and 2 hydraulic hoists, controller cable at No. 4 turntable, mobile crane, and roof of Outdoor Machinery Inspector's office. Three staff injured. Blackfriars Goods traffic handled at Southwark and Bricklayers Arms Depots.

Southwark Street Bridge (No. 407) 22.15*: carrying four running lines and two sidings on each side, the bridge had been struck by an HE and six lines collapsed into the street below, along with four wagons and a sludge-tender. Remaining two sidings also damaged. Holborn and Blackfriars stations closed. Down Local line reopened for steam trains only 1/6. Down and Up Through lines not cleared until 15.30 2/6. West side sidings soon made available for freight trains (by SLW) through to Loughborough Junction, but Up Local line over bridge not restored until 13.00 29/6, when current restored to Local lines from 16.30.

Nunhead – Lewisham, Breakspeare Road bridge: UXB buried behind pier. Line closed, so not available for freight or diverted passenger trains.

Blackfriars Junction – Elephant & Castle 02.40: HE in Glasshill Street put Local lines out of alignment and damaged conductor rails. Repaired 11.00 24/4.

*From Lt. Col. Mount's Report: "This is the most comprehensive damage of a girder bridge I have yet seen". Two of three girders (span 90ft) carrying four running lines collapsed into the roadway. A third girder, carrying some sidings on east side, was pushed off abutments at one end. Also, considerable damage done to one of two main girders of separate bridge carrying the two 'Market Sidings' on west side. Latter bridge restored first, with trestling and leaving space for the double tram track. Siding lines slewed into the running lines to provide a single line for freight traffic. Meantime, trestling and steel joist weigh-beams to restore Up and Down Main lines and then the Local lines to be tackled.

On 26 May, Mount reported that three tracks in operation, over steel trestling kindly lent by War Office. Trestling required for fourth track would be recovered from Blackfriars Road Bridge, also damaged in the raids. Rebuilding of bridge urgent, but required 1,000 tons steel: War Office, nor as before LMSR, cannot provide any more trestling at present, so SR CME being prevailed upon.

The Blackfriars main power signalbox close by, which had already suffered fire damage on 16/4 and was under repair, was completely destroyed. Four men, occupied hand-signalling, were sheltering in a steel bell-type refuge but killed by blast. Spare 24-lever power frame installed temporarily to work junctions either side of bridge.

Bridge 98 between Blackfriars Junction and Elephant & Castle repaired 11.00 25/4, but owing to the other damage no traffic could pass yet. Moreover, Local lines at McLeod Street Bridge (Elephant & Castle – Walworth Road) damaged 14.30 24/4, when arch collapsed from damage on 16–17/4. Lines reopened 10.45 26/4. Thus goods traffic was restored in 15 days and other traffic in stages of 22, 42 and 70 days.

"It appears that the enemy has made several attempts to put the MWL at Blackfriars out of use, and with other recent incidents at the river bridges it may indicate deliberate attack on cross-Thames communications."

SE Lines:

London Bridge – St Johns 21.36: All TC and signalling failed. Traffic at standstill until restored 01.15.

Barnehurst – Crayford/Slades Green 22.55: Large crater near lines at Perry Street Fork Junction and signalbox damaged. Signalman unhurt, but one staff injured near Inspection Shops. Up line clear 12.15 20/4, then SLW. nwr 16.30 21/4.

Belvedere – Erith, Pembroke Crossing 23.05: LM exploded. Down line, signalbox and gatehouse damaged, but both lines blocked owing to damage and debris from fire at adjacent factory. Clear by 16.15 23/4.

Selhurst 22.58: Retaining wall and ARP shelter damaged.

Elmer's End 23.53: HE damaged station and sub-station; wagons derailed. One staff injured. nwr 12.40.

Southwark Park Junction – North Kent East Junction: UXB found at Rotherhithe Road Bridge. Four of six Eastern Section lines closed, and evening services curtailed by 75%, with LPTB providing substitute bus services. On Central Section, three lines closed by UXB during day and reasonable service run, but Down Local line closed later in day. Screen of wagons placed while BDS at work, then only No. 3 Down, No. 1 Up, Down Local and both lines on Bricklayers Arms Branch remained closed, until 15.10 28/4.

Charlton – Charlton Lane Crossing 01.00: HE on Down side cut telecom and HT cables. Traffic run by TIW, until 21/4.

Bricklayers Arms Goods 03.13: Numerous IB fell. Invoice shed and canteen damaged. Eight wagons badly damaged, 11 road vehicles destroyed or damaged.

Plumstead: Goods shed and offices damaged.

Maze Hill 01.05: Both lines blocked by damage. Clear 21/4 for steam 12.30, electric 16.30.

Belvedere 02.00: HE damaged shelters on Up platform, throwing debris over both lines. Station closed. Reopened 18.00 28/4 and shuttle service provided to Dartford.

Addiscombe 02.30: HE nearby damaged roof and platforms.

Elmstead Woods 02.45: Station damaged by blast from HE in approach road.

Bricklayers Arms Goods 03.13: IB destroyed glass canopy of 'G' Shed. Six wagons burnt out, two damaged. One Scammell tractor, five trailers, one horse-cart and another vehicle burnt out. Roofs of offices, staff-rooms and motor maintenance shops damaged by fire and water.

Plumstead – Abbey Wood 03.30: Both lines and telecom blocked by debris from HE damage off railway. nwr 17.00 21/4.

Mottingham 03.45: Signalbox windows blasted, substation damaged.

UXB: Charing Cross 02.45: UXLM, rendered harmless 16.45; Holborn – Blackfriars 03.02: UXLM, rendered harmless 09.13; New Cross Gate – Brockley 04.32: UXLM, rendered harmless 11.05; London Bridge 06.00: removed?; Abbey Wood 06.00: UXB two feet from Down line;. East Putney – Wimbledon (over West Hill Tunnel) 12.35: screened 17/4 and suspended District Line trains then passing 15 mph from 12.55 18/4, removed 21/4; 18/4: Sanderstead 18.00, removed 16.15 23/4. Blackfriars – Elephant & Castle. 18.35 29/4: DAB found that fell 22.10 19/4 15 yards from Up side in school playground,[70] removed 18.00 3/5. Elmstead Woods 2/5: DAB (presumed fallen 19/4) found 100ft from Down side, removed 4/5 without interference with traffic.

On the Saturday morning (19 April) the SR had reported: "Considerable improvement in passenger services in London, and freight almost normal", and "At Charing Cross, No. 1 platform now available for not more than seven coaches." However, at the weekend the situation must have been dire.

The LMSR reported that traffic from the Midland Division to the SR (Eastern Section) was being diverted owing to damage on the MWL, and this continued on 21–23 April. The land-mine explosion at Kensal Green on 19 April had stopped all freight from Willesden to the SR and GWR. Restrictions on all traffic to Willesden, in force since 7 April, were lifted on 24th.

An LNER report of 28 April confirmed that GE Suburban services were badly disrupted by damage at many points. HE at Stratford had blocked all lines at Western Junction and damaged the signalboxes there and at Central Junction. The Main Local

lines were in order at 09.15 20/4, Fenchurch Street lines clear 16.00, signalling restored 07.25 21/4. Meanwhile, Stratford – Liverpool Street passengers were conveyed by road services. However, as Bow Road Bridge was seriously damaged the Fenchurch Street service was still suspended on 28/4. Two UXB at Ilford had stopped all traffic. One bomb was removed 10.00 21/4, and at 16.30 traffic allowed to pass on all lines at extreme caution. Then from 05.30 24/4 Military had complete occupation for removal of second bomb, with Local lines handed back 15.20 with 5 mph SpR; Through lines still out of use on 28/4 pending completion of work on the bomb. Meanwhile, trains for Stratford and Liverpool Street were diverted all the way round via Seven Kings West Junction, Newbury Park and Woodford, and a local service arranged Manor Park – Liverpool Street, with bus service Ilford – Manor Park. Furthermore, on 20/4, damage at Chadwell Heath and discovery of two UXB beside lines at Brentwood necessitated stopping all traffic and instituting special bus service Shenfield – Gidea Park, while main line trains diverted via Witham and Bishops Stortford to Liverpool Street. At 16.30 21/4, permission was received for trains to run over Down Through and Up Local lines at Brentwood and although bomb remained this working continued until 28/4 with services restricted as necessary. On the North Woolwich Branch, all trains were still terminating at Canning Town.

On the SR, in the 17 days to 7 May, a great deal was achieved but some blockages remained. Belvedere – Erith was completely blocked (until 10/5) by UXB of 20/4 and there was partial blockage on several other lines. At Blackfriars Junction (Southwark Street Bridge 407), an Up line was made available for steam trains from 00.50 5/5, another UXB threatening traffic having been removed on 3/5 and at Elephant & Castle the Down Through line was clear 3/5 but platform not yet available owing to damage.

One week after the raids normal services were being run into all the London terminals, except for three. At Charing Cross, 405 of services were running; Blackfriars and Holborn remained closed, but two passenger lines were expected to be available within a week, although operations would be hampered by the destruction of the Blackfriars power signalbox. A single white line became available across Southwark Street and was used for the important freight traffic exchange with the LMSR and LNER via the MWL.

Nevertheless, the extensive damage on the SR, as well as stopping from the night of 19/20 April the freight from the LMSR and LNER over the MWL and Blackfriars Bridge, interrupted most freight from the LNER (Southern Area). However, a restricted amount of traffic was run via Sandy, Calvert and Northolt Junction to the Eastern Section, or via Harringay and Gospel Oak or Sandy, Yarnton and Reading to the Central Section.

After 20 April, London was virtually free of attack for three weeks while the Luftwaffe turned their weight onto Plymouth, Portsmouth, Liverpool, Belfast, Clydeside and many other targets well away from London. This allowed the railways to recover briefly.

21/4/41

LNE: Tidal Basin: Owing to UXB, Palace Gates – North Woolwich trains terminated Canning Town.

ELR Line: Spitalfields hoist out of action. Trains worked via Liverpool Street (reverse).

23/4/41

LNE: West India Dock Bridge, Millwall Branch 09.00: UXLM, traffic suspended, until detonated 17.15 24/4.

24/4/41

LNE: Ilford 05.30: All lines closed to allow Military to deal with UXB. Traffic diverted via Woodford.

Waterloo. Southward view after extensive damage on the north side towards the North Sidings, suffered at 9.35pm on 5 January 1941. In the foreground are the footbridges linking the concourse to the lifts down to the Underground Bakerloo and Northern Lines. Behind is the Armstrong lift for the Waterloo & City Line vehicles and the ventilation shaft.

Waterloo, Necropolis Station. The consequences of a direct hit in the dreadful night of 16/17 April 1941. This was the station on the south side used before the war for conveying coffins and mourners to Brookwood Cemetery.

Blackfriars Junction. The Luftwaffe could hardly have hit a bull's-eye better than this one, achieved with a parachute-mine on the evening of 19 April 1941, this south-east view being taken two days later. It is the bridge over Southwark Street just south of Blackfriars Bridge, carrying four major lines of the SR Eastern Section off that bridge immediately before they divide at Blackfriars Junction for London Bridge Station and beyond and for Loughborough Junction etc.

Above left Southwark Street Bridge. View towards Blackfriars Goods, after the raid of 19/20 April 1941. At 10.15pm a heavy bomb caused the girders of both Through lines and the Down Local line leading to Blackfriars Bridge to collapse into the street.

Left Southwark Street Bridge. View towards Blackfriars, taken on 25 May 1941. On the left is Blackfriars Goods station and the west side girders for the Market Sidings appear to have been repaired. In the centre are the temporary trestles for the two Through lines and the Up Local lines. On the right is the Down Local, not at that time restored for electric trains although a conductor rail seems to be in place. The tower on the right housed a hydraulic hoist for lowering wagons to sidings below.

Above Southwark Street Bridge. Scene on 11 May 1941, three weeks after almost complete destruction of the bridge on the night of 19/20 April 1941. The temporary trestling, part steel part timber, is supporting the East Sidings (originally leading to the Blackfriars passenger station of 1864-85). The Down Local line is in the foreground and beyond is the Market Siding on the girder. There seems to be a remarkable air of calm, considering this was the day after another very heavy raid.

Paddington. A parachute-mine had fallen in the night of 16/17 April 1941 in the approach drive alongside Eastbourne Terrace. The scene, westwards from Praed Street, shows some of the resulting destruction, which embraced many of the GWR offices and facilities along Platform 1. It was just as well the incident occurred at 2.40am, but even so 16 were killed and 94 injured. The mess was cleared up in about four days.

Fenchurch Street. Repairs in progress on the front of the station, four months after the heavy raid of 10/11 May 1941.

London's Last Major Raid

On the night of 10/11 May London suffered another massive attack, which as it turned out was the last of the 1940–41 Night Blitz. Between 23.30 and 04.15, 507 bombers dropped 711 tons of HE and 86,200 IB, which caused one conflagration (at Elephant & Castle), 10 major and 46 serious fires. The bombers killed a record 1,436 people and seriously injured 1,792.[71] Although the tonnage dropped was less than in the big April raids, the damage caused was even worse: 71 Key Points were affected, including 33 factories and works. Six important factories and the Lambeth Cold Store were destroyed. West Ham Power Station (97,000 kW) received damage that required a year to repair and the damage to sub-stations and the distribution system exceeded any previously achieved. There was such damage to gas mains that 200,000 consumers were affected and restoration of supply took two months. Numerous major water mains were broken and pressure was very low for a week. Telephone communications were cut for some time owing to severe damage at Faraday House, the London Trunk Exchange. Road traffic through the city was blocked entirely for two days and to some extent for three weeks; cross-river traffic was normal after five days but Southwark Bridge was closed for two months. More than 50 important buildings were damaged, notably the Houses of Parliament, War Office, Westminster Abbey, St James's Palace, the Ministries of Aircraft Production, Pensions and Works, the British Museum, Tower of London, Royal Naval College, St Clement Dane's Church and six others. Hospitals struck included: Vincent Square Children's, Mile End, Poplar, Royal Eye (Southwark), St Luke's (Chelsea), St Mary Abbot's (Kensington).

10–11/5/41 (Saturday – Sunday, reports combined)

GW: South Lambeth: HE blocked road entrance to depot.

East Acton – Wood Lane (E&SB) 00.42: HE on track. Milk train ran into crater, blocking both steam lines by derailment of locomotive[72] and six wagons. LPTB lines also damaged, but service restored 14.20 12/5. nwr on steam lines 11.00 15/5.

Paddington Goods 01.12: HE in yard damaged vans and lorries, also offices and other buildings. One staff injured.

West London Carriage Sidings 01.15: Twelve coaches burnt out. Cables cut, affecting signal lights and TC, but Block not affected. Traffic diverted from Main to Relief lines.

Paddington 01.30: HE on Platform 13 line damaged stairs to booking-office and blocked Platforms 13 and 14. 01.45–02.55: All signalling and lighting failed. Signalling supply partially restored in evening. One staff and one other killed, 19 staff and 63 others injured. Debris cleared 12/5, Platform 14 reopened 19.00 12/5, No. 13 06.00 14/5. From early 13/5, shuttle LPTB service Hammersmith–Paddington (using Platform 14), extended to Baker Street 11.00. Also HE fell near Platform 15, blocking Nos 15 and 16 lines and signals, but these restored 16.00.

Royal Oak 01.30: Up Main, Up Relief and Carriage lines damaged, but cleared 12.00. Down Carriage line cut, and 30 coaches damaged. Three Goods lines blocked and 11 wagons damaged, but cleared 17.00. Wall of cutting of H&C under GW demolished and debris fell on electric lines, cleared 13/5. Retaining wall in Ranelagh Bridge Loco Yard badly damaged.

Old Oak Common East Box: Signal cables cut.

Smithfield: Goods depot, warehouses, cartage offices, walls etc. damaged. Access blocked by debris and not restored until 27/8, fully by alternative routes 6/10.

LMS: Willesden No. 1 23.50: IB fell on a coach in NLR bay. Coach and wagons set on fire on Down WLR. But "normal at 00.10"!

Euston No. 4 23.50: IB fell on track. Fast and Slow lines closed, but Fast lines clear 00.15.

Poplar: Platforms, signalbox, Goods offices, Foreman's, Yardmaster's and power houses damaged. Several craters in sidings

Bow: Sidings and eight wagons damaged.

Old Ford: IB damaged shed, motor vehicles and merchandise.

Canning Town Goods: Provender shed and garage badly damaged.

St Pancras 00.15: HE between Platforms 3 and 4 penetrated to King's Cross Tunnel connecting Midland with Metropolitan lines, completely blocking tunnel. Another bomb penetrated at north end between Platforms 6 and 7, exploded underground and formed camouflet. Station roof and coaching stock damaged. One passenger killed and two injured – in shelter. Platforms 5–7 were available 13/5, but ground began to subside. Two sets of 58ft girders put in to carry the two roads (Nos 6 and 7). The station had to be closed, but services resumed 19/5 into all platforms except Nos 3 and 4. (These were shortened 100ft and reopened 5/6). All expresses and most locals then run, although some locals terminated Kentish Town and a few cancelled. The Tunnel lines were interlaced and reopened as a single line from 21.30 27/5. Normal two-way working was not restored until 20.00 28/12/41.

Somers Town Goods: Two HE in HL penetrated to LL. Buildings and roof damaged, 19 roads blocked.

Highbury & Islington 00.20: HE blocked all lines. Five coaches of empty electric train badly damaged and motorman killed. Block to Canonbury cut. All traffic stopped. No. 1 lines restored 08.40, No. 2 lines 14.10, but no traction supply to electric lines. Freight trains passing.

Leytonstone 00.45: HE in High Street damaged stairways and platforms.

Kentish Town 00.55: HE on Nos 1 and 2 Cattle Dock Sidings.

St Pancras Goods 01.00: UXB by canal, so yard closed until 05.30.

Euston, Hampstead Road Bridge 01.00: All lines blocked by debris. Roof of Up side Carriage Shed damaged. One staff injured. Two EMU badly damaged. On 12/5, Up Fast line clear 10.18, Down Fast 05.30, Up Slow 07.05, Down Slow 20.55, and two roads in Carriage Shed available.

Camden Goods 02.15: HE on Regulator's Office. HE penetrated tunnel of Empty Stock line. Four staff killed and seven seriously injured. Yard and Up and Down electric lines closed. Up line clear 17.20 11/5, Down clear 18.20 12/5.

Devons Road Loco and Carriage Sheds 04.45: Several coaches damaged, and debris strewn over running lines. nwr 09.00 12/5.

Shoreditch 06.00: Fire under arches blocked No. 2 lines, until 16.10.

Haydon Square Goods: Closed owing to damage in early morning. (Line from Stepney blocked anyway).

Tredegar Road Milk Depot (Victoria Park – Bow): Three roads blown out.

LNE: Stratford Market 22.30: HE on Down Main between platforms. Station buildings damaged and station closed. Passenger trains passing over Goods lines. nwr 13.00 11/5.

Holloway 00.00: IB destroyed Glassblower's Shop adjacent to Yardmaster's office. Other IB in Carriage Sidings dealt with by Home Guard and staff.

Fenchurch Street 00.00: HE on and near station. Refreshment room and other buildings severely damaged. Platform 1 blocked by debris and three coaches of 00.20 to Shoeburyness damaged by fire. One person injured. nwr 16.20 13/5.

Temple Mills 00.05: HE seriously damaged lines. All traffic stopped. Coal, Suburban and Blackwall Yards, also reception road for Colchester and Cambridge traffic on Down side, all out of use. Down side restored temporarily 11/5, but Hump frame damaged. All running lines except Up Goods clear 06.00. nwr not until 16/5.

Devonshire Street – Coborn Road 00.25: Overbridge on fire. Traffic stopped until 01.00, when Local lines reopened. Up Through line reopened 01.50, Down Through 03.00.

Spitalfields 01.00: HE in yard stopped all working. All lines except Up Through in order 05.30. Spitalfields water-softener damaged. No trains in/out of yard owing to damaged sidings. Hoist road damaged, four-arch span demolished. Several motor vehicles damaged and five wagons burnt out. Hoist lost power, but restored at low pressure 16/5. nwr 17/5.

Tottenham – Northumberland Park 01.00: HE damaged 42 yards of private siding.

ELR Line (LPTB) 01.25: Line closed owing to damage to Rotherhithe tunnel, and station.

Marylebone 01.45: IB set fire to roof over booking-hall and north end of Platform 2. Fire Brigade arrived at 03.55 and fire under control 04.20. Station roof badly damaged, but offices affected only by water. Three HE in Goods Yard destroyed building housing hydraulic and other machinery. Stores, three coaches and seven motor vehicles lost. Working of depot restricted also by damage to track, turntable and wagons. Traffic diverted to Neasden as required.

Finsbury Park – Canonbury 02.00: Overbridge damaged. Lines closed until 16.00, then SLW Canonbury – Finsbury Park No. 1. nwr not until 12.00 26/5.

Stepney East – Gas Factory Junction 03.00: Bridge over Commercial Road damaged and Up line blown out. Traffic stopped. Woodford – Fenchurch Street trains terminated at Ilford until 14/5, LMS trains at Bromley. SLW from 13/5.

Limehouse Junction: Bridge damaged. Line (freight only) closed until 28/5; alternative routes used.

King's Cross 03.15: HE on station demolished 75ft of main station block on western side facing Platform 10, including buffet, grill room, Hotels Department stores, RTO's office and a number of Headquarters offices. Serious damage to adjoining sections to north and south, including Booking and Enquiry Offices,[73] Ladies 1st Class waiting-room, Gentlemen's lavatories and offices above. Large section of retaining wall of Platforms 7 and 8 demolished together with five bays of roof. Much debris and large girders covered south end of Platforms 10, 8, 7 and 6, and measures to secure remainder of western roof and eastern side made rapidly. Two booking-clerks escaped with slight injury, but many people buried under debris of Buffet and RTO's office. Troops assisting and more called for. One locomotive[74] and 15 coaching stock damaged. At first, only Local station and Platforms 1, 2 and 4 remained usable. Platforms 7 and 8 in use 12/5, but all not fully in use until 27/5. Meanwhile, Tea Room on Platform 10 used as Temporary Booking office, and a buffet car placed by the buffers as temporary Refreshment room. On 11/5, known casualties were reported as four staff (firewatchers) and five Servicemen killed. A further body was recovered on 13/5, and the bodies of a fire-watcher and a military policeman recovered 19/5, also (on 20-21/5) two Scots Guardsmen. Gap in western side remained for many months and Station not fully repaired until after the war, at a cost of about £3,125,000 in today's money.

Liverpool Street 03.30: Numerous IB set fire to west side. Clock-tower gutted, and General offices, Refreshment and Grill rooms and booking-office seriously damaged, also Tea Room on footbridge and offices for 175ft on south side. West Side station required immediate temporary repairs and roofing. (Cost of repairs about £2,000,000 at present-day prices). All platforms except No. 1 available by 11.40, although fires not under control until 14.00 same day. One staff died from smoke. Enfield services terminated Hackney Downs and passengers changed to Chingford trains. Loughton trains terminated Stratford and passenger changed to Gidea Park trains.

 Bishopsgate 05.30: Fire in trader's office. One staff injured extinguishing IB. South Box temporarily vacated.

 Poplar Docks Depot: Damaged, but reopened 11.30 12/5.

 Cable Street Depot, Leman Street: HE blew out Up Slow and damaged several arches. Fast lines blocked by debris, cleared on 12/5. Slow lines in order 16.20 16/5.

 Blackwall Branch: Both lines blown out at Millwall, Limehouse and Bridge 545 on curve. IB damaged offices at Blackwall. SLW eventually possible on Limehouse Curve from 11.00 26/5.

SR (Western Section):

 Feltham Junction – Feltham Yard 23.50: All lines blocked by large crater. Cleared 14.15 11/5.

 Feltham Marshalling Yard 23.50: Three HE on Up Departure Sidings, blocking Nos 1–12 and 17 – 21. Engineer's Depot considerably damaged. Three staff injured. All clear 16.00 13/5.

 Twickenham: Sub-station damaged and one staff injured.

 Loco Junction 00.10: 18.30 (10/5) Weymouth – Waterloo express damaged by fire and still standing 09.40. (Report at 12.30 stated one coach of train returning empty from Waterloo uncoupled there and left to burn out).[75]

 Waterloo 00.15: All lines closed. General Offices on Windsor side, also Bonded Warehouse and Building Department beneath Platforms 1–10, damaged by fire and still burning 06.00 11/5. Crater in North Sidings. Four staff injured in fires; later, one staff and two other people killed in Lost Property arch.

Waterloo was really badly affected this time*. HE fell on Platform 1 and all lines were blocked by damage to arches under Platforms 1–3 and by fire in arches under all platform lines. "Asphalt melting and unable to get near yet to examine." Fire spread during day under all platforms and reached north side by evening. It was still raging 22.35 12/5. At 06.25 14/5 it was reported out but only under Platforms 1–11. It was not extinguished until late on 15/5. Two men had been killed and another badly burned. Up Main Relief and Through lines and connections to Nos 9–12 platform lines damaged. General Offices, warehouses and stores also damaged. HE near signalbox, another near Lambeth Road Bridge and crater in North Sidings. Roof of old Boiler-house and of W&C sub-station damaged. At switchboard most junction and PO lines down. Calls made via Paddington and Hounslow, until emergency line to Woking available 08.50. No current at sub-station as feeders from Clapham Junction damaged. No traction signalling or lighting.

 With the ensuing problems with DAB and the restoration of the power for the points and signalling, it is not surprising that the station was only partially opened even by 21.15 16/5, when Platforms 6 and 7 were available. Main line suburban services recommenced running through to Waterloo at 06.00 17/5 (at 5 mph), nwr from 22/5. Platform 13 reopened 13.00 18/5, Nos 4 and 5 18.00 21/5, Nos 18–21 18.15 23/5. Up Main Relief and Through lines clear 20.15 23/5. Windsor Line platforms (Nos 18–21) reopened 18.15 23/5. Platforms 10, 11, 16 and 17 reopened 17.00 25/5, Nos 8 and 9 15.15 26/5, Nos 14 and 15 14.15 27/5. No. 12 not reopened until 11.30 5/6. No. 3 platform not reopened until 03.00 11/8 and Nos 1 and 2 not reopened until 06.00 21/9.

 *From Lt.Col. Mount's Reports: Raid of 10/11 May burnt out remainder of old offices; a trailer-pump might have saved Waterloo Station. As it was, one small bomb exploded at basement level inside one of the 25ft arches carrying the station and destructive fire broke out in arches, many let out for storage of spirits in bond. Heat from burning spirit very intense, resulting in calcining of brickwork of piers and arches to up to nine inches. Arches extending width of station half destroyed. However, sufficient substance left in piers to carry joist girders: these thrown across from pier to pier, enabling weight of traffic carried independently of arches.

 Repairs to arches took time, but traffic resumed in fortnight. Piers of arches repaired in brickwork, to release temporary steel joists urgently

wanted elsewhere. Altogether 240 men of Company's staff specially mobilised for the emergency. Initially two tracks dealt with in 2½ days by gang of 40 with breakdown crane to lift RSJ's into position (two under each rail, overlapping on each pier). 1,000 tons steel used, leaving Company with only small reserve. Arches therefore repaired quickly, War Office sending 50 bricklayers and Contractors extra 20 men. Arches (three spans each 820ft x 25ft) repaired by driving bolts through piers to bind new to old brickwork, then made up with concrete. To save time, shuttering and pier repairs applied only under each track; arching under platforms stiffened with ribs later.

 By mid-August 1941, walling of north side complete and 300 of 1,500ft of arching, with steel scaffolding and timber shuttering going forward in sections. A secure and permanent job ensured, lest whole station collapse in future. "The fire might well have caused such a catastrophe and that the vast amount of spirits left unconsumed by the fire ought to be moved away without delay."

 Vauxhall 00.15: HE damaged Engineer's office, station, buffet, No. 1 (timber) platform and arches 59–63. Failure of signalling and lights. DAB between Down Main Local and parapet wall, removed 10.35.

 Nine Elms Loco 00.15: Crater in Nos 7 and 8 Shed roads and in Foundry road. One locomotive[76] damaged by HE and several wagons burnt. One staff injured extinguishing fires in Factory.

 Nine Elms Goods: 'B' Shed on fire.

 Waterloo – Vauxhall 15.10: Undiscovered UXB exploded, damaging Up Windsor line and blocking Down Windsor Through line with debris. Down Windsor line clear 10.25 13/5 – from Waterloo only 12.00 17/5. Up Windsor line not clear (for steam trains only) until 17.15 21/5.

 Vauxhall 15.10: DAB reported in street on Up side, so Up Windsor Local line blocked. Bomb cleared 12.00 13/5, but unable to reopen Windsor lines until cable repairs completed. At midnight, another UXB reported under far end of No. 8 platform, so BDS blocked all lines. However, bomb discredited 18.00 and Waterloo traffic resumed 13/5.

 Waterloo & City Line: No current for pumps in morning, owing to flooding after DAB exploded in Queen Victoria Street. Pumps restored at 21.15, but lines remained flooded. UXB near Bank also to be removed before service restored 06.00 26/5.

SR (Central Section):

 Tulse Hill 23.15: Signalbox windows smashed by HE off premises.

 Clapham Junction: IB fell into coach of 23.46 EMU Victoria – West Croydon; thrown out by passengers!

 Selhurst – Gloucester Road Junction: All lines blocked. Local lines clear 17.00.

 West Norwood – Gipsy Hill: Both lines blocked, but clear at 15.00.

 Peckham Rye – Nunhead/Queen's Road (Peckham): Both lines on each route blocked by severe damage to Cow Lane (rail-over-rail) Bridge 430. SL lines clear 11.30 12/5, Catford Loop lines 17.55 16/5 (5 mph).

 Queen's Road (Peckham) – Peckham Rye: Both lines blocked by damage to Kirkwood Road Bridge. Clear 12.00 12/5.

 Old Kent Road Junction – Queen's Road (Peckham): Both lines blocked by damage to Surrey Canal Bridge and/or (according to reports) Old Kent Road Bridge. Clear at 12.00 12/5, when SL service restored London Bridge – Battersea Park.

 London Bridge (Central and Eastern): Station building extensively damaged. Nos 12, 15, 17, 20, 21 platforms blocked by damaged trains, Nos 14 and 16 by bomb damage. Signal and traction current supplies failed. Platforms 17, 18, 20 and 21 out of use. Down side parapet wall thrown across tracks near Peek Frean's. 13.10: SM reported: (a) HE had dropped on girders of No. 13 platform, windows of 8-car train blown out; a 4-BIL train in No. 15 also badly damaged. (b) Another HE exploded on station buildings near Post Office. Four DAB suspected: (i) Platform 21, station end; (ii) UX oil-bomb on ballast of No. 16; (iii) on No. 3 Down line

London side of No. 298 points. (These three cleared 12.30). (iv) between Down Through and Down Local (Central Section); this exploded 14.00. Wagon screens set up to allow use of Platforms 12–16 and 20–21, although latter damaged and not in use until 15.45 13/5. 18.10: SM reported all Eastern Section lines clear, except Nos 1 and 2 Down still blocked by debris from Peek-Frean's factory, also DAB. Wagon screen placed 18.40, allowing use of all other lines. No. 2 line clear 07.55 13/5, No. 1 not until 11.00 21/5. Platforms 17 and 18 restored 12.05 15/5 after removal of UXB.

London Bridge – New Cross Gate/New Cross: Down Local and Down Through Central and No. 3 Down Eastern lines blocked by damage to arch, but all reopened 12.00.

New Cross Gate – Surrey Docks: 'In' and 'Out' ELR lines, Down Local and three sidings blocked by damage and debris. Cleared 11/5.

New Cross Gate: Nos 3–5 'New Sidings' (at 1m. 0c.) and Nos 8–12 Down Goods Sidings (at 2m. 30c.) blocked by damage and debris from exploded DAB. Cleared 16/5.

Battersea Park 00.30: All lines blocked by debris on tracks from HE on adjoining property. Clear 21.20.

Victoria (Central) – Battersea Park 00.40: Incline road blocked by damage to arch. Clear 11.20 12/5.

Denmark Hill 00.50: Station damaged by LM on adjoining property.

Victoria (Central and Eastern) 01.00: Up Main and Up Relief lines (Eastern Section) blocked. Five DAB: (i) large one penetrated roof near SM's Office onto Platforms 7 and 8; (ii) on Platform 10; (iii) on Platforms 1 and 2, cleared 16/5; (iv) two in forecourt, Eastern side, cleared 11.00 17/5. Entire station closed, including Underground. Central side reopened 12.40 12/5, but with Platforms 9–12 out of use owing to DAB on No. 10; Nos 13–17 being used; passengers using Buckingham Palace Road entrance. This DAB exploded at 01.40 13/5, damaging platform and some screening wagons. Platforms 9 and 12 clear 13/5, the rest 15/5. Up Central Main line clear 11.10. Up Eastern Main line clear 15.50 15/5. Victoria (Eastern) reopened 17.00 16/5.

Clapham Junction – Wandsworth Common 01.00: All lines blocked at New Wandsworth by debris of boundary wall. Local lines clear 03.50, Main lines 07.25, but all wires down so TIW, until restored 16.15.

Wimbledon – Merton Park 02.15: Footbridge and signalbox damaged. Both lines blocked, but clear 07.00.

Purley – Kenley 03.20: Both lines blocked by damage. Clear 12.45.

Norwood Yard 03.30: HE blocked 'In' and 'Out' Goods and Electric lines. Selhurst end of sidings damaged. One electric line clear 07.30, 'In' Goods 17.00, 'Out' Goods clear 12.00, 'Out' electric line 17.00 12/5. 'In' electric line clear 15.00 13/5.

Selhurst – Gloucester Road Junction 03.30: Both lines blocked by HE. No current. Clear 17.00.

SR (Eastern Section):
LC&D Lines:
Holborn Viaduct 23.00: Fire gutted station buildings, damaged roof. Bridge decking, timbers and buildings at Holborn LL burnt out. Fires in offices on both sides of station. Debris on lines. "Underbridges may be affected." All lines blocked. 03.00: Staff evacuated. Station still on fire 19.00. On 12/5 all lines in station still blocked by debris. Up Local line to Snow Hill clear 12.45 14/5, then MWL freight worked by SLW via Up Local line and through Market Siding to Blackfriars Junction. Down Local line clear 12.00 14/5, Up Local line into station restored 12.00 1/6. Emergency crossings at Ludgate Hill not used as signalling out of use.

Blackfriars – Elephant & Castle 23.00: HE between Down and Up Local lines, damaging arch adjoining Bridge 396. One Down line reopened 17.00 16/5. Track slewed from Local to Through, then trains regaining Local at Elephant & Castle, where both Local lines clear and slewed to connect back with Through lines. Local lines and single Market Siding regained by crossings at Blackfriars Junction. Up Local at Bridge 396 restored 10.50 29/5, Down Local 12.00 1/6.

Blackfriars 23.00: All lines at station blocked. 03.00: Station on fire. HE damaged River Bridge under Down and Up Loop lines. Platform lines and Through lines not reopened until 15.50 25/5, Down Local not reopened until 15.30 2/6. Nos 1 and 2 Bay lines not reopened until 11.00 9/8. Blackfriars Junction Box destroyed – not replaced by temporary box until 12.15 2/6; permanent Box on 9/10/42.[77]

Elephant & Castle 23.10–03.30*: Station buildings struck by two HE and all lines blocked, with four bridges damaged and tracks hanging down from arches. Station and signalbox[78] completely gutted. Four staff (one LNER) seriously injured. Four bridges damaged, including arch under Local lines at Hill Street Junction. Local lines clear 17.00 16/5 and slewed into Through lines there, so providing one Up and one Down line Blackfriars Junction – Loughborough Junction. Platforms back in use morning 1/9. Slewing removed and all Through and Local lines not back to normal until 12.45 2/6. (Otherwise reported dates were: Lines slewed over at both sites 10.50 30/5, then Up Local at Blackfriars Junction clear, Down Local 12.00 11/6).

*From Lt.Col. Mount's Report: Whole station, many of viaduct arches, and the buildings each side, e.g. Spurgeon's Tabernacle, burnt out. Obviously deliberate attack on Circus, which however not hit although many surrounding buildings badly damaged. By August only small outlay spent to bring two platforms and railway approaches into normal use.

Longhedge 00.45: Stores Department buildings destroyed by fire.

Shortlands – Beckenham Junction 00.55: Lines damaged, no current. Clear 06.10. nwr 18.35 12/5.

Loughborough Junction 02.35: Signalbox roof damaged by debris.
SE Lines:
London Bridge – Spa Road: Nos 1 and 2 lines blocked by damage. No. 2 clear at 07.55 13/5. No. 1 clear 11.00 21/5.

Deptford Lift Bridge – New Cross Gate Yard: Down Wharf line blocked, but clear 16.20.

Metropolitan Junction – Cannon Street: Local lines damaged at Bridge 36 (Southwark Street), also Metropolitan Siding, but Up line clear 20.00. 'In' line to Cannon Street blocked by damage to Bridge 37. Clear 10.40 14/5.

London Bridge – Charing Cross: Signal current failed. Restored 20.05 12/5.

Catford Bridge – Lower Sydenham 00.55: Both lines blocked by damage. Lines cleared 12.00 12/5.

Bricklayers Arms 01.08–02.00: Nos 1–6 roads in 'L' section blocked by HE. Other bombs damaged several roads serving 'G' and 'J' Yards, but in order 18.00.

West Wickham 00.20: HE fell on platform. Both lines blocked. Station windows smashed. Porter missing. Lines clear 15.35, but no current until 15/5.

Borough Market Junction 00.22: All lines blocked and lights failed. Found in order 06.00, reopened 16.45.

Plumstead, Polytechnic Sidings 00.30: Two 8-car trains damaged by blast. Windows smashed at signalbox.

Greenwich – Maze Hill 00.45: Both lines blocked by damage to retaining wall. Not restored until 20.30 25/5.

Waterloo Eastern – Charing Cross 03.00: Down Local and both Through lines blocked by damage at Belvedere Road Bridge and to pier on Thames Bridge*. Down Local line clear 16.45. Through lines not cleared until 09.45 5/10.

*From Lt.Col. Mount's Reports and others: Heavy bomb made large crater in river-bed about 30ft upstream of one of the two piers supporting Hungerford (Charing Cross) Bridge in middle of river. At first no harm to railway suspected, but when track above abruptly found out of alignment several 2½-inch vertical cracks discovered each side of pier. Evidently much of end carrying outside girders undermined, so two railway tracks closed. Calculated that the pier carried dead load of 7,000 tons, so dead-plus-alive load was double that allowed: girders had moved out two inches, although without much movement of cross-girders. Temporary dolphins (posts) driven in river-bed to relieve the two outer main girders of live load, so enabling traffic to resume, slowly. Sheath of interlocking steel piles driven around damaged portion of pier into river-bed and suitable ties constructed to secure displaced and intact portions of pier and prevent further lateral movement – and the trains continued to pass.

> Waterloo Eastern – Metropolitan Junction: HE blocked Up Local line. Cleared 17.00.
>
> Elmer's End 03.15: HE hit 3-coach EMU in Down bay, damaging station buildings and substation. All lines blocked by debris. Current cut off. SM severely shocked. Lines clear 15.35, but Down bay not until 16.00 20/5.
>
> Greenwich – Maze Hill 03.30: HE on track. Both lines blocked. Not clear until 23.30 25/5.
>
> Cannon Street 03.55: Terminus buildings and roof damaged by fire. 04.20: Locomotive[79] and several vehicles demolished by HE on No. 8 'In' line. Debris all over platforms. Station closed.[80] Three corridor sets derailed in West Siding and eight-car set damaged in East Siding. 13.15: Running lines in order, but station unusable owing to debris. Platforms 1–5 cleared 17.30, but no traction current. Indeed roof still on fire 24 hours later. Platforms 1–5 reopened 05.00 14/5, No. 6 10.30 15/5, No. 7 10.30 16/5, No. 8 09.35 17/5. Signalling power supply not restored until 08.30 15/5.
>
> West Norwood – Gipsy Hill 04.15: Both lines blocked by damage. Down line clear 09.15, Up 14.40.
>
> Blackfriars – Elephant & Castle 00.00, but Down and Up Through lines cleared same day; Borough Market Junction 00.22– 16.45; Shortlands – Beckenham Junction 00.25–06.10; London Bridge 01.00–?; Elephant & Castle – Loughborough Junction 01.00–06.00; (Cables found damaged 02.30 near Penrose Street).

Main lines closed for examination included:

London Bridge, Cannon Street, Holborn Viaduct, Blackfriars, Waterloo, Charing Cross and Elmer's End sub-stations: Cables damaged, so no traction or signalling current, but restored at Cannon Street and Elmer's End early 12/5.

Other UXB: Victoria – five: on concourse (removed 15.15 16/5), Platform 1 (14.45 16/5), Platform 10 (screened 12/5), two in East forecourt (removed 01.55 13/5, 01.00 17/5). London Bridge – two: near Artillery Street (removed 11/5), between 'C' and 'D' sections (screened 11/5, removed 15/5); Spa Road – exploded 11/5. Birkbeck – Beckenham Junction, in track 01.20, cleared 12.00 20/5; Crofton Park – Catford – two on Down line (near Bridge 467, made harmless 15/5; near Bridge 465 (found exploded), lines clear 16.45 15/5; New Cross Gate Sidings near Carriage Lighting Shops, screened, not affecting running lines.

12/5/41

SR: Waterloo – Vauxhall 13.30: Up Windsor and Down Windsor Through lines blocked, owing to dangerous state of wall of Field's factory alongside. Declared safe 13/5 and signalling restored for normal running 15/5.

Waterloo & City Line: UXB exploded in Queen Victoria Street, but line still closed owing to lack of current. Traction supply restored 18.30, but line still closed. No current for pumps in morning, owing to flooding. Pumps restored at 21.15. Current supply restored 18.30 23/5. DAB found at Bank 19.15, another on 22/5. Both removed 25/5.

Abbey Wood – Belvedere 18.45: UXB of 20/4 detonated, but both lines blocked. Clear 14.25 13/5.

Signal current failed at midnight to Charing Cross, Metropolitan Junction, Borough Market Junction and London Bridge. Restored at London Bridge 00.17, rest 03.30 – except Metropolitan Junction – Cannon Street not until 10.30 30/7.

14/5/41

LNE: Routes via MWL to Hither Green and Bricklayers Arms reopened 16.30, but traffic limited until 16/5. (See SR).

SR: Holborn LL – Blackfriars 17.40: Route now available for MWL traffic via London Bridge, but Up Local at Blackfriars not safe, pending demolition of premises alongside. A Midland goods train stranded on Up Local removed 12.45. At 21.50 SLW instituted over Down Local Holborn – Ludgate Hill, thence over Up Local and Market Siding to Blackfriars Goods, but to/from Blackfriars southward possible only via Metropolitan Junction owing to blockages on Loughborough Junction route.

Loughborough Junction – Cambria Junction 20.15: Down line clear 14.00, but Up trains running under special arrangements as only one train at a time can pass over bridge.

15/5/41

SR: Holborn Viaduct – Blackfriars 14.40: SLW stopped, owing to unsafe vaults beneath Ludgate Hill old station. SLW restored over Local line 07.57 16/5. Through (Loop) lines at Blackfriars open for electric trains 15.00 25/5, also all platforms at Holborn in use.

When the main Blitz came to an unexpected end after that last raid in May 1941, the railways in London were not really in such a bad way. Although St Pancras, Holborn Viaduct and Blackfriars were not reopened for a few more days and Waterloo and Charing Cross were under serious difficulties, all passenger termini and main stations were functioning and would be operating normally within a month or so. A few main Goods stations had been very badly damaged and more or less put out of use, including Poplar and Somers Town on the LMSR, Marylebone and Royal Mint Street on the LNER and parts of Nine Elms and Bricklayers Arms on the SR. Several lines would be partially blocked for some time to come, notably the NLR at Highbury and over the viaducts to Broad Street, the Midland Tunnel at King's Cross and the Blackfriars – Loughborough Junction important elevated route on the SR. Nevertheless, freight traffic was able to cross London fairly normally. Passengers were often delayed, but were able to get to and from work etc. considerably more easily than they had in the previous autumn.

Opposite top Victoria (Central). Two days after the raid of 10/11 May 1941, railwaymen cheerfully work with Army men of a Bomb Disposal Squad – although it seems as if a bomb has gone off and thrown rails over the wagons. The site is probably on the Platform 10 line looking outward to Elizabeth Bridge.

Opposite Elephant & Castle. Devastation of the Down Through platform after the raid of 10/11 May 1941. Part of the overall roof has fallen down.

King's Cross, 11 May 1941, inside the wrecked booking hall, the first floor roof having collapsed.

King's Cross. Later on 11 May 1941, after a large bomb had exploded at 3.15am in the main booking hall and blown out a substantial chunk of the West side, including other facilities on Platform 10 and offices above. The view is westwards over to a glass-less roof of St Pancras Station – also struck the same night.

Opposite King's Cross. Roughly the same view as opposite, two months later, with clearance and essential repairs now done. On the right the front of the Suburban Station is visible behind the scaffolding.

Elephant & Castle. View towards Loughborough Junction, two days after the disaster of 10/11 May 1941, the station being situated on the important elevated four-track ex-LC&D City line of the SR (Eastern Section). Two large bombs had struck the station – only five days after it had been reopened after damage on 16/17 April. Men are hard at work and have already cleared the wrecked buildings on the Up Through/Down Local platform. Some of the overall roof of the Through platforms is left, but there is a large gap in the Up Local platform where evidently a bomb has gone through the arch over Walworth Road.

Holborn Viaduct Station. Havoc in the small concourse, two days after the devastation of the station and the hotel above in the raid of 10/11 May 1941. Believe it or not, the station was already open again, but damage down the line prevented any trains being run for several more days. The station remained more or less like this until it was completely rebuilt in 1963.

Holborn Viaduct to Blackfriars. View to Blackfriars station, two days after the raid of 10/11 May 1941, past the remains of Ludgate Hill station, which closed in 1929 but survived the Blitz – the ugly 1860s tower had supported its roof. The roof of Blackfriars is devoid of glass and adjacent commercial buildings are shattered. On the right are the girders of the bridge over Ludgate Hill.

Holborn Viaduct. As above the devastated concourse two days after it was gutted on 10/11 May 1941.

St Pancras. After the night of 10/11 May 1941. The wreckage as seen from the approach road by Platform 4 over to No. 1. It looks as if the horse-box still has an occupant.

St Pancras. View from Platform 4 to No. 1 and the entrance, featuring the gaping hole made by a bomb that went through to the tunnel underneath about midnight 10/11 May 1941.

Somers Town Goods, St Pancras. General view westwards of wreckage in yard after the same raid.

Two months after the destruction of Southwark Street Bridge on 19/20 April, all tracks have been restored and London was granted a rest from the heavy air raids for an extended period of time.

The Respite: Mid-1941 to the end of 1943

After the great raid of 10/11 May 1941, the Blitz was virtually over. For a long time London endured no further significant attacks at all. In 1941, only a fairly minor raid on the night of 27/28 July caused casualties (especially in Poplar).

It was then really not until 1943 (17/18 January) that the enemy raided London again. This was still only a 'training' attack (in two waves, 40 and 50 planes), on the Royal Docks. Significant damage was done (eight medium fires, 78 people killed) and total immobilization of Blackwall Point Power Station, but the bombs were scattered owing to improved defences and enemy inexperience. A similar ineffective night raid was made on 3/4 March, but on that occasion a dreadful stampede on the escalator at Bethnal Green Underground station/shelter

killed 173 people. An unexpected low-level attack in daylight on 20 January by 22 FW 190 fighter-bombers was far more effective, with 53 fatalities,[81] though a repeat on 12 March was much less successful. Small 'nuisance' attacks by fighter-bombers were kept up during 1943 over many parts of the country, the London Region being visited on about 25 occasions. Their effects on London were in general slight, but bad incidents included the burning of the Mount Pleasant GPO Sorting Office on 17 June and the killing of 76 people in the Putney Dance Hall on 7 October. Apart from the January 1943 attack, for 2¾ years little damage or inconvenience due to enemy action was experienced by the railways in London and most incidents reported were fairly trivial.

28/7/41

LMS: Old Ford 03.20: HE in Up Goods yard blew rail onto Up line. Latter clear 05.15, Goods Yard 11.55.

Channelsea Junction 03.30: LMS lines blocked by debris from HE on south (LNE) side.

South Bromley – Poplar 03.30: Lines blocked by fire at Spratt's factory. nwr 06.00 28/7.

LNE: Stratford, Channelsea Junction and Fork Sidings 03.10: HE on Cairns' premises blew crane and girders onto railway, blocking all lines. Signalbox damaged and Block down. Damage to 21 coaches. Traffic suspended Victoria Park – Stratford LL. SLW 08.00, nwr 16.00 29/7.

SR: Feltham 02.40: In Yard Up Hump Box and eight sidings damaged. Two staff injured. Both lines damaged Feltham Junction – Feltham East, also bridge over River Colne. UXB reported. nwr 18.55.

25/8/41

LMS: Stonebridge Park – Harlesden 06.45: Further subsidence affecting Up Electric line, so SLW over Down Electric. Steam shuttle operated Wembley – Euston to supplement electric service. At 18.50 a loco derailed on Up Electric, so line blocked again. From 20.45 traffic running over Up Electric at 5 mph. Closed again for repairs, 10.30–14.00 25/8.

1942

10/2/42

LMS: Walthamstow – Leytonstone 10.35: House, previously damaged in Blitz, subsided, blocking Up line. SLW (freight only) until 12.00. Buses substituted Leytonstone – Blackhorse Road, until passenger service restored 14.50 12/2, with SLW over Down line. Up line reopened 12.30 18/2.

28/7/42

LMS: Old Ford 02.50: Explosion of AA shell injured one staff.

SR: Erith – Crabtree Crossing 03.33: Shrapnel cut telecom, until 08.40.

1943

17/1/43 (Sunday)

LMS: East Ham 21.15: AA shell damaged roof of Platform 9. Traffic run over Up line. No delays. nwr in morning 18/1.

SR: Blackfriars – Elephant & Castle 20.30: HE buckled Up Local line. Block failed 20.36 – 00.11 (18/1). Lines reopened 19/1, 04.20 (steam), 11.10 (electric).

Peckham Rye 20.49: Station glass damaged by blast from HE nearby.

Tulse Hill 20.51: Block to Peckham Rye failed until 00.10, also Peckham Rye – Denmark Hill until 02.30.

New Cross Gate 22.15: Wagons and sleepers set on fire and damaged.

18/1/43

LNE: Leman Street 05.00: AA shell exploded under bridge on Down Fast line. Traffic diverted to Slow line under caution. nwr 09.40.

Lord's Tunnel, near Marylebone 07.40: DAB exploding on Lord's Cricket Ground caused debris to fall in tunnel. Lines clear, but owing to another UXB, all passenger trains in/out Marylebone suspended. Trains terminated at Harrow or Neasden and passengers diverted onto LPTB as far as West Hampstead, thence by bus. Booked service recommenced from Neasden Emergency Platform with 14.05 (Marylebone) to High Wycombe; Met&GC Joint trains also operated from this platform. Certain additional services run from Paddington in lieu. UXB removed 17.00, but tunnel wall damaged. Debris cleared and nwr 22.00.

Marylebone Goods Yard 08.00: Large UXB found in Hinchcliffe Sidings, so all working stopped. Although UXB not removed, all work resumed 19/1, except for barge traffic.

On 20/1 UXB in Hinchcliffe Cripple Siding prevented work in coal yard and barge wharf. On 29/1 at 16.30, nwr except Hinchcliffe and Foster's Yards.

Forest Gate 10.45: AA shell damaged Down Slow line. All traffic suspended until 11.15 while Engineer in possession.

SR: Charlton 10.00: UXLM closed Maze Hill and Blackheath lines, also part of goods yard from 13.50. Up services terminated Woolwich Arsenal, thence buses provided. Greenwich lines reopened 17.30, North Kent lines and goods yard 18.21.

Isleworth – Syon Lane 10.30: Up line damaged by AA shell. Trains run at caution until nwr 14.00.

Kidbrooke – Eltham Well Hall 10.56: Both lines blocked on account of five UXB. Services terminated at these stations and buses provided between. nwr 14.47, but lines closed again 11.08 23/1, with SLW from 24/4. Two UXB removed 17.20 4/2.

20/1/43

GW: Surrey Commercial Docks: GW motor vehicle destroyed in air raid while delivering. Crew uninjured, but those in another – undamaged – vehicle hurt.

SR: North Kent East Junction Box 12.32: Slight damage caused by blast from HE's off Up side.

Norwood 12.45: Loco yard machine-gunned. One locomotive[82] slightly damaged. No casualties.

21/1/43

SR: New Eltham – Sidcup 15.24: Lines closed, by UXB from 17/1. Buses substituted. SLW 14.10 22/1. nwr 14.50 28/1.

23/1/43 (Saturday)

SR: Kidbrooke – Eltham Well Hall 11.08: UXB found near Up side, so all traffic stopped. Screen of wagons put on Up line, then SLW at 5 mph 14.41 until nwr 17.25 4/2.

1/3/43

SR: Old Kent Road Junction – Queen's Road, Peckham 12.15: Crack found in Old Kent Road underline bridge – presumably caused by earlier air raid damage, making it unsafe for Down line. Cancellations or diversions imposed until 16.45, then Down line reopened at 10 mph SpR.

3/3/43

LMS: Willesden, Brent Sidings South End 21.23: HE damaged four wagons. nwr 12.00 4/3.

SR: Honor Oak Park 21.02: AA shell blocked Up and Down Main and Down Local lines. All cleared 00.45, nwr 13.00 4/3.

Old Kew Junction 22.30: Rail buckled on Up line by AA shell. SLW from Brentford from 05.10 until nwr 07.15 4/3.

North Kent East Junction 22.38: Greenwich lines closed owing to UXB. nwr 23.05.

4/3/43

SR: Upper Sydenham: Substation damaged.

5/3/43

SR: Parks Bridge Junction – Hither Green 10.42: During removal of UXB of 11/40, Down Local line closed; 5 mph SpR on other lines. Down Dartford Loop trains run via Bexleyheath, with shuttle Lee – Dartford and buses for other passengers. Down Local reopened (5 mph) 22.28 6/3. UXB removed and nwr 12.10 7/3.

6/3/43 (Saturday)

SR: Hither Green: UXB found in Up Yard near No 7 road, affecting parts of Nos 6, 7 and 9 roads. Down Local blocked, 5 mph SpR on other lines, until 10.23. Blocked again 11.45 7/4, while UXB detonated, then nwr 12.10.

12/3/43

LNE: Seven Kings: 07.17 local train Gidea Park – Liverpool Street machine-gunned. No damage or casualties.

Ilford 07.35: HE in vicinity of Carriage Sidings, damaging Goods office and signalbox windows.

Goodmayes 07.41: Goods train in Down Yard machine-gunned.

17/4/43 (Saturday)
LNE: Bounds Green 00.15: HE in vicinity damaged wires and No.2 Control circuit with Knebworth. Block failed to Gordon Hill, restored 07.45.
SR: New Cross Gate 01.15: HE exploded in Millwall Football Ground. Debris thrown onto Deptford Lift-Bridge – Old Kent Road Spur line. nwr 07.53.

28/4/43
LMS: Dunloe Street, near Broad Street 22.34: Timbers on fire stopped traffic on No.2 Up and Down lines. Electric services terminated at Dalston Junction until 04.35.

17/5/43
SR: Crofton Park 01.20: HE blew out windows of station and signalbox. Parcels office and Porters' room damaged.
Waterloo 07.40: Electric train derailed outside station, blocking Up Main Local line and causing loss of current to Platforms 1–7 lines, also affecting W&C line. Normal current 08.50. nwr 14.25. [This incident possibly not due to enemy action].

20/5/43
LNE: Temple Mills 02.10: AA shell exploded in No.5 road of carriage sidings, damaging three coaches and track.

22/5/43 (Saturday)
SR: Sanderstead – Upper Warlingham 03.30: AA shell-burst caused Block failure. Traffic operated by TBW, until nwr 09.20.

13/6/43 (Sunday)
LNE: Stratford, Channelsea Carriage Sidings 03.00: HE fell between Nos 13 and 14 roads, striking wagon of oil. Much damage to rolling stock by fire. One quad-set and five wagons destroyed. Fire extinguished by 04.52, but all communications cut at Channelsea Junction Box and blast damage at Stratford station, and to Central, Fork Junction and Loop Junction Boxes. No.13 road reopened 11.30, but telecom not restored until 04.45 14/6.

15/6/43
GW: South Greenford Halt – Drayton Green Halt 00.50: HE damaged waiting shelters and telegraph wires.

15/9/43
SR: Nine Elms 22.10: AA shell exploded in Central Yard, damaging six wagons (one by fire).

7/10/43
LMS: Hampstead Heath – Gospel Oak 22.00: HE blocked both lines. Down clear 09.30, Up (for freight only) 12.00 8/10. Electric services reversed at Finchley Road and Gospel Oak, with buses between. nwr 16.00. Freight working GW – Temple Mills especially affected. From 20.00 8/10, passenger service restricted to hourly to allow clearance of freight traffic.
LNE: Highgate, Park Junction 22.00: HE badly damaged track and cut cables. Service resumed in morning under SpR. nwr 16.45 8/10.
SR: Bromley South 21.00: HE on Up Dock siding. Small crater and cut telecom to Shortlands. One passenger and one staff killed; seven passengers and two staff injured. TIW, until telecom restored 06.10, Block 11.10 8/10.
Forest Hill 21.00: HE in goods yard damaged Down Local line, siding and retaining wall.
Hinchley Wood – Claygate 21.00: HE nearby damaged Up line. All telecom cut Hampton Court Junction – Claygate. Line repaired 05.18, then TIW. nwr 09.17.

8/10/43
LNE: Stratford, Chobham Farm Junction 10.20: Locomotive derailed, blocking Up and Down Goods and Down Main lines. SLW Loughton Branch Junction – Polygon Box.

King's Cross 02.45: One staff killed and another injured near No. 10 platform. Cause not stated.
SR: Bricklayers Arms – New Cross Gate in night: AA shells made seven three-foot craters in bank on Down side, but lines not affected.

17/10/43 (Sunday)
GW: West Drayton 01.30: HE behind yard damaged static water tank. Repaired 18/12.

18/10/43
SR: Herne Hill Sorting Sidings 10.45: UX AA shell blocked No.3 siding until 16.00. Siding closed again for digging 08.30 26/10. Reopened 12.00 11/11.

19/10/43
LNE: Sudbury Hill 22.25: HE adjacent to station. Block and telecom cut to Sudbury & Harrow Road. nwr 15.50 20/10.

21/10/43
LMS: East Horndon – Upminster 01.04: HE blew out Up line. Passenger trains diverted via Tilbury. SLW 03.52 East Horndon station – Canon Box, until nwr 10.00.
LNE: Woodford 01.32: AA shell damaged crossing-gates and wires. nwr 09.00.
SR: Sidcup – New Eltham 01.00: HE damaged Block and telecom, also Sidcup station. Telecom restored 12.00 21/10.
Lee 02.55: Both lines blocked by UXB. Buses substituted Mottingham – Grove Park. nwr 09.20.

28/10/43
Of numerous incidents involving barrage balloons or their cables, this one deserves mention. At 05.52 between Honor Oak and Lordship Lane (SR), a balloon fell right in front of the 05.46 EMU Crystal Palace HL to Holborn Viaduct, but the driver saw it and was able to stop the train. The current was cut off and the branch services cancelled only until 07.07.

5/11/43
SR: Raynes Park – Malden 22.35: UXB 50 yards from Down side. SpR 5 mph all traffic. At 11.10 6/11, BDO instructed all traffic be stopped until wagon screen provided on Down Local line. Set up 12.28, when Through and Up Local lines reopened, with main-line trains diverted.[83] Screen removed and Down Local reopened (5 mph) 21.42 9/11. UXB made harmless and nwr 15.10 20/11.

6/11/43 (Saturday)
SR: Addiscombe 21.50: Station damaged by HE nearby.

1/12/43
SR: Kingston – Teddington 20.05: AA shell cut traction cables near Kingston Junction Box. Current failure on Down side, including Kingston bay line. nwr 00.01.

18/12/43 (Saturday)
SR: Chelsfield – Knockholt 22.28: HE on track blocked both lines, also electricity pylon brought down and cables strewn across line. At Knockholt, windows smashed and Down siding damaged, also two wagons, a ballast-brake and horse-box damaged. Local trains reversed at Chelsfield and Knockholt, with buses provided between. Main-line trains diverted via Swanley, Otford and Sevenoaks. nwr (15 mph SpR) 15.36 19/12, lifted 11.00 11/1/44.

20/12/43
LNE: Devonshire Street, Mile End 06.00: Local lines blown out by HE that fell in Lower Yard. Reception line and slip damaged. Staging in girder bridge carrying Local lines dislodged and seriously damaged. Staff mess rooms, two platelayers' huts and weighbridge hut damaged, also one locomotive, 26 wagons and one coach. All telecom and lighting damaged, but repaired by 13.00. Three staff injured. Traffic over Local lines suspended until 09.00, then run at 15 mph. Meanwhile trains run at caution over Through lines, with Loughton trains diverted to Fenchurch Street.

Paddington. The Little Blitz: at about 1am on 22 March 1944 a large bomb fell through the roof onto Platforms 6 and 7. The view of the havoc, taken from Platform 8 looking across to Platform 1, shows men just starting to clear up, while passengers alight from a train almost as if nothing had happened. Only "some services were cancelled", and things were back to normal four days later.

The Little Blitz

Early in 1944, the Germans attempted a limited reprisal for the devastation they themselves were suffering from Allied bombing. In the face of Britain's greatly improved defences, with just some 400 bombers (including a few HE177 'heavies' and a variety of new navigation aids), they put on another succession of night raids of short duration, mainly on London – Operation 'Steinbock' (for us, the 'Little Blitz'). In this offensive, unlike in 1940–41, the Luftwaffe proved decidedly inept. They usually chose cloudy nights and bombed from high altitudes, attacking London on 14 occasions. They commenced on 21/22 January, when it was intended to drop 500 tons of HE, but actually only 32 tons fell on the capital; similar pathetic outcomes resulted on 29–30 January and 3–4 and 13–14 February. Much more successful were the two attacks made on 18–19 and 20–21 February. In these, 428 people were killed and two major and seven serious fires caused. Several factories were wrecked and seven hospitals were hit, also the Treasury and St Paul's School (Hammersmith). Further less serious raids occurred on 22–23 and 23–24 February and 69 more people died in London. In March attacks were made on 14/15, 21/22 and 24/25, but with limited success: about 335 tons of bombs in all were dropped and about 110 people were killed. The last raid of the series was on 18/19 April (53 tons, 39 killed).

Damage and disruption was suffered by the railways in the Little Blitz, although usually it was not very serious – and quite often due to our own very vigorous anti-aircraft-fire.

January 1944

2/1/44 (Sunday)
LMS: Euston 19.30: Points damaged by HE at No. 2 Box, blocking Up Fast and Up Slow. nwr 04.00.

5/1/44
SR: Barnes Bridge – Chiswick 23.10: Suspected UXB in foreshore under bridge on Surrey side. SpR 5 mph on both lines, but UXB discounted and nwr 09.05 6/1.
Norwood Yard 19.51: Explosion of AA shell damaged shunters' lobby and lamp room.

15/1/44 (Saturday)
SR: Chessington – Tolworth: UXB suspected 40 yards from Up line. Trains terminated Tolworth and buses provided on to Chessington. Later found to be an exploded shell, but lines not reopened until 15.09 16/1.

21/1/44
LMS: Purfleet Rifle Range Halt – Rainham 21.05: HE 75 yards from line brought down all wires. TIW applied. nwr 09.40 22/1.
SR: Maze Hill – Westcombe Park 21.27: HE damaged Down line. Both lines closed, but Up line found to be clear. Porter seriously injured by shrapnel. nwr 04.48 22/1.

22/1/44 (Saturday)
LMS: Kentish Town, in night: HE damaged railway wall at Gainsford St. Poplar 08.50: Up and Down lines blocked by four UXB near coaling wharf between East India Quay and Poplar Central. UXB removed and nwr 13.40 26/1.

LNE: Chingford 04.00: Both lines blocked by derailment of light engine. 03.58 Local to Liverpool Street ran into the obstruction, and two passengers injured. Liverpool Street services turned round at Wood Street, with buses thence to Chingford. Both lines clear 11.00 and trains passed at caution until nwr 14.00. [Enemy action?]

Hadley Wood 05.10: Driver of 21.40 express Leeds to King's Cross on emerging from Ganwick Tunnel saw IB falling on line. Train was stopped in tunnel and 20 IB extinguished by enginemen, then train resumed at caution. nwr 06.10, but UXB found near Ganwick Tunnel, so passenger trains diverted via Hertford North while freight trains allowed to pass at 5 mph. Buses provided New Barnet – Potters Bar. Passenger services restored (SpR 5 mph) 23/1 with 11.05 ex-King's Cross and 12.36 ex-Hitchin. nwr after UXB put in 'Category C' 16.30 23/1.

SR: Victoria, Grosvenor Road Carriage Sidings 04.31: IB set fire to roof of coach. Extinguished 05.52.

Beckenham Junction – Shortlands 10.30: Two UXB near line. Both lines closed, but reopened 12.50 after bombs found of "small calibre". However, on 2/2 UXB found 25 yards from Up side, removed 16.30.

Malden – Norbiton 15.50: Both lines closed after hole found near Up line. Subsequently ascertained hole due to AA shell, so nwr 17.09 (15 mph SpR on Up line until 10.00 29/1).

29/1/44 (Saturday)

LMS: Poplar: HE heavily damaged buildings and two signalboxes.

LNE: Leytonstone 21.15: Two HE fell. One fell on station subway, where some passengers trapped. After wreckage cleared 31/1, reported that four people killed, two injured (all members of public). The other bomb fell 70 yards south of station, destroying SM's office and arcade and damaging waiting-rooms. Lines blocked. Buses substituted Leyton – Snaresbrook (Leyton – Leytonstone from 1/2). Damage cleared and craters filled 31/1. Lines reopened 12.00 2/2, but station not until morning of 7/2.

Stoke Newington 20.45: Station damaged by AA shell, also wires down. Communications restored 31/1.

Temple Mills 21.15: IB in Yard. Only damage to wires between South and North Boxes. nwr 11.00 30/1.

Gidea Park – Harold Wood 21.00: 'Missile' – later found to be UX AA shell – on Southend Road overbridge. All traffic stopped until 23.35.

SR: Clapham Junction 09.05: AA shell exploded on Platform 12, damaging windows and roof stanchion.

Bricklayers Arms 21.00: HE nearby damaged Mileage and Weighbridge offices, 'L' shed and shunters' cabin, also Mercer's Crossing Box.

Erith 21.15: HE damaged both lines and Up platform. UXB in Down goods yard, not affecting traffic. Down line reopened 06.05, then SLW until Up reopened (15 mph SpR) 09.53. UXB removed and nwr 10.30 30/1.

Belvedere – Erith 21.15: HE nearby damaged crossing-house at Pembroke Road. British Plasterboard Siding at Crabtree damaged; 12 wagons shut in and slightly damaged.

Mottingham 21.20: HE nearby damaged station buildings on Up and Down sides.

Victoria 21.20: BB cables fell across Eastern Section Carriage Shed and all lines over Grosvenor Road Bridge. All cleared 22.22.

31/1/44

SR: Waterloo 03.25: Barrage balloon down on signal gantry near station and all lines closed. Main lines reopened 04.10, Local lines 06.00.

February 1944

4/2/44

LMS: Dagenham Dock: HE damaged Foreman's and shunters' cabins also several wagons.

Rainham 06.10: HE blocked Through lines. Down line clear 11.50. nwr 13.50.

LNE: Romford – Chadwell Heath 05.10: Down Local line damaged by AA shell. Traffic worked over Down Through line. nwr 08.47.

Goodmayes 05.10: IB caused six fires in coal dump.

SR: West Dulwich 05.30: Extensive damage to station by HE off railway.

Belvedere – Greenhithe, Barnehurst – Dartford 05.30: HE caused failure of current. Lines closed for examination. Buses substituted. Current restored by 10.30.

Crayford Creek Junction 05.44: HE damaged signalbox and apparatus. Signalman injured. From 10.30, traffic resumed Slades Green Junction – Crayford Spur 'A' Box[84] under TIW, then Slades Green Junction – Crayford Creek Junction signalled by TBW until normal 18.00 including Crayford Creek Junction – Crayford Spur 'A'. At 16.10, traffic resumed Perry Street Fork Junction – Crayford Creek Junction, signalled by TBW. Normal 19.00.

Slades Green 05.45: HE damaged Inspection Shed and Repair Shop, also smashed windows of 12 electric sets. Carriage-washing machine and staff canteen also damaged.

Crayford Creek Junction – Crayford Spur 'A' Box 19.15: Block instruments and bells failed again. Rectified 09.45 5/2.

6/2/44 (Sunday)

LNE: Stratford early morning: Exploding AA shell damaged CME's Tool Shop and fractured gas main.

13/2/44 (Sunday)

GW: Paddington, Westbourne Bridge Box 20.50: AA shell exploded on Up Carriage line, damaging water main, also Block and telecom. Down Carriage line out of use also until 22.10. Block and telecom restored 02.45, Up line 03.40, then nwr.

19/2/44 (Saturday)

GW: Old Oak Lane Bridge (North Acton – Viaduct Junction) 01.00: HE damaged both lines and telecom. Down line clear 12.00 21/2, Up line 08.00 28/2.

Goldhawk Road (H&C) 01.15: HE partly demolished bridge. Lines damaged. H&C service not restored until 17.00 9/3.

Paddington 01.30: Five wagons (four loaded and one empty) damaged by IB. One soldier injured by falling IB. nwr 02.25.

LMS: West Hampstead (Mid.) 00.40: HE practically demolished station buildings and all lines blocked. Down Local line clear 02.00, Up Local 02.45. Down Fast clear 12.20 19/2. All lines in order 14.50 21/2, but station still closed owing to damage.

Gospel Oak 01.05: Station buildings and platforms set on fire. Lines blocked. Up clear 01.45, Down 02.45. UXB in Goods yard 08.35, removed 12.00 20/2.

Canonbury 01.30: Station buildings badly damaged by HE and fire, also wood panels of overbridge. Block and telecom destroyed. All lines blocked. No. 1 lines soon cleared, but No. 2 (Electric) lines closed until 10.48 21/2. Electric service operated Broad Street – Dalston and Highbury – Richmond/Watford, with buses Highbury – Dalston. Station remained closed until 3/4.

Kilburn High Road 01.33: Brake van and empty wagons damaged and cables burnt by IB. Block and signalling cut. nwr 09.20 21/2.

Kilburn High Road – Queen's Park 04.30: UXB found. All traffic stopped until 05.00, when working resumed over steam lines only at 5 mph. Up Electric line reopened 08.00 with SLW. SpR on steam lines withdrawn in evening. On 19/2, UXB "fired last night" but Down line still closed, until 10.45 20/2.

Highgate Road: Several wagons of freight train in station damaged by fire. Station closed until 12/3.

Broad Street, Kenley Street stables: HE killed two horses and injured others.

Haydon Square 05.40: UX AA shell found in depot and all working stopped.

Mortimer Street Junction 05.52: UXB by signalbox, blocking LL lines from Kentish Town and Midland Division – T&H line. Trains worked over HL, Kentish Town Junction – Junction Road. Also power supply to Kentish Town Locomotive Depot cut, disabling coaling plant until overnight 19–20/2. UXB removed and nwr 05.20 20/2.

Kentish Town, HL line 08.30: UXB found. Freight trains only allowed past. Passenger service run Upper Holloway – Barking only. Goods lines Hendon – St Pancras affected, also to T&H line. UXB cleared and nwr 13.00.

Kentish Town, Highgate Road Junction: UXB on Gospel Oak side of signalbox. All traffic stopped on T&H line and Western Division. UXB cleared and nwr 13.00.

Kentish Town, Carlton Road Junction – Mortimer Street Junction: UXB discovered behind wall 11 yards from HL line – but all traffic stopped already by above-mentioned UXB. UXB cleared and Up line reopened 09.35 20/2. Down line repaired and nwr 12.00.

LNE: Bishopsgate 01.00: Wagon of meat destroyed by fire from IB.

King's Cross, Top Locomotive Shed: Two UXB found, but no interference with working. Also two UXB in Goods yard.

SR: Point Pleasant Junction 00.50: HE fell on factory and much debris fell on track. Damage to signalbox and apparatus. All lines closed. Up Trains terminated Barnes. Passengers conveyed on to Clapham Junction by buses. Reading trains diverted to main line via Chertsey. Local lines reopened 09.35, with TBW. Through lines clear 11.25. No traffic until Block restored on Local lines 17.45 19/2, on Through lines 10.40 20/2, then nwr Clapham Junction – Putney. Signal repairs on East Putney line completed and nwr 16.20 20/2.

White Hart Crossing (Barnes – Mortlake) 00.50: Crossing Box damaged by HE and all telecom failed. TIW in operation. (It later transpired that there was "no interference to traffic")!

Wimbledon 01.05: HE in East Goods Yard damaged sidings and many wagons. Telecom to East Putney destroyed. Damage put Nos 2–5 sidings out of use and prevented use of Nos 1 and 2 LPTB Platform lines. Latter reopened 10.00. Nos 2 and 3 roads in sidings not reopened until 17.30 29/2, No. 4 16.30 1/3, No. 5 17.00 2/3.

Cannon Street 01.05: AA shell damaged No. 6 Platform line.

Plumstead – Abbey Wood 01.10: HE made large crater in track, blocking both lines. Freight train standing on Down line and its locomotive[85] partly fell into crater. Driver and fireman seriously injured. Four wagons damaged. All telecom destroyed. Three UXB also suspected, but later discredited. Down line clear and Block restored 10.45 20/2. SLW 11.20, until nwr (10 mph SpR) 14.43. In meantime, trains reversed Plumstead and Belvedere, with buses between. Gillingham trains diverted via Dartford Loop. nwr 14.30 2/3.

20/2/44 (Sunday)

GW: Paddington 22.00: Roof, top floor and new wing of Hotel damaged by fire from IB. Footbridge on Lawn damaged by fire and train indicator burnt out. Fire damaged Alfred Road garage and 12 vehicles, also Westbourne Park New Transit Shed and Mercer's Shed. One person killed, two seriously injured (one died later).

West Brompton (WLER) 22.00: Telecom destroyed. nwr 17.15 21/2.

North Acton – Hanwell – West Drayton 22.00: Telecom destroyed. Restored 17.15 21/2.

Latimer Road (H&C) 22.15: Station and signalbox damaged by HE. Metropolitan services, already suspended to Hammersmith, now reversing at Ladbroke Grove. SLW instituted 17.50 21/2 and service extended to Shepherds Bush. SLW extended to Hammersmith 24/2 with SpR. nwr not until 16.30 14/4.

Wood Lane (E&SB) 22.15: Extensive damage by HE and IB. LPTB

service suspended to Ealing Broadway. nwr 08.35 23/2.

Shepherds Bush (WLR) 22.30: HE damaged Exhibition Hall, sidings etc. Owing to UXB, depot vacated 16.30 21/2 until 26/2.

LMS: Kentish Town, City Sidings 22.07: Two compartments of suburban stock burnt out by IB. nwr 23.30.

Barking East: AA shell exploded near Stoney Road Bridge, damaging fencing, power cables and signal wires. Wires repaired 01.30 21/2.

LNE: Gordon Hill 08.55: Both lines blocked owing to suspected UXB. Shuttles run King's Cross – Gordon Hill and Crew's Hill – Hertford North, until 18.10 when BDO found only UX AA shell.

Manor Park 22.00: HE at entrance of Goods yard badly damaged Goods and other offices, also Moy's coal office completely destroyed. Signalbox damaged and switched out. nwr 09.45 21/2.

New Southgate 22.10: Signalbox, lamp room etc. damaged by IB.

SR: Spa Road 22.03: 21.22 EMU Dartford – Charing Cross struck by blast while passing. Many windows blown out, but no injuries.

Nine Elms Goods Depot 22.05: Damaged by fire, but extinguished by 02.15 were: 'H' and 'J' Sheds, Warehouse and Bonded Stores, General offices, several wagons, one road motor vehicle. Also damaged: Sheet & Rope factory, 17 wagons, seven road tractors, merchandise in 'H' and 'J' Sheds, South African Wine Co's store, electric crane on wharf, barge loaded with paper, many telephones.

Nine Elms Locomotive Depot 22.05: HE and numerous IB fell near Shed, blocking Nos 1, 3 and 4 roads. Coaling plant and main water tank damaged and several locomotives derailed or damaged.[86] Six motor vehicles and 17 wagons damaged. Coaler back in use and Nos 3 and 4 roads clear 11.45 27/2.

Stewarts Lane Depot 22.05: Numerous IB fell on Depot and Longhedge Works, damaging buildings and two wagons. Coal stocks ignited.

East Putney 22.05: IB fell through roof of empty train.

Whitton – Feltham 22.10: HE damaged both lines. Up clear for steam 06.45 21/2, Down 12.45. Current restored and nwr 13.05 21/2. Station buildings and signalbox damaged, also HT cables, resulting in failure of all TC at Feltham Junction and Feltham East and West Boxes, train indicators at Up and Down Humps and lighting of offices and yard. Rectified 16.28 21/2.

Nunhead – Peckham Rye 'B' 22.10: Blast caused failure of certain signalling at both Boxes. nwr 09.15 21/2.

Balham Intermediate Box 22.15: HE nearby blew out signalbox windows. Block out, until 23.40.

Chiswick 22.20: Lines blocked by damage. Station buildings and signalbox blasted. Lines reopened 08.00 23/2 and signalling repaired, but three UXB, so nwr not until 7/3. Combined disruption at Whitton and Chiswick entailed diverting Reading trains via Chertsey. Windsor services terminated Hounslow. Buses to Twickenham; special buses also covered interrupted section of Hounslow Loop.

UXB: Barnes – Barnes Bridge 22.30, removed 09.30 6/3; Southfields – East Putney 23.30, found to be IB 10.25 21/2; Clapham Junction – Earlsfield (traffic allowed to pass). One of Barnes UXB discredited 26/2, but lines remained closed. One removed 14.00 27/2, the third 13.45 4/3. nwr eventually 09.30 6/3.

Temporary failure of traction current occurred at several places. Most were short-lived, but failure Hounslow – Kew Bridge not restored until 07.05, and Twickenham – Feltham until 13.05 21/2.

London Exchange routes closed until 12.45 21/2: Battersea – Brent via Barnes, Feltham – East Goods via MWL.

21/2/44

LMS: Falcon Lane Goods Depot: Several craters found and Military stated lines unsafe, so working suspended. nwr 22/2.

LNE: Gordon Hill – Crews Hill 08.55: UXB on running lines, so both closed. Shuttle service arranged, but BDS eventually reported it was exploded AA shell, so nwr 18.10 (!).
SR: West Wickham 24.00: HE damaged station and signalbox.
UXB: Bricklayers Arms Goods 09.00, closed entrance to Depot, removed 12.35; Wandsworth Common, Down platform line closed and SpR on Local lines, later found to be exploded AA shell, cleared 14.40; East Putney 20.40, near signal-box, found to be phosphorus type, nwr 21.35.

22/2/44
Very severe Freight Restrictions currently in force on all Railways except SR.
LNE: Hornsey: Lines to Locomotive Shed damaged by AA shell, blocking in locomotives. nwr 10.00.
SR: Lewisham, Parks Bridge Junction 00.15: HT cable damaged by AA shell fouled Loop lines. Removed 03.30.
Mortlake 00.20: Booking office and roof damaged by IB, also wires severed. Traffic suspended until fires extinguished 02.00.
Nunhead 00.25: HE damaged cables, causing TC failure Elephant & Castle – Nunhead/Sydenham Hill. HSW in operation until restored 09.05.
Crayford Spur 'B' Box 00.35: Signalbox damaged by HE and communication failed Crayford Station – Dartford Junction. Signalman sustained shock. TIW in operation. Dartford Loop lines closed 00.35–04.15. Telephone restored 09.10, Block restored and nwr 14.00.
Feltham Yard 00.40: Cattle Dock gutted by fire from IB. Yard closed 01.00–07.20 owing to UXB at Ashford end. Exchange routes to East Goods, Willesden, Neasden and Brent closed in consequence.
Staines 01.05: HE caused CEB Grid to fall across locomotive. Lines blocked until 04.35.
Lee – Mottingham 02.45: Block cut by shrapnel damage to wires. TBW until rectified 20.30 23/2.

23/2/44
GW: Hanwell & Elthorne: SpR 5 mph over Wharncliffe Viaduct, owing to UXB nearby. Bomb discredited and nwr only at 16.51 27/2.
Chelsea & Fulham (WLER) 22.30: HE damaged (disused) station buildings.
LNE: Victoria Dock (PLA): HE by No. 3 Shed, south side. Foreman's hut burnt out.
Silvertown Tramway: Owing to bomb damage in Vinesta's Works, high chimney unsafe and traffic not allowed to pass. nwr 15.00 27/2.
Northolt Park 10.30: UXB discovered in Down line 100 yards from station and traffic stopped, but BDO authorised SLW 13.30 on Up line. Some trains diverted over Met&GC route, and shuttles run to Northolt Junction and Sudbury Hill. Restricted passenger service restored 16.00 until bomb removed 27/2.
Winchmore Hill 11.05: UXB 70 yards from line, so SpR 5 mph. Bomb rendered harmless and nwr 16.30 29/2.
SR: Feltham 01.00: Main lines and Yard closed owing to UXB. Cleared and nwr 10.15.
Old Kent Road Junction – Peckham Rye 'A' Box 13.28: IB caused failure of communications, so TIW. TBW 17.26, then nwr.
Beckenham Junction 22.00: AA shell exploded in Goods yard, cutting lines and damaging signalbox. Goods shed reopened 16.00 24/2.
Barnes East Box 22.13: Signalbox badly damaged by HE, closed and Block cut. Down Local line closed owing to state of signalbox. Traffic suspended owing to two UXB suspected opposite damaged East Box, but discredited 08.50. Down local line reopened 10.10 24/2, at 'caution'.
Hampton Wick 22.40: Station premises set on fire, also 22.28 EMU Kingston – Shepperton in platform. Guard injured, also one passenger injured and died later.
Teddington 22.40: Lines blocked by debris. nwr 00.35 24/2.

Berrylands 22.50: IB set fire to Up side booking office and Down side waiting room. 22.30 Waterloo – Dorchester express stopped 20 minutes to assist.

24/2/44
LMS: Acton Wells Junction 22.10: Lines blocked by debris from houses, until 03.10 25/2.
Euston 22.10: IB damaged two coaches in Carriage Sidings.
Walthamstow – Leyton 22.30: Block cut, until 09.35 25/2.
South Acton – Hammersmith Branch 22.30: Single goods-only line blocked by debris. nwr 11.30 25/2.
SR: Vauxhall – Queen's Road, Battersea 22.05: All traffic stopped owing to damage to Arch 64 and Down Windsor Local line and loss of current. Main Through, Windsor Through and Down Windsor Local lines cleared 03.53, current restored 04.03 and all lines clear 10.50 25/2. However, only Down and Up Main Through lines used at first (with HSW), then from 13.50 Windsor Local and Through lines. Current restored, Main Local lines reopened and nwr 16.25 25/2. SpR on Up Windsor Local line not lifted until 16.00 11/8.
Nine Elms Goods 22.05: Damage to Transfer Shed, Stationery Stores and other buildings, including stables where six horses seriously injured.
Vauxhall – Loco Junction 22.05: Blast struck 21.59 EMU Waterloo – Hampton Court passing over Wandsworth Road Bridge on Down Local line. Two staff killed and seven passengers injured in train; seven staff injured in yard below. Considerable damage to signalling severely dislocated Waterloo services. Most trains terminated Wimbledon or Clapham Junction, until evening rush-hour, 25/2.
Hither Green 22.07: Down Dartford Loop line and Down and Up lines 'A' Box – Hither Green Station closed, owing to explosion of AA shell. All lines reopened by 23.10. Signalling failed at 'A' Box, so HSW until nwr 02.15 25/2.
Brentford 22.10: HE nearby damaged station buildings and SM's house.
Kew Bridge 22.10: HE damaged retaining wall.
Wimbledon 22.10: AA shell exploded in station approach (LPTB side). Five casualties, with one killed.
Norwood Junction/Fork Junction – East Croydon 22.12: IB damaged traction supply, Block and stores.
Waterloo 22.15: AA shell exploded on roof over Platform 17, damaging platform. One staff and six passengers injured.
Stewarts Lane 22.40: Signalbox and rolling stock damaged by IB.
Waterloo – Loco Junction 22.42: Signalling failed. Restored 03.25 25/2.
Fulwell – Hampton: UXB near Burtons Road bridge. Lines closed. 25/2: Another UXB near Park Road bridge. One removed 27/2. SLW over Up from 04.55–16.20 28/2 for digging, again on 29/2, with SpR meantime. nwr not until 11/3.
Other UXB: Dundonald Road Crossing (Wimbledon – Merton Park) 12.40: Both lines closed, but only 50 kg bomb so reopened 15.45, then another of 250 kg further off required SpR 5 mph, clear 14.15 7/3.

25/2/44
LNE: Wood Green 01.15: Bomb crater over tunnel, so 10 mph SpR. nwr 10.50.
Traffic for SR (Western Section) severely restricted owing to damage at Clapham Junction and Acton. nwr 11.20.

29/2/44
SR: Lower Sydenham – New Beckenham 21.40: HE nearby cut telecom Up side. TBW until Block restored 00.20 1/3.
UXB: Southfields – East Putney 20.10: Bomb from 24/2 30 yards from Down side; traffic passing at caution while BDS working. Subsequently found to be an IB, so nwr 12.30 1/3.

March 1944

1/3/44
LNE: King's Cross Goods, early morning: AA shell exploded on Potato Market office and destroyed it.

2/3/44

SR: Brockley 02.55: HE damaged station footbridge. Debris blocked all four lines. nwr 05.25.

Streatham Hill 03.00: IB damaged three compartments of an EMU.

New Eltham 03.12: HE nearby smashed station and signalbox windows and destroyed all communications with Mottingham and Sidcup, so TIW. TBW restored 09.25, Block 10.33.

Brockley Lane 03.15: HE caused failure of signals and points. Lines available 05.20, Block restored 14.20, Up line signalling 15.20, Down line 18.15. Meanwhile, owing to suspected UXB (later found to have exploded), traffic Nunhead – Hither Green suspended until 12.50.

Plumstead – Abbey Wood 03.17: HE near track destroyed all communications, so TIW. nwr 14.50.

Elmstead Woods 03.20: IB caused extensive damage in Surveyor's office (evacuated from London), with loss of valuable records.

Lewisham – Parks Bridge Junction 04.38: Courthill Loop lines closed owing to UXB. nwr 12.50 2/3, but digging operations on 19/3 exploded phosphorus bomb, necessitating closure of Up Loop 07.00–14.35, with SpR 5 mph on Down line, until 16.00 20/3.

St John's 10.10: Collected from embankment New Cross – St John's, one of several IB exploded and injured three Engineer's staff.

Grove Park 10.20: UXB on Down Local line. Other lines (including Bromley Branch) closed progressively up to 12.19. All cleared 15.25.

14/3/44

LMS: St Pancras 23.05–23.40: HE and IB in Cambridge Street and Churchyard Sidings. Wires down and Block failure Cambridge Street – Dock Junction. Also, two UXB near Cambridge Street Box, where signalman injured. All traffic stopped and trains terminated/started Kentish Town, with buses to/from St Pancras. Block restored 00.20. Two UXB removed and Fast lines clear 10.50. Other lines clear and nwr 11.55 15/3.

Hatch End – Bushey & Oxhey 23.15: IB on line caused Block failure on all lines and of telecom Willesden – Tring. All lines blocked until working resumed 00.02, at 'caution' on Slow lines.

SR: Brentford 23.02: IB in goods yard, extinguished 23.30. Brake-van and footbridge damaged.

Shortlands Junction 23.09: Signalbox damaged, also substation. Block instruments failed, so TBW.

15/3/44

LMS: St Pancras Goods 00.20: Accounts Office destroyed by IB fire. Three staff injured. Stables burnt and four horses injured.

Commercial Road 01.10: IB set fire to two warehouses (one on hire to US Authorities).

Brent Sidings 12.25: UXB suspected between Nos 7 and 8 roads Up Sidings, necessitating screens of wagons in Nos 6–9. Other sidings unaffected. Subsequently discovered to be AA shell, which was removed 17.47, then nwr.

SR: Pouparts Junction – Clapham Junction 'B' Box 00.50: Conductor rail on Up Local line displaced by AA shell, which exploded 23.25. Main and Down Local lines closed until 01.37. Up line reopened 02.05 16/3.

Waterloo – Clapham Junction 00.50: Down Main Local and Main Through lines closed until 03.06, owing to un-ignited parachute flare on track.

Waterloo 'A' Box 02.20: Several IB showers on roof. Little damage, but one staff injured. Up Main Through line closed until 03.05 owing to rocket shell case embedded in track.

London Freight Exchange routes via MWL closed LMS (Midland) – Hither Green, Bricklayers Arms and Herne Hill. Alternative routes used.

16/3/44

GW: Paddington 13.45: Two 500 lb UXB found off railway near Ranelagh Bridge. 5 mph SpR on all lines. nwr not until 17.30 26/3.

17/3/44

GW: Paddington 12.00 (cf. 16/3): Down Main No. 1 Engine & Carriage line and Parcels Spur line closed. Down trains proceeded through yard at 5 mph and out at Westbourne Bridge Box, but UXB discredited and nwr 11.00 19/3.

22/3/44

GW: South Lambeth 01.00: HE damaged several roofs.

Paddington 01.05. HE fell between Platforms 6 and 7 at buffer end. Extensive damage to track and Platforms 4–8 out of use. Also. Station roof, buildings and coaching stock damaged by blast. Phosphorus bomb fell on Platform 9, setting fire to many mailbags. Also small bomb fell on Platform 11, damaging track, but failed to explode and was removed 10.15. "Some services cancelled". No. 4 line restored 07.00, No. 5 at 17.15, Nos 6 and 7 17.30 26/3.

LMS: Poplar Goods Depot 01.00: Many IB fell in 'A' Yard. Goods offices and stables gutted. Two horses killed and five injured. Timber footbridge connecting 'A' and 'B' Yards also destroyed. 'A' Yard out of use owing to suspected UXB – later found to be exploded IB. Passenger services Dalston Junction – Poplar terminated at Bow until 08.00. Freight traffic suspended. East Quay open 12.00. Midland side open and freight traffic moving 13.30. Coal and marshalling sidings to PLA and LNE (GN Section) remained open, but 'A' Yard, West Quay and New Dock cut off by damage to road bridge. nwr 13.00 24/3.

LNE: Chadwell Heath 01.20: AA shell exploded on Down Local line, moving track six inches. nwr 06.00.

Crouch End 01.50: Blast from HE nearby smashed station windows. Also destroyed Block and telecom Ferme Park No. 7 – Park Junction, Highgate. nwr 05.55.

SR: Hither Green Loco Depot, in night: Many IB fell, damaging roof, floor and two locomotives,[87] also telephone wires and cables.

Orpington 'A' – Petts Wood Junction 01.06: HE nearby damaged footbridge and cut all communications between these signalboxes. All lines closed for examination until 03.00, then TIW. Telephone restored 09.40, Block 12.00.

Vauxhall 01.15: Up Windsor Local line and Archer Street Bridge damaged by HE. All three Windsor lines closed. Debris from adjacent premises thrown onto Main Local lines, and all Main lines closed until 02.35. Up Main Through closed again 02.45–03.45 for clearance of debris. Reading and Windsor trains reversed Clapham Junction, with bus service to Waterloo. Windsor Local lines reopened 16.00, Through lines next day, all with 5 mph SpR. nwr not until 16.00 6/6.

Vauxhall – Loco Junction 01.15: Debris damaged point-rodding. Repaired 11.45 23/3.

Nunhead 01.30: Roof of booking office and platform canopy damaged by IB.

Eltham Well Hall 01.35: IB damaged wagon in goods yard.

Welling 01.40: IB on station and goods yard. Ladies' room, signalbox and three wagons damaged.

Grove Park 10.20: Owing to suspected UXB in bank on Down side opposite signalbox, Down Local line closed, also Up Local line at 11.05. All services worked over Main lines, 5 mph SpR. However, both Main lines closed 12.00 and evacuation of signalbox ordered 12.19, so trains diverted via Mid-Kent line and Bromley North branch closed. Bus service provided Hither Green – Chislehurst. Bomb later found exploded already, so nwr 15.25.

25/3/44 (Saturday)

SR: Beckenham Junction 00.05: AA shell exploding near Down siding broke windows of empty electric stock.

Elmer's End – Eden Park 00.10: IB set fire to Stanhope Grove Bridge. Current off on both lines, until 01.55.

Temple Mills 15.15: PAC in Loughton Yard, blocking six sidings; crater 15 x 30ft. 60 wagons damaged, with 16 destroyed. S&T Shop windows and instruments damaged, also windows in Leyton station. Stratford Control circuits Nos 4–6 cut. No casualties. Control circuits repaired 19.30 27/6, remaining three 12.00 28/6. All normal 15.00 29/6.

SR: East Putney 05.30: Station buildings and signalbox damaged.

27/6/44

LMS: Highbury 12.50: Station badly damaged by FLY. Several staff slightly hurt. No.1 (steam) lines blocked, owing to unstable buildings. Electric trains running on No.2 lines, but not stopping. No.1 lines clear 14.30. Normal 17.45.

Finchley Road – West Hampstead 05.35: Windows broken and all lines closed for examination until 09.50.

LNE: Hornsey – Wood Green 00.50: Blast from FLY smashed windows and displaced foundations of Carriage Shed, also windows of 10 coaches. Damage to Wood Green station and three signalboxes.

Clapton 15.20: FLY off railway near Down side in front of Goods offices, caused damage and cut wires. No. 4 Control circuit cut.

SR: Clapham 00.20: Signalbox badly damaged by PAC off railway property. Buildings damaged on Up Slow line and threatening Up Relief line, which was also closed 09.30.

Bricklayers Arms Junction 02.35: All Central Section lines blocked, also Bricklayers Arms Branch. Down Local line clear 12.40, other lines by 16.25. Damage was caused by FLY near signalbox at New Cross Gate Sidings, where windows blown out and Block destroyed. Signalman suffered shock. Block restored 16.30.

Deptford Lift Bridge Box 02.35: Structural damage done and all telecom cut. Signalman suffering shock.

Grove Park 04.00: PAC off railway property damaged signalbox. Block failed, but restored 08.30.

Walworth Road 22.42: FLY exploding nearby blocked all lines with debris. Through lines only clear 05.44. Up Local line cleared for steam 09.00, for electric trains and Down for both 14.30 28/6. Block failure also between Brockley Lane, Nunhead, Herne Hill, Denmark Hill and Peckham Rye until 23.45. 21.50 EMU Wallington – Holborn had many windows broken. Two staff and 25–30 passengers injured, two seriously. Block failed to Walworth Road Coal Sidings Box, so TBW. Freight exchange by MWL stopped until 05.54 28/6.

28/6/44

GW: Old Oak Common 12.30: Blast from FLY damaged Wagon Shop and smashed windows of East Box.

LMS: Finchley Road (Mid.) 05.35: Signalbox damaged. All lines closed, until 09.50.

South Tottenham (T&H) 11.45: FLY damaged offices, stables etc. at Goods Depot.

LNE: Tottenham 11.50: Three FLY off railway damaged windows at Tottenham West and South Junctions, Lea Bridge and Temple Mills North Boxes.

Wood Green 13.25: FLY off railway slightly damaged No.1 Box and cut No.2 circuit to Knebworth Control. Restored 29/6.

SR: Streatham Hill 01.06: FLY 200 yards away badly damaged station.

Clapham 13.43: FLY off railway extensively damaged goods and passenger stations. Debris on track and all lines closed. Reopened 14.50 (5 mph SpR), but SL trains not calling owing to debris on platform. At 15.40 SL lines again closed, owing to unsafe awning. One staff severely injured. Down SL line clear 15.40 29/6, Up 15.30 30/6.

Beckenham Hill 13.55: FLY off railway damaged station roof, windows and ceilings.

29/6/44

SR: Ladywell 02.04: Debris blocked both lines. Clear 07.40.

Beddington Lane 07.20 and 09.00 (two FLY): Halt and signalbox damaged by blast.

Wimbledon 10.32: FLY fell on empty EMU in No. 1 Carriage Siding, badly damaging train and killing motorman; two other staff injured. Ramp at west end of flyover carrying Up Local line damaged, also Down and Up East Putney lines. Debris on all lines. Lines reopened: Up and Down Through 12.30 for steam, 13.52 for electric trains; Down Local 15.50; East Putney lines for steam 14.00, electric trains 16.38; Up Local (10 mph SpR) 14.15 30/6. SpR not withdrawn until 16.00 22/9. No.1 Carriage Siding reopened 11.30 5/7.

Coombe Road 17.30: Station buildings severely damaged.

30/6/44

GW: Wood Lane (E&SB) 16.30: FLY off railway damaged steam lines at junction with United Dairies Siding, destroyed Wood Lane ground-frame and brought down wires North Acton – Viaduct Junction. Block restored 20.00, lines clear 21.30.

GW&LNE: Northolt Junction West 02.30: Block to Ruislip & Ickenham failed. nwr 16.00.

LMS: West Ham 00.10: Damage done at station, signalbox and Plaistow Loco.

Walworth Road Depot 00.15: Damaged (see SR below). nwr 13.30.

Romford 20.40 (see also LNE): FLY blew out single Upminster line 30 yards from station and destroyed ground-frame controlling LMS/LNE connecting line. Normal services to Upminster from 13.09 1/7.

LNE: Barkingside 15.50: FLY off railway did considerable damage to station.

Romford 20.40 (see also LMS): FLY temporarily blocked Up and Down Through lines. Traffic diverted to Local lines until 21.41.

SR: Walworth Road 00.15: FLY on Down side close to Bridge 381 badly damaged conductor rail supports, closing all lines. Local lines reopened for freight 03.00. Current restored 10.30 and Up line clear 12.05, Down Through at 13.00 (10 mph SpR).

Bickley 01.15: FLY fell on Down Local line, blocking all lines. Two 8-car EMU's in sidings badly damaged. Down Through and Up Local lines reopened 13.00, Up Through 13.40. nwr 20.10.

Greenwich 07.25: FLY off railway blocked both lines with debris and smashed windows. One staff seriously injured. Lines clear 09.00.

Nunhead 09.33: FLY off railway damaged cables and blocked both lines, also telecom to Peckham Rye. Lines reopened 10.55. TIW until 13.30, then nwr. Power also failed at Victoria, until 12.10.

Streatham Hill 10.25: FLY off railway damaged station roof, electric train, Inspection Shed and signalbox. Two carriage cleaners badly cut, others suffered shock.

Bromley Junction – Beckenham Junction 13.42: Both lines blocked by damage to Beckenham Road bridge (Birkbeck). nwr 18.19.

Wandsworth Common 14.25: FLY off railway blocked all lines and damaged wagons of passing freight, killing the guard. Through lines clear 15.39, Local lines 19.07. Signalbox windows smashed and shunter, driver and signalman suffered shock. All communications to Balham cut. TIW until nwr 19.05.

Bickley Junction 15.00: FLY off railway broke 10 windows in empty 13.04 EMU Victoria – Sevenoaks.

July 1944

1/7/44 (Saturday)

GW: Park Royal 06.30: Considerable damage by FLY near main line to signalbox and Old Warehouse in Goods depot, also several offices, cabins and 20 wagons.

Longhedge Junction (WLER) 16.05: Debris on line and minor damage.

LMS: Canonbury Junction 20.15: FLY fell adjacent to Down line, damaging wires and cutting Block Willesden Junction – Barnsbury. Traffic resumed 21.05.

Mill Hill 23.35: FLY fell near signalbox, breaking windows. Signalman injured. Damage to waiting-room, booking-office and SM's house.

LNE: Stratford, Abbey Gates 04.32: FLY nearby damaged signalbox and cut Control circuits until 08.50. nwr 17.35.

Alexandra Palace 07.02: Blast damaged station buildings. Glass smashed in waiting push-pull train and empty stock in sidings.

Stepney, Salmons Lane Bridge 18.20: Girders shifted slightly, so trains run at caution, until 09.45 2/7.

SR: Victoria 02.59: FLY fell close to Eastern Section carriage sidings near Grosvenor Road Bridge. Extensive damage to stock, glass of shed and boundary wall.

Beckenham Junction 03.07: Extensive damage to station buildings and SM's house. SM to hospital with shock.

Addiscombe 09.18: Both lines blocked by debris from FLY off railway, until 09.37. PW hut damaged. Windows smashed in signalbox, carriage shed and booking-office. nwr 14.03.

Welling 10.31: Debris blocked both lines. Station buildings and platforms damaged and signal blown down. Telecom and wires cut. Two staff injured. Lines and Block restored 14.03.

Greenwich 12.30: FLY on Lovibond's factory on Up side towards London. Station and platforms extensively damaged. Windows smashed in 11.48 EMU ex-Cannon Street. Five people, including booking-clerk, seriously injured; many others less seriously. After station buildings made safe, lines reopened 17.30 but station remained closed until 16.00 3/7. Current supply cut Sand Street – Plumstead and North Kent East Junction – Maze Hill; reinstated 14.44 and 18.30 respectively.

Shortlands 13.00: FLY 100 yards from Down platform. Station premises damaged and blast smashed windows in departing 12.31 EMU Holborn – Sevenoaks. Train proceeded to Bromley South, where one passenger taken to hospital. Others were cut and several suffered shock. Train taken out of service.

Angerstein Wharf 13.10: FLY on Harvey's factory by railway. Entrance to Harvey's and United Glass Bottle Co's Sidings blocked by debris and wires cut.

Streatham Hill 14.40: FLY fell 75 yards from Down side at Balham end, damaging carriage-washing machine and breaking windows of empty EMU.

Beckenham Junction 16.33: FLY nearby damaged station buildings and house, also signalbox. nwr 17.18.

Pouparts Junction – Longhedge Junction 20.50: FLY adjacent to lines blocked both. Clear 11.45 2/7. Longhedge Junction and Queen's Road Boxes damaged, destroying Block on WLER. Down Main Local line Queen's Road – Clapham Junction closed owing to displaced conductor rail. All traffic stopped in area while lines examined, until 22.10.

Waterloo – Vauxhall 23.34: Windows smashed in leading vehicle of 23.31 EMU Waterloo – Strawberry Hill. No injuries. All lines closed until 00.10 2/7 for examination, then 5 mph SpR.

2/7/44 (Sunday)
LMS: Maiden Lane Junction 12.45: All glass in signalbox smashed, also in York Road and St Pancras Junction Boxes. Signalman in Maiden Lane Box injured. Batteries for Block destroyed.

SR: Wimbledon Chase 00.10: Station buildings damaged. Lines blocked until 06.30.

New Cross Gate 02.15: Down and Up Main, Down Local and Deptford Wharf lines blocked, also Nos 1 and 2 sidings. Much damage to coaches in sidings. Main lines and No.2 siding clear 06.50. Down Local line 08.32, Deptford Wharf line and No.2 siding clear 18.00.

3/7/44
GW: Kensington Addison Road (WLR) 15.28: Damage to rolling stock in station, also glass and signals. Five milk tankers damaged.

LMS: Wembley 19.08: FLY fell on track and blocked all lines. Sudbury Junction Box damaged, telecom all out, also Block and TC instruments. Fast lines clear 19.45, Slow lines 20.15. From commencement 4/7, electric service Willesden – Euston and Bushey – Wembley, otherwise steam trains covering for electric service. nwr Sudbury Junction Box 09.00 4/7. Down Electric line clear 16.00, Up 18.15 4/7.

LNE: Custom House 16.25: FLY on PLA property damaged station and signalbox. Four wagons blown over and two damaged in Docks area. Trains cautioned, until 17.35 4/7.

SR: Battersea Wharf: FLY damaged Goods shed and offices.

Mitcham – Morden Road Halt 02.30: Blast damaged Goods shed and Emergency Repair Depot.

West Croydon – Waddon/Waddon Marsh Halt 04.15: Up Sutton line and Mitcham lines blocked by debris. Sutton line clear 07.10, Mitcham Goods line 10.00, single passenger line 11.30. Electric staff restored 17.00.

Streatham Junction South 04.35: All lines blocked by debris and signalbox damaged. Mitcham Junction lines reopened 10.10, Tooting lines 10.25. At Eardley Sidings, 51 vehicles damaged, including five Pullman cars and two Casualty Evacuation Trains. All telecom destroyed. nwr 17.30.

Lewisham Junction – Blackheath 07.02: Both lines blocked by debris of retaining wall, until 17.50. Lewisham Junction Box damaged and Block cut. nwr 19.00.

Maze Hill 07.40: Damage done to station buildings and windows of empty stock.

Lewisham Junction 17.02: Windows of booking-office smashed. Failure of train-describer, Block and phone St John's – Blackheath. Telecom restored 18.00, remainder 19.00.

Ewell West – Epsom 18.36: Both lines blocked after FLY fell near track. Stone's siding demolished and wires cut. Ground-frame and line clear 21.00, with TBW. nwr 14.24 5/7.

Clock House – Elmer's End 19.08: Block failed until 20.28. nwr 09.00 4/7.

Nunhead 23.59: FLY 15 yards off railway caused failure of power points and Block to Brockley Lane and Bellingham. Points rectified 01.30.

4/7/44
GW: Brentford Dock: FLY did considerable damage to buildings, sheds and hydraulic plant.

LNE: Snaresbrook 12.46: SM's house and offices damaged by FLY that fell at Eagle Lane.

Finsbury Park 19.30: FLY near station caused Block failure Harringay Up Goods – Finsbury Park No. 6. Restored 23.59.

SR: Sydenham Hill – West Dulwich 04.22: FLY nearby cut telecom and Block West Dulwich – Herne Hill South. TIW until 10.10.

Waterloo 08.50: Explosion of FLY nearby smashed windows of signalbox and substation. 08.17 EMU ex-Chessington South struck by blast and 12 windows broken. One passenger injured.

Morden South 08.52: FLY near line blasted station buildings and signalbox. 08.41 EMU Wallington – Holborn Viaduct had several windows broken, but no casualties.

Earlsfield – Wimbledon 10.03: FLY fell on track near Durnsford Road, damaging Through and Local lines. Through lines reopened 14.10, but only on TIW until some telecom restored 16.45, at 18.00 still only by TBW. At Wimbledon Park Depot, staff canteen, female carriage-cleaners' mess room and foreman's hut all damaged. Electric stock damaged in Repair Shop and in traffic sidings. Several staff cut by glass. Down Local line clear 19.35, Up Local 22.30 (15 mph SpR over flyover, until 5/7). Signalling restored 23.30.

Norbury – Thornton Heath 11.12: All Main and Local lines damaged by FLY on Up side. Local lines reopened 11.40, Main lines 12.50.

Ewell West – Epsom 18.40: Both lines blocked by FLY. Buses provided, until nwr 21.45.

5/7/44

LMS: Somers Town, St Pancras 14.20: FLY fell in Ricketts Wharf coal depot. Five lines at Somers Town damaged, but four restored by morning 7/7. Access to Milk Depot and Coal Wharf also blocked. Milk Shed damaged. Engineer's crane damaged by fire. 67 wagons damaged or derailed. Hydraulics at LL put out, but restored 7/7. Nine staff and two horses injured.

St Pancras Passenger Station: Slight damage to offices on Platform 7. Windows smashed at Station and Junction Boxes. Three empty coaches damaged, also LMS property in Midland Road and St Pancras Road. Twelve passengers suffered minor injuries or shock; one female staff and one Refreshment Room staff injured. At Euston House, superficial damage on ground and fifth floors.

LNE: Leytonstone 17.55: FLY 100 yards from station damaged windows and ceilings of waiting room and parcels office. Eleven windows broken on 16.48 train Epping – Liverpool Street, but no casualties.

SR: Sydenham Hill – West Dulwich 04.22: Blast damaged Block and telecom. nwr 10.10.

Sutton 05.40: FLY nearby damaged Langley Road bridge and two others. Lines reopened to Mitcham Junction 07.20, Wallington (5 mph SpR) 08.30. All telecom cut, so TIW until 09.30. Block restored 11.25.

Balham 12.50: FLY adjacent to station blocked Down Local line until 18.04. Down Local platform unusable and station buildings badly damaged. One staff injured. Line reopened 15.30 6/7.

Reedham 17.00: FLY 50 yards from station damaged railway cottages and station.

Victoria 18.10: FLY off railway damaged roof of CME's office and smashed windows and doors of substation. Substation attendant injured. nwr 16.10 6/7.

Deptford – Greenwich 18.10: FLY off railway damaged arches, blocking lines, which were reopened (10 mph SpR) 20.00. Block cut, so signalling by TBW. Hut used by Home Guard demolished, also tool shed and cables damaged. nwr 20.30.

Woodside – Elmer's End 19.20: FLY off railway blocked both lines with debris and cut telecom. Line clear 20.37, for TIW. At Woodside, windows of booking-hall and signalbox smashed.

6/7/44

LMS: Kentish Town West 06.45: Nearby FLY damaged 100 yards of conductor rail Kentish Town Junction – Kentish Town West Boxes, also several wagons of passing freight. nwr 09.50.

LNE: Silvertown 06.50: FLY in North Woolwich Road blocked lines and damaged 14 wagons. nwr by 17.00.

SR: Lordship Lane 06.45: Station buildings damaged. Debris on line.

7/7/44

LMS: Victoria Park 23.57: FLY in Hackney Wick Road damaged wires and Block in Victoria Park Box. TIW, until 11.15 8/7.

SR: Wimbledon – Merton Park 01.35: FLY nearby closed line until 02.55. Gatehouse windows at Dundonald Road Crossing damaged, also windows of Wimbledon 'B' Box.

Catford Bridge – Lower Sydenham 12.42: FLY caused Block failure until 13.50 8/7.

New Cross 14.35: Up ELR Goods line blocked by FLY on Cold Blow Siding at Bridge 58, which was damaged. Ground-frame badly damaged. East London Up Junction Box, Yard Inspector's office, shunters' lobby, CME Mess, Stores and offices, and empty electric and steam stock damaged. Trains stopped on ELR lines. ELR Goods line not reopened until 18.05 27/9.

Streatham Junction South – Mitcham Junction 15.37: FLY exploded between Down line and Eardley Sidings, displacing both conductor rails. All telecom failed, so TIW until 18.45, although lines reopened 17.23. Considerable damage to stock in Eardley Sidings. Three Engineer's staff injured. Current failed also Mitcham – Mitcham Junction, but restored 17.00.

West Dulwich 21.30: Station buildings blasted.

8/7/44 (Saturday)

LMS: Leyton 12.40: Much blast damage to Goods offices etc.

SR: Charing Cross 00.40: FLY fell close to river bridge. Damage done to windows and telecom including train-describers to Metropolitan Junction. Restored 04.15.

Chipstead 23.35: Station buildings and telecom damaged by blast from FLY. Lines reopened 00.42.

9/7/44 (Sunday)

LMS: Barking 14.45: FLY in Stevenage Road damaged Little Ilford No. 2 Box and Inspector's office in Yard. Damage done to 50 electric and 25 steam coaches in Little Ilford South Sidings and to wall of Carriage Shed.

LNE: Neasden 11.20: FLY fell on and demolished C&W Shop, offices and stores, Chief Electrical Engineer's Shop and staff canteen. Serious blast damage done to Neasden South Box, PW office and store, S&T Engineer's cabin and store, Terson's (contractors) shed, roof of Locomotive Shed and railway cottages. Damage to 80 yards of sidings. Rolling stock damaged or destroyed included six carriages, 34 wagons, two service vehicles and a Decontamination Unit. Out of 30 staff working in Shop, three killed, one missing, 13 sent to hospital (two died later) and four treated on spot; six canteen contractor's staff also injured. Lighting in Down Yard out, so emergency generators used. Destruction of overhead wires cut all communications. Block and telecom restored to Marylebone and Harrow 14.00, remainder (and lighting) 18.00. Improvised canteen provided from a kitchen-car and two saloon coaches.

Crouch End 12.07: FLY near Down line towards Highgate blasted station and railway cottages.

Rectory Road 14.30: FLY nearby caused damage to station.

SR: Nine Elms 00.30: FLY near Yard damaged Stationery & Printing Office, South Viaduct Box, Sheet & Rope Factory, 'H' and 'J' Sheds, Arches 50–57 and Yonder Hill saw-mills.

Lewisham 00.55: Windows smashed at station and Parks Bridge Junction Box.

Welling – Falconwood: FLY fell 50 yards from Up line – but did not explode. Both lines closed and trains terminated at Eltham Well Hall and Bexleyheath. Diversions via North Kent line. Bomb made harmless by 12.25 10/7.

Hinchley Wood – Claygate 23.50: Debris from FLY off railway blocked both lines. Clear 06.45, but telecom cut, so TIW until 12.16 10/7.

10/7/44

LNE: Thames Wharf Junction 09.20: FLY 75 yards away damaged Thames Wharf Junction Box. Signalman suffered shock. Goods office damaged and two staff injured.

Ferme Park Yard and Hornsey 15.09: Blast smashed windows of several signalboxes.

SR: Purley 05.11: Blast from FLY caused failure of electricity supply, for traction until 06.40, for signalling until 13.41 (generators used). Signal supply normal 05.45, traction 06.58 11/7.

West Wickham 14.25: Blast from FLY caused extensive damage to station and signalbox.

Forest Hill 17.38: Blast from FLY smashed signalbox windows, but blocked lines only for 10 minutes!

Bromley South 19.30: Windows smashed in 18.51 EMU Holborn – Sevenoaks, injuring three passengers. Windows of signalbox also broken.

11/7/44

GW: Royal Oak 14.41: FLY caused considerable damage to station, Westbourne Bridge Box, Goods shed, stores, offices etc.

LMS: Maiden Lane Junction 14.46: Lines from Camden Town blocked by debris until 15.00. Signalbox windows smashed.

SR: Cheam 09.30: FLY nearby blocked lines with debris until 09.50. Station and signalbox damaged and signalman suffered shock. Telecom to Ewell East cut, so TIW until phone restored 10.40. Block restored 13.40. Block to Sutton West also partially cut and Up trains signalled by TBW. nwr 19.38.

Crystal Palace LL 18.10: FLY caused considerable damage to station, also to one EMU.

12/7/44

LNE: Grange Hill 17.00: FLY fell in goods yard, blocking Up and Down lines. Booking-office demolished and staircase made unsafe. After clearance of lines, trains passed through without stopping, until nwr 16.30 13/7. Meanwhile, buses provided Chigwell – Hainault.

SR: Forest Hill – Sydenham 15.25: FLY fell between Down Local line and sidings at south end of Forest Hill station. All traffic stopped. Lines reopened 17.35–20.00.

Merton Abbey Goods 15.30: FLY in Board Mills damaged goods office. Two clerks injured.

Hither Green Sidings 'B' and 'C' Boxes 16.50: Blast caused Block failure, smashing windows in 'B' Box. Signalman suffered shock. Block restored 17.45.

North Kent East Junction – New Cross 16.57: FLY fell near Down Local line. All lines closed by debris, but clear 17.33!

Peckham Rye 19.15: FLY struck and badly damaged Cow Lane Bridge (rail-over-rail). Eastern Section lines to Nunhead and Central Section lines from Queen's Road all blocked. Current cables damaged. Access to LMS depot blocked. Exchange freight on Eastern Section diverted. Lines reopened (temporarily) for rush-hour 17/7, fully only from 16.00 21/7. Catford Loop reopened (10 mph SpR) 15.30 22/7. nwr not until 07.30 24/7.

Victoria 19.15: Signals failed, due to Peckham Rye incident (see above). Central Section trains terminated Clapham Junction, Eastern Section trains operated by HSW. nwr 21.45.

13/7/44

SR: Victoria (Central) – Pouparts Junction 15.42: Signalling failure, until 17.50. Victoria (Eastern) – Factory Junction 15.47: Signalling failure, until 17.28.

Sydenham – Crystal Palace LL 20.08: Telecom cut. TIW until 01.40 14/7.

14/7/44

SR: Selhurst 08.50: FLY fell nearby, while one Up and one Down train in station. Windows of both trains smashed. Several passengers and a guard injured. Telecom cut, so TBW until 12.26.

15/7/44 (Saturday)

LNE: Liverpool Street 15.40: FLY in Old Broad Street smashed windows and damaged Old Building and Hotel, also ceiling of West side booking-hall. No interference with traffic and no casualties.

SR: Freight exchange routes still blocked.

London Bridge 14.00: Windows of signalbox blown out. Other damage caused, including to a train. No casualties.

Nine Elms 15.18: FLY fell in Gas Works on Up side, damaging windows in New Warehouse and Locomotive Shed. Fireman of freight train injured.

16/7/44 (Sunday)

LMS: Bow Road Goods 12.15: Considerable damage to offices, also Devons Road Loco Depot.

LNE: Devonshire Street 16.55: FLY nearby blew out East and West Boxes, and blocked Through lines with debris. Four vehicles burnt out, five others damaged. Track in yard badly damaged and work stopped. Block and telecom cut East – West Boxes. Through lines reopened 17.15 and normal working 18.35 although telecom not restored until 22.35. Two

roads in yard restored and nwr from 18.00 17/7 – but less two roads, fully restored 10.00 19/7. 22/7: Retaining wall unsafe, so Nos 7 and 8 roads closed again.

SR: Wimbledon 00.15: FLY exploded directly on station, causing extensive damage to station buildings and blocking Up Local line and Nos 1–4 (LPTB) platforms with debris. Five staff taken to hospital and five others suffered shock. Six passengers in LPTB train cut by glass. Through lines closed for examination until 01.15. SpR of 5 mph over other lines. Up Local line cleared 14.30. Platforms 2 and 3 clear 17.15 then nwr, but Platform 1 not reopened until 20.20 20/7. SpR not removed until 16.00 27/10.

London Bridge 10.28: FLY fell in street near station. All Central and Eastern lines closed. One staff injured. Damage to brick arches feared, but not serious, so nwr 11.27.

Raynes Park – Malden 11.12: FLY fell on track, blocking all lines. Damage done to HT cables, causing loss of traction, signalling and Block supply for varying periods at Motspur Park, Chessington South, Hampton, Feltham, Gunnersbury and Richmond. Damage done to station, SM's house, coal merchants lobby and Sports Club. Lines reopened by 18.35, with 15 mph SpR on all lines except Up Local until 16.00 18/7, but nwr not until 12.00 20/7.

Queen's Road, Battersea 19.25: FLY nearby caused extensive damage to signalbox. Blast also smashed windows at station and in 18.28 EMU Tattenham Corner – Victoria. Many (including the guard) injured, nine passengers and a woman porter taken to hospital and 23 (including the motorman) given First Aid.

17/7/44

GW: Brentford Goods 05.30: Extensive damage done by FLY to warehouses, offices and some wagons.

LNE: King's Cross Goods 05.50: FLY did considerable damage to Potato Market, also General, Enquiries and Outwards offices.

Marylebone 10.45: FLY severely damaged Station Box, tracks, shunters' cabin etc., empty stock and wagons in Goods yard. Retaining wall badly fractured. Passenger station closed, but Platforms 3 and 4 reopened to limited service 15.30. One staff killed and 12 injured (one later died). Normal services from morning 23/7.

18/7/44

LMS: Dalston Western Junction 08.15: FLY nearby caused failure of traction current and Block, but alternative supply available 08.28!

Upton Park – Plaistow 16.30: Three rear coaches of LPTB District Line train blasted.

Barking – East Ham 18.20: FLY exploded near Down Local line, and windows of LPTB train broken. Points and Nos 2 and 3 roads blocked until 19.02.

LNE: Stamford Hill – Stoke Newington 18.20: Blast damaged Manor Road Sidings and Stoke Newington Boxes. Telecom cut. nwr 21.25.

SR: Elmer's End – Eden Park 07.50: FLY near Elmer's End station caused damage there, at signalbox and at sub-station. Telecom cut, until 10.15, but lines clear 08.05.

Teddington 18.25: FLY damaged SR motor-van and injured driver.

Merton Park – Morden Road Halt 22.30: Halt extensively damaged. Single line closed until 23.10. Telecom and Block failed Merton Park – Mitcham, so PMW until 07.15 19/7.

19/7/44

LNE: Snaresbrook 15.45: Station buildings and SM's office damaged by blast of FLY 100 yards away.

SR: West Dulwich 07.50: Station extensively damaged by blast.

Cannon Street 08.40: Extensive blast damage at Station and Hotel. SM and several passengers injured.

20/7/44

GW: Park Royal 10.25: Extensive damage by FLY in Estate, to factories, Goods offices, Electricity Centre, Salvage depot, etc.

LMS: Rainham 11.10: FLY fell on Sewerage Farm Bridge, blocking both lines. Telecom and Block cut. Buses substituted Rainham – Barking. Up line clear 15.15, then SLW until nwr 18.00.

LNE: Poplar Dock 00.25: FLY on PLA property damaged offices and mess room. Cartage vehicle damaged. Driver and two female guards killed.

Chingford 04.30: FLY 10 yards from embankment cut telecom to Wood Street. nwr 11.30.

North Woolwich 04.45: FLY damaged signalbox and station.

New Cross Gate Goods 05.00: FLY damaged Goods Agent's offices, Goods station and track at Canal Junction. ELR closed until 07.15 21/7.

21/7/44

GW: West Ealing 11.45: Glass etc. damaged at station, goods depot, also Longfield Avenue and West Ealing signalboxes.

LNE: Tottenham 14.30: FLY nearby cut telecom and Control circuits. Restored 17.35.

Lea Bridge – Temple Mills 14.45: FLY 10 yards from Down line brought down wires and disabled Block. TIW until nwr 18.35. At Temple Mills, damage to offices etc. and four wagons. Breakdown of machinery at Wagon Shops. Lighting failed at Cambridge Heath, Hackney Downs and Seven Sisters.

SR: Gipsy Hill in night: Blast caused extensive damage to station.

Thornton Heath 02.10: FLY nearby. Down sidings obstructed by debris. Windows smashed at signalbox, footbridge, booking-office and Porters' room.

Waterloo – Loco Junction 02.15: All lines closed for examination after FLY fell outside Hay Yard, Nine Elms Goods. All except Up and Down Local lines reopened 06.27, pending repair of parapet of Wandsworth Road Bridge. Up Local line reopened 13.38, Down 16.15 21/7. Considerable damage done in Nine Elms Goods to 'A' Shed, Hay Yard, New Warehouse, Empties offices, porters' lobby, weighbridge and stables. Four staff firewatchers injured, one seriously.

New Cross Gate 04.45: FLY fell in Carriage Sidings New Cross Gate – Cold Blow Lane. All lines closed until 06.30, after Down freight train hit and caught fire – 15 wagons damaged. Also 104 coaches (24 electric) damaged. East London Junction and New Cross Gate Yard Boxes damaged and Block cut. Staff lobbies also damaged. Four staff injured. Block restored 14.50.

Mitcham Junction 07.50: Footbridge and windows of signalbox and station damaged.

Deptford 07.50: Nine wagons damaged by blast from FLY.

Nine Elms Goods and Vauxhall 12.20: Blast smashed windows at Vauxhall station, also buildings including Brunswick House and 'A' Shed. In Hay Yard, Empties office, lobby, weighbridge, stables and arches damaged. Seven female staff suffered shock.

Earlsfield 13.22: Glass smashed at station and signalbox, also windows of 13.07 EMU Waterloo – Dorking North.

Lower Sydenham 15.40: Wall of booking-hall damaged and signal-box windows smashed.

Bickley Junction – St Mary Cray 22.35: FLY 150 yards away caused Block failure and smashed windows of St Mary Cray Box. nwr 09.32 22/7.

22/7/44 (Saturday)

LNE: Brimsdown 03.00: FLY in six-foot blocked Up and Down lines. Signalbox demolished and signalman injured. SM's house and station damaged, wires down. Local trains curtailed to Hertford East – Enfield Lock and Ponders End – Stratford, with buses between. Crossing-gates smashed and several wagons, six lorries and a one-ton mobile crane damaged. Lines cleared 15.15, telecom and Block 16.15. nwr not until 17.50 27/7.

SR: Blackheath 07.00: Windows smashed at booking-office, 'A' Box, and in coaches in carriage sidings.

23/7/44 (Sunday)

LNE: Clapton 05.00: FLY off premises damaged retaining wall and tunnel entrance. Station and wall at Hackney Downs also damaged.

SR: Cannon Street 04.10: FLY fell in roadway outside station, damaging roof, windows and doors at station, also windows of an EMU. Platforms lines 7 and 8 blocked by debris, until 19.00.

Victoria (Eastern) – Factory Junction 15.19: FLY nearby damaged Stewarts Lane Box. Down Main line blocked by debris, until 16.11. Signalbox lad suffered shock.

24/7/44

LMS: Queens Park – Kilburn (High Road) 04.45: FLY in Cambridge Road blasted windows of 22.00 (Sunday) express Blackpool – Euston, causing 55 casualties. Train stopped for the few more severe ones being taken off the train at Kilburn.

Dalston Junction 18.30: FLY near railway damaged windows of New Inn Yard Box. Signalman suffered shock. Fire near line, so trains run at caution. nwr 20.00.

Purfleet, Saw Mill Crossing 20.00: FLY on track, causing crater and damage to 45 wagons in military freight train. Diversions via Ockendon Branch. Two shunters and a guard suffered shock. Shuttle service Barking – Purfleet and Tilbury – Grays. nwr 16.10 25/7.

Becontree 23.35: FLY nearby smashed windows of station and LPTB electric train.

LNE: Bishopsgate 18.30: FLY in Great Eastern Street injured four staff and smashed windows at Depot and at Liverpool Street Station.

Manor Park 18.30: FLY blocked all lines and extensively damaged Down side of station. Six staff injured. Diversions via Woodford and Fairlop Loops until 19.05, when Through lines restored. Then normal, except trains not calling at Manor Park. Down trains calling from 15.30 25/7, with nwr 18.00.

Stratford 23.25: FLY near Up side smashed windows of Central and Western Junction Boxes and blasted Goods station buildings.

Noel Park 23.55: Weighbridge and ground-frame damaged, also coaching stock.

SR: Deptford 00.25: Station damaged.

Loughborough Junction 00.30: Station damaged, also arches.

25/7/44

LMS: Bow 00.45: FLY outside damaged station buildings.

26/7/44

LNE: South Woodford 01.45: Signalbox extensively damaged by FLY 500 yards away.

North Woolwich 07.00: Blast blew out windows of two local trains on move, also at station. One staff injured.

SR: Wandsworth Common 04.20: FLY 300 yards from Up side damaged station, station house and signalbox. Damage also at LMS goods yard.

27/7/44

LMS: Euston 02.10: Down side Carriage Shed and one coach damaged.

Victoria Park 17.57: FLY off property smashed signalbox windows and cut Block to Homerton. nwr 20.45.

SR: Herne Hill – Tulse Hill 01.15: FLY 50 yards from Down side damaged Croxted Road bridge. Debris blocked both lines until 08.17. TIW in operation. nwr on Up 12.30, Down 16.30.

Plumstead Sidings 17.00: FLY off premises considerably damaged goods shed and offices.

Wallington 17.55: FLY near station damaged Up side buildings, signalbox and goods shed, also cut telecom to Sutton. 17.18 EMU Victoria – Epsom Downs badly damaged by blast and 25 passengers injured (three taken to hospital). Lines closed until 18.25, then TIW to Sutton. Telecom restored 19.30, Block 21.00.

Blackheath 17.58: Station buildings and 'A' Box damaged by blast.

Brockley Lane – Lewisham Junction 18.00: Both lines blocked and telecom cut. At Lewisham station, buildings damaged. nwr 10.30 28/7.

West Norwood 19.32: Junction signalbox damaged, also York Hill bridge and West Norwood station. Lines closed for demolition of adjacent house until 20.35.

Kenley – Whyteleafe 23.05: Conductor rails damaged and telecom cut. Debris blocked both lines. Lines clear 07.30, Block restored 11.00, telecom 17.00 28/7.

28/7/44

LMS: East Horndon, Duncan West Box 04.08: Block and telecom cut. Lines closed until 06.11.

LNE: Forest Gate 09.55: FLY nearby damaged station and SM's house, blocking all lines. Through lines cleared 10.10, Local 10.20. nwr (with caution) 22.10.

Devonshire Street 21.50: FLY near entrance to Mile End Goods Yard damaged shunters' cabin and wires and smashed glass at West Junction Box. nwr 06.00 31/7.

Marylebone 21.55: Goods offices and stables damaged.

SR: Victoria (Central) 13.30: Signalbox windows and roof of carriage cleaners' lobby badly damaged.

Charing Cross 21.43: FLY in Thames broke shutters and station clock.

29/7/44 (Saturday)

GW: West Brompton (WLER) 23.15: FLY fell on retaining wall between District Lines and WLER, destroying Up WLER and slewing Down line. Girders of WLER fell on District track, causing current surge and disruption over Underground system. All telecom cut. Down line clear and SLW Chelsea – Lillie Bridge 08.30. Block restored 16.30 30/7. GW/LMS London exchange traffic then resumed, but some diversions still necessary. SLW ceased 18.30 30/7, then nwr (5 mph SpR).

LMS: Dalston Junction 10.32: Debris blocked Up and Down electric lines. Seven lengths of Down line displaced. Electric services to Broad Street suspended and passengers conveyed by bus. nwr 16.30.

West Brompton (see also GW above) 23.15: Signalbox badly damaged. All traffic to/from SR via Kensington being worked via Kew East Junction.

LNE: Bethnal Green 00.01: Blast damaged station and new East Box.

SR: Denmark Hill – Peckham Rye 00.15: Coping stones fallen at Peckham Rye end of Grove Road Tunnel blocked all lines. Peckham Rye station also damaged. Eastern Section lines reopened 02.29, Central Section lines 04.45 (15 mph SpR) nwr 07.05.

Nine Elms Yard 14.30: FLY off premises damaged windows of New Warehouse, Wharf offices, Agent's office, Brunswick House and clerical dining-rooms.

Forest Hill 18.35: All lines blocked after FLY exploded in bank, with rails displaced, cables cut. Telecom cut and Block failed. Up lines reopened 19.30, Down Main 21.00, Down Local 22.10. Telecom restored 18.40 30/7.

Hither Green 18.40: All lines blocked by FLY off premises adjacent to subway entrance at London end. Damage done to roof of Up Through platform, subway and windows of 'A' Box. All lines blocked by debris and all communication to 'A' and 'B' Boxes cut. Four passengers on Up Through platform killed and six seriously injured. Down Local line reopened for steam 19.21, for electric trains 21.23. Dartford Loop lines reopened 20.13, Up Local line 21.23, Through lines 15.50 30/7. Telecom restored 23.30, Block on 30/7 – Local lines 10.00, Main 15.50.

Tulse Hill 21.40: FLY near railway damaged signalbox and an overline bridge, blocking both lines. Signalbox unusable, so no traffic to/from Leigham Junction. Lines to Herne Hill reopened 10.50 30/7. Tulse Hill – West Norwood Junction clear 09.30 31/7, but not in use before 1/8 owing to damage to signalling. At 06.00 1/8, no signals in use and points being hand-worked and clipped. TBW Tulse Hill – Knights Hill/Herne Hill Boxes. No communication Tulse

Hill – Leigham Junction, and lines used only for empty stock by TIW. Block restored 18.00 1/8. Down and Up London Bridge lines between station and junction reopened 21.30. Spur lines to Leigham Junction remained out of use owing to damage to signalbox.

Merton Park 23.00: Debris thrown onto both lines by FLY off premises. Signalbox, booking-office and station-house damaged. Conductor rails displaced. Telecom cut Merton Park – Wimbledon 'B' Boxes. Lines clear 02.50 30/7 but for steam only, for electric 08.30. Telecom restored 11.00 30/7. PMW to Mitcham until 16.00.

30/7/44 (Sunday)

GW: Old Oak Common 23.50: FLY off premises damaged East Box, Carriage Sheds and Post Office Stores, also Yardmaster's office, old Lifting Shops and three LMS coaches.

South Lambeth Goods 23.50 (see SR): FLY at Stewarts Lane forced closure of depot, already extensively damaged earlier.

LMS: West Ham 00.10: Signalbox damaged but just workable. Slight damage at Plaistow Loco Shed. Signalmen at West Ham and Plaistow Sidings Boxes suffered shock but carried on.

SR: Thornton Heath 13.00: FLY off premises extensively damaged station and SM's house.

Sutton West Box – Wimbledon 'C' Box 16.12: FLY near line cut telecom, so TIW, until nwr 20.38.

Cannon Street 18.19: Blast from FLY off premises on west side damaged windows and doors of station and signalbox, also coaches. Three passengers received minor injuries.

Lee Junction – Mottingham 23.45: FLY nearby blocked both lines with debris. Signalling apparatus at Lee Junction Box damaged and all communications cut. TIW, until phone restored 07.22 at Hither Green 'A' and Mottingham Boxes, then TBW. Lines reopened (5 mph SpR) 03.53 31/7. Block bells restored between Hither Green 'A', Lee Junction and Mottingham Boxes by 12.06 31/7, but Block still out at Lee Junction, so HSW.

Stewarts Lane 23.50: FLY in Hampton's yard blocked with debris all Central and Eastern Section lines. Down and Up Eastern and Down Central lines clear 05.00 31/7, but signalbox badly damaged and unworkable, and signalman badly shaken. TIW Stewarts Lane – Victoria/Longhedge Junction/ Factory Junction. Owing to suspected underline bridge damage, Down Main and Local lines Victoria Eastern – Factory Junction closed 00.19. Main lines reopened (5 mph SpR) 06.10 31/7, Up Relief (10 mph SpR) 06.45 for light engines only, adjacent building being unsafe, but later open (10 mph SpR) for all traffic on Main and Up Relief lines. Phone restored 10.00 31/7, then TBW. All traffic out of Battersea Yard cancelled 00.05–06.00 31/7. All points and Block and most signals restored 18.00 31/7. Central Section Up line not reopened until 18.35 4/8. Most SpR removed by 6/8. Considerable interference with Exchange traffic.

31/7/44

LNE: Goodmayes 00.30: FLY nearby damaged buildings, also East and West Boxes.

Wembley Hill 06.00: Blast damaged station, SM's house and railway cottages.

August 1944

1/8/44

GW: Chelsea Basin Depot (WLER) 14.30: FLY exploded in Thames opposite stables. Main wall damaged and unsafe. Damage done to box-wagon, also Yardmaster's, Goods and other offices.

LMS: Commercial Road Goods 10.05: Damage to windows and doors by FLY in Whitechapel High Street. 15.30: Another FLY in Nos 1 and 2 roads necessitated closure of depot with all tracks out of use. Wagon hoist at south end demolished, probably out of use for months. Extensive damage to offices and warehouse. Fourteen LMS staff, also 19 USA personnel, sustained injury or shock. HL partially restored 2/8, LL 12.00 2/8.

LNE: Leman Street 15.35: Blast damage to buildings on Up and Down platforms. (Station already closed).

Spitalfields Yard 16.00: Blast damage to buildings.

SR: Selsdon 07.00: FLY damaged station buildings and SM's house. One staff injured.

Welling 07.05: FLY smashed windows of signalbox and booking-office. One passenger slightly injured. Signalling failed until 08.50.

Lordship Lane 10.20: FLY – with engine running – fell on track, forming 10ft crater and damaging track, station buildings and subway. One staff killed. nwr 16.30 2/8.

New Cross 14.15: FLY damaged station.

2/8/44

LMS: Barking, Ripple Lane No. 1 Box 02.20: Damaged by blast. Signalman suffered shock.

Gospel Oak 04.20: Nearby FLY blasted No. 1 Box, also booking-office windows and walls.

Plaistow Loco Depot 05.00: Considerable damage to buildings. Roof over Nos 1, 2 and 8 roads destroyed and canteen collapsed.

LNE: Temple Mills 06.45: FLY in carriage sidings near South Box on Down side. Nos 4–7 roads blown out. Operations on Down side suspended until 09.00. Block and telecom out of use until 10.00. Yard-master's house and six railway cottages damaged. Damage to 53 coaches (four destroyed) and 18 wagons. nwr 17.30.

SR: Feltham 04.15: Station extensively damaged by FLY nearby.

Kingswood & Burgh Heath 08.32: FLY nearby damaged windows of booking-office, ladies' waiting room, station house and signalbox.

Plumstead 13.00: FLY exploded 200 yards from Down side. Station and signalbox extensively damaged. Signalman injured but stayed at his job. Damage to empty stock in Up sidings, also goods shed and general offices.

3/8/44

LMS: St Pancras Goods 02.55: Blast damaged Delivery Office, weigh-bridge, granary and stables.

Poplar 'B' 03.00: FLY damaged track, six wagons and lock gates. Repairs done at low tide. Winding-gear damaged and windows of offices and lock-man's cabin smashed.

Willesden 10.25: Windows smashed in No. 8 Box and Brent North Box. Phone cut in Inspector's office.

LNE: Angel Road 00.15: Signalbox windows smashed. Block to Northumberland Park Box cut. One staff injured. nwr 09.00.

Leyton 01.45: Station damaged and windows of signalbox smashed.

Poplar Dock and East India Dock 03.00: Damage to Goods offices and mess rooms. Windows smashed at Poplar and Brunswick Junction Boxes.

SR: Balham Junction 00.45: Signalbox windows smashed. Lines closed until 01.40.

Lewisham 00.50: Extensive damage to station by blast.

Eltham Well Hall 01.15: Station buildings and signalbox badly damaged. All telecom failed to Blackheath and to Welling, so TIW. Telecom restored 05.14, Block 09.40.

Loco Junction 04.48: Extensive damage to windows and frames in signalbox. SR Road Motor Repair Shops damaged. nwr 06.05.

Sidcup 04.50: Station buildings badly damaged and both lines blocked by debris. Block to Mottingham and to Crayford cut. Lines reopened 05.40 with TIW. Block restored 11.30, telecom 14.30.

West Norwood – Gipsy Hill 05.15: Both lines blocked by debris from damage to Gipsy Road bridge, but clear 06.05. All telecom cut, so TIW until TBW 09.25, Block restored 14.50.

Bricklayers Arms 07.20: Damage to 40 yards of bridge wall, office buildings, roof of East Yard stables and Mercers Crossing Box, also 25 wagons and containers. nwr 14.00.

Mitcham Junction – Mitcham Common Crossing Box 08.15: FLY exploding nearby blocked both lines with debris. Station damaged. Both lines reopened 08.55, but all communications destroyed. TIW, until 10.38 when phone restored. Block restored Mitcham Junction – Mitcham 12.45, Mitcham Common 16.20.

Penge East – Beckenham Junction 11.30: All communications destroyed, so TIW until phone restored 13.40, Block 15.45.

Eltham Park – Falconwood 11.45: FLY caused telecom failure Eltham Well Hall – Welling. TIW until phone restored 13.50. Block restored 16.45.

4/8/44

LNE: Temple Mills Yard 16.35: FLY nearby demolished six Company's cottages and severely damaged Yardmaster's office and house, also South Junction Box. Windows and doors smashed in S&T and Engineer's stores and offices, C&W Shops and nine coaches.

SR: Lower Sydenham 15.45: FLY nearby extensively damaged station buildings, also HT cables.

Raynes Park – Motspur Park 19.01: 18.47 EMU Waterloo – Effingham Junction damaged by blast from FLY 50 yards from Up line. Train taken out of service Motspur Park. One passenger killed and 24 injured. (Eight taken to hospital and numerous others received First Aid). West Barnes Crossing Box damaged.

5/8/44 (Saturday)

SR: London Bridge (Eastern) 03.50: Blast smashed windows in signal-box, offices and two EMU. nwr in 30 minutes.

6/8/44 (Sunday)

LMS: Elm Park 03.30: FLY near Up Through line damaged porters' room and brought down wires. nwr 11.20.

LNE: Custom House 05.50: Station buildings damaged.

East Smithfield Goods 13.45: Damaged by FLY falling at St Katherine's Dock.

SR: Plumstead 03.35: Windows of Goods office smashed and foundations shifted.

London Bridge 03.50: Windows of signalbox and two empty EMU smashed.

West Dulwich 17.04: FLY fell directly on Down platform. Buildings on fire. Passengers in waiting-room slightly injured. Train damaged. Station closed. Block cut Herne Hill South – Sydenham Hill – Penge East. Restored 15.59 7/8. Station reopened 04.00 9/8.

Sydenham Hill 17.10: Another FLY falling between platform and tunnel struck rear of 16.54 EMU Victoria – Orpington, causing damage and injury to passengers. Tree blown across tracks. Lines closed Herne Hill – Penge East. Traffic diverted via Nunhead, with shuttle Shortlands – Penge East.

7/8/44

LMS: Poplar 06.20: Loop Line Junction Box severely damaged by blast. Repaired 9/8.

LNE: Poplar Dock 06.13 (see also LMS): Blast damaged offices and shed.

East India Dock 11.30: Blast damaged Company cottage and tenants' premises.

SR: Raynes Park – Malden 10.58: FLY nearby brought down wires and caused short-circuits. All lines closed until 11.37. Phones restored 13.35 8/8.

Plumstead, Church Manor Way Crossing 11.14: Damage to ground-frame controlling private siding, shunters' lobby, phone room, crossing-keeper's box and gatehouse.

8/8/44

LNE: Tufnell Park Goods 06.40: FLY near goods yard damaged wall and offices, also 14 wagons and two brakevans.

SR: Barnehurst – Perry Street Junction 23.15: FLY at bottom of embankment blocked Up and Down lines, displaced conductor rails and damaged cables and wires. Both lines reopened for steam 00.43, electric 01.00 (5 mph SpR) with TIW. Block restored 11.28. nwr 17.00 9/8.

9/8/44

SR: Forest Hill 06.35: FLY nearby blocked Up line with debris, for just 20 minutes.

11/8/44

SR: Herne Hill – West Dulwich 07.32: FLY 40 yards from Down side, 200 yards from Herne Hill South Box damaged bridge parapets both sides. All telecom failed Herne Hill South – Sydenham Hill. Lines reopened 08.35 (5 mph SpR), with TIW until Block restored 15.00.

13/8/44 (Sunday)

LNE: Maryland 06.20: Blast damaged station and debris blocked lines, but cleared 06.25![93]

SR: Streatham Hill 07.53: FLY damaged windows of signalbox, roof of Electric Sheds and door of CME's office.

14/8/44

LMS: Hampstead Heath – Gospel Oak 04.25: FLY nearby damaged Gospel Oak Box, severing Block and telecom. Lines reopened 05.05 at caution. nwr 11.00.

Somers Town Goods 07.00: FLY fell in HL coal bays on Down side near St Pancras Junction Box, penetrating to LL, damaging track, girders and Nos 15 and 16 roads and causing crater and fire. St Pancras Junction Box and Block instruments extensively damaged. Windows smashed also in St Pancras Station and Somers Town Boxes. All three signalmen suffered badly from shock, but remained on duty. Many wagons damaged, wires down and telecom cut between Station and Junction Boxes. However, trains run in and out at caution. At St Pancras Goods Depot, damage done to No. 20 (HL) and Nos 15 and 16 (LL) roads. Retaining wall of HL badly damaged, along with coal merchants' tenancies, weighbridge and stables. nwr 08.00 – nevertheless![94]

LNE: King's Cross 07.00: FLY at St Pancras Junction (see LMS) smashed windows of Inwards offices and Locomotive Shed, also did damage at Camley Street coal drops. Also windows and doors smashed at passenger station.

SR: Elmstead Woods – Grove Park 07.03: FLY nearby damaged fencing and wires. Block repaired 12.00.

15/8/44

LNE: Newbury Park 02.40: FLY damaged windows and wires at signalbox. nwr 15.00.

Temple Mills 02.40:[95] Wires down and No. 4 telephone circuit out of order. Restored 15.40.

Hackney Marshes (Clapton – St James' Street) 14.25: Explosion of FLY cut Chingford Control circuit until 15.45.

Forest Gate 17.59: FLY nearby superficially damaged signalbox and station. Ticket-collector injured by blast and died before reaching hospital.

SR: Queen's Road, Peckham 15.45: FLY exploded near track, blocking both lines. Block cut Old Kent Road Junction – Peckham Rye 'A'. Block restored 12.30 16/8. nwr (15 mph SpR) 18/8. However, on 4/9 repair of damaged bridge required 15 mph SpR. nwr 08.00 21/8.

16/8/44

LMS: Ripple Lane Yard 21.06: FLY between fence and No. 7 road slewed Nos 5–7 by four feet. Extensive damage done to stock. Telecom down between Up Sidings, No. 1 Box, Plaistow and Shoeburyness. nwr 23.00.

LNE: Hoe Street, Walthamstow 10.00: FLY smashed windows at station. Debris on line cleared in seven minutes!

Snaresbrook and South Woodford 19.11 and 19.17: Two FLY exploding nearby[96] caused damage to station buildings and put telecom to Eagle Lane Box out of order.

SR: Deptford Wharf 07.15: FLY in Royal Victualling Yard damaged warehouse, also North and South Boxes.

Lower Sydenham 18.20: FLY nearby severely damaged station. SM injured, but stayed on duty.

New Cross Gate – Brockley 18.31: FLY exploded in bank near Vesta Road overbridge. Debris strewn over all four lines and all telecom cut. Lines clear 19.15, then TIW until phone restored 21.00. Windows damaged in passing EMU. One passenger injured but continued journey after treatment. nwr 17.00 17/8.

17/8/44

LMS: Falcon Lane Goods, Clapham Junction 13.30: FLY fell at Wandsworth Road entrance, damaging stables, motor lorry, windows of offices, also demolished No. 230 Lavender Hill (LMS property). Two staff seriously injured.

SR: Clapham Junction 13.30 (see also LMS above): Blast damaged Relay Room, 'B' Box, subway and arches.

18/8/44

LNE: Poplar Dock 07.15: FLY smashed windows of Goods Agent's office and Millwall Junction Box.

20/8/44 (Sunday)

LNE: Wood Street, Walthamstow 16.15: FLY nearby caused failure of colour-light signals Clapton – Chingford, also superficial damage at station. Emergency circuit for signals working and trains running at caution. nwr 23.00.

SR: Ravensbourne – Shortlands 06.29: Both lines blocked by FLY damaging Bridge 490. Up line conductor rail displaced and all telecom destroyed. Lines clear (5 mph SpR) 08.20. Telecom restored 14.55. nwr 15.15.

21/8/44

LMS: Kensal Green 12.35: FLY in roadway near station damaged station buildings. Station closed. Traffic passing 17.00 (SpR 15 mph through tunnel). Station reopened morning 24/8. Kensal Rise: Same FLY blasted doors and windows.

Acton Central 13.10: FLY in roadway damaged station buildings and signalbox. Woman guard and Junior Booking Clerk cut by glass.

SR: Fulwell – Hampton 12.30: Uxbridge Road bridge damaged.

Chiswick 14.47: Blast from FLY nearby extensively damaged station buildings and SM's house.

Strawberry Hill 20.00: Blast damaged station building, signalbox and Carriage Sheds.

22/8/44

LMS: Shoreditch 12.30: FLY near station (closed in 10/40) damaged signalbox windows, skylight of staircase from Platform 1 and hoarding on Up side. No casualties.

LNE: Cambridge Heath 12.30: Parapet wall brought down by FLY, blocking all lines with debris. Suburban lines clear 13.30, Down Fast 13.55, Up Fast clear and nwr 15.15. Meanwhile, passengers used existing road services.

SR: West Norwood Junction – Leigham Junction 07.29: Blast from FLY covered both lines with debris, but clear 07.40. However, all telecom cut, so TIW until 09.30 when phone restored. nwr 13.00.

23/8/44

LNE: Sudbury & Harrow Road 08.00: FLY near station brought down footbridge, blocking Up Slow and Up Main lines and cutting Block. Damage to points and signalling, also 14 wagons. SLW 11.30 over Down line to Sudbury Hill, with TIW. nwr 16.25.

SR: Twickenham 04.45: Blast damage to East Box, goods offices, shed and stables.

Herne Hill Sorting Sidings 20.53: Explosion of FLY nearby broke most of windows in passing 20.43 EMU Holborn –

Wallington, causing injury to five passengers (two serious). Train taken out of service at Wallington. Blast also damaged roofs and windows of Yardmaster's, Foreman's and C&W Examiner's offices. Cables damaged, causing failure of TC and electric lighting, affecting Herne Hill Station and North, South and Sorting Sidings Boxes. TC restored 21.45 at Sorting Sidings, but not elsewhere, so HSW in operation. All repaired and nwr 13.58 24/8.

24/8/44

LMS: West Hampstead 07.45: FLY nearby smashed windows of Finchley Road Box and damaged goods offices and weighbridge.

LNE: Farringdon Street Goods 08.00: Blast damaged three warehouses on old HL, wall of LL and temporary office. Working impeded.

Stratford Market 18.50: Blast smashed windows and damaged five tenanted warehouses.

SR: Malden – Berrylands 18.40: FLY fell between Down Local and Down Kingston lines 300 yards west of Malden station. Conductor rails of Down Local, Through and Kingston lines displaced and pieces of bomb jammed between conductor and running rails of Down Kingston line. Cables damaged, causing failure of traction current on all lines Raynes Park – Hampton Court Junction, also Malden – Norbiton. Failure of colour-light signalling Malden – Hampton Court Junction and Block Malden – Malden Crossing Box. All lines Malden – Surbiton and Down line Malden – Malden Crossing closed 18.40. Up Local and Through lines Surbiton – Malden clear for steam traffic 19.39. Current restored 21.14, when also both Down lines reopened for all traffic, with SpR until 12.00 30/8. Down line Malden – Malden Crossing reopened for all traffic 21.55. SpR 10 mph on Down Local lines Malden – Berrylands/Malden Crossing. TBW Malden – Hampton Court Junction until 05.43 25/8, when colour-light signalling restored using emergency diesel set. Generator failed 12.31 25/8, so TBW again until 16.00.

27/8/44 (Sunday)

LNE: Stratford 07.00: Blast damaged Lea Junction Box and buildings in Carriage Sidings.

29/8/44

SR: Sunbury 13.10: Blast from FLY nearby smashed windows at station and signalbox, also ceilings of station house.

30/8/44

LMS (T&H): Harringay Park 01.15: FLY nearby damaged signalbox windows, also booking-hall and office. Signalman injured.

31/8/44

LNE: Beckton Tramway, near Custom House 10.55: FLY nearby damaged signalbox and wires. nwr 16.45.

SR: Falconwood 10.02: FLY exploded back of Down platform, damaging station buildings and emergency HT supply lines. Both lines blocked by debris. One passenger seriously injured. All telecom destroyed Eltham Well Hall – Welling. Phone restored 12.23, Block 16.20. Both lines reopened 16.06, but Down platform not available until 17.30. Meanwhile Down trains not stopping. Damage to HT feeders affected supply to Barnehurst, Dartford and Northfleet substations, so evening business services reduced on North Kent, Bexleyheath and Dartford Loop routes, also Dartford – Gravesend. Current restored sufficiently for 'series' running of normal business service 21.05. nwr 10.13 1/9.

September 1944

8/9/44

SR: Chiswick 18.40: 'Explosion' nearby superficially damaged station. This was in fact the first V-2 Rocket (BIG BEN), although not admitted officially for two months.[97]

On 14 September, a report to the SR Finance Committee sum-

marised the effects of the V-1 offensive. The SR had experienced 490 FLY incidents (over half in the London Region) in 78 days; 83 blockages had occurred and all but one (the Down Local line on Charing Cross Bridge) had been cleared. Twelve of their staff and 37 of their passengers had been killed (157 and 423 respectively injured); in the same period the other Railways (including the LPTB) had had seven staff killed and no passengers killed, with 146 and 89 passengers and others injured.

16/9/44 (Saturday)

LMS: Barking, Ripple Lane Box 06.05: Blast from FLY blocked Up and Down Tilbury lines with debris and cut wires. Passenger services diverted via Upminster, with buses Dagenham Dock – Barking. nwr 11.35.

17/9/44 (Sunday)

LMS: East Ham 06.10: Following "three explosions" (actually a Rocket) in vicinity, a large container was found on the platform, said by ARP to contain acid: it burst open, releasing foaming white liquid which set fire to sleepers.[98] Traffic stopped on all lines, three until 07.10, the fourth until 08.30.

24/9/44 (Sunday)

SR: Addlestone – Chertsey 21.55: FLY displaced Down line conductor rail and severed all telecom Addlestone Junction – Lyme Crossing Box. Windows smashed in four EMU in Chertsey Up Sidings. Lines reopened 00.33, with TIW Addlestone Junction – Lyme Crossing. nwr 11.17 25/9.

October 1944

20/10/44

SR: Norwood Junction 20.10: Blast from Rocket at South Norwood damaged station buildings, Loco Shed and goods shed, also smashed glass in North Box.

26/10/44

LNE: Lea Bridge 08.15: Blast from Rocket in Walthamstow damaged signalbox and crossing-house.

Palmers Green 18.45: Rocket fell on Up platform as 18.20 local Finsbury Park – Hertford North arriving. Station badly damaged. 14 passengers and three staff injured (nine seriously). Crater in track and all communications severed. Lines closed Grange Park – Wood Green and buses substituted. King's Cross – Hertford service terminated Wood Green. Shuttle services run Welwyn Garden City – Hertford North and Hertford North – Grange Park. On 27/10, full suburban service King's Cross – Palmers Green; bus service Palmers Green – Winchmore Hill; shuttle service Winchmore Hill – Hertford North. nwr 19.02 27/10.

SR: London Bridge – Bricklayers Arms Junction 08.40: Rocket exploded 20 yards from Up SL line, near Southwark Park Road bridge. Several lines blasted out of alignment and 200 yards parapet wall blown onto track. SL lines and Up Local line closed. 09.10: Through and Down Local lines also found displaced, so closed. Blast damaged two electric trains, injuring a motorman and one passenger. Four passengers in 08.25 Charing Cross – Tonbridge[99] reported minor injuries upon arrival at Tonbridge. Through and Down Local lines reopened 09.55–10.18, SL lines 12.02 (SpR of 5 mph over Up). Up Local under 5 mph SpR until 07.52 12/11 and under possession of Engineer 10.00–15.00 until further notice. During blockage, suburban services terminated New Cross Gate/Peckham Rye. Passengers conveyed by LPTB buses New Cross – Nunhead. Some main-line services diverted Victoria and others terminated East Croydon.

27/10/44

LNE: Churchbury 03.50: Blast from FLY damaged Up and Down lines and telecom. nwr 11.00.

SR: Hither Green Sidings 23.47: Rocket in Lewisham damaged Yardmaster's office and shunters' lobby, also five brake vans and several wagons in Down Sidings. Wires brought down and all communications cut Sidings 'B' – 'C' Boxes, so TIW until phone restored 03.30. nwr 12.00 28/10.

28/10/44 (Saturday)
SR: New Cross 11.07: Rocket (mid-air burst!)[100] in Deptford slightly damaged station buildings, also badly damaged railway house in Railway Grove.

Peckham Rye 18.20: Rocket in Camberwell near Central Section Down line between 'A' and 'C' Boxes caused slight damage to Platform 4 roof and Electricity Dept North Repair Shop.

30/10/44
LNE: Royal Victoria Dock 12.31: Rocket on south side of Dock near No. 2 Shed. Damage to six wagons, Clyde Wharf Shed (Silvertown) and Foreman's office.

Forest Gate – Maryland 12.30:[101] Rocket fell in Forest Lane near Up side. Windows broken in Maryland Box. Debris on line, so traffic on Up Through run at caution. nwr 14.30.

31/10/44
LNE: Thames Wharf Junction 18.40: Rocket explosion in Victoria Dock cut No. 6 Stratford Control circuits. Working resumed 19.00, but owing to damage at Docks operations restricted until 06.00 1/11 when nwr on PLA. Circuits restored and nwr 14.30 1/11.

SR: Purley – Kenley 06.48: FLY caused loss of current on Down line Purley – Warlingham substation, but restored 07.22. Telecom and Block also destroyed. TIW until Block restored 09.30. Superficial damage at Purley Station, South Box and Divisional Engineer's office.

Deptford Wharf 07.40: Rocket in Surrey Commercial Docks damaged boiler house, hydraulic plant, general office, warehouse, railway cottage, canteen and North Box.

November 1944

1/11/44
SR: New Cross Gate – Brockley 18.25: Rocket explosion in Deptford 200 yards from Down Local line damaged windows, roofs etc. of two passing EMU. One passenger injured. No damage to track. Control phone circuits damaged, but restored by 22.45.

2/11/44
SR: Surbiton – Hampton Court Junction (HCJ) 03.30: Rocket explosion breached Down embankment 50 yards London side of HCJ Box. All lines blown out of alignment and Down and Up Hampton Court lines also out of use, with wing-wall of fly-over carrying Down line damaged. Signalbox damaged. Signalman injured but stayed on duty. Main-line services diverted and electric services terminated Surbiton, Esher and Claygate. Special buses operated Hampton Court – Esher/Claygate. Through lines reopened 16.00 (steam only), by TIW Surbiton – HCJ, by TBW HCJ – Esher West. Through, Up Local and Up Hampton Court lines reopened for electric trains 18.00 and road services from Esher and Claygate withdrawn. Down Local and Down Hampton Court lines reopened 13.00 3/11, with severe SpR on all lines. Special bus service Hampton Court – Surbiton withdrawn 10.00 3/11. Signalling normal 17.00, but still TBW on Down lines at first. SpR on Down Through and Local lines withdrawn 12.00 22/11. SpR over Down Hampton Court line not withdrawn until 16.00 15/12.

3/11/44
SR: Hither Green Sidings 04.40: Explosion of Rocket in 'C' section, making crater 30 x 20ft. Section closed, also 'B' section by debris. All lines between 'B' and 'C' Boxes closed until 05.43. No damage found, but all communications destroyed between these Boxes, so TIW. All communications restored 13.30 and 'B' section reopened 15.45 3/11. Ladies' lava-

tory destroyed and damage done to Yardmaster's office, RCH office, Police office, Decontamination Room and Up Side shunters' lobby. Seven vehicles destroyed, 103 damaged (32 badly). Ten staff injured and several others sent home with shock. Some London Freight Exchange routes closed and certain traffic diverted to Herne Hill and Blackheath, also Bricklayers Arms. Exchange traffic normal 3/11. 'C' section sidings (except Nos 1–3 roads) clear 6/11. nwr 16.00 8/11.

4/11/44 (Saturday)
LNE: Ilford 11.00: Blast from Rocket in golf-course nearby smashed windows of signalbox, Parcels office and berthed carriages.

5/11/44 (Sunday)
SR: Balham 07.45: Rocket in Tooting Bec blasted Balham Intermediate Box and cut gas supply.

London Bridge – Bricklayers Arms Junction/North Kent East Junction 10.55: Rocket in Galley Wall Road, Bermondsey demolished Southwark Park Road bridge, which carries SL and Up Local lines. Remaining Central Section lines (Up and Down Through and Local) damaged. Signals, TC and telecom also put out of use on Central and Eastern Section lines. Latter closed until 11.35, then TIW until 12.40 when phones restored. Subsequently TBW London Bridge – North Kent East Junction. Telecom restored on Central Section London Bridge – Bricklayers Arms Junction 12.40. Down Local and Up Through lines reopened 17.13 (5 mph SpR) with TBW. Down Through line (Central Section) reopened (5 mph SpR) 18.52, but with TBW. Normal signalling restored on Eastern Section lines 18.26. Normal Block signalling restored London Bridge – Bricklayers Arms Junction 08.15 6/11. Through lines and Down Local line not reopened until 07.10 6/11, Up Local line 07.52 13/11. SL lines reopened 15.00 14/11, but SpR not removed until 16.00 21/2/45).

6/11/44
SR: Albany Park 14.58: Rocket in Bexley near line smashed windows, doors and covered way at station.

10/11/44
LMS: Haydon Square Goods 14.10: Blast from Rocket in Goulston Street damaged windows and ceilings at five offices and warehouse, also at Commercial Road Goods. No casualties.

LNE: Hornsey 08.15: Rocket at entrance to Goods Yard demolished weighbridge and coal offices, severely damaged Goods office, also damaged station, SM's house, canteen etc. and four signalboxes. One person injured. Owing to unsafe chimney at station, all traffic run at caution 10.20, until 16.30 11/11.

SR: Beckenham Junction 01.53: FLY nearby damaged station. In goods yard, lamp room burnt out, two wagons damaged and windows smashed in signalbox and in electric stock, also six SR road vehicles damaged. Track undamaged, but telecom to Shortlands cut, restored 11.45 11/11.

12/11/44 (Sunday)
LMS: West Ham 22.02: Rocket fell at Abbey Mills Lower Junction (see LNE below), damaging roof of West Ham station, and minor damage to buildings. Windows also smashed in Upper Abbey Mills Box.

LNE: Abbey Mills Lower Junction 21.56 (see LMS above): Blast damaged signalbox. Telecom and Block cut. Restored 09.00 13/11.

13/11/44
LNE: Stratford 05.10: Rocket fell Billet Carriage Sidings (High Meads) alongside Paint Shop, severely damaging carriages outside, also many inside. (31 coaching vehicles and six wagons totally destroyed; about 160 coaches and many wagons damaged). Electricity supply severely damaged. Considerable damage done to Carriage Lifting and Engine Repair Shops, Fire Station and General offices. Signalboxes

blasted at High Meads, Loughton Branch, Chobham Farm and Loop Junctions, and telecom severed. All lines blocked at High Meads Junction, stopping LMS – LNE traffic via North London line and Temple Mills – Colchester direction. Four staff injured and three suffered shock. Suburban passenger services affected by locomotives delayed off shed by blockage at High Meads Engine outlet. nwr Temple Mills to LMS 09.00, to Colchester line 13.25

14/11/44

LMS: Kentish Town Junction – Gospel Oak (NLR) 01.00: FLY nearby partially demolished wall. Wires damaged at junction. Infirmary stables at goods depot damaged. Trains allowed past at caution. nwr 04.30.

SR: Petts Wood 06.17: Rocket exploded on Up side, blasting many windows of EMU, but no injuries. Down line Block cut Orpington 'A' – Petts Wood Junction, so TBW until rectified 11.00.

Eltham Well Hall 08.40: Rocket 200 yards from line damaged station, signalbox and windows of EMU. Fifteen persons injured at station (nine seriously).

15/11/44

LNE: Crowland Box, Chadwell Heath – Romford 05.12: Blast from Rocket in Romford smashed signalbox windows. Block and telecom cut, including Control circuits. Six wagons damaged.

Cambridge Heath 05.55: Blast from FLY extensively damaged station buildings.

17/11/44

LNE: Stratford Works 00.05: Blast from Rocket in Buxton Road damaged Boiler Shop, Brass Foundry and Brass Stores.

Channelsea Junction, Stratford 04.53: Rocket exploded near Channelsea Junction, blowing out several lines and telecom. Signalbox and signalling heavily damaged, also carriage stock in Channelsea Sidings. Shunters' cabin set on fire. Shunter killed and others injured. Goods Delivery office, Agent's office, Goods Shed, mess room and lavatory all damaged. The locomotive[102] of a train of empty tank cars received virtually direct hit. Two brake-vans and a wagon destroyed; one wagon and about 180 coaching vehicles in sidings badly damaged. Driver, fireman and two shunters killed; two signalmen, foreman shunter and one shunter injured, also six enginemen less seriously. Up and Down lines Lea Junction – Fork Junction clear 09.00, Channelsea Junction – Stratford Central Junction Down line 12.45, Up line 14.25. On 18/11, Up line Channelsea Junction – Stratford Western Junction clear 14.25, Down line 16.45. Telecom restored 15.00, but HSW continued.

18/11/44 (Saturday)

LNE: Barkingside 11.16: Rocket in Aldborough Road 1,000 yards away smashed windows of waiting-room, porters' room and signalbox.

20/11/44

SR: Bickley 21.18: Rocket in Southborough Lane nearly a mile away damaged Bickley Station and Bickley Junction Boxes, also Chislehurst sub-station.

21/11/44

GW: Latchmere Junction (WLER) 23.12: Blast from Rocket in Battersea Park Road smashed signalbox windows. Block failed, restored 15.33 22/11.

25/11/44 (Saturday)

LNE: New Cross (Gate) Goods 12.26 (see SR below): Blast from Rocket damaged windows and doors.

SR: New Cross Gate[103] 12.26: Blast from Rocket in New Cross Road nearby caused considerable damage to windows etc. at station, South and Yard Boxes, Locomotive Shed and CME's Workshop. Debris on Up Local line, cleared 12.40. Two male staff killed, two female carriage cleaners missing. One staff seriously injured.

December 1944

1/12/44

LNE: Muswell Hill 18.26: Rocket exploding on Down side cess by viaduct arch nearest station, extensively damaged station, SM's house and viaduct, also tenants' offices in goods yard. Crater 50 x 20 ft. Both lines blown out, Up line slewed out five feet. Damage to LPTB cables over viaduct, telecom and Block Alexandra Palace – Cranley Gardens. No casualties. 18.25 train from Alexandra Palace held and stabled. From 07.00 2/12, 30-minute service provided Finsbury Park – Muswell Hill, with buses Muswell Hill – Alexandra Palace. Lines reopened 17.15 3/12. nwr 05.00 4/12.

2/12/44 (Saturday)

SR: Waterloo 20.30: Blast from Rocket in River Thames by Waterloo Pier damaged station roof and signalbox.

8/12/44

LNE: Woodford 03.30: Blast from Rocket 150 yards from station cut wires and Block Woodford – South Woodford. TIW until Block and telecom restored 11.10.

9/12/44 (Saturday)

LNE: Bush Hill Park 07.45: Blast from Rocket in Enfield close to station did some damage. Phone circuits cut, in order 12.45.

10/12/44 (Sunday)

SR: Belvedere – Erith, Pembroke Road Crossing 00.38: Blast from Rocket in Lower Road badly damaged gatehouse and smashed windows of signalbox.

12/12/44

SR: Elephant & Castle – Blackfriars 04.25: Explosion of Rocket nearby[104] threw debris onto track, blocking all lines and short-circuiting traction current, Through lines clear 05.02, Local lines 05.16. Waterloo: Windows smashed of signalbox and SM's offices, also sub-station.

17/12/44 (Sunday)

LNE: Lea Bridge 16.02: Blast from Rocket 25 yards from station damaged District Goods Manager's office and signalbox. Booking-clerk injured. Station wall made unsafe. Water main burst, flooding track in station. Local services diverted, also Up Goods line closed owing to danger of wall collapsing, which it did 18.30. Water turned off 18.00, cutting supply to Temple Mills. nwr 18.35, at caution until 20.20.

19/12/44

SR: Honor Oak Park 23.25: Blast from Rocket close by in Boveney Road damaged station and smashed windows of signalbox. Lines closed for examination until 02.12.

21/12/44

LMS: Barking – Dagenham 16.15: Blast from Rocket in Basedale Road close to railway caused some damage at Becontree station, failure of Block and signals. Negative rail in Up line broken. Rail replaced 17.30. Shuttle service provided Upminster – Dagenham 17.15–17.30. All Block in order and nwr 19.25.

23/12/44 (Saturday)

SR: Falconwood – Welling 18.49: Rocket fell in Northumberland Avenue near Up side, uprooting electricity pylon. Cables strewn across lines. Lines clear of debris 23.50, but Intermediate colour-light signals out of action until 00.45 24/12.

January 1945

2/1/45

SR: New Beckenham 12.15: Rocket in Lennard Road severely blasted signalbox and station.

3/1/45

LNE: Bush Hill Park 08.40: Rocket falling 20 yards away badly damaged station and District Passenger Manager's office, where four staff injured.[105] Station buildings also damaged.

SR: Catford – Crofton Park 20.20: FLY exploded ¼ mile from Up side. Failure of Block Nunhead – Bellingham. TBW until Block bells restored 22.06. Block restored 23.00.

4/1/45

LMS: Dalston Junction 16.10: Blast from Rocket in Woodland Street damaged station buildings and smashed windows of EMU in sidings and of signalbox. Debris fell on track. nwr 16.46.

6/1/45 (Saturday)

SR: Nunhead 13.48: Blast from Rocket nearby in Kitto Road smashed windows at station and signalbox. Debris on track, so caution until 15.00.

Peckham Rye – Denmark Hill 22.48: Rocket exploded between North and South Electric Carriage Sheds, making a large crater. South Shed badly damaged and small transformer station demolished. North Shed damaged at Peckham Rye end. Extensive damage electric coaching stock: two destroyed, three badly damaged, 22 lesser damage. No casualties. All lines blocked by debris. Down Catford Loop line reopened 23.45, Up Loop 13.00 7/1, SL lines reopened 14.00 7/1. All telecom destroyed 'C' Box – Tulse Hill and 'B' Box, and 'C' Box – Denmark Hill, so TIW Peckham Rye – Denmark Hill. Block restored 'C' Box – Tulse Hill 08.30, 'B' Box – Denmark Hill 14.00 7/1. Train maintenance was diverted to Slades Green and Durnsford Road Depots.

7/1/45 (Sunday)

SR: Teddington – Hampton Wick 02.16: Blast from Rocket close to Fairfax Crossing Box blocked both lines. All telecom destroyed. Signalman badly shaken, slightly injured. Trains terminated Teddington and Kingston. Passengers used bus and trolley services. Shuttle trains operated Shepperton – Strawberry Hill. Lines clear 08.25, with TIW until nwr 14.00.

8/1/45

LMS: West End Lane 16.33: Rocket exploded on track 200 yards west of station, blocking all NLR lines. Embankment of LPTB Metropolitan lines gouged away at south end of bridge over NLR and Up LPTB lines slewed towards Down lines and blocked.[106] Windows broken in 10.08 express Bradford – St Pancras passing on Midland main line nearby. Substation damaged and electrical apparatus put out of order. TC Euston – Camden also failed. Electric services reversed Brondesbury/Hampstead Heath. NLR freight traffic diverted via Chalk Farm. Freight on following exchange routes suspended: LNE (GE) – SR (LSW) via Temple Mills and Old Oak (LMS); LNE (Ferme Park) – GW (Acton); LNE (Temple Mills) – GW (Acton) via Victoria Park. Traffic using alternative routes. nwr 16.35 9/1.

LNE: Marylebone – Harrow-on-the-Hill: Following blockage of LPTB lines at Kilburn at 16.33 (see LMS above), shuttle service run on LNER to clear passengers.

9/1/45

SR: New Beckenham and Clock House 10.50: Blast from Rocket in Beckenham blew out temporary repairs at both stations, also at Kent House.

13/1/45 (Saturday)

LMS: Campbell Road Junction – Devons Road, Poplar 07.08: Explosion of Rocket blocked Tilbury lines at Bromley and NLR lines at Devons Road, closing access to Devons Road Loco. Freight train in Up Sidings badly damaged. Wagon shops at Bow Works destroyed. Blast damaged LPTB train at Bromley station, injuring 30 passengers (one died next day). Damage to Bow Loco Works superficial, but one employee seriously injured and six shocked. Tilbury lines clear 11.25, Devons Road section 13.40.

LNE: Wood Green 02.30: Rocket exploded south of station, blowing out all Up running lines and some Carriage Sidings. Down Slow No.1 uncertain, Down Slow No.2 available, Down Goods

blocked by debris, but no casualties. Considerable damage to Wood Green station buildings, Nos 1–4 Boxes, Carriage Shed and associated buildings; vacuum-cleaning shed demolished. Serious damage to 55 coaching stock. SLW 05.15–10.30 over Down Slow No.2 Hornsey – Wood Green, then special working of Down trains over Down Slow No.2 and Up trains over Down Slow No.1. Up main-line trains run (extremely delayed) over it until 09.15, others diverted.[107] Up Main line restored 12.10. Suburban services cancelled King's Cross – Wood Green. Hatfield trains reversed New Southgate, Hertford trains at Bowes Park. Restricted suburban passenger service later. Shuttle service Bowes Park – Hertford North; suburban passengers directed to LPTB at Bounds Green and Arnos Grove. Up Main line clear 12.10, Down Goods 14.00, Down Main, Up Slow and Up Goods 15.55. Up Carriage line Wood Green No.4 – Hornsey Up Goods Box out of order until 16.15 14/1. Outer Suburban service resumed normally 17.30, Inner Suburban 19.30. Block restored 15.00, but Control and Trunk telephone circuits out of order until 16.15 14/1. Up freight traffic suspended. Exchange with SR affected by incident, but limited exchange via MWL, also via Harringay, from 17.00. nwr 06.00 15/1.

Palace Gates and Noel Park 02.30: Blast damage also at both stations. Normal on 15/1.

14/1/45 (Sunday)

LNE: Finsbury Park 02.15: FLY nearby smashed windows at station and Nos 5 and 6 Boxes. Lines declared clear 02.50. Five Suburban and one Outer Suburban carriage sets damaged.

SR: Walworth Road – Camberwell 01.56: FLY fell 50 yards from Up Local line near Bridge 371. Bridge coping thrown onto all four tracks. Wires brought down and signal power supply cut. Through and Down Local lines reopened by 07.25. Up Local line reopened 08.56, by TIW until phones restored 12.25 and Block 14.55, then nwr.

Mitcham Junction 01.58: FLY exploded on track, damaging both lines and destroying all telecom. Windows at Mitcham Junction station blasted. Trains operated to either side of obstruction and linked by buses. Telecom restored 13.36. nwr 14.35.

20/1/45 (Saturday)

SR: Maze Hill 19.23: Blast from Rocket nearby damaged station buildings and signalbox. Both lines blocked with debris. Two staff seriously injured. Stock in sidings damaged. Telecom destroyed to North Kent East Junction and Charlton. Traffic diverted as necessary. Lines clear 12.00, telecom 12.35 21/1.

23/1/45

LMS: Dagenham Dock – Rainham 19.15: Blast from Rocket in New Road nearby smashed windows of coaches and cab of locomotive of 18.36 local Fenchurch Street – Tilbury.

SR: Hither Green Sidings 08.39: Blast from Rocket in Hither Green Cemetery near Up side smashed windows of 'C' Box. Signalman suffered shock.

24/1/45

SR: Greenwich – Maze Hill 16.20: Blast from Rocket in Church Street damaged retaining walls on either side, blocking both lines with debris Greenwich Station – Greenwich College tunnel. 16.14 EMU Cannon Street – Gillingham ran into debris and leading vehicle derailed. No casualties. Passengers detrained and taken along track to Greenwich station. Greenwich line trains diverted via St John's and Blackheath. Passengers for Deptford, Greenwich, Maze Hill and Westcombe Park diverted to ordinary buses. Damage to retaining walls delayed re-railment and lines reopened (15 mph SpR) 15.30 25/1. SpR withdrawn 19.00 13/2.

26/1/45

LNE: Gidea Park 09.56: Blast from Rocket (mid-air burst) at Ardleigh Green nearby blew out windows of two empty suburban trains in Carriage Sidings, also cut telecom wires.

Fairlop 14.45: Blast from Rocket in Fencepiece Road nearby damaged station and signalbox. Five staff slightly injured.

SR: Clapham Junction – Wandsworth Town 10.40: Blast from Rocket nearby blew out windows of eight empty coaches in Carriage Sidings.

29/1/45

LMS: Canonbury – Dalston Junction 10.02: Blast from Rocket (air-burst in Islington) blocked all lines with debris, but nwr 10.25.

February 1945

1/2/45

LNE: Stratford and Stratford Market 03.04: Blast from Rocket in Barnby Street near railway smashed windows at both stations and severely damaged LNER Printing Works.

2/2/45

SR: Nunhead – Crofton Park 08.22: Blast from Rocket in Finland Road 200 yards from Down side caused failure of Up line Block, also broke windows at St John's Box. Block rectified 10.55.

4/2/45 (Sunday)

LNE: Ilford 15.05: Blast from Rocket nearby[108] smashed windows at station and signalbox, also damaged eight coaches and C&W hut at Aldersbrook Sidings. Cables and wires severed. Ilford booking-clerk suffered shock.

5/2/45

LNE: London Fields 02.40: Rocket in Mare Street damaged Helmsley Road bridge and station. All lines blocked with debris. Buses substituted Hackney Downs – Liverpool Street. Chingford and Cambridge line trains diverted via Stratford. Enfield trains terminated Hackney Downs. nwr 06.15 5/2.

6/2/45

SR: St Mary Cray – Swanley 09.48: Rocket exploded 20ft from Down side, ¼ mile towards Swanley, making crater 9 x 40ft. Down line blocked and all telecom destroyed. SLW until 11.32, when double-line operated with TIW. Phone restored 14.00, Block 16.50, then nwr.

7/2/45

LMS: Dagenham Dock – Barking 12.10: Rocket exploded in Ripple Lane Down Sidings. Crater 120 ft x 40 ft. Damage to 22 wagons (some loaded). No casualties. Main lines blocked, so Up services diverted over Up Reception Sidings and Down services via Upminster. Down line reopened 15.55, nwr 16.25.

8/2/45

LNE: Cambridge Heath 10.55: Blast from Rocket very close in Parmitter Street severely damaged station. Woman porter cut by glass.

Ilford 12.37: Rocket exploded in Ley Street[109] 15 yards from over-line bridge on Down side, blocking all four lines with debris. Serious damage to station buildings and SM's house. East side booking-office closed. Six staff suffered shock or minor injuries. Through and Up Local lines clear by 13.30, Down Local 14.55. Later reported wall leaning towards line, so trains run at caution until 16.00 11/2.

10/2/45 (Saturday)

LMS: Purfleet Rifle Range 16.01: Blast from Rocket nearby damaged station buildings. Block failed on Up line, restored 22.07. Station closed until morning 12/2.

LNE: Leytonstone 08.25: Blast from Rocket in Lemna Road damaged station buildings. Signalman received cuts but remained on duty. Traffic stopped for only 20 minutes.

11/2/45 (Sunday)

LNE: Clapton 14.53: Explosion of Rocket 100 yards away in Lea marshes badly damaged signalbox. Bridge over River Lea cracked, so trains running at caution. nwr 06.00 28/2.

SR: Crofton Park 22.00: Explosion of Rocket in Marnock Road right by Up side blocked both lines with debris. Signalbox and station damaged, also lengthman's hut. Down line clear 01.45, Up 02.45. Block Nunhead – Bellingham restored 10.55 12/2.

12/2/45

LNE: Stratford 23.05: Explosion of Rocket in Marsh Hill, Hackney[110] caused damage at Loco Running Shed oil store.

13/2/45

LNE: Noel Park 16.44: Explosion of Rocket in Gladstone Avenue nearby severely damaged station buildings.

Goodmayes 23.00: Five-foot portion of Rocket that exploded in air over Dagenham fell on Up Local line. All four lines blocked by debris, but clear in 30 minutes.

14/2/45

LNE: Marylebone 17.12: Mid-air explosion of Rocket resulted in casing and mechanism damaging bridge over Regent's Canal, track and Goods Yard Box, also Down Slow line. Lines closed for examination until 18.09. Working into Goods Yard interrupted, but passenger survives not interrupted. nwr 20.00 15/2.

Hackney Downs 22.31: Explosion of Rocket in Sigdon Road close by damaged station and smashed signal box windows.

15/2/45

SR: Barnehurst – Perry Street Fork Junction 07.05: Explosion of Rocket in Thames Lane, 30 yards from Up side, damaged cables, windows and frames in Perry Street Fork Junction Box, also Slades Green Inspector's Shop, and telecom. One signalman sent home with shock. Block failed to Barnehurst, Slades Green and Crayford Creek Junction. Traction current lost. Down Bexleyheath line trains reversed Bexleyheath or Barnehurst until current restored 08.30. Phones restored 10.00, all Block 11.35.

17/2/45 (Saturday)

LNE: Blackwall 05.37: Explosion of Rocket in Leamouth Road, Poplar led to damaging fire in 'B' Warehouse (rented by Instone's) Severe damage done to several other warehouses, buildings and stables, also seven wagons and four road vehicles.

18/2/45 (Sunday)

LNE: Ilford 04.25: Explosion of Rocket in Ley Street threw debris over all four lines. Goods shed damaged. nwr 05.18.

Blackwall and Canning Town 14.40: Explosion of Rocket in air over Poplar damaged office buildings at Blackwall and station at Canning Town.

SR: Mottingham – New Eltham 19.54: Explosion of Rocket in Felhampton Road, half a mile from Up side, damaged two emergency feeder cables. Restored in 30 minutes.

19/2/45

LMS: Blackhorse Lane, Walthamstow 14.18: Blast from Rocket[111] close by damaged mechanical horse and Baun's premises. Driver and woman attendant seriously injured.

SR: Erith 07.42: Blast from Rocket in Slades Green Road smashed windows of North End Sidings Box. Block failed, but restored 09.05.

20/2/45

LNE: Ilford 11.42: Blast from Rocket nearly a mile away in Uphall Road damaged station – once again.

Gidea Park 20.35: Explosion of Rocket close by destroyed all telecom and threw debris on track. Station windows smashed. All traffic stopped. nwr 21.43, but telecom not restored until 14.30 21/2.

22/2/45

SR: Greenwich – Maze Hill 22.50: Explosion of Rocket in Straightsmouth, 25 yards Greenwich side of overline bridge. Bridge damaged and both lines blocked by debris from retaining walls on either side. Greenwich station windows smashed. Traffic diverted via St John's and Blackheath. Passengers for stations Deptford – Westcombe Park directed to ordinary buses. Both lines reopened 14.45 24/2 (15 mph SpR until 26/2).

26/2/45

LMS: West Ham, Manor Road Sewage Bridge 20.35: Explosion of Rocket in Plaistow Down Sidings damaged West Ham station and signalbox, also positive rail on Down Local line. Nos 5, 7 and 8 roads, with 29 wagons and five brake-vans damaged. Bus service introduced 20.45 Bow Road – Barking, while Engineer had possession of line until 22.45. One staff and one passenger slightly injured.

LNE: Temple Mills Yard 18.28: Explosion of Rocket blew out five roads and blocked nine with debris in Loughton Yard, destroying 22 wagons and damaging 50. Windows smashed in 139 coaches. Block and telephone wires destroyed, HT cable damaged. Railway cottages, Police office and Blacksmith's shop damaged. On 27/2, four roads still out of use and acceptances still restricted. nwr not until 16.00 4/3.

March 1945

2/3/45

SR: Orpington 12.12: Blast from Rocket in Knoll Rise, 440 yards from Down side, damaged station buildings and Divisional Offices. One staff injured.

3/3/45 (Saturday)

SR: Belvedere – Abbey Wood 04.40: After explosion in mid-air over Abbey Wood Road, casing of Rocket fell on and damaged HT cables on Down side.

5/3/45

LMS: Rainham – Purfleet 22.40: Explosion of Rocket in Wilfred Avenue, 30 yards away blocked Up and Down lines with debris and caused failure of Block and telecom. Lines clear 23.32. Block and telecom in order 09.45 6/3.

SR: Deptford 11.10: Explosion of FLY extensively damaged station, warehouses, signalboxes and offices. Five staff injured.

6/3/45

SR: Sidcup – Bexley 00.58: Rocket in Cheshunt Avenue, ¼ mile from Down side caused failure of Block and sub-station damage. Lines closed, but reopened 02.53 after clearance of debris. Block restored 09.00.

7/3/45

LNE: Angel Road – Pickett's Lock Box 06.01: Explosion of Rocket blew out both lines and damaged coal train in No.3 Reception line. Up freight traffic stopped. Passenger trains diverted via Churchbury branch. Shuttle service Cheshunt – Ponders End, buses to Angel Road. Down Main line clear 16.00, Up Main 16.55 (both at caution). All telecom severed. Control circuits restored 10.00 7/3, rest 17.00 12/3, then nwr.

SR: North Kent East Junction 03.30: Rocket exploded 50 yards from Up side, demolishing large block of Railway flats in Folkestone Gardens. No damage or injuries on Railway and lines closed only 15 minutes, but 51 people in flats killed and 72 injured (39 seriously). SpR 15 mph from 06.30, while men working on damaged buildings. Slight damage to signal wires and several windows broken in Bricklayer's Arms Junction Box. Six windows and clock in North Kent East Junction Box broken and 11 telephone circuits cut. Circuits restored 15.25. SpR over Nos 1 and 2 Down and Nos 2 and 3 Up lines until 08.00, and Nos 3 Down and No.1 Up lines until 13.40.

Westcombe Park 08.35: Rocket exploded in Engineer's Department Works on Up side, severely damaging works and station buildings, also 11 wagons. Three staff killed, one seriously and 14 slightly injured or shocked. Glass broken in Angerstein Junction Box and signalman slightly injured but stayed on duty. Telecom destroyed Maze Hill – Charlton Junction. TIW until telecom restored 14.40.

On 8 March 1945 occurred one of the worst V-2 incidents of the war. The rocket fell directly on the great Smithfield Meat Market on the corner of Farringdon Road and Charterhouse Street and penetrated to the railway beneath before exploding. The Market was crowded and great masses of concrete and girders fell down. 110 people were killed, 123 seriously injured.

8/3/45

LMS: West Smithfield Market 11.02 (see LNE below): Blast from Rocket at Farringdon Market damaged doors and windows of LMS offices. Motor-van driver injured and female conductor missing.

LNE: Farringdon Goods 11.03: Rocket fell on Market above and penetrated through to LL. No. 3 road, Nos 2–4 docks, cranes, turntables, loading-banks and three motor-trailers buried in debris. Considerable damage to warehouses and offices. Retaining wall at corner of Charterhouse Street collapsed. Traffic diverted to other Depots. Depot partially reopened only on 22/3. nwr not until 06.00 3/5.

SR: St Mary Cray 04.40: Explosion of Rocket in Up side station approach damaged station buildings and cut HT cables. Loss of current St Mary Cray – Swanley and Dunton Green – Sevenoaks. Lines closed for examination until 05.50, but all telecom failed St Mary Cray Junction – St Mary Cray Boxes, so TIW until telecom restored. Current restored 06.20, telecom 15.30, then nwr.

Holborn Viaduct 11.03 (see LNE above): Blast from Rocket at Smithfield damaged windows of Holborn LL Box and premises of Holborn Viaduct Station. nwr 11.20.

Blackheath 12.05: Explosion of Rocket in Wemyss Road nearby caused severe damage to station buildings and signalboxes. Four staff injured. Some windows of departing EMU broken. Five passengers slightly injured. nwr 12.40, nevertheless.

9/3/45

SR: Charlton Junction 04.27: Explosion of Rocket in Victoria Way caused blockage of North Kent lines Angerstein Wharf Junction – Charlton and Greenwich lines Maze Hill – Charlton. All telecom destroyed on both routes. Trains diverted via alternative routes. Special buses provided New Cross – Woolwich. Greenwich lines reopened 14.58, North Kent lines 18.45 (15 mph SpR until 09.00 24/3). Telecom restored 14.21.

10/3/45 (Saturday)

SR: Elmer's End – Eden Park 00.01: Explosion of Rocket 150 yards from Down side necessitated closure of lines until 01.02. All telecom destroyed Elmer's End – West Wickham. Traffic worked 'under emergency regulations'. nwr 10.51.

16/3/45

LNE: Willesden Green 02.40: Explosion of Rocket in Dartmouth Road on Metropolitan side of railway severed cables. Automatic signalling failed on Marylebone line on Down side from Kilburn and Up side from Neasden until 08.30. Lines clear 04.00, but passenger services restricted. nwr 10.30.

17/3/45 (Saturday)

LMS: Dagenham Dock, Ripple Lane Down Sidings 22.26: Rocket made 50 ft crater and damaged 21 wagons and three brake-vans. Damage to No. 8 road and No. 1 Box.

18/3/45 (Sunday)

LNE: Canning Town 00.39: Blast from Rocket in goods yard caused considerable damage at Canning Town and Blackwall.

21/3/45

SR: Syon Lane – Brentford 09.36: Rocket exploded in Packard's Heston factory 100 yards from Up side. Both lines blocked with debris. Down Line conductor rail damaged, windows at Syon Lane broken. All telecom destroyed Brentford – Wood Lane Crossing Box. Hounslow Loop services terminated Brentford and Hounslow. Passengers conveyed by LPTB buses between. Other services diverted. Lines available (Down for steam only) 12.00, Up clear for electric 13.10, when also telecom restored. Owing to fire in adjacent factory, SpR 5 mph until 15.25.

23/3/45

SR: Crofton Park 01.40: Mid-air explosion of Rocket[112] damaged roof of Down platform and Down line blocked by part of missile until removed by ARP 03.30.

24/3/45 (Saturday)

LNE: Poplar Dock 01.30: Explosion of Rocket in Stewart Street nearby damaged railway buildings and Poplar Dock and Millwall Junction Boxes.

26/3/45

SR: Chislehurst 15.23: Explosion of Rocket in Tudor Close, 80 yards from Up side, damaged station and goods shed. One staff seriously injured.

27/3/45

LNE: Pickett's Lock 00.23: Explosion of Rocket in Edmonton Sewage Works nearby caused Block failure. Restored 06.30.
Spitalfields 07.21:[113] Explosion of Rocket in Vallance Road nearby smashed windows of granary point and shunters' cabins, also empty stock train in Bethnal Green station. One staff slightly injured.

Incidents of Minor Damage caused by V-1 and V-2

Many missile incidents (240 of the 745) entailed quite minor damage on the railways – mainly smashed windows. Although making life very uncomfortable especially for the signalmen, the flow of traffic was not significantly affected, so they are not listed here individually. Before September 1944 the damage was caused by a blast at a distance from a FLY, after that date it was usually from a Rocket. The 240 comprised 18 on the GWR, 34 on the LMSR, 79 on the LNER and 109 on the SR.

Waterloo. Wreckage at Platform 21 (Windsor side) on 23 June 1944, after a V-1 had flown across the station at 9.30am and exploded in the North Sidings. Hundreds were frightened but 'only' one was killed and 20 seriously injured.

Victoria (Eastern). The scene on 25 June 1944, after a V-1 had exploded on the Eastern Section offices and entrance off Wilton Street – fortunately about 2am when few people were around. Nevertheless there were a number of casualties, as well as structural damage.

Victoria (Eastern). A closer view of the damage on 25 June 1944.

Cow Lane Bridge, Peckham Rye. View westward on 19 July 1944, with reconstruction well in hand a week after a V-1 exploded on this bridge, which carried the ex-LC&D Catford Loop line over the ex-LB&SC SL lines from London Bridge. Peckham Rye station is in the distance to the left, the Loop line curving and dropping down to connect with the SL lines there. Beams are being placed on temporary timber trestling and a cable bridge is already in place. Note that all the men in the scene are actually doing something.

Wimbledon. The wrecked concourse on the LPTB side of the station, on 16 July 1944 after a V-1 had landed directly on it, mercifully just after midnight – there were only about 15 people hurt and none killed. If it had been rush-hour …!

Hungerford Bridge. View to Charing Cross Station, some ten weeks after a V-1 had landed slap-bang on the river bridge at 4am on Sunday 18 June 1944. It 'took out' a substantial section, which included the two Local lines and also the footbridge on the downstream side – fortunately at a time when hardly anyone would have been around. Repairs are well in hand, with trestling built up from the river bed. Trains were running again later the following day, on the Through lines off picture to the left, and on the Local lines – gingerly – a month later.

Hungerford Bridge, Charing Cross. An upstream view, also on 5 September 1944. Note the substantial temporary structure erected to allow access from the water.

A large crater cut both ex-GN Enfield branch lines after a V-2 rocket had exploded at Palmers Green during the rush-hour at 6.45pm on 26 October 1944. Men were hard at work the next day, restoring the services to normal by 7pm that evening. The carnage might have been even worse than stated in the text, for a Down train leaving was almost as near as the one shown in the illustration. A number of houses were very badly damaged in adjacent roads. Moreover, an Up train was also approaching, but the alert driver was able to stop 100 yards from the explosion. It makes one realise that train drivers – even more than the rest of us – 'carried on', not knowing when they might run into a crater or when something awesome would drop out of the blue and wipe them out.
C.C. Herbert/NRM

Grange Hill. View towards Chigwell and Woodford (on the Hainault Loop) the day after a V-1 had struck at 5pm on 12 July 1944. They are almost ready to serve passengers.

Brimsdown. A V-1 had exploded at 3am on 22 July 1944 slap on the Cambridge main lines by the signalbox on the London side of the station. The view is northward with the wrecked signalbox in the centre and scores of people milling around and working to clear up the mess.

Ilford. View towards the station and London after a V-2 had exploded at 12.35pm on 8 February 1945 very close to the Down Slow line. Believe it or not, the lines were clear by 3pm.

Serious Accidents *not* due to Enemy Action

The primary topic of this book is the effect of enemy air raids on the railways, but some serious accidents in the London Region should be mentioned, although ostensibly unrelated to the exigencies of the war.

12/10/40 (Saturday)
On the LMSR at Sudbury Junction at 19.15, the locomotive[115] and all coaches of 12.00 express Liverpool – Euston derailed and overturned after striking parcels barrow allowed to run off platform at Wembley. Driver, fireman and five passengers killed, nine seriously injured. All lines blocked, but Up Slow soon brought into use for meat, fish and other trains of perishables. Down Fast cleared on 13/10, but not for "normal traffic" until 14.35 15/10. Meanwhile some traffic diverted to Midland Section or to LNER.

12/11/40
On the SR at Woolwich Arsenal at 07.09, two electric trains collided on a stretch with SLW on the Up since damage on 7/10. One motorman seriously injured and four passengers less so.

14/11/40
King's Cross 00.00: Brake-van and four wagons of train off SR derailed 50 yards from end of Hotel Curve Tunnel. The breakdown train entered the tunnel 04.20 and at 05.40 its locomotive derailed at same place! Moorgate local trains cut back Finsbury Park.[116] nwr 12.15 and heavy freight backlog cleared. Meanwhile at 02.30 Gas Works Tunnel flooded and partially closed, so blocking Down Slow and Down Main No. 2, but clear 09.10.

18/3/41
A bad collision – probably not due directly to enemy action – occurred at Leyton (LNER) about 07.30. The 06.42 local Ilford – Liverpool Street [via Woodford] collided in fog with 07.01 local Loughton – Liverpool Street. About 75 people hurt, but none fatally. Shuttles run Leytonstone – Loughton. Through trains to Liverpool Street started Snaresbrook and ran via Woodford Loop. Buses Maryland – Leytonstone. nwr 09.45 19/3.

20/4/41
Although just after two very heavy air raids, the serious accident at St John's (SR) at 18.31 seems not due directly to enemy action. The loco and five coaches of the 18.15 express Cannon Street – Dover – Ramsgate derailed on London side of the station. Fireman killed and Driver badly injured. Two passengers slightly injured. All four lines blocked. Traffic terminated Catford Bridge, Hither Green, Blackheath. Cause unknown. Later, trains terminated Peckham Rye and New Cross Gate, with special buses between. Signal current failed, so HSW necessary into London Bridge (Central) until 20.50. Traction current restored 22.40. Re-railing completed at 19.27 21/4. Local lines reopened 22.10 21/4, Through lines 18.50 22/4.

4/11/42
Serious accident at Waddon (SR) 06.05. Two EMU collided on Down Platform line. One coach derailed. Both lines blocked until 16.25. One motorman killed, two passengers injured. Traffic diverted and buses provided West Croydon – Wallington, connecting with shuttle electric service Wallington – Epsom Downs.

6/12/42 (Sunday)
Victoria (Eastern) 20.47: Light-engine collided with 20.35 express leaving for Ramsgate. Locomotive of express derailed. Both locomotives and one coach damaged. No injuries to passengers, but driver of light-engine seriously injured. Eastern Section Down Main and Relief lines blocked, but clear 04.08 7/12.

16/3/43
Liverpool Street 12.22: 07.35 express ex-Cromer ran into buffers Platform 10. Injuries to 20–30 passengers (two serious).

29/4/43
Victoria (Central) 08.45: 07.12 ex-Tunbridge Wells West collided with buffers Platform 17. Leading coach telescoped, locomotive blocked line. Several casualties, including fireman and guard. nwr at 12.00.

10/6/43
King's Cross 13.19: 08.40 express ex-Cleethorpes ran into buffer-stops Platform 8. One coach damaged. Three passengers injured, but "No interference with working."

25/10/43
Camden Town 11.05: Shunting locomotive and eight wagons ran out of control and collided with Maiden Lane Box, partly demolishing it. Nos 1 Up and Down and No.2 Up lines blocked. No.2 Up line clear 13.00, permitting restricted electric service and some freight. nwr 20.00.

15/1/44 (Saturday)
Ilford 19.25: Very serious accident in dense fog. 14.40 express Norwich to Liverpool Street (headed by B12/3 4-6-0 No. 8564) ran into rear of 14.33 express ex-Yarmouth. Nine people killed (three US Servicemen), 30 injured. Through lines blocked. nwr 14.30 17/1.

21/8/44
Wood Green 17.30: First four coaches of 17.21 local Finsbury Park – Gordon Hill derailed and locomotive fell down embankment onto Down Goods line. Five passengers injured (one seriously). Driver seriously injured and fireman suffered shock. Down Hertford line trains diverted through Engineer's yard. Locomotive and coaches re-railed 06.30 22/8, then normal suburban services operated. Down Goods line reopened 12.00 23/8.

30/8/44
Unusual accident, South Harrow Tunnel (Sudbury Hill – Northolt Park, LNER GC Section) 03.45. Owing to design weakness, very occasionally the fireboxes of the US Army S160 2-8-0 collapsed, violently. (These were on loan to UK Railways in 1942–44). This was one of those occasions.[117] Both lines blocked. Driver and fireman seriously injured, fireman dying later.[118] SLW was put in operation Sudbury Hill – Northolt East 06.05. nwr 08.50.

29/12/44
Romford 18.15: 17.20 local Chelmsford – Liverpool Street ran into rear of freight. Guard in brake van killed. Several wagons telescoped. Local lines blocked.

18/1/45
Rickmansworth (Met&GC) 10.31: LNE freight collided with LPTB (Metropolitan) passenger train. Three coaches telescoped. Both lines blocked. One passenger suffered shock. Down line clear 11.30, then SLW to Chorley Wood until nwr 17.07.

4/2/45
Unusual and serious accident, King's Cross 18.05:[119] 18.00 express to Leeds (17 coaches, 590 tons hauled by A4 Pacific No. 2512) after entering Gas Works Tunnel ran back owing to locomotive slipping. (Exceptionally heavy trains of those days sometimes slipped to standstill on greasy incline up through tunnel, but on this occasion crew of the express unaware – owing to darkness and smoke – that their train actually going backwards). The reversing train split on points and part collided with coaches of 19.00 express to Aberdeen standing at Platform 10. Two rear coaches of Leeds train derailed, one lying broadside, one leaning against signal-bridge. Bridge brought down with all cables carrying power to West side (suburban station and Down Metropolitan line). Leading coach of Aberdeen train damaged. Locomotive of Leeds train a total failure.

Two men killed in overturned coach; 20–30 cases of shock and slight injuries. Local Station, Down Slow, Down Main No.2 and Passenger Local lines all blocked. Main Station only available at Platforms 1–5. Inner Suburban trains terminated Finsbury Park[120] and passengers transferred to LPTB services. Outer Suburban trains also terminated Finsbury Park as necessary. Hertford trains terminated Bowes Park if required. Central portion of signal gantry, carrying all power signal wires, had to be moved, wires disconnected and run underground. "This will necessitate HSW for some considerable time". (Actually restored in 18 days, and HSW needed for West side signalling only). Broadside coach removed 09.05 5/2, but entry to Platforms 7 – 17 and all signalling on Departure side still out of use. Down Slow restored 13.45 5/2, but trains restricted to 14 coaches – to 16 from 9/2. MWL traffic restored 15.20 5/2, but suburban services still terminated Finsbury Park. Restricted Outer Suburban services resumed 6/2. On 12/2, Outer and Inner Suburban services resumed working into Platforms 6 – 15, with "HSW as necessary". On 21/2, Arrival side working normally, with departures from Platforms 16 – 17 operating by HSW. Otherwise, signalling in main-line station normal 09.45 21/2.[121]

Bow Locomotive Works. Serious damage in the Erecting Shop after the raid of 19/20 April 1941. The locomotives all look very Midland; one of the two 4-4-0s on the left is No. 515.

Conclusions

Considered in retrospect and in light of the massive damage and disruption later achieved by the Allied bombing of enemy railways – albeit with very much greater forces, the Germans were not very successful in disrupting the railways. Nevertheless, air raids, air raid warnings and the blackout did seriously hamper the railways' ability to move traffic generally, particularly in London and the South of England. Although the Luftwaffe were unable during their night raids to bomb specific railway targets, it does seem that bombs may have been aimed deliberately at areas in London where they might do some serious damage, for example around Blackfriars Bridge. However, their bombing was not very effective. The number of reports of damage and delay on the railways as a whole due to enemy action rose from 32 in June 1940 to a peak of 1,317 in September, fell back to 176 in February 1941 and rose to a lesser peak in 1941 of 564 in April. A measure of the inefficacy of all that bombing, and of the efficiency of repair work, is that railway facilities were affected for more than 24 hours in only 15–20% of instances and in only about 3% for more than a week.

Over the whole of Britain, during the 5½ years of aerial warfare, the Railways reported more than 9,000 cases of damage and delay. Some 3,600 of these incidents interfered only slightly with traffic facilities, but in 5,600 cases there was damage or delay. In nearly 250 cases, working arrangements were affected for more than a week, but over 90% caused interruption of services for less than 24 hours. The enemy destroyed eight locomotives and damaged 484. The number of passenger vehicles demolished was 637 and no fewer than 13,487 were damaged. Freight rolling stock also suffered severely: 3,321 wagons were reduced to scrap and 20,294 required repair.

The destruction of railway assets was serious enough, but was probably not so extensive as the German High Command hoped to effect. Unhappily, the attacks on the main-line railways and the LPTB lines killed 900 people and injured 4,450. Included in these totals are 395 railwaymen killed and 2,444 injured. The heaviest death toll (300) was on the SR; it was 225 on the LPTB lines, 170 on the LNER, 126 on the GWR and 72 on the LMSR. Nevertheless, all these facts pale almost to insignificance when compared with the death and destruction suffered on the railways of the enemy, and in the Soviet Union, France and many other countries in the war.

The night raids of 1940–41 were prolonged for much of the night, and all the more disruptive owing to the long hours under 'Alert' conditions. It was particularly hard on people's nerves – and on the working of the railways. There was the Black-Out to be contended with, which severely restricted – and made more hazardous – outside work such as shunting even in the absence of Alerts. Also, until some easement was allowed in November 1940, during Alerts trains were stopped to allow any passengers to take shelter, then allowed to proceed at 15 mph – freight trains at 10 mph. From February 1941, trains were no longer stopped or restricted in daylight, but at night they still had to stop then proceed at 30 mph. Nevertheless, many instances still occurred of trains running into craters or obstructions, and it was only in 1943 that a rule was made that if signalling failed during a raid in darkness, fog or snow, all trains were to stop until the line had been reported safe. During the V-1 offensive, signalmen at boxes in or approaching the London area warned drivers by showing a white board with a black arrow pointing upwards. To discourage workers running for shelter immediately on hearing the Red Alert roof spotters were appointed, who in the London Region gave warning to main stations and signal-boxes of 'imminent danger' when Flying Bombs were 15 miles off. Nevertheless, key staff such as trainmen and signalmen responsible for the immediate safety of other staff and the public were expected to – and did – remain at their posts even when warned of imminent danger. They tried to keep the trains moving at all costs: so long as a signalman could see no obstruction and his instruments were working to his adjacent Boxes, he did not (after November 1940) stop a train by putting his signals to danger – he hoped for the best, with the result that not a few trains ran into craters or debris in the dark.

Passenger Traffic

Sixty and more years later there are few people still living who can remember personally how it was to live and work in London during the Second World War. Most people today have grown up in a world dominated by the motor car and most of them possess one (at least). London is almost unique in that people who work in the Central London area travel there by train; in Britain as a whole, 85% of people travel to work by car. People complain constantly about the 'unreliability' (mainly in terms of precise punctuality) and discomfort (mainly really due to the other passengers) of their regular journey to work. If they possibly can, they use their cars for any other journeys, short or long, in spite of usually being unable by a large margin to predict how long a journey by car will take and the real but not obvious dangers of driving. Similarly, over 90% of goods traffic now goes by road. The clear advantage of the lorry, as with the private car, is the door-to-door transit, even though and in spite of the motorway network it is no quicker nor in overall terms cheaper than rail transport.

Back in WW2 (and before) the railways were by far the most important mode of inland transport. They were operated by competent men aware of their responsibility to keep the system running at all costs, with in the main a strong sense of pride in their work. This is underlined by the perhaps tedious repetition in this account of the duration of interruptions of traffic after war incidents. In those days, if a railway line was blocked it was of the utmost importance to restore normal working as quickly as possible. Otherwise, people would freeze or starve; utilities and factories would grind to a standstill. The contrast with the present day is amazing. If an interruption of railway operations occurs nowadays, for whatever reason trivial or not, it takes of the order of ten times longer to restore normal working than it did in WW2, and at a phenomenal cost – mainly in wages. Much of this disparity is due to 'Health & Safety' considerations, but fundamentally it is due to the perceived non-essentiality of the public transport network and to related public attitudes. Major routes are closed for repairs routinely at weekends: e.g. long stretches of the West Coast Main Line at the height of the summer holidays for renovation – but who cares? – 'We'll go by car anyway'.

In WW2 people were forced to endure delay and disruption of their journeys, and they took it in their stride. Looked at from the eyes of those living now, it seems quite incredible that bombing by the enemy rarely resulted in the closure of major London stations and main lines for more than a few hours, if at all. Most of the termini were so large that they could 'absorb' a remarkable number of explosions of the relatively small HE bombs (mainly 250–500 kg) used by the Luftwaffe, without having to be closed to passengers. UXB were much more effective.

The London area had many trying experiences, by piloted aircraft in the Blitz of 1940–41 and the Little Blitz of 1944, then to attacks by missiles after June 1944. For the Railways, it was worst for the Southern, serving South London and suburbs. This Railway suffered severely, not only because of geography, but also to some extent from its relative modernity: in the London area and down to the South Coast the SR had already been electrified and in part also equipped with modern power signalling. The fact that the electrification was by conductor rail made the railway less vulnerable than it might have been if the overhead system had been used. However, the SR had its own electricity supply, separate from the National Grid (50 c/s frequency), so when the generating station (25 c/s) at Durnsford Road (Wimbledon) was seriously damaged in October 1940, half of its capacity was lost and the Western Section suburban services had to be curtailed much more than if power could have been taken from the Grid.

On most of the SR lines in Inner London, the numerous bridges and viaducts were a particular handicap during the war, although multiple tracks and the variety of routes usually allowed for some traffic to pass. A direct hit on a viaduct section by 500 kg or more of HE, or the presence of a UXB, could involve closure of a whole multi-track section for many days. Heavy repairs and the rapid erection of temporary structures were necessary, whereas even a crater on a stretch of plain track could be dealt with in a few hours. The passenger services of the SR were also handicapped by being to a large extent electrified and therefore vulnerable to interruption of power supply. Even if track was not damaged, wires and cables often were, rendering lines inoperable by failure of signalling and immobilizing electric services. Blockages were also quite often caused by barrage balloons and/or their cables. Anyway, even if not known to have been hit by enemy missiles, important routes had often to be closed for varying periods on many occasions during and after air raids or V-weapon incidents, for general examination for obstructions – especially for UXB.

Waterloo, London's largest terminus, with its 21 terminal platforms in the main (Western Section) part and four through platforms in the adjoining Eastern ('Junction') Station, was an easy target for the Luftwaffe. During the war it received well over 40 direct hits from HE bombs and countless IB. Heavy damage was caused during at least eight raids and relatively lesser damage in another eight or so. To begin with, the terminus was closed from 7 September 1940 for no less than 12 days following almost complete destruction of the approaches, and very soon afterwards for another two days. There were subsequently several raids that disabled at least a major part of Waterloo, such as 9 December when on the north side a bomb penetrated to the W&C and put that line out of use for three months. Then the terminus was unusable for eight days after the 29 December raid. In 1941 it closed for 13 hours on 8 March, 36 hours on 17–18 April and for six days after the massive fire on 11 May.

The approach to Waterloo from Clapham Junction, of four miles all above the houses and over about 30 bridges and viaducts, was frequently subject to damage at multiple sites. Until the end of 1940, it was rarely free of blockage somewhere, especially on the Windsor Lines side. In the later raids, the approaches were blocked often, if intermittently. There were eight tracks, from south to north: Down and Up Main Local, Down and Up Main Through, Up Main Relief, Down Windsor Local, Down Windsor Through, Up Windsor. Along the way were the great yards at Nine Elms; nearer Clapham Junction were a maze of railways and yards that crossed and interconnected with each other. When Waterloo was closed, not only passengers from the South-West suburbs and beyond had to find other ways to get into London, but also outwards parcels and mails accumulated in enormous quantities. After being sorted, they were sent by road to Wimbledon, Esher or Woking. Also the nightly Newspaper trains left from Clapham Junction, Wimbledon or even Surbiton.

It was a similar story with London Bridge and its elevated approach of nearly four miles from Spa Road, Bricklayers Arms Junction or North Kent East Junction. This had 11 tracks, from north to south: Eastern Nos 1–3 Down, Eastern Nos 2 and 1 Up, Eastern/Central Down and Up Main and Up Local, Central (SL) Down, Up Main and Up Local. There were few times during the Blitz when all these lines were completely clear of damage or UXB, but also rarely was London Bridge Station, being in two main parts, entirely closed: 29 December 1940 was an exception, when devastation of the Central Section part and UXB entailed closure for 3½ days – while trains were still running through the Eastern part.

Victoria was more vulnerable, because there were 'only' nine tracks (four Eastern, five Central) on its approaches over Grosvenor Bridge. It presented a large target and received a proportionate share of bombs. One or other of the two sides of the terminus were closed for up to five days, mainly owing to UXB as physical damage was not great. Fortunately, the elevated approaches to Victoria were not often blocked. However, in the Blitz Victoria had the misfortune of 'receiving' in its forecourt a crashing German bomber and later a V-1. Waterloo also was severely damaged by a flying bomb .

Of the smaller SR termini, Charing Cross was battered the most often. It was only ever closed completely for a few hours, although at one time it struggled with two platforms for three weeks and the Local lines were out of action for many months. This was on account of major damage to the bridge over Blackfriars Road on the four-track elevated approach, also to the Hungerford (River) Bridge during the Blitz and later by a flying bomb. Waterloo Eastern was also shattered in one particular raid. Likewise, Cannon Street was blasted in the May raid but was working (skeletally) four days later. Holborn Viaduct was gutted in the same raid, but along with Blackfriars came to life again when the approach lines over all those bridges were restored 15 days later.

When the lines to/from London Bridge were cut, no doubt journeys were prolonged, but rarely entirely aborted because SER line passengers could usually switch to LC&DR lines, at least into Victoria, and vice-versa. Passengers on the Central Section could choose to travel via Victoria or London Bridge. As matters turned out, they would have found Victoria less often blocked. Central Section commuters could also switch to LC&DR line or Western Section services if necessary. However, if they tried to get into London by the ex-LC&D Blackfriars (City line) route this was more often than not obstructed. The destruction of the big bridge at Blackfriars Junction over Southwark Street on 20 April 1941 was the culmination of a succession of major and prolonged blockages of the route down to and beyond Loughborough Junction.

The problem with South London was that the LPTB had really only one Underground line (Northern) that penetrated far enough to act as a trunk route for suburban passengers. Their main alternative, the tram routes, were very susceptible to severance by bombing. Moreover, South Londoners were seriously inconvenienced by the closure of the Tube tunnels under the Thames, which occurred whenever there was an Alert and was almost continuous during the two months of night raids during the Blitz and then again in June and July 1944 owing to the FLY. It was also very inconvenient when the W&C 'Drain' was put out of action for nearly three months from December 1940. North of the Thames, most of the tramways had already been converted to trolleybus routes, while the Underground served most areas other than the North-East suburbs. The Underground was usually able to take the passengers impeded by obstructions on the main-line railways, although this hardly applied to the LPTB District Line in East London which on the surface ran parallel to the LT&S line of the LMSR. Passengers using the Tube lines in the evening or early morning, however, had to make their way around the masses of Shelterers!

The main-line termini on the north side of the Thames were all bombed on several occasions, but in the main their approaches were generally less vulnerable than were those of the SR. Euston was perhaps the most fortunate. It was severely damaged on only one occasion and was never closed completely, although the electric services into Euston were interrupted some 15 times. (The longest blockage was for a week and passengers were accommodated by steam services meanwhile). Paddington was badly hurt twice, but each time it carried on. Liverpool Street was severely damaged on several occasions but the whole station never closed for more than 17 hours; rather, only one or other part of it was affected. Its busy (steam) suburban services were, however, often interrupted by obstructions down the line. King's Cross was badly damaged on 11 May 1941 but was not closed then, and only briefly on a couple of other occasions when enemy action cut the approach lines.

It was rather different with the smaller termini. Marylebone, with only a double-track approach, was closed for three days, later for two spells each of a month or so, after the breaching of the shallow tunnels on the approach. However, most of its passengers could use the Metropolitan instead, making use of the temporary interchange station at Neasden. Broad Street, in spite of a four-track approach, was isolated several times (once for a month) by damage to the viaducts from Dalston Junction at several places.

Fenchurch Street was not itself badly damaged but was closed (or the services into it suspended) several times owing to bridge damage or UXB on its fairly restricted and partly elevated approaches, the principal route running into Fenchurch Street, the LMSR's LT&S Line being briefly blocked on numerous occasions.

St Pancras was unlucky. It was struck and severely damaged on five occasions, often closed for at least a day and once for five days. Passengers were no more inconvenienced than having to use the Tube to/from Kentish Town, in the same way as King's Cross passengers were catered for at Finsbury Park.[122] On two of those nights a bomb penetrated to the tunnel on the important link between the Midland main line and the MWL at King's Cross: it took four days to restore traffic on the first occasion; on the second total blockage lasted 16 days and it was 7½ months before normal double-line working resumed.

One should also remember that rail travellers in London during the Blitz and the V-weapons offensive had sometimes to contend with more than delays and diversions, and the risk of sudden death everyone had to accept. There were quite a number of occasions when HE affected passenger trains in transit, as the record shows. (Sometimes the Luftwaffe even machine-gunned trains, but this was largely out in the country). Fortunately, being in a train was not a serious risk in this regard: far more so was taking shelter under the railway arches, which were not meant to be shelters but were often believed to be.

Freight Traffic

Bomb damage, and the presence of UXB on or near the lines, had cumulative effects in slowing down the movement of railway traffic and reducing railway capacity. At any time, London was a major bottleneck in terms of inland rail transport. When London terminals were put out of action or London goods depots destroyed, loading, unloading and marshalling were impeded throughout the country and the movement of traffic suffered. Traffic had to be 'stopped back', freight trains moved more slowly and wagon turnover was retarded. The congestion spread to other lines and steadily reduced the efficiency of the railway system as a whole. It was just as well that the Germans did not persist with their Blitz on London but spread it widely over other British cities. Their raids on London, heavy as they were, were usually so spaced out that the disruption and congestion they caused could be overcome betweenwhiles.

Perhaps the greatest problem of all was to distribute enough coal to meet the needs of South London and South-Eastern England, for this traffic had to be got across the Thames. During September/October 1940, 25–50% of line capacity in the neighbourhood of the river crossings was out of action because of air raids. The number of wagons exchanged from north to south of the river fell to little more than 25% of the July 1940 figure. The whole of Southern England was, like London, a coal consuming area drawing the bulk of its supplies from further north, albeit now to some extent from South Wales. Normally a good deal was moved by sea to the South Coast ports, but the dangers to shipping in the North Sea and the Channel were so great that a large part of the sea-borne supplies had to be curtailed. Instead the coal was sent by rail, and in February 1940 the celebrated scheme of 'Convoy' coal trains was introduced: at yards in the coalfields 'Block' trains were made up for one or two destinations only, some 250 or more 'Convoy' trains per week being scheduled to run through from North to South without intermediate marshalling. This coal traffic, together with ever-increasing merchandise traffic, had to be passed from the LMS and LNE systems to the GWR and SR at various exchange junctions, such as Bordesley, Banbury and Reading. If at all possible, it would not be routed through London.

From September 1940, not only the capacity of the railways became markedly reduced by damage in the London area, but also sea-borne supplies were being hampered by slower discharge of ships in the Thames, by bad weather and by convoy delays. It seemed at the time that the limit of inland transport capacity to carry coal to London and the South had been reached: road transport could give no great relief, except for very short hauls and the canals could only make a trifling contribution. In the 36 weeks ending 8 September 1940, total loaded wagon-miles on all the railways was 27% higher than in the corresponding period in 1939 (coal, 33%),[123] and the industrial and military build-up was moving ever more freight from the North to destinations in the South and South-West. There were few good cross-country routes by which it could move, so this traffic tended to become concentrated in the London area. There it had to be exchanged from the Northern lines to the Southern system over lines that were inadequate for handling intensive freight traffic. In 1940, the capacity of lines that had been adequate in the summer became insufficient in the new and difficult traffic situation of the autumn and winter months. For example, at the end of September 1940, owing to damage to the approaches to the Thames crossings, the number of wagons exchanged between the LMSR and SR in the London area was less than a quarter of what it had been six months earlier.

Other than for the heavy traffic to/from the Docks, industry and population on the north side of the Thames Estuary, the Thames crossings in the London area constituted the pinchpoints for traffic for South-East England. The evolution of the railway system had not resulted in crossings capable of conveying a substantial flow of freight over the Thames without major deviation. They were confined to the Chelsea and Barnes Bridges in West London, and the Blackfriars Bridge that connected the LPTB 'MWL' with the Eastern Section of the SR. During the war, the LPTB ELR tunnel, linking the LNER at Spitalfields with the SR at New Cross, was largely discounted on account of its limited capacity, location and vulnerability, so the three bridge crossings bore the brunt of the cross-river traffic. The Chelsea Bridge took over 70 per day but trains had to be of restricted length and had to run the gauntlet of the MWL and the long elevated stretches of the SR so often blocked by enemy

action. (Kew Bridge could take some of the Feltham traffic otherwise routed over Barnes Bridge, but none was scheduled and could really only be run in the dead of night, because otherwise it was very busy with suburban passenger traffic).

The ring lines round the west and north sides of London were of vital importance for freight and wartime special traffic. The WLR/WLER, between Willesden LMSR (Western Division) and Old Oak Common GWR and Latchmere/Clapham/Longhedge Junctions, conveyed traffic for destinations on the SR in South London, Kent and most of Sussex. It embraced a southward extension of the NLR with the SR, also linking with the N&SWJ line that connected to the LMSR (Midland Division) and the LNER (GC Section). The WLR/WLER was cut frequently, but in spite of most of it being only two-track the longest interruptions were two of five days and one of ten in September/October 1940.

The NLR route was also blocked on very many occasions. This carried prodigious freight and special traffic, squeezed in between local electric services. It conveyed traffic off the WLR/WLER and from the LMSR via Willesden Junction and Camden Town, from the GWR and SR via the N&SWJ, and from the LMSR Midland Division, to the LNER (GN and GE Sections), the Docks and LT&S destinations such as Tilbury, via Temple Mills Yard and Stratford or via Gospel Oak and the T&H Line. There were four tracks on the middle stretch of the NLR and total blockages never exceeded a few days, but bridge and other damage caused partial blockage for long periods. The Gospel Oak – Forest Gate route was rarely totally blocked for more than a few hours, but it was reduced at Leyton and Wanstead Park to a single line for periods of up to six weeks.

Considering the concentration of air attacks on East London and the Docks, lasting damage to the network of railways in that area was surprisingly limited. Along with goods stations in the Docks, the four-track LNER line from Stratford to North Woolwich serving the Royal Docks was very severely damaged in the first big raids of 7–8 September 1940, when it was out of action for at least two weeks; later it was blocked occasionally. The NLR line to Poplar and the West/East India Docks complex was obstructed many times. These interruptions were not as serious as they might have been, for much of the Port of London traffic had been diverted to West Coast ports. It was more serious in 1944 during Operation Overlord, when many Flying Bombs were falling in the area while supplies were being loaded for Normandy.

Before the war there was concern that severe bombing of London would disrupt the vital movements across the Thames bridges in the capital. More particularly, the great dip of the MWL under the Metropolitan Line between King's Cross and Farringdon might flood due to fracture of massive sewers and mains; in the event such flooding did occur on one occasion and the MWL were blocked by other damage on several occasions during the Blitz. In December 1939 nearly 2,000 wagons were passing per day across Blackfriars Bridge, two-thirds from the LNER (GN) and one-third from the LMSR (Midland Division). Therefore right at the outset, to facilitate cross-London traffic over Blackfriars Bridge, new connections were put in between the MWL and the Metropolitan (passenger) lines at King's Cross, to allow traffic to be diverted in emergency to the ELR line; also a new crossover was inserted at Ludgate Hill to enable either half of Blackfriars Bridge to be used. As we have seen, during the Blitz the route over Blackfriars Bridge proved very vulnerable on account of destruction of bridges on the elevated sections of the SR.

The overriding requirement was to keep the traffic moving, and for this an extra 100 miles of journey was acceptable, at least for coal and provided wagons were not tied up or sidings choked. New links to facilitate cross-London transit were brought into use in 1940, and indeed proved necessary. The first really viable alternative route off the LNER (GN) to the MWL went by the loop (built in the First World War and resuscitated in March 1940) from Harringay to the T&H, then by another restored loop at Gospel Oak to the NLR. Several trains a day could be diverted this way via Temple Mills, the T&H Line, Gospel Oak and the WLER to Norwood or Hither Green on the SR.

Diversion well away from London altogether was preferable. Thus for example, the GWR at Old Oak Common was overburdened, so coal from South Wales and the Bristol District to the SR Central Section was sent instead via Salisbury and Havant. For North/South traffic, routes were created based on the existing and new junctions of the LMS Cambridge – Bletchley – Oxford line and the GWR from Oxford through Reading. On the Cambridge – Oxford line, loops were built in 1940 from the LNER (GN) main line north of Sandy and to the LNER (GC) main line at Calvert, also a new LMS – GW connection was put in at Oxford. Southbound freight traffic in general (not only coal) for the important Solent area or for the SR Central Section via Chichester, was run onto the GWR at Oxford, thence via Reading West and Basingstoke. (From Calvert, traffic followed the LNE (GC) route to Northolt Junction, thence onto the GWR or via Neasden and the N&SWJ to the SR at Kew Bridge). Later, the heavy flow of traffic off the GWR to/from the SR, which otherwise would have passed through London, was carried by a new main-line connection opened in 1941 at Reading. Less useful was a link put in at Staines between the GWR and the SR, to give a route for traffic from the LNER via Banbury, Sandy, or Calvert or from the LMSR via Bletchley, through Oxford to reach the SR. However, in practice the route was rarely used, probably only at the most critical times in the Blitz.

Restriction Orders

Already early in the Blitz, damage to critical link lines in London was having a most serious effect on the transfer of traffic between north and south of the Thames. For instance, the GN Section of the LNER normally forwarded 50–60 trains to the SR each day, but on 11 September 1940 there were 5,000–6,000 wagons held up on the LNE system awaiting transfer. A stop therefore had to be put on the loading of all traffic forwarded over the LNER and destined for the SR Central and Eastern Sections. The usual exchange routes between the LMSR and SR Central and Western Sections had also been seriously compromised and a very considerable quantity of traffic was held up in the LMS yards, although some relief was gained by exchanging traffic with the SR at Feltham. This was the initial reaction to the Blitz and anticipated difficulties that recurred in the coming months, to which the Railways adapted.

One way was by the REC issuing Restriction Orders to stop temporarily the loading of freight traffic for certain routes and destinations where congestion or disruption was occurring. The following list (dated 18 September 1940) indicates the situation early in the London Blitz. Much longer and more drastic Restriction Orders came to be imposed later on.

LMSR: All traffic for Poplar (LNW and MR), including coal for barging or otherwise; all coal and coke (except loco coal and block[124] coal for LMS stations Cheltenham to Bristol, Avonmouth and branches, and for GW line between Cheltenham, Gloucester and Bristol. (This was because traffic normally routed through London was being diverted that way). All traffic for Canning Town. Traffic for LT&S Line via Western Division was closed, and all except coal was to be diverted as above; coal was to be blocked back and held until further notice. Then all traffic including coal[125] for SR Eastern and Central Sections was stopped, followed by all traffic to Grays and Purfleet, then by all traffic (including coal) for many LNE stations and the Docks in East London, next for the LMS depots at Brixton, West Kensington, Walworth Road, Wandsworth Road and Thames Wharf. Next, all traffic to SR Central Section via Midland Division routes, then also coal via Willesden. Finally, all traffic from Western Division or from GWR to LNER via Temple Mills.

GWR: All traffic via Acton for Poplar (GW and LMS) and Victoria & Albert (GW and LMS), also all stations on the LT&S; all traffic (including coal) for South Lambeth; all traffic for SR Central and Eastern Sections via all junctions.

LNER: All traffic LMS to LNE via Nottingham (Sneinton Junction). (This prevented diversion of LMS traffic to the LNER, which was already overburdened). All coal including block coal to GW line via Banbury. (This put a stop for the time being on coal from the North-East to London and beyond being diverted from its normal route by the LNER).

Subsequently, Restrictions also tended to be placed on forwarding certain traffics to London goods depots during periods of Alerts, notably during the V-weapons offensive.

Part of an SR Report made on 24 September 1940 when matters were at their most worrying reads:

"Between 7 and 23 September the SR had no less than 275 blockages (116 due to bomb damage, 159 due to UXB), nearly all in the London area. Every London passenger terminus had been closed at one time or another – but not all on any one day. There was interference with freight working by closure for a time of various London depots and some marshalling yards and also by blockage on some of the exchange routes with other Companies. The additional facilities worked out for alternative routes for use in the event of demolition of Thames bridges had proved valuable, but the energetic steps by the Chief Engineer and his staff in effecting temporary repairs have in most cases resulted in the lines being available for traffic within a few days – often only hours – of the occurrence. Full advantage has been taken of the assistance from the Army RCC. ... The position today ... is that every SR London passenger terminal is open and, in the suburban area, only 13 stations are without a train service.[126] The main trunk routes are all available to traffic, with the exception of an interruption between two stations on the Hastings line. The London goods depots are open, necessarily with some restriction on traffic. The marshalling yards are working and our inflow of wagons from other Companies is equal to that of the same period last year. The staff of all grades throughout the railways continues to show exceptional qualities of endurance, courage, cheerfulness and resource even in exceptionally dangerous and trying conditions, and there is no doubt that the fine leadership of the Departmental and Divisional Officers has contributed very largely to maintaining the spirit of teamwork throughout the line."

Bibliography

The following is a brief list of books recommended for background to the facts about the Railways and the London air raids.

Bell, R., CBE (1946). *History of the British Railways during the War, 1939–45.* London: The Railway Gazette.

Crump, N. (1947). *By Rail to Victory. The Story of the L.N.E.R. in Wartime.* London: The London and North Eastern Railway.

Darwin, B. (1946). *War on the Line. The Story of the Southern Railway in War-Time.* London: The Southern Railway Company.

Jackson, A.A. (1969). *London's Termini.* Newton Abbot: David & Charles Publishers Ltd.

Royle, T.W. (1943–45). *History of the London Midland and Scottish Railway in the Second World War,* Volumes I – IV. Unpublished, but held in typescript at the National Archives at: RAIL421/9 also RAIL418/197–200.

Savage, C.I. (1957). *Inland Transport* (History of the Second World War, Civil Series). London HMSO and Longman Green.

White, H.P. (1963). *The Regional History of the Railways of Great Britain, Volume III, Greater London.* London: Phoenix House.

For topographic details of London railways, the series of booklets published from 1986 by Middleton Press at Midhurst are recommended. They now cover all the termini and suburban lines. Also recommended for railway details are the Alan Godfrey Maps, published at Gateshead in recent years, being reprints (at 1:4340) of Ordnance Survey 1:2500 maps of 1914 (and earlier) and now covering most of London.

There are numerous books about London in the Second World War. A thorough bibliography is given in: Creaton, H. (1998). *Sources for the History of London 1939–45: a Guide and Bibliography.* London: British Records Association. Those studied by this author include:

Calder, A. (1969). *The People's War: Britain 1939–45.* London: Jonathan Cape.

Collier, B. (1957). *The Defence of the United Kingdom,* London: HMSO and Longman Green.

Gardiner, Juliet (2004). *Wartime Britain 1939–1945.* London: Headline Book Publishing.

Home Office (Civil Defence Department), Key Points Directorate, London (1948), *Chronicle of Main Attacks on Great Britain and Northern Ireland and of their effect on the vital National War Effort (1939–1945).* (See NA HO201/42).

Longmate, N. (1981). *The Doodlebugs.* London: Hutchinson.

O'Brien, T.H. (1955). *Civil Defence,* London: HMSO and Longman Green.

Ramsey, Winston G. (Ed.) (1987–90). *The Blitz, Then and Now,* Vols. 1–3. London: Battle of Britain Prints International.

Ray, J. (1996). *The Night Blitz 1940–41.* London: Arms and Armour Press.

Ziegler, P. (1995). *London at War 1939–1945.* London: Sinclair-Stevenson.

––––––––––

Endnotes

1. It was also considered as 'reprisal' for the RAF's recent achievement in getting British bombers as far as Berlin. It was preceded by a 'practice' run on the night of September 5/6.
2. Officially, by the German Oberkommando der Wehrmacht (OKW), on 12 October.
3. This fact led to the introduction of radio communication between a number of important control centres.
4. Preserved at the National Archives (NA) in the following: REC Daily Situation Reports: AN2/1095–1122; Monthly Lists and Summaries, also giving casualty numbers: AN2/500-504,509–512, also MT6/2758.
5. Especially the following NA files: AN2/582, 810-811; RAIL250/776; RAIL390/1192; RAIL421/9; RAIL648/ 89–92, 103–116; MT6/2749, 2751, 2761-2764; HO192, HO198/206, HO199, HO201/42, HO203.
6. Not included are incidents on the Whitechapel & Bow section of the LPTB, owned jointly with the LMSR, which was primarily part of the Underground system although traversed in part by goods trains. Several incidents on the Central London (E&SB) LPTB line are also omitted if not affecting the GWR. There were also some incidents on the Metropolitan Lines running parallel to the LNER between Finchley Road and Harrow-on-the-Hill, which apparently did not affect the LNER so are not mentioned.
7. For example, three derailments occurred in one week in March 1944 at King's Cross, each requiring passenger trains to be terminated at Finsbury Park for several hours.
8. See NA RAIL648/89–92/103–116.
9. The logbook prior to 14 September 1940 was not, unfortunately, acquired by the NA. Consequently, there are more gaps in the accounts recorded here of the events of early September, especially regarding restoration of normal working.
10. E4 0-6-2T No. 2504.
11. N 2-6-0 No. 1811.
12. A 'major' fire was defined as one requiring more than 30 pumps; a 'serious' fire 11–30 pumps. A 'conflagration' was a 'major' fire which was spreading.
13. On 7/9, all District/Metropolitan Line services east of Whitechapel were suspended from 17.45. Stepney Green station was severely damaged.
14. Other reports state that it fell in the Maori Sports Ground, 200 yards from the railway.
15. 'Schools' 4-4-0 No. 900 'Eton'.
16. With respect to Poplar and Victoria & Albert Docks and South Lambeth, these restrictions remained in force for many weeks.
17. I should think so – presumably by HSW!
18. Including O1 2-8-0 No. 3462 and other engines.
19. Preserved at NA AN2/582, together with other reports made in those darkest days of September 1940.
20. Including G6 0-6-0T No. 257.
21. Were lines really closed two weeks?
22. Probably several DAB involved: it is not clear from reports which exploded spontaneously, or when, and therefore for how long station was closed. See also 16/9/40
23. *Reports of Chief Civil Engineers and/or of Lt.Col. Mount (Chief Inspecting Officer to the MoWT).
24. This was at the time when Britain was so short of steel that urban iron fencing was being dismantled everywhere and melted down.
25. Discrepancy not resolved.
26. The main part of a Dornier Do17Z that had been shot up, most of the crew having bailed out beforehand – although one was beaten up by angry crowds in Kennington.
27. There must have been more to it than that.
28. SR C 0-6-0 No. 1720 and LNER J52 0-6-0T No. 4056.
29. The rush of water into the Wembley Brook carried forward into the gardens of the houses beyond and drowned several people in their Anderson shelters.
30. Lt.Col. Mount's report stated that there had now been five attacks on the Depot, in which four other engines had been badly damaged.
31. Officially 1/12/40.
32. Misunderstanding arose between the SR and the LCC about whether the footbridge should be made safe, but in the end it was, especially as the Underground under the river was closed during Red Alerts.
33. 4-6-0's Nos 5662 and 5709.
34. 'Schools' 4-4-0 No. 912 'Downside'.
35. Officially 21/10/40.
36. 'Schools' 4-4-0 No. 936 'Cranleigh'.
37. 0-6-0T Nos 8754 and 8767.
38. 4-6-0 No. 6122 'Royal Ulster Rifleman'
39. There seem to have been no casualties, except that the bombs fractured a major gas main and a number of people sheltering under the old Grosvenor Road station were taken to hospital with gas poisoning and a C&W Carriage Examiner died.
40. H 0-4-4T 1321.
41. It had been damaged the night before at Euston and this was probably the only time it was diverted throughout the war!
42. On 21/10/40, Uxbridge Road Station and the line Latimer Road Junction – Uxbridge Road Junction were closed, also St Quintin Park and the WLER stations at West Brompton, Chelsea & Fulham and Battersea
43. LMS 0-6-0T No. 7395.
44. N1 0-6-2T No. 4571.
45. Not mentioned by LMSR but must have applied to them as well.
46. But they managed to carry on in the meantime with a UXB there
47. 2-6-2T No. 6111.
48. O1 0-6-0 No. 1051.
49. The Railways were beginning to use wireless communication as a back-up.
50. J1 4-6-2T No. 2325.
51. A parachute-mine – 50 casualties; graphically described in *The Blitz Then and Now* (Vol. II, pp.328–9).
52. Summary reports indicate that there were two bombs concerned here, in two adjoining carriage yards.
53. Full service restored 15/4/41.
54. The incident is described vividly in Darwin's *War on the Line*.
55. See *The Blitz Then and Now* (Vol. II, pp 348–9, with several photographs.
56. E5 0-6-2T No. 2583.
57. Presumably including Christmas.
58. It seems that the enemy held off on Christmas and Boxing Days, as there were not even Alerts.
59. These premises housed 300 staff of the Traffic Manager's Department, who had to be transferred to Waterloo and elsewhere, also much valuable documentation was consumed in the fires.
60. This was when compulsory Fire-Watching duty was introduced.
61. Bank station was so badly damaged by HE falling in the concourse that it was not reopened until 17/3/41.
62. In Bishopsgate four buses were badly damaged, a driver and a conductor were killed and three others injured.
63. From a single raider, which dropped a very large (2,500 kg.) bomb that caused massive residential damage over a ¼-mile and killed 80 people.
64. Shadwell & St George's East (HL, LNER), also Leman Street, stations were officially closed on 7/7/41.
65. 4-6-0 No. 4961 'Pyrland Hall'.
66. 'Lord Nelson' No. 852 'Sir Walter Raleigh', and 'Schools' No. 927 'Clifton'.
67. Station closed before the war (1934).
68. ?Abbey Mills Upper Junction.
69. E1 4-4-0 No. 1497.
70. "If lines not already closed by destruction of Southwark Street bridge, traffic would have been allowed to pass at 15 mph"!
71. In addition a bomb from this raid, which waited until 6 June 1942 to explode, killed another 19.
72. 4-6-0 No. 5936 'Oakley Hall'.
73. All cash (about £4,000) was recovered (really?), but all the ticket stock was destroyed.
74. N2 0-6-2T No. 4761.
75. This seems a confused story: it is unlikely that the same train was set on fire twice, i.e. before and after depositing passengers at Waterloo!

76 T14 4-6-0 No. 446 – beyond repair.
77 Until the permanent signalbox was commissioned, electric services to Holborn Viaduct were restricted to 60% of normal.
78 A new signalbox was opened on 2/6/41.
79 'Schools' 4-4-0 No. 934 'St Lawrence'.
80 Bombs also penetrated to the Underground lines and blocked them.
81 Including 38 children and six teachers killed by a direct hit on a school at Catford.
82 E3 0-6-0T No. 2169.
83 Presumably via Richmond.
84 The Crayford Spur, between the North Kent and the Dartford Loop Lines with 'A' and 'B' Boxes controlling it, was put in during the war (11/10/42), to facilitate traffic between Woolwich Arsenal (Plumstead Sidings) and Hither Green Yard.
85 C 0-6-0 No. 1071.
86 K10 4-4-0 No. 380; 4-6-0's: N15 Nos 751, 755, 775 and 776, N15X No. 2328, S15 No. 841; Q1 0-6-0 No. C15; D1 0-4-2T No. 2289.
87 C 0-6-0's Nos 1054 and 1245.
88 The passenger service from Broad Street via Dalston had been suspended from 5 May 1944 anyway, although a bus service was substituted until 23/4/45.
89 Pilotless aircraft
90 Higham, Major J.B. and Knighton, E.A. (1955). Movements (War Office Monograph Series), War Office, London. (See NA WO277/17)
91 C 0-6-0 No. 1593.
92 C2X 0-6-0 No. 2549.
93 Some mistake here.
94 It seems much more likely that the damage occurred on the previous day!
95 It would seem that this was the same V-1, but it is about two miles between Newbury Park and Temple Mills.
96 One at Sylvan Road, the second at Wanstead Place off High Street – within 600 yards of each other!
97 Indeed, so anxious were the authorities not to reveal any enemy success with their Secret Weapons that the secret Ministry of Home Security Intelligence Summary No. 3666 for 12 hours ending 06.00 Saturday 9th September 1944 (see NA HO203/15) was worded as follows: "During the early part of the period missiles believed to be long range rocket bombs have been directed against this country. Some damage and a small number of casualties, including 3 persons killed, have been reported. For Security reasons it has been decided that, for the present, locations will not be given. Important Notice. It has been decided that the special security measures for which the signal BIG BEN CONFIRMED was devised will not be taken for the present, and accordingly the signal BIG BEN CONFIRMED has not been issued."
98 Presumably phosphorus.
99 The locomotive, L1 4-4-0 No. 1759, suffered slight damage.
100 Strangely, this was not unusual.
101 Two missiles fell at the same time within a mile or two!
102 J17 0-6-0 No.8200, which was damaged beyond repair.
103 The V-2 that fell on a crowded Woolworth's and killed at least 160.
104 The 'Official' list (NA HO198/177) locates this V-2 at 'Bethlehem Royal Hospital', but this was on Lambeth Road about half a mile from the railway referred to, so there is confusion.
105 Offices already evacuated from Hamilton House, Liverpool Street now had to return there.
106 A Bakerloo Line train was blasted, injuring 12 passengers (one seriously).
107 Just how they were diverted is problematic.
108 Either one that fell in Wanstead Park Road at 15.04 or one that burst in the air over Ilford at 15.08!
109 This was a bad incident in a busy street, 14 people dying.
110 This was over a mile away, and much nearer Homerton LMS station, but the LMSR apparently reported no damage.
111 Off the railway this rocket caused 17 deaths plus 20 missing.
112 The remains of the Rocket was reported as falling at Deptford at that time.
113 This Rocket did much more damage with casualties on LPTB Shoreditch – Whitechapel line.
114 This one fell a few hundred yards from the author when he was at College.
115 'Patriot' 4-6-0 No. 5529.
116 Officially, LNER (and LMSR) suburban trains to Moorgate had ceased to run in October 1940 anyway.
117 No. 1707, working the 03.30 empties Neasden – Woodford. See Over Here: the Story of the S160, by R.N. Higgins (1980), Rochdale: Big Jim Publishing Ltd., also *Allied Military Locomotives of the Second World War*, by R. Tourret (1995), Abingdon: Tourret Publishing.
118 After the locomotive had been fitted with a new boiler and returned to Neasden in May 1945, the men there refused to steam it, but it was sent to work in France like the others, ending up working in Turkey.
119 The Report by H.M. Inspector of Railways (Major G.R.S. Wilson) was published in full in *The Railway Gazette* (10 August 1945, pp. 151–153).
120 For the umpteenth time, actually.
121 During the repair work, the power cables that had just been placed underground were accidentally severed! Hence the second resort to HSW, also to the confused records as to the sequence of resumption of normality.
122 During the Blitz, Up expresses to King's Cross used to stop at Finsbury Park anyway – for the nervous who couldn't wait to get 'Underground'.
123 Coaching train-miles were down by about 30%.
124 Block trains for single destinations, under the 'Convoy' system set up in February 1940.
125 This was a drastic measure, a severe threat to supplies for heating and power in London and the South-East.
126 This is a remarkably positive attitude in view of the grim prospects for the immediate future!

Index

Page numbers in italics refer to photograph captions

88, 89, 103, 110, 111, 124, 136
Ferme Park Yard 39, 40, 47, 76, 108, 115, 124
Finchley Central 23
Finchley Road (LMS, Midland) 26, 113, 121
Finsbury Park 24, 25, 28-30, 32, 41, 47, *68*, 72, 89, 114, 121, 123, 124, 133, 136, 140, 141
Forest Gate 13, 19, 28, 32, 76, 102, 118, 120, 137
Forest Hill 20, 29, 30, 78, 103, 112, 115, 116, 118, 120
Forty Hill 11
Fulwell 18, 40, 43, 44, 107, 120

Gallions (PLA) 12
Gas Factory Junction 12, 16, 20, 47, 75, 89
Gidea Park 27, 42, 43, 81, 90, 102, 105, 125
Gipsy Hill 11, 16, 17, 25, 42, 90, 92, 117, 119
Gloucester Road Junction, Croydon 38, 90, 91, 111
Goldhawk Road 105
Goodmayes 12, 22, 29, 32, 33, *63*, 73, 103, 105, 118, 125
Gordon Hill 27, 32, 80, 103, 106, 107, 133
Gospel Oak 22, 30, 31, 33, 43, 79, 81, 103, 105, 106, 119, 120, 123, 137, 138
Graham Road, Hackney 22
Grange Hill 11, 17, 116, *131*
Grange Park 11, 33, 121
Greenford 29, 30, 33, 37, 40, 44, 103
Greenwich 17, 21, 22, 40, 91, 92, 102, 113, 114, 115, 124, 126
Grosvenor Bridge 14, 16, 28, 114, 136
Grosvenor Road 14, 16, 18, 24, 25, 33, 78, 105, 140
Grove Park 28, 39, 42, 44, 74, 78, 79, 103, 108, 113, 120
Gunnersbury 23-25, 32, 34, 35, 40, 116

Hackbridge 14, 25, 36, 42
Hackney 12, 13, 22, 46, 76, 115, 117, 120, 125
Hackney Downs 13, 22, 28, 33, 41, 90, 117, 125
Hackney Wick Goods 11, 31
Hadley Wood 28, 105
Haggerston 15, 22, 37, 41, 73, 77
Hainault 44, 116, *131*
Hall Farm Junction 40
Hammersmith 16, 40, 72, 88, 106, 107
Hampstead Heath 30, 35, 103, 120, 124
Hampton 18, 40, 43, 44, 107, 122
Hampton Court 29, 35, 45, 103, 107, 122
Hampton Court Junction 11, 24, 26, 29, 30, 39, 44, 103, 112, 121, 122
Hampton Wick 14, 29, 44, 107, 124
Hanwell & Elthorne 25, 39, 44, 107
Harlesden 19, 25, 27, 37, 102
Harold Wood 72, 105
Harringay 26, 47, 76, 79, 81, 114, 124, 138
Harringay Park 23, 26, 44, 73, 121
Harrow & Wealdstone 35
Harrow-on-the-Hill 29, 39, 102, 140
Hatch End 79, 108
Haydon Square Goods 14, 16, 21, 27, 46, 73, 74, 89, 105, 111, 122
Haydons Road 36, 40
Hayes (SR) 17-9, 28, 39, 76, 79, 112
Hayes & Harlington 29, 32, 35, 37, 43
Hendon (LMS) 21, 29, 71, 73, 106
Herne Hill 16-9, 21, 24, 25, 33, 36-7, 41, 45, 48, 71, 74, 76, 78, 103, 108,

111, 113, 114, 117-9, 120-2
Highams Park 20, 31, 109
Highbury & Islington (LMS) 31, 75, 76, 89, 92, 105, 113
Highgate 105
Highgate Road 16, 30, 31, 43, 105, 106
Highgate 16, 80
High Meads, Stratford 22, 41, 45, 72, 122
Hinchley Wood 12, 17, 30, 103, 115
Hither Green 14, 16-8, 31, 34, 37, 39, 44, 45, 74, 76, 78, 79, 92, 102, 107, 108, 111, 112, 116, 118, 121, 122, 124, 133, 138, 141
Hoe Street, Walthamstow 11, 27, 80, 120
Holborn Viaduct 15, 16, 18, 24, 38, 39, 41, 45, 47, 72, 78, 79, 91, 92, *96*, *97*, 103, 112, 114, 126, 136, 141
Holloway 22, 72, 89
Homerton 15, 19, 21, 27, 79, 117, 141
Honor Oak 14-6, 20, 38, 44, 103
Honor Oak Park 20, 42, 46, 78, 102, 123
Hornchurch 11, 12, 73, 77, 111, 112
Hornsey 39, 40, *70*, 107, 113, 115, 122, 124
Hounslow (SR) 25, 26, 36, 43, 90, 106, 127

Ilford 13, 16, 19, 32, 33, 36, 37, 42, 45-7, 73, 75, 77, 79, 80, 81, 89, 102, 110, 112, 115, 122, 125, *132*, 133, 141
Isleworth 102

Junction Road 16, 22, 27, 36, 106

Kempton Park 14
Kenley 11, 42, 43, 44, 91, 109, 118, 122
Kensal Green 28, 30, 32, 40, 43, 81, 120
Kensal Rise 20, 43, 120
Kensington, Addison Road 17, 22, 30, 36, 41, 43, 114, 138
Kent House 17, 24, 30, 44, 78, 124
Kentish Town and Junctions (LMS) 17, 20, 22, 23, 25, 28-33, 36, 40, 43, 89, 104, 106, 108, 115, 123, 136
Kentish Town West 23, 115
Kew Bridge 16, 18, 24, 31, 39, 42, 106, 107, 137, 138
Kew East Junction 27, 118
Kew Gardens 23-5, 35, 40, 44
Kidbrooke 16, 22, 28, 45, 74, 102
Kilburn & Brondesbury (LPTB) 19, 43, *67*, 124
Kilburn High Road 17, 28, 32, 34, 39, 105, 117
King's Cross 13, 15-7, 20, 21, 25, 26, 28, 29, 31-3, 36, 37, 41, 42, 45, 72, 73, 74, 77, 89, 92, *94*, *95*, 103, 105-7, 111, 112, 116, 120, 121, 124, 133, 136, 137, 141
Kingston 30, 34, 103, 107, 121, 124
Kingswood & Borough Heath 14, 36, 119
Knights Hill 46, 48, 118

Ladbroke Grove 25, 36, 41, 72, 106
Ladywell 16, 19- 21, 38, 39, 41, 46, 113
Latchmere Junction 18, 26, 32, 33, 36, 41, 47, 123, 137
Latimer Road 19, 23, 36, 38, 40, 42, 106, 140
Lea Bridge 13, 20, 29, 37, 40, 42, 74, 75, 109, 113, 117, 121, 123
Lee 14, 17, 31, 34, 39, 44, 75, 102, 103, 107, 112, 118
Leigham Junction 14, 25, 118, 120
Leman Street 13, 16, 18, 20, 44, 45,

72, 74, 90, 102, 119, 140
Lewisham 12, 14, 16-8, 20, 22, 34, 36, 37, 44, 46, 48, 75, 76, 80, 108, 111, 112, 114, 115, 118, 119, 121
Leyton (LMS) 19-21, 26, 43, 107, 115, 137
Leyton (LNE) 18, 19, 44, 72, 105, 113, 119, 133
Leytonstone (LMS) 19, 21, 22, 26, 31-3, 75, 76, 89, 102
Leytonstone (LNE) 11, 39, 105, 115, 125, 133
Lillie Bridge Yard 17, 19, 36, 118
Limehouse 89, 90, 93
Little Ilford Sidings 16, 79, 115
Liverpool Street 12, 13, 15, 31, 37, 39, 41, 42, 47, *64*, *66*, 72-5, 80, 81, 89, 105, 110, 116, 117, 125, 133, 136, 141
Loco Junction 15, 17-9, 23, 31, 38, 40, 42, *49*, 77, 90, 107, 108, 117, 119
London Bridge 14, 17-22, 28, 29, 31, 33-5, 37, 38, 40, 42, 45-8, *53*, 73-6, 78-81, 83, 90-2, 112, 116, 118, 119, 121, 122, 133, 136
London Fields 13, 17, 21, 30, 125
Longhedge Junction 14-9, 23, 24, 32, 35, 36, 79, 91, 113, 114, 118, 137
Lords 43, 102
Lordship Lane 16, 103, 115, 119
Loughborough Junction 14, 16, 18, 21, 24, 25, 36, 40, 41, 45, 46, 48, *52*, 78, 80, 83, 91, 92, 117, 136
Loughton Branch, Stratford 20, 22, 28, 72, 74, 75, 103, 123
Lower Sydenham 11, 17, 22, 40, 74, 78, 91, 107, 115, 117, 119, 120
Ludgate Hill 91, 92, *97*, 137

Maiden Lane 16, 32, 37, 72, 114, 115, 133
Malden 11, 13, 22, 26, 28, 34, 38, 39, 44, 73, 103, 105, 116, 119, 121
Malden Manor 13, 41, 44, 109
Manor Park 15, 16, 81, 106, 117
Manor Way (PLA) 119
Maryland (Point) 24, 43, 80, 120, 122, 133
Marylebone 16, 17, 19, 23, 24, 26, 44, 73, 76, 77, 89, 92, 102, 116, 118, 124-6, 136
Maze Hill 22, 34, 35, 48, 71, 72, 75, 81, 91, 92, 102, 104, 114, 124, 126
Merton Abbey 11, 17, 36, 38, 116
Merton Park 11, 31, 36, 38, 91, 107, 115, 116, 118
Metropolitan Junction 16, 19, 24, 25, 29, 30, 35, 37, 39, 73, 74, 79, 91, 92, 112, 115
Mildmay Park 20, 79
Mill Hill 11, 38, 114
Mill Hill East 27
Millwall 12, 13, 75, 81, 90, 120, 127
Minories Goods 15, 111
Mitcham/Mitcham Junction 11, 14, 20, 25-7, 31, 35-9, 42, 43, 73, 78, 114-9, 124
Mitre Bridge 21, 26, 43, 71
Moorgate 29, 33, 133, 141
Morden Road Halt 114, 116
Morden South 114
Mortlake 15, 16, 20, 25, 31, 106, 107
Motspur Park 11, 28, 109, 116, 119
Mottingham 16, 31, 34, 39, 41, 81, 103, 105, 107, 108, 118, 119, 125
Muswell Hill 123

Neasden (LNE) 19, 24, 27, 29, 36, 39, 42, 46, *69*, 73, 77, 79, 89, 102, 107, 115, 126, 136, 138, 141
Necropolis, Waterloo 77, *83*
New Barnet 21, 75, 105

New Beckenham 17, 38, 78, 107, 123, 124
Newbury Park 23, 81, 120, 141
New Cross/New Cross Gate 13-8, 20, 22, 23, 28, 33-6, 38, 39, 42, 43, 46-8, 75, 76, 78-81, 91, 92, 102, 103, 108, 112-7, 119-23, 126, 133, 137
New Eltham 20, 22, 30, 72, 102, 103, 108
New Southgate 38, 43, 106, 124
New Wandsworth 33, 34, 47, 91
Nine Elms 16-8, 20, 22, 25, 26, 29-31, 33, 35, 38-43, *48*, *49*, *51*, 74, 77, 90, 92, 103, 106, 107, 112, 115-8, 135
Noel Park 28, 72, 117, 124, 125
Norbiton 13, 22, 26, 38, 44, 105, 121
Norbury 38, 48, 112, 114
North Acton 17, 24, 25, 30, 35, 37, 105, 106, 113
North Dulwich 38, 46, 78
North Harrow 26, 27
North Kent East Junction 14, 17, 31, 36, 41, 42, 46, 48, 75, 76, 81, 102, 114, 116, 122, 124, 126, 136
North Kent West Junction 14, 18, 19, 38
North Pole Junction 43, 71
North Sheen 20, 25, 35, 44
Northumberland Park 46, 75, 89, 119
North Wembley 43
North Woolwich 13, 23, 27, *63*, 71, 72, 74, 80, 81, 112, 115, 117, 137
Norwood (Junctions, etc.) 11, 14, 17, 22, 34, 36, 38, 40, 41, 80, 91, 102, 104, 107, 111, 112, 121, 138
Nunhead 14-6, 20, 22, 23, 25-7, 75, 80, 90, 106-8, 110, 112-4, 116, 119, 121, 124, 125

Ockendon 117
Old Ford 20, 21, 77, 89, 102
Old Kent Road Junction 17, 24, 74, 75, 78, 90, 102, 107, 120
Old Kew Junction 25, 102
Old Oak Common 15, 21, 23, 27, 29, 30, 36, 37, 41-3, *55*, 71, 89, 113, 118, 124, 137, 138
Old Oak Lane Halt 79, 105
Orpington 19, 34, 37, 38, 41, 71, 79, 108, 119, 123, 126

Paddington 12, 14, 20, 22, 26, 27, 30, 32, 42, 44, 46, 72, 76, 79, *86*, *87*, 88, 90, 102, *104*, 105, 106, 108, *109*, 136
Palace Gates 13, 36, 39, 72, 81, 124
Palmers Green 121, *131*
Park Junction, Highgate 18, 36, 74, 78, 81, 103, 108
Park Royal 14, 21, 24-6, 31, 34, 42, 113, 116
Parks Bridge Junction 14, 16, 17, 20, 34, 44, 102, 107, 108, 111, 115
Peckham Rye 15, 18, 23, 26, 33, 40, 46-8, 74, 76, 80, 90, 102, 106, 107, 113, 116, 118, 120-2, 124, *129*, 133
Penge East 14, 17-9, 20, 30, 42, 46, 112, 119
Penge West 17-20, 42
Perivale 15, 21, 30
Perry Street Fork Junction 20, 80, 105, 120, 125
Petts Wood 19, 20, 28, 29, 34, 37, 38, 41, 78, 108, 123
Pickett's Lock 73, 74, 126, 127
Pinner 27, 39
Plaistow & West Ham Goods 45
Plaistow 12, 16, 18, 20, 22, 31, 45, 72, 73, 75, 79, 113, 116, 118-20, 126
Plumstead 14, 15, 31, 39, 72, 73, 81, 91, 106, 108, 114, 117, 119, 141